# Selected Chinese Cases on the CISG

This book series intends to provide a comprehensive and systemic analysis of Chinese cases on the CISG to show international legal scholars and practitioners not only the judicial interpretation and application of the CISG in China but also the scholastic understandings of and approaches to it. This series will fill the gaps relating to the lack of understanding of Chinese cases on the CISG and complement the discussion and analysis of the CISG in leading commentaries on the CISG, which is already endorsed by world renowned scholars in this filed.

Another aim of the series is to identify whether there is a special Chinese approach to the interpretation and application of the CISG. If the answer is in the affirmative, it will examines whether Chinese courts prefer to apply the CISG, whether Chinese parties prefer to choose the CISG as the governing law, whether the application of the CISG in China promotes its wider adoption and application by other countries and whether the Chinese approach will contribute to the uniform interpretation and application of the CISG at the international level.

In addition, the series will highlight the similarities and differences between the Chinese approach to the interpretation and application of the CISG and the approaches adopted by courts in other jurisdictions and discuss which approach is more preferable and valuable to the further development of a uniform sales law. It will also compare the similarities and differences of the understanding and interpretation of the CISG between Chinese and foreign scholars which may affect the approach to be adopted by a court. Both will prompt foreign legal practitioners and companies to reconsider whether they should choose the CISG as the governing law of the contract when doing business with companies the place of business of which is in China.

Peng Guo · Haicong Zuo · Shu Zhang
Editors

# Selected Chinese Cases on the UN Sales Convention (CISG) Vol. 3

Springer

*Editors*
Peng Guo
Swinburne Law School
Swinburne University of Technology
Melbourne, VIC, Australia

Haicong Zuo
Law School
University of International Business
and Economics
Beijing, China

Shu Zhang
Deakin Law School
Deakin University
Geelong, VIC, Australia

ISSN 2731-3573 ISSN 2731-3581 (electronic)
Selected Chinese Cases on the CISG
ISBN 978-981-99-6853-4 ISBN 978-981-99-6851-0 (eBook)
https://doi.org/10.1007/978-981-99-6851-0



This Springer imprint is published by the registered company Springer Nature Singapore Pte Ltd.
The registered company address is: 152 Beach Road, #21-01/04 Gateway East, Singapore 189721, Singapore

Paper in this product is recyclable.

# Foreword

This volume is an essential resource in understanding how China and its courts regulate international sales, including under the Convention for the International Sales of Goods [CISG]. Much of China's case law on international sales is difficult to identify, comprehend and synthesise in English, given language, cultural and legal barriers. This volume provides a detailed compendium of Chinese judicial decisions. It also offers an invaluable synthesis of how Chinese courts construe international sales laws not limited to the CISG. The beneficiaries are both those who are trained and untrained in the Chinese civil law tradition and who seek access to finely synthesised resources on sales law.

Accentuating this volume's importance is China's centrality as a participant in international trade and investment. Impelled by its ever-expanding Belt and Road Initiative [BRI], China has ascended into a salutary leader in international commerce within several decades. It is now the largest inbound and second largest outbound investor state globally. Once a struggling developing state, it is both the origin and destination of multiple import and export transactions that traverse the global economy today and most likely, tomorrow.

This volume addresses these fast-growing developments both expertly and comprehensively. It details cases in which Chinese courts apply the CISG in diverse contexts. It does so by highlighting key applicability issues as well as the interpretation of specific CISG articles in Chinese civil law. In so doing, it encapsulates the insights embodied in multiple Chinese judgments, along with the capacity of Chinese courts to identify and express them. In doing so, it demonstrates the significance of those judgments to the regulation of international sales.

It is a pleasure to know that Peng Guo and Shu Zhang who both completed their Ph.Ds. under my supervision are making this essential contribution to the global importance of China in relation to the CISG. Their collection, translation and publication of the Chinese jurisprudence surrounding the Convention add enormous value as a legal resource to comprehending the significance of the existing literature on the subject.

I highly recommend this volume to all readers interested in China's salient contributions to the law governing international sales.

Sydney, Australia
June 2023

Emeritus Professor, Dr. Leon Trakman,
LLM, S.J.D. (Harvard)

# Preface

The United Nations Convention on Contracts for the International Sale of Goods (CISG)[1] has now 95 signatories.[2] It is one of the most successful texts prepared by the United Nations Commission on International Trade Law (UNCITRAL). It represents a landmark in the course of the unification of international trade law and has a significant impact on domestic law reforms in many countries, such as China.

Cases are considered a crucial source of learning; however, so far, no serial Chinese casebooks on the CISG have been published. Also, even though there are many Chinese cases on the CISG, there is no comprehensive and systematic analysis of these cases. In addition, scholars from different countries have noticed the existence of a large number of Chinese cases and realised their potential value in the promotion of the uniform interpretation and application of the CISG; however, the language barrier has hindered access to the cases and subsequently their potential influence on and contribution to the global jurisprudence of the CISG. All this guarantees the high value and usefulness of the publication of a series of *Selected Chinese Cases on the CISG* to make them assessable to the rest of the world.

The primary aim of this series is to, for the first time, provide academics, judges, legal practitioners and law students with an important source to locate Chinese CISG cases. Although existing databases on CISG cases, such as the CISG-Online database,[3] the Unilex database,[4] the Albert H. Kritzer Pace CISG database[5] and the UNCITRAL CLOUT database,[6] have some Chinese cases, the coverage is relatively limited. This series, therefore, intends to provide a comprehensive collection of Chinese CISG cases.

[1] *United Nations Convention on Contracts for the International Sale of Goods*, opened for signature April 11, 1980, 1489 UNTS 3 (entered into force January 1, 1988) (CISG).

[2] https://uncitral.un.org/en/texts/salegoods/conventions/sale_of_goods/cisg/status.

[3] https://cisg-online.org/home.

[4] https://www.unilex.info.

[5] https://iicl.law.pace.edu/cisg/cisg.

[6] http://www.uncitral.org/clout/index.jspx.

The second aim is to track down the development of court practices about the CISG in China. It is of great importance to perceive how Chinese courts understand, interpret and apply the CISG, which will provide guidance to domestic and international businessmen to predict and avoid potential problems and enhance predictability and certainty in the resolution of emerging disputes regarding the CISG in a proper and effective manner.

The third aim is to conduct a systematic study of Chinese CISG cases. Both Chinese and international scholars and practitioners will provide comments on the cases. They will provide a scholarly and practical analysis of the CISG from different perspectives and identify the similarities and differences between the Chinese approach and the approaches adopted in other jurisdictions when appropriate.

We hope that this series will add China's contribution to the uniform interpretation and application of the CISG globally.

Hawthorn, Australia — Peng Guo
Beijing, China — Haicong Zuo
Geelong, Australia — Shu Zhang
July 2023

# Contents

**JiedongXian Yuequn Aquatic Products Development Ltd. v. Inland Sea Inc.** ........ 1
Max Siying Wu

**Beijing Chenguang Huilong Electronic Technology Development Co., Ltd. v. Thales Communications & Security S.A** ........ 9
Max Siying Wu

**Entreprise P. Boucher v. Henan Yuanfeng Leather Products Co., Ltd.** ........ 19
Bruno Zeller

**Ri xx Development Co., Ltd. v. Hong Kong Bang xx Development Co., Ltd.** ........ 23
Max Siying Wu

**U.S. Tire Imports Inc. v. Qingdao Guangming Tyre Co., Ltd.** ........ 31
Jie Luo and Fang Gu

**WuXi Hengfeng Electronic Products Co., Ltd. v. Symban Lighting Corporation** ........ 37
Ye Xia

**Western Mining Group (Hong Kong) Company Limited v. Hanchang Industry Co., Ltd., Shanxi Fuyuan International Commerce Co., Ltd.** ........ 45
Max Siying Wu

**Shanghai X Colour Printing Co., Ltd. v. Y** ........ 53
Bruno Zeller

**Ningbo Bridge Import & Export Co., Ltd. v. The Money Consultants Inc.** ........ 57
Junmin Zhang

**Shanghai Jiamupu Industry Co., Ltd. v. Moraglis S.A.** ................ 63
Xiaojun Chen and Peng Guo

**GINO Co., Ltd. v. Beijing Ji Nuo Si Trading Co., Ltd.** ................ 69
Xiaojun Chen and Peng Guo

**Dou Ya Trading Co., Ltd. v. Liaoning Hua Xi Group & Liaoning Hua Yi Clothing Co., Ltd.** ................ 73
Xiaojun Chen and Peng Guo

**Nanjing Overseas Wood Co., Ltd. v. Trans-Pacific Trading Ltd.** ........ 77
Xiaojun Chen and Peng Guo

**A Company v. B Company** ................ 81
Xiaojun Chen and Peng Guo

**A Co., Ltd. v. B Co., Ltd.** ................ 85
Peng Wang and Yueshan Liu

**Bongsan Stone v. Fujian Nan'an Lianfengmei Stone Co., Ltd. and Xiamen Yuxin Xingye Import and Export Trade Co., Ltd.** .......... 97
Wenjing An

**Rubberflex Sdn Bhd Co., Ltd. v. Fujian Agricultural Materials Group Xiamen Import and Export Co.** ................ 107
Xu Yan

**Tradeways S.R.L Co., Ltd. v. Xuchang Foreign Trading Co., Ltd.** ...... 113
Xu Yan

**YT Tech Corporation v. Yantai Haiwan Plastic Products Co., Ltd** ...... 121
Charles Caishun Guo, Wenjing Lin, and Charlie Xiao-chuan Weng

**Hangzhou X Insulation Materials Co., Ltd. v. Y Electric Wire Industrial Co., Ltd.** ................ 131
Edgardo Muñoz

**Balance Industry Co., Ltd. v. Cixi Chenyang Packaging Co., Ltd.** ...... 137
Benjamin Hayward

**Daewon GSI Co., Ltd. v. Zhejiang Wuyi Tea Industry Co., Ltd.** ........ 153
Charles Caishun Guo, Wenjing Lin, and Charlie Xiao-chuan Weng

**Hangzhou Thousand-Island Lake Tiantu Needlework Co., Ltd. v. Huatai Group of America, Inc. and Wenzhou Gongmei International Trade Co., Ltd.** ................ 159
Chaolin Zhang, Junkai Fan, and Peng Guo

**Choi Wonkyu v. Xu Chunhua** ................ 171
Sarah Xiao Xun, Charles Caishun Guo, and Wenjing Lin

**Tong v. Kaiping X Stainless Steel Products Ltd.** . . . . . . . . . . . . . . . . . . . . . . 179
Benjamin Hayward

**Knoles & Carter La Piel, Inc. v. Richina Leather Industrial Co., Ltd.** . . . 191
Shao Long and Sichen Lu

**Castronics Precision Metals (Tianjin) Co., Ltd. v. Boram Hi-Tek Co.,** . . . . . . . . . . . . . . . . . . . . . . . . . . . . . . . . . . . . . . . . . . . . . . . . . . . . . . . . . 201
Hongzhi Hu

**Castronics Precision Metal (Tianjin) Co., Ltd. v. Boram Hi-Tek Co., Ltd.** . . . . . . . . . . . . . . . . . . . . . . . . . . . . . . . . . . . . . . . . . . . . . . . . . . . . . . 209
Junmin Zhang

**Nanjing Dingfu Toys & Gifts Co., Ltd. v. Michyvic S.L., Yu Hai** . . . . . . . . 215
Sarah Xiao Xun, Charles Caishun Guo, and Wenjing Lin

**XX Co., Ltd. (China) v. XX Company (Spain)** . . . . . . . . . . . . . . . . . . . . . . . 223
Peng Wang and Yueshan Liu

**Shanghai Yuqing Clothing Company v. Corporate Funding Partners** . . . . . . . . . . . . . . . . . . . . . . . . . . . . . . . . . . . . . . . . . . . . . . . . . . . . . . 233
Mengsha Yang

**Jiaxing Haoneng Packaging Co., Ltd. v. Print-Service Ltd.** . . . . . . . . . . . . 243
Hongzhi Hu

**Guangzhou Fanyunanxing Limited v. J & H International Inc. & Merion Kitchenware (Suzhou Industrial Park) Co., Ltd.** . . . . . . . . . . . . . . 249
Kaiwei Cui and Peng Guo

**Taiwan Semiconductor Co., Ltd. v. Shenzhen SANG DA Bai LI Electric Co., Ltd.** . . . . . . . . . . . . . . . . . . . . . . . . . . . . . . . . . . . . . . . . . . . . . . . . 259
Shaotang Wang

**Cai Puzhong v. Huang Xiaobin, Liu Liya** . . . . . . . . . . . . . . . . . . . . . . . . . . . 263
Shao Long and Suqing Shi

**A/S Harald Nyborg Co., Ltd. v. Wuxi Anjiu Automatic Vehicle Co., Ltd.** . . . . . . . . . . . . . . . . . . . . . . . . . . . . . . . . . . . . . . . . . . . . . . . . . . . . . . 269
Kaiwei Cui and Peng Guo

**Wooree ETI Co., Ltd. v. Beijing Shiyuanda Electronic Technology Co., Ltd.** . . . . . . . . . . . . . . . . . . . . . . . . . . . . . . . . . . . . . . . . . . . . . . . . . . . . . . 279
Long Shao and Sichen Lu

**Wooree LED CO., Ltd. v. Beijing Shiyuanda Electronic Technology Co., Ltd.** . . . . . . . . . . . . . . . . . . . . . . . . . . . . . . . . . . . . . . . . . . . . . . . . . . . . . . 289
Junkai Fan, Chaolin Zhang, and Shu Zhang

**KOYJ Co., Ltd. v. Beijing Shiyuanda Electronic Technology Co., Ltd.** . . . . . 297
Geng Wang and Shu Zhang

**m.c.or-shy Ltd. Company v. Hangzhou Fuming Refrigeration Technology Co., Ltd. and Hangzhou Silk Garment Import and Export Co., Ltd.** . . . . . 305
Kaiwei Cui and Peng Guo

**Grand Resources Group Co., Ltd. v. STX Corporation** . . . . . 315
Peng Wang and Yueshan Liu

**Guangzhou Gulangma Co., Ltd. v. WS Invention Trade Gmbh** . . . . . 329
Shao Long and Siyuan Yu

**Allied Pacific Motor (Malaysia) Sdn. Bhd v. Chongqing Jieyadi Technology Development Co., Ltd.** . . . . . 339
Alex Wan

**P.H. "PODLASIAK" Andrzej Cylwik v. Yiwu Entuo Import and Export Firm** . . . . . 347
Alex Wan and Peng Guo

**Index** . . . . . 355

# Editors and Contributors

## About the Editors

**Dr. Peng Guo (Editor-in-Chief)** is a Lecturer in Law at the Swinburne University of Technology. He has worked across several Australian universities and has held visiting positions at different European universities. He has received scholarships and fellowships awarded by renowned research institutions and international organisations, including the Max Planck Institute for Comparative and International Private Law, the International Institute for the Unification of Private Law (UNIDROIT), the Swiss Institute of Comparative Law and the European Union. His research interests lie in comparative contract law, international sale of goods, international commercial arbitration and technology and legal education.

**Dr. Haicong Zuo (Editorial Board)** is a Professor in the Law School at the University of International Business and Economics (UIBE). Prior to joining UIBE Law School, he was Dean and Professor at the Law School of Nankai University and Professor at the Law School of Wuhan University. His research interests include, but are not limited to international commercial law, WTO law, international economic law and international dispute resolution. He has published on various topics in a number of books and leading journals in both Chinese and English and has chaired or co-chaired different research projects funded by various stakeholders.

**Dr. Shu Zhang (Editorial Board)** is a Senior Lecturer in Commercial Law at Deakin Law School, Deakin University (Australia) and coached Deakin Law School's Vis Moot team. Prior to joining Deakin Law School, Dr. Zhang was a Postdoctoral Fellow at the Chinese International Business and Economic Law Initiative, Law School, University of New South Wales (Australia). Her research interests include international commercial law, dispute resolution and international arbitration, as well as comparative contract law. She also completed internships at both the Australian Centre for International Commercial Arbitration (ACICA) and the Chinese International Economic and Trade Arbitration Commission (CIETAC). She is also admitted to practice in New South Wales, Australia. She obtained her Ph.D. in Law from the University of New South Wales (Australia), and her LLM, LLB and B.A. in Economics (Double Degree) from Peking University (China). She has published various manuscripts in leading journals in this area, such as the *Journal of Contract Law*, *Vindobona Journal of International Commercial Law and Arbitration* and *China Quarterly*.

## Contributors

**Wenjing An** North China Electric Power University, Baoding, China

**Xiaojun Chen** Wincon Law Firm, Qingdao, China

**Kaiwei Cui** University of International Business and Economics, Beijing, China

**Junkai Fan** Qingdao Maritime Court, Qingdao, Shandong, China

**Fang Gu** Zhongnan University of Economics and Law, Wuhan, China

**Charles Caishun Guo** Quanzhou Intermediate People's Court, Quanzhou, China; Fujian High People's Court, Fuzhou, China

**Peng Guo** Swinburne University of Technology, Melbourne, VIC, Australia

**Benjamin Hayward** Monash Business School, Department of Business Law and Taxation, VIC, Caulfield East, Australia

**Hongzhi Hu** Nankai University, Tianjin, China

**Wenjing Lin** The Primary People's Court of Shishi City of Fujian Province, Shishi, Japan;
Shishi Primary People's Court of Fujian Province, Quanzhou, China

**Yueshan Liu** Nankai University, Tianjin, China

**Shao Long** University Hunan University, Changsha, Hunan, China;
Hunan University, Changsha, Hunan, China

**Sichen Lu** University Hunan University, Changsha, Hunan, China;
Hunan University, Changsha, Hunan, China

**Jie Luo** Zhongnan University of Economics and Law, Wuhan, China

**Edgardo Muñoz** School of Law, Universidad Panamericana, Guadalajara, Jalisco, Mexico

**Long Shao** Hunan University, Changsha, Hunan, China

**Suqing Shi** Hunan University, Changsha, Hunan, China

**Alex Wan** Swinburne University of Technology, Melbourne, VIC, Australia

**Geng Wang** University of International Business and Economics, Beijing, China

**Peng Wang** Nankai University, Tianjin, China

**Shaotang Wang** Nankai University, Tianjin, China

**Charlie Xiao-chuan Weng** University of New South Wales, Sydney, Australia

**Max Siying Wu** Dacheng Law Offices, LLP, Guangzhou, China

**Ye Xia** Tianjin, Hexi District, China

**Sarah Xiao Xun** Guanghua Law School, Zhejiang University, Hangzhou, China

**Xu Yan** General Times Center, Beijing, China

**Mengsha Yang** Tianjin University, Tianjin, China

**Siyuan Yu** Hunan University, Changsha, Hunan, China

**Bruno Zeller** University of Western Australia, Crawley, WA, Australia

**Chaolin Zhang** Qufu Normal University, Rizhao, Shandong, China

**Junmin Zhang** Shanghai Normal University, Shanghai, China

**Shu Zhang** Deakin University, Geelong, VIC, Australia

# JiedongXian Yuequn Aquatic Products Development Ltd. v. Inland Sea Inc.

**Max Siying Wu**

**Case Information**

**Case Name:** *JiedongXian Yuequn Aquatic Products Development Ltd. v Inland Sea Inc.*

**Seller:** Inland Sea Incorporated
**Place of Business:** United States of America

**Buyer:** JiedongXian Yuequn Aquatic Products Development Ltd.
**Place of Business:** China

**Details of First Instance:**
**Court:** Jieyang Intermediate People's Court
**Date of Decision:** N/A
**Case No.:** (1999) Jie Zhong Fa Jing Chu Zi No. 65
**Judges:** N/A

**Details of Second Instance:**
**Court:** Guangdong High People's Court
**Date of Decision:** 10 October 2004
**Case No.:** (2004) Yue Gao Fa Min Si Zhong Zi No.84
**Judges:** Yuyu WANG (Justice), Ji LI (Deputy Justice), Haibin HAN (Deputy Justice)

M. S. Wu (✉)
Dacheng Law Offices, LLP, Guangzhou, China
e-mail: seawing2002@126.com



P. Guo et al. (eds.), *Selected Chinese Cases on the UN Sales Convention (CISG) Vol. 3*, Selected Chinese Cases on the CISG,
https://doi.org/10.1007/978-981-99-6851-0_1

**CISG Applied:** Yes
**Key CISG Provisions Interpreted and Applied:** Articles 1(1), 18(1), 23

**Case Abstract**

The buyer and seller entered into a one-year term Sole Agency Contract in 1996, for the exclusive agency of sale of artemia cysts in China, under which the buyer would purchase from the seller, and sell as the seller's agent, at least 40 tons of artemia cysts. The price of the artemia cysts was left to be determined upon negotiation according to market conditions prior to the shipment of each batch of goods. One third of the price was to be paid before shipment and the rest within 60 days upon receipt of each batch of goods. Yuequn Hong was the legal representative of the buyer when executing the contract, and was also the legal representative of JiedongXian Yuequn Aquatic Products Development Ltd. ('Yuequn Ltd.') during the execution and performance of the contract. Immediately after the conclusion of the contract, Yuequn Hing sent purchase orders to the seller in the name of the buyer and Yuequn Ltd. respectively. Yuequn Hong corresponded with the seller via letters and facsimile, with his signature on each, for placing orders and business transactions.

After the shipment of the goods, there was one statement of account issued by the seller to the buyer's agent, who then translated and forwarded it to Yuequn Hong, stating the amount of the outstanding payment for 12,100 cases of artemia cysts. While the invoices and air consignment notes for the goods were all issued to the buyer, the seller considered it was Yuequn Ltd. that had failed to pay the amount due. The seller then filed to the court of first instance, claiming the unpaid value and interest from Yuequn Ltd., and that Yuequn Ltd., the buyer, and Yuequn Hong should be held jointly liable.

Yuequn Hing replied that he was acting as the legal representative of the buyer instead of himself to execute the contract with the seller. Yuequn Ltd. stated in defence that it was not the contracting party of the contract, had not established any contractual relationship with the seller, and had not received any goods from the seller. The buyer argued that it had made full payment to the seller for all the goods delivered but did not receive the other 12,100 cases of goods. The three defendants all requested the Court to dismiss the seller's claims. The disputing parties had not agreed on any governing law in their contract or during the course of their dispute.

The court of first instance held that it was an arrearage dispute under the sales agency contract, and as the contracting parties had not agreed on the governing law, the laws of the People's Republic of China should be applied in this case, based on the doctrine of most significant connection. The Court considered that the statement of account and the other evidence mutually confirmed, in combination with the correspondence and testimony of the sales representative of the seller, that the statement of account could prove that the buyer owed the seller payment for the goods. Regarding the contracting parties, Yuequn Hong represented the behavior of the buyer, and neither Yuequn Ltd. nor Yuequn Hong took the role as buyer according to the evidential materials. For these reasons, the court of first instance ruled that only the buyer should pay the seller.

The buyer appealed. The court of appeal held that notwithstanding the name of the contract, the rights and obligations of the parties match the characteristics of the sales contract, thus the nature of the contract should be sales instead of an agency contract. Hence, the court of appeal rectified the view of the court of first instance and determined that this was a contract dispute relating to the international sale of goods. In regard to the governing law of this dispute, art 142(2) of *the General Principles of Civil Law of the People's Republic of China* ('GPCL'), released in 1986, stipulated that 'International practice may be applied on matters for which neither the law of the People's Republic of China nor any international treaty concluded or acceded to by the People's Republic of China has any provisions.' Article 1(a) of the CISG provides that '[t]his Convention applies to contracts of sale of goods between parties whose places of business are in different States: (a) when the States are Contracting States'. Since the parties in the dispute have their places of business in China and the USA respectively, both of which are Contracting States to the CISG, the CISG should be applied. Thus, the court of appeal held that the court of first instance was incorrect in applying the domestic law of China in this case.

Regarding the substantive issue of whether the seller had established a contractual relationship with Yuequn Ltd. and Yeuqun Hong, the court of appeal held that according to art 12 of the CISG, a contract is concluded at the moment when an acceptance of an offer becomes effective in accordance with the provisions of the CISG. The purchase order of Yuequn Ltd. and Yuequn Hong submitted by the seller was an offer, however the seller could not prove if there was a statement or other conduct by the seller indicating assent to the offer. Hence it was insufficient to sustain the seller's claim that Yuequn Ltd. and Yuequn Hong concluded a sales contract with the seller. Furthermore, according to art 87 of the GPCL, which stipulates that '[w]hen there are two or more creditors or debtors to a deal, each of the joint creditors shall be entitled to demand that the debtor fulfill his obligations, in accordance with legal provisions or the agreement between the parties; each of the joint debtors shall be obliged to perform the entire debt, and the debtor who performs the entire debt shall be entitled to ask the other joint debtors to reimburse him for their shares of the debt', the court of appeal maintained the view that joint liability only applied when it was expressively agreed by the debtors or provided by law. Obviously, this was not the case in this dispute. Therefore, the court of appeal ruled against the seller on the claim that the buyer, Yuequn Ltd. and Yuequn Hong should bear joint and several liabilities.

Regarding another substantive issue, whether the buyer owed the seller payment for the goods, the court of appeal held that the evidence produced by the seller lacked probative force. The sales representative of the seller was not deemed to represent the buyer for agency by estoppel, and the buyer should not be responsible for the sales representative's conduct. In the end, the court of appeal ruled against the seller entirely.

## Commentary to the Key Issues Related to the CISG

### Issues

Issue 1 The Applicability of the CISG

Issue 2 The Applicability of Domestic Law Along with the CISG

### Comments

### Issue 1 the Applicability of the CISG

#### I. Chinese Court's Approach to Find the Law on Merits of the Dispute

Influenced by a significant civil-law tradition, when dealing with international civil and commercial cases, Chinese courts generally employ a private international law approach in finding the *lex causae*, under which they will follow the choice of law rules in *lex fori, i.e.,* the domestic law of the People's Republic of China. Typically, the court will start with the first step of classification, *i.e.,* to identify the nature of the dispute at hand. As a preliminary question to finding *lex causae*, classification of the nature of the dispute has logically no other option but to be conducted according to the domestic civil and commercial law of China. Where the dispute is identified as one arising out of a commercial contract, with international element(s) involved, the court will have to consider whether there are any international legal instruments that should be applied. If not, the court should follow the 'proper law' method in conflict of law rules, which requires the judge to first determine if there is any consented choice of law governing the merits of the dispute by the parties, in absence of which the judge shall then follow the principle of the 'most significant contact' and find the law of the jurisdiction with the maximum contact, or say, the most characteristic connections, to the enforcement of the disputed commercial contract.

#### II. Classification of the Dispute

In this case, classification of the dispute by the Court is definitely a key element to have determined the *lex causae*. Unlike the decision of the first-instance court, notwithstanding the name and appearance of the contract being a Sole Agency Contract, the court of appeal found that it was actually an international sale of goods contract. The deal was that the buyer should purchase from the seller and sell as the seller's agent a certain amount of goods, which contained the purchase of goods as a main part of the contract. The court of appeal relied on the relevant domestic law of China, specifically the Contract Law, and has compared the traits of the disputed contract with the definitions and descriptions by the Contract law to recognize which type of contract is at hand. It is laudable for the court of appeal to have rectified the misjudgment of the court of first instance and reached a just classification of the dispute.

## III. The Application of CISG

Once dispute had been classified as one of international sales of goods, the Court will naturally look at the applicability of the CISG as the most important and frequently applied international legal instrument in the field, to which China is a Contracting State.

Regarding the pre-emptive and direct applicability of the CISG, according to art 1(1)(a) of the CISG, when the places of business of both contracting parties are in different Contracting States, the CISG shall directly or autonomously apply, irrespective of the conflict of laws rules of the forum State.

This case was a dispute over a contract for the international sale of goods. As the places of business of the parties were located within a Contracting State of CISG and the parties did not expressively exclude the application of the CISG, therefore the CISG should be applied. However, the court of first instance failed to consider the autonomous and pre-emptive application of the CISG under such circumstances. Instead, it determined that, given the parties did not choose the applicable of law, the law of the People's Republic of China should be the governing law of the case in accordance with the doctrine of most significant relationship, which was incorrect. It should also be noted that the court of first instance regarded this case as a dispute over a sales agency contract instead of a contract for the international sale of goods, which may have led to the erroneous application of law. One of the prerequisites for the application of the CISG is that the dispute is one under a contract for international sale of goods; if the court is to determine that the nature of the disputed contract is not one for international sale of goods, there is no room for application of the CISG. From this perspective, one may not draw an easy conclusion that the court of first instance did not have an accurate understanding of the pre-emptive application of the CISG.

During the appeal, the Court of Appeal rectified the Court of First Instance's view on the nature of the contract, and regarded that the contract between the parties was one for international sale of goods. When considering the governing law of the case, the Court of Appeal referred to art 142 of the General Principles of Civil Law, although it did not use it as the legal basis for applying the CISG in its reasoning. Instead, the Court of Appeal held that the CISG should be applied with priority through directly analyzing whether the application conditions of the CISG had been satisfied or not.

In judicial practice, some courts consider art 142 of the General Principles of Civil Law as the legal basis for the pre-emptive application of the CISG, such as in Judgment (2007) Lu Min Si Zhong Zi No. 6, Judgment (2004) Hui Zhong Fa Min San Chu Zi No. 297, Judgment (2013) Xia Min Chu Zi No. 277, and even Judgment (2007) Yue Gao Fa Min Si Zhong Zi No. 274 which was also made by Guangdong High Court in the same period. Some courts apply the CISG by quoting art 142 as a starting point. In this way, the courts first determine that the governing law should be Chinese the law, and then quote art 142(2) of the General Principles of Civil Law as a reference path to the CISG. In spite of applying art 142 of the General Principles of Civil Law, some courts exclude the application of the CISG on this ground, such as in Judgment (2010) Hu Gao Min Er (Shang) Zhong Zi No. 78.[1]

During the phase of specific law application, after the governing law has been chosen, there might typically be another issue in the application of the CISG. This is the parallel application of domestic law. Even after correctly choosing the CISG as the governing law, courts are still prone to neglect the priority of the CISG and instead to apply domestic law, or apply the CISG in the same manner as the domestic law.[2]

In this case, however, after choosing the applicable law, the Court of Appeal did not overlook the priority of the CISG, but specifically analyzed and made conclusions on certain issues pursuant to the provisions of the CISG. For example, despite both the CISG and domestic laws having regulations regarding the method of contract conclusion, the Court of Appeal determined whether the contract was effective directly pursuant to art 23 of the CISG, which reads '[a] contract is concluded at the moment when an acceptance of an offer becomes effective in accordance with the provisions of this CISG.' Thus, according to the principle of preemptive application of the CISG, the Court determined that a contract is concluded when the promise comes into effect, even though there is no material difference between the CISG and domestic law on this issue. It should be noted that, despite the relevant regulations of the CISG being basically adopted as the provisions of the Contract Law 1999 of China on offers and promises, perfection and supplementation have been made to some legal systems as well by combining with the practical situation of China. Therefore, with respect to the constitutive elements of effectiveness, withdrawal, and cancellation of offers and promises, as well as the mode of contract conclusion, differences still exist. Since it is not involved in this case however, no more discussion on this is made.

**Issue 2 the Applicability of Domestic Law Along with the CISG**

The Court of Appeal did not entirely exclude the applicability of domestic law, even though it regarded the CISG as the governing law. Since there are no express regulations on the determination of the nature of the contract, apparent authority (recognition of the representative of the company) and joint and several debts in the CISG, the Court of Appeal determined its judgment applying the respective domestic laws.

Article 7(2) of the CISG is the basis for the domestic law to fill the blank in a situation where the CISG is preemptively applicable. Article 7(2) concerns the issue of filling loopholes, i.e., how to deal with a matter of international sale of goods which falls within the jurisdiction of the CISG, but no express regulation can be found in it. However, art 7(2) does not directly provide that the domestic law of the country where the court is located should be directly applied in dealing with any matter for which there is no express provisions in the CISG, instead it provides that '[q]uestions concerning matters governed by this CISG which are not expressly settled in it are to be settled in conformity with the general principles on which it is based or, in

[1] He [1], p. 21–22.

[2] Yang [2], p. 63–64.

the absence of such principles, in conformity with the law applicable by virtue of the rules of private international law', which means, in filling the gaps in the CISG, judges and arbitrators are required to solve issues following the general principles on which the CISG is based. Only where no such general principles can be found does art 7(2) permit reference to the applicable national law, i.e., the law applicable by virtue of the rules of private international law, to solve these questions.

The so-called general principles, however, are quite general, vague and difficult for every party to explore and infer the possible results. That leaves ample scope for applying domestic laws. Law practitioners with a background of the civil law system are familiar with applying the general principles, e.g., the principle of good faith stipulated by law, and specific provisions of domestic law to fill in the blanks of the CISG. For example, in dealing with the deposit issue in Civil Judgment (2019) Min Min Zhong No. 578, the Fujian High People's Court held that 'Given that CISG does not stipulate any deposit system, or define the punitive general principle for default, pursuant to Article 41 of the Law of the Application of Law for Foreign-related Civil Relations of the People's Republic of China, which read 'parties may agree on the law applicable to the contract. Otherwise, the laws of the place frequently resided by the party whose performance of obligations best reflects the characters of the contract or other laws most closely related to the contract shall apply', which means the laws of the place where the contract is performed, i.e. the People's Republic of China, can be applied in solving the issues.'; The same wording was used in the reasoning of the Tianjin High Court in its Civil Judgment (2019) Jin Min Zhong No. 90. In this case, the internal logic of the court of appeal should be so, although the Court did not state the reasons for directly applying the domestic law.

In summary, in the application of the CISG, the Court of Appeal adhered to the principle of preemptive application of the CSIG, and in the application of domestic law, it followed the principle of 'indirect application dominates while direct application supplements', which deserves credit.

## References


1. He, X. Y. (2017). the Divergence and Countermeasures of the Applicability of CISG in Courts of the Free Trade Experimental Zone. *International Business Research*, 38(01), 19-29
2. Yang, M. S. (2020). *Research on the Preemptive Application of United Nation CISG on Contracts For The International Sale Of Goods*. Law Press


**Max Siying Wu** is a senior partner in Dacheng Law Offices (Guangzhou), a PhD of International Law in Wuhan University, and was formerly a judge in Guangdong Provincial High People's Court hearing commercial cases involving foreign interests. He has published a personal monograph the Unification of International Commercial Contract Law: Grounds, Aims and Approaches, and also participated in several scholarly writings, eg. International Business Law. He is appointed as Executive Council Member of International Law Research Institute of Guangdong

Law Society, Secretary-general of Cross-border Investment Legal Services Committee of Guangdong Lawyers Association, Member of Foreign-related Legal Services Committee of Guangzhou Lawyers Association, Mediator of Guangzhou Mediation Center for Financial Disputes, Arbitrator of eight commercial arbitration institutions in China including Guangzhou Arbitration Committee and Shenzhen Court of International Arbitration. He is also an Extramural Postgraduate Tutor of Guangdong University of Finance & Economics, and research fellow of the institute of Legal Theories & Practices of Sun Yet-sen University. He is honored as one of the Guangdong and Guangzhou Leading Lawyers on Foreign-related Legal Services.

# Beijing Chenguang Huilong Electronic Technology Development Co., Ltd. v. Thales Communications & Security S.A

**Max Siying Wu**

## Case Information

**Case Name:** *Beijing Chenguang huilong Electronic Technology Development Co., Ltd. v Thales Communications & Security SA*

**Seller:** Thales Communications & Security SA
**Place of Business:** France

**Buyer:** Beijing Chenguanghuilong Electronic Technology Development Co., Ltd.
**Place of Business:** China

**Details of First Instance:**
**Court:** Beijing No.2 Intermediate People's Court
**Date of Decision:** 2004
**Case No.:** (2003) er Zhong min Chu Zi No.07936
**Judges:** N/A

**Details of Second Instance:**
**Court:** Shanghai High People's Court
**Date of Decision:** 18 March 2005
**Case No.:** (2004) Gao Ming Zhong Zi No. 576
**Judges:** Fengju Jin (Presiding Justice), Li Zhang (Justice), Hong Rong (Justice)

M. S. Wu (✉)
Dacheng Law Offices, LLP, Guangzhou, China
e-mail: seawing2002@126.com



P. Guo et al. (eds.), *Selected Chinese Cases on the UN Sales Convention (CISG) Vol. 3*, Selected Chinese Cases on the CISG,
https://doi.org/10.1007/978-981-99-6851-0_2

**CISG Applied:** No
**Key CISG Provisions Interpreted and Applied:** No

**Case Abstract**

On 7 November 2002, the Shandong Provincial Government invited tenders for a radio equipment project. In order to participate in the tender, Beijing Chenguanghuilong Electronic Technology Development Co., Ltd. ('BCETD') contacted the Project Manager of Thales Communications & Security SA ('Thales') and requested Thales to provide BCETD with the antenna needed for the tender. On 18 November 2002, the Project Manager of Thales signed a Letter of Authorization, in which Thales authorized BCETD to act as its agent to handle matters in connection with the tender. On 26 November 2002, the Project Manager of Thales sent an email to BCETD concerning 'ANT194A and ANT184A' (the subject of the email), informing BCETD that the antenna price could be CIF €54,600, and introducing considerations such as the warranty period and delivery terms. BCETD later submitted the Letter of Authorization and won the tender. On 3 March 2003, BCETD entered into a Procurement Contract with the relevant government agency of Shandong Provincial Government. However, Thales had so far failed to deliver the antenna to BCETD, resulting in a breach of contract by BCETD under the Procurement Contract and liability to pay the liquidated damages. BCETD sued Thales to assume liability for breach of contract.

There was no agreement as to the governing law between the parties regarding the dispute before litigation. During the first instance proceedings, BCETD stated that it chose to apply the law of the People's Republic of China and the CISG, while Thales chose to apply the law of the People's Republic of China. The Court of First Instance therefore held that, since both parties had chosen Chinese law as the governing law, pursuant to the principle of party autonomy, the governing law in this case should be Chinese law. As to whether a contract had been established between the parties, the Court of First Instance held that with the facts that Thales issued the Letter of Authorization, sent emails to BCETD, and BCETD won the tender on the basis of these documents, it could not be concluded that a contract of sales had been established between the parties. Therefore, BCETD had no right to hold Thales liable for breach of contract, and Thales should only undertake the liability for *culpa in contrahendo* (**liability for wrongs in conclusion of contracts**).

Both BCETD and Thales appealed against the judgment of the Court of First Instance. As to whether the CISG should be applied or not, the Court of Appeal held that, although the CISG should be applied automatically and pre-emptively in accordance with art 142 of the General Principles of Civil Law, providing the parties do not exclude it, Thales made it clear during the first instance proceedings that Chinese law should be applied but not the CISG, and BCETD did not demonstrate the difference between Chinese law and the CISG. Thus, Chinese law should be the governing law of this case. As to whether a sales contract had been established between the parties, the Court of Appeal held that the Letter of Authorization only represented that Thales agreed to supply the antenna, and the email did not detail the product model, the model quoted and the specific port of CIF. Moreover, even

BCETD itself did not deem that a contract had been concluded, as it had subsequently repeatedly requested to conclude a contract with Thales.

Finally, the Court of Appeal concluded that, in accordance with the Contract Law of the People's Republic of China ('Contract Law'), the sales and purchase contract relationship between the two parties had not been established, and therefore BCETD had no right to hold Thales liable for breach of contract. Thales only had to undertake the liability for ***culpa in contrahendo***.

## Commentary to the Key Issues Related to the CISG

### Issues

Issue 1 The Applicability of the CISG

Issue 2 Any Difference between the CISG and the Contract Law in Regard to the Offer of contract?

### Comments

### Issue 1 The Applicability of the CISG

#### I. Legal Basis for the Automatic and Pre-emptive Application of the CISG

As to the automatic application of the CISG, in the *Digest of Case Law on the United Nations Convention on Contracts for the International Sale of Goods* ('DOCL') which is compiled by United Nations Commission On International Trade Law ('UNCITRAL'), it is interpretated that, according to art[1] (1)(a)[2] of the CISG, if the places of business of both parties to a dispute over international contracts for sales of goods are in different countries, and both of those countries are Contracting States to the CISG, the Convention is 'directly' or 'autonomously' applicable.[3] From the perspective of Chinese law, after China formally became a Contracting State to the CISG in 1986, the Supreme People's Court issued in 1987 the Circular on Transmitting Certain Issues of the MOFTEC in Connection with the Implementation of United Nations Convention on Contracts for the International Sale of Goods.[4] Published by the Ministry of Foreign Economic Relations and Trade of People Republic of China in the same year, it states, 'the contracts for sale of goods reached between the Chinese companies and the companies in the aforementioned countries (except Hungary) will automatically apply to the provisions of the Convention and the disputes or litigations arisen should be also settled under the Convention, unless otherwise agreed.'

[1] *United Nations Convention on Contracts for the International Sale of Goods*, opened for signature 11 April 1980, 1489 UNTS 3 (entered into force 1 January 1988), (CISG).

[2] CISG Article 1 (1): This Convention applies to contracts of sale of goods between parties whose places of business are in different States: (a) when the States are Contracting States.

[3] United Nations Commission on International Trade Law (UNCITRAL) [1], p. 5.

[4] Circular of the Supreme People's Court on Transmitting Certain Issues of the MOFTEC in Connection with the Implementation of United Nations Convention on Contracts for the International Sale of Goods (Fa (Jing) Fa [1987] No. 34), December 10, 1987.

Therefore, whether pursuant to the CISG, DOCL (compiled by UNCITRAL) or the Circular of the Supreme People's Court of China, when the places of business of the parties to the international contracts for sales of good are in different countries and both of those countries are Contracting States to the CISG, the CISG shall be automatically applied, with no need for the parties to agree on it specifically.

As to the preemptive application, theoretically speaking, the 'power distribution theory' developed in the 1990s holds that domestic law merely regulates the domestic civil legal relationship, and it lacks the ability to regulate the international commercial relations. Since the value embodied in domestic law is more to safeguard the sovereignty of a country, it is prone to overlooking the rightful adjustment to the interests of the parties. For this reason, compared with the domestic law of a country, international commercial conventions are more suitable for resolving international business disputes.[5] In art 1(3)[6] of the CISG, it is expressly stipulated that the CISG can be applied without considering the specific rules of conflict. When interpretating art 1 of the CISG, DOCL first mentions that 'convention prevails over recourse to private international law', that is, under the traditional mode, in the case of an international situation, courts resort to the private international law rules in force in their country to determine which substantive rules to apply. Pursuant to the provisions of the CISG, the application of the Convention prevails over the recourse to the forum's private international law rules. Hence, in those countries, however, where international uniform substantive rules are in force, such as those set forth by the Convention, courts must determine whether those substantive international uniform rules apply before resorting to private international law rules at all.[7]

From the perspective of the domestic law of China, a civil-law tradition has heavily influenced the common habit of courts of China, in that they always follow a private-international-law approach when finding the *lex causae* in international commercial cases, and always need to look at reference terms in domestic law of China as a 'doorway' to the application of international legal instruments, be it an international commercial convention that is meant to be applied directly and pre-emptively. This has provoked some controversy, since such a traditional approach would entirely ignore the direct and pre-emptive applicability of many international conventions such as CISG and the Montreal Convention. Article 142(2) of the GPOCL[8] was one such reference term, in fact the most frequently visited 'doorway', which provides '[w]here the provisions of an international treaty which the People's Republic of China has concluded or has acceded to differ from civil laws of the People's Republic of China, the provisions of the international treaty shall apply, with the exception of those articles to which the People's Republic of China has declared its reservation.'

---

[5] Yang [2], pp. 18–24.

[6] CISG: Article 1 (3): Neither the nationality of the parties nor the civil or commercial character of the parties or of the contract is to be taken into consideration in determining the application of this Convention.

[7] United Nations Commission on International Trade Law (UNCITRAL) [1], p. 4.

[8] General Principles of Civil Law of the People's Republic of China (Order of the President No. 37), January 1, 1987.

According to this term, it is clear that international conventions (such as the CISG) have application priority to domestic law where any difference exists. However, as for whether a difference is a prerequisite for applying the CISG preemptively, GPOCL art 142 provides no clear answer. In the point of view of many scholars, the differences between the CISG and the domestic law of China should not be a prerequisite for the pre-emptive application of the CISG, since this contradicts the meaning of becoming a Contracting State of the CISG. This has been indicated in the preamble of the CISG as 'removal of legal barriers in international trade.' In addition, differentiating the regulations of the CISG and the domestic law of China lacks not only standard but feasibility. What constitutes the difference? The wording or the purpose of legislation? If the court has to determine a difference between the CISG and domestic law before applying the CISG, it will naturally tend to apply domestic law immediately, and will easily ignore the different regulations of the CISG. Therefore, even if ambiguity remains in art 142 of the GPOCL, the CISG should be applied pre-emptively without considering whether there is a difference.

Another outstanding issue in the application of the CISG by Chinese courts is that, even when CISG art 1(a) is satisfied, the court may still determine the governing law by the principle of party autonomy or the doctrine of the closest connection in accordance with art 145 of the GPOCL,[9] arts 3 and 41 of the Law of the People's Republic of China on the Application of Laws to Foreign-related Civil Relations[10] and art 126(1) of the Contract Law.[11] Such errors exist in the decisions made by the court of first instance and the court of appeal in this case. The ambiguity of art 142 of the GPOCL is one reason for this. Another reason for such error is that Chinese courts are unfamiliar with the conditions under which the application of the CISG is excluded, and therefore they often arbitrarily determine that the CISG has been excluded from application.

The issues brought about by the problematic art 142 of the GPOCL have currently been eliminated thanks to the coming into effect of the Civil Code of People's Republic of China (Civil Code) on January 1, 2021, and the abolition of the GPOCL

[9] General Principles of Civil Law of the People's Republic of China (Order of the President No. 37), January 1, 1987, Article 145: Unless otherwise stipulated by law, the parties to a contract involving foreigners may choose the law applicable to the handling of disputes arising from the contract. If the parties to a contract involving foreigners have not made a choice, the law of the country of closest connection to the contract shall be applied.

[10] Law of the People's Republic of China on the Application of Laws to Foreign-related Civil Relations (Order of the President No. 36), April 1, 2011, Article 3: The parties concerned can explicitly choose the laws applicable to civil relations involving foreigners in accordance with what the laws. Article 41: The parties concerned shall negotiate and choose the applicable laws for the contracts. If the parties concerned have not made a choice, for the party whose fulfilment of obligations can best realize the contract features, the laws of his regular residence or other laws which have the closest relationship to the contract shall apply.

[11] Contract Law of the People's Republic of China (Order of the President No. 15), October 1, 1999, first paragraph of Article 126: Parties to a contract with a foreign element may nominate the law to be applied in the handling of contractual disputes, except where laws provide otherwise. Where the parties to a contract with a foreign element fail to nominate the law of the contract, the law of the country with the closest connection to the contract shall be applied.

at the same time. The Civil Code contains no reference term similar to art 142 of the GPOCL, and the Judicial Interpretations to the Law of the People's Republic of China on the Application of Laws to Foreign-related Civil Relations has also removed its former art 4 which played the same role of 'doorway' as art 142 of the GPOCL. Consequently, there is presently no longer any such 'doorway either existing or needed in the law of China for the direct and pre-emptive application of CISG.

## II. Whether a Unilateral Objection Constitutes Effective Exclusion of the CISG

The CISG stipulates the exclusion of its application in art 6[12]; however, it does not define the point of time and form of exclusion. Both the court of first instance and the court of appeal in this case held that the CISG has been excluded on the basis that no agreement was reached between the parties on the application of the CISG during the trial. The court of first instance held that Thales' choice to apply Chinese law constituted an effective exclusion of the CISG, and therefore the CISG should not be applied according to the principle of party autonomy. The court of appeal held the same view that the CISG has been effectively excluded. The opinions of the courts in this case are obviously erroneous, but the same opinions are commonly held by Chinese courts in judicial practice. For example, in Civil Judgment (2007) Hu Gao Min Si (Shang) Zhong Zi No. 6, the High People's Court of Shanghai Municipality also held that the objection of one party to the application of the CISG alone constituted the effective exclusion of the CISG.

According to the provisions of the CISG, it can only be excluded by 'the parties', which means excluding the application of the CISG requires mutual agreement of both parties. UNCITRAL also clearly indicates in the DOCL that 'opting out requires a clear, unequivocal and affirmative agreement of the parties'.[13] In addition, regarding the point of time of express exclusion, UNCITRAL does not state in the DOCL that the exclusion mutually agreed upon by both parties during the trial is invalid. On the contrary, UNCITRAL cites relevant German cases holding similar views, including CLOUT case No. 122 [Oberlandesgericht Köln, Germany, 26 August 1994], CLOUT case No. 292 [Oberlandesgericht Saarbrücken, Germany, 13 January 1993], CLOUT case No. 331 [Handelsgericht Kanton Zürich, Switzerland, 10 February 1999], and Schweizerische Zeitschrift für Internationales und Europäisches Recht, 2000, 111.[14] Therefore, regarding the issue of point of time of express exclusion, UNCITRAL to a large extent respects the autonomy of both parties, however, the exclusion should be subject to the mutual agreement of both parties.

The opinion of the courts in this case apparently deviates from the legislative purpose of the CISG to allow excluding its application merely by the unilateral expression of exclusion intent by one party. The most important purpose and significance of the CISG as an international commercial convention is to unify the legal

---

[12] CISG: Article 6: The parties may exclude the application of this Convention or, subject to article 12, derogate from or vary the effect of any of its provisions.

[13] United Nations Commission on International Trade Law (UNCITRAL) [1], p. 33.

[14] United Nations Commission on International Trade Law (UNCITRAL) [1], p. 36.

rules on disputes over contracts for international sales of goods. The CISG also serves to increase the predictability of judgment results for traders from different countries in international trading, as the CISG shall be applied automatically and preemptively if the places of business of the parties are in different Contracting States to the CISG and the parties do not agree to exclude the application of the CISG. If one party is entitled to exclude the application of the CISG by unilateral objection after the dispute occurs, the party which is in a disadvantaged position under CISG rules will always try to enable the application of a governing law which is more favorable to it by excluding the application of the CISG. Allowing the occurrence of such a situation by courts will undoubtedly increase the unpredictability of legal rules for disputes over contracts for international sales of goods, which totally deviates from the legislative purpose of the CISG as well as the purpose of China in becoming a Contracting State to the CISG.

In summary, if the requirements stipulated in CISG art 1(a) have been met, and the parties have not agreed to exclude the application of the CISG, the CISG should be applied automatically and pre-emptively. However, as the court of first instance and the court of appeal did in this case in determining whether the CISG was applicable, instead of first investigating the possibility of CISG application, Chinese courts in judicial practice often refer to party autonomy, the closest connection or any other international conflict rules to determine the application of law, or simply regard the unilateral objection as the effective exclusion of the CISG. The main reason for the continuation of this issue is that Chinese courts are still not familiar with the CISG, and therefore they are inclined to apply the Contract Law.

**Issue 2 Are There Any Differences Between the CISG and the Contract Law in Regard to the Offer of Contract?**

The main reason for the Ccourt of First Instance and the Court of Appeal holding that no sales contract was established between BCETD and Thales is that the Letter of Authorization and the email sent by Thales did not constitute an offer under the Contract Law. Although the Courts did not apply the CISG in their judgments, which was an error in the governing law, in this case there was no difference between the conclusions reached by the application of the CISG and of the Contract Law regarding whether an effective offer existed.

According to art 14(1)[15] of the CISG, an effective offer must meet the following three conditions: (1) such proposal shall be addressed to one or more specific person(s); (2) the offer shall indicate the intention that the offeror is willing to be bound by the offer; and (3) the contents of the offer should be sufficiently definite. The requirement of 'sufficiently definite' in art 14(1) of the CISG means the proposal

[15] CISG: Article 14(1): A proposal for concluding a contract addressed to one or more specific persons constitutes an offer if it is sufficiently definite and indicates the intention of the offer or to be bound in case of acceptance. A proposal is sufficiently definite if it indicates the goods and expressly or implicitly fixes or makes provision for determining the quantity and the price.

indicates the goods and expressly or implicitly fixes or makes provision for determining the quantity and the price. As for the Contract Law, art 14[16] also states that an offer requires: (1) the offeror intends to be bound by the offer; and (2) the content shall be concrete and precise. Obviously, the Contract Law issued in 1999 is greatly affected by the CISG, though a specific offeree is not expressly required under the Contract Law. As for the requirement of 'concrete and precise content', the Contract Law does not provide a clear explanation like the CISG. On the contrary, according to art 88 of the GPOCL,[17] the provisions of the quality, duration, location, and price of the contract can be determined by stipulated methods. Therefore, from the perspective of the provision of the Contract Law, in addition to the subject and quantity of the goods, the clarity of other contents of an offer are either deemed as not necessary or can be determined through regulated methods. However, it does not mean that the requirements of an effective offer under the Contract Law are looser than the requirements of the CISG. Article 12 of the Contract Law[18] lists eight elements that are generally contained in a contract. Even though this provision does not constitute a compulsory regulation, it increases the requirements of clarity of the content, since Chinese courts will take those elements into consideration when determining whether an effective offer exists.

In this case, from the perspective of the CISG, the Letter of Authorization and the email sent by Thales do not meet the condition of art 14(3), i.e., the content in these documents does not meet the requirements of 'sufficiently definite'. Firstly,

[16] Contract Law of the People's Republic of China (Order of the President No. 15), October 1, 1999, first paragraph of Article 14: An offer is an expression of intention to conclude a contract with another person, and the said expression of intention shall satisfy the following requirements: (1) its content shall be concrete and precise; and (2) it shall be stated clearly that, upon the offer being accepted by the offeror, the offeror shall be bound by his or her expression of intention.

[17] General Principles of Civil Law of the People's Republic of China (Order of the President No. 37), January 1, 1987, Article 88: If the contract stipulations concerning quality, duration, location or price are unclear and cannot be determined by reference to relevant articles in the contract and if the parties, moreover, are unable to reach agreement through discussion, the following provisions shall apply: (i) If the quality requirements are unclear, the contract shall be performed in accordance with State quality standards. In the absence of State quality standards, it shall be performed in accordance with usual standards. (ii) If the term of performance is unclear, the debtor may fulfil its obligations to the creditor at any time. The creditor may also demand at any time that the debtor fulfil its obligations, but shall allow the other party the necessary preparatory time.

(iii) If the place of performance is unclear and the payment of money is involved, performance shall be in the place in which the party receiving the payment is located. If the place of performance is unclear in other respects, performance shall be in the place in which the party fulfilling the obligation is located. (iv) If the agreement with regard to price is unclear, the contract shall be performed in accordance with a price set by the State. In the absence of a State-set price, the contract shall be performed with reference to the market price or the price of a similar item or the standard of payment for a similar category of labour.

[18] Contract Law of the People's Republic of China (Order of the President No. 15), October 1, 1999, first paragraph of Article 12: The parties shall agree on the content of a contract, and in general the following matters shall be included: (1) the title or full name and the residence of each party; (2) the subject matter; (3) quantity; (4) quality; (5) price or remuneration; (6) period, place and methods of contractual performance; (7) liability for breach of contract; and (8) methods of dispute resolution. In concluding a contract, the parties may consult model contract instruments of various kinds.

the model of antenna was not clearly stated in the documents, and no provision can be used to determine this, as the subject of the email from Thales to BCETD was 'ANT194A and ANT184A'. Hence, the model of the antenna equipment was yet to be determined by both parties. Secondly, no specific quantity of goods was given in the documents, and no provision can be used to determine it. From the perspective of the Contract Law, a similar conclusion cannot be drawn either, since the subject and quantity of the goods are not available. Additionally, the Court of Appeal specifically mentioned in its judgment that BCETD had repeatedly urged Thales to subsequently sign a contract, which contradicted BCETD's claim that the contract had been validly established.

Therefore, although there are errors in the application of law by the Courts, as to whether an effective offer exists, the application of the CISG and of the Contract Law will both reach a negative conclusion.

## References

1. United Nations Commission on International Trade Law (UNCITRAL). (2016). *UNCITRAL Digest of Case Law on the United Nations Convention on Contracts for the International Sale of Goods*. https://uncitral.un.org/en/case_law/digests
2. Yang, M. S. (2020). *Research on the Preemptive Application of United Nation CISG On Contracts For The International Sale Of Goods*. Law Press

**Max Siying Wu** is a senior partner in Dacheng Law Offices (Guangzhou), a PhD of International Law in Wuhan University, and was formerly a judge in Guangdong Provincial High People's Court hearing commercial cases involving foreign interests. He has published a personal monograph the Unification of International Commercial Contract Law: Grounds, Aims and Approaches, and also participated in several scholarly writings, eg. International Business Law. He is appointed as Executive Council Member of International Law Research Institute of Guangdong Law Society, Secretary-general of Cross-border Investment Legal Services Committee of Guangdong Lawyers Association, Member of Foreign-related Legal Services Committee of Guangzhou Lawyers Association, Mediator of Guangzhou Mediation Center for Financial Disputes, Arbitrator of eight commercial arbitration institutions in China including Guangzhou Arbitration Committee and Shenzhen Court of International Arbitration. He is also an Extramural Postgraduate Tutor of Guangdong University of Finance & Economics, and research fellow of the institute of Legal Theories & Practices of Sun Yet-sen University. He is honored as one of the Guangdong and Guangzhou Leading Lawyers on Foreign-related Legal Services.

# Entreprise P. Boucher v. Henan Yuanfeng Leather Products Co., Ltd.

**Bruno Zeller**

### Case Informatiion

**Case Name:** *Entreprise P. Boucher v Henan Yuanfeng Leather Products Co., Ltd.*

**Seller**: Entreprise P. Boucher
**Place of Business:** Canada (Not Confirmed)

**Buyer:** Henan Yuanfeng Leather Products Co., Ltd.
**Place of Business:** China Mainland

**Case of First Instance:**
**Court:** Henan Province Xinxiang Municipal Intermediate People's Court
**Date of Decision:** 13 August 2007
**Case No.:** (2007) Xin Min San Chu Zi No.30
**Judges:** Yanbin Tu, Lin Wang, Yuguang Ding

**CISG Applied:** No
**Key CISG Provisions Interpreted and Applied:** N/A

### Case Abstract

In August 2006, Entreprise P. Boucher ('Boucher') brought a claim for the unpaid amount under a sale of goods contract before the Zhengzhou Intermediate People's Court ('IPC') against Henan Yuanfeng Leather Products Co., Ltd. ('Yuanfeng').

B. Zeller (✉)
University of Western Australia, Crawley, WA 6009, Australia
e-mail: bruno.zeller@uwa.edu.au



P. Guo et al. (eds.), *Selected Chinese Cases on the UN Sales Convention (CISG) Vol. 3*, Selected Chinese Cases on the CISG,
https://doi.org/10.1007/978-981-99-6851-0_3

Yuanfeng disputed the jurisdiction of the Zhengzhou IPC, which then ruled that the case should be heard by Xinxiang IPC. In March 2007, Yuanfeng brought a counterclaim against Boucher.

Boucher claimed that, in May 2005 they (as the seller) reached an oral agreement with Yuanfeng (as the buyer) on the sale of 10 containers of wet blue cattle hides. The goods were delivered and accepted by Yuanfeng between August and December 2005. The price of the goods, USD $437,800, however, was never paid by the buyer.

Yuanfeng responded that the sale of goods contract did not exist due to the non-existence of a written contract. As the parties' domiciles were in Canada and China, which were ontracting States of the CISG, the CISG should apply. Due to China's reservation to art 11 of the CISG on the formality of the international sale of goods contracts, the contract was not formed. Thus, Yuanfeng had no obligation to pay. Further, Yuanfeng argued that the contract between these two parties was actually for Yuanfeng to provide labour and work to process the cattle hides, so they placed a lien against the goods until the processing costs were paid.

Yuanfeng further brought a counterclaim against Boucher for all costs they had paid, and losses they had suffered, in accepting and processing the cattle hides.

The Court held that:

The parties failed to choose the applicable law for this contract. Thus, the applicable law should be determined pursuant to art 126(1) of the Chinese Contract Law (1999), which provided, 'in the absence of the parties' choice, the law applicable to a contract should be the law of the place having the closest connection with the contract'. The contract in dispute was signed and performed in China, and the disputed subjects were also in China. Thus, Chinese law should apply.

The Court further examined the nature of the contract and determined that it was a sale of goods contract, based on the contract and other materials submitted by Yuanfeng to Zhengzhou Customs. Based on that determination, the Court upheld Boucher's claims and rejected Yuanfeng's counterclaim pursuant to the Chinese Contract Law (arts 159 and 107).

### Commentary on the Key Issues Related to the CISG

#### Issues

Issue 1 Is the Outcome comparable to a CISG Decision?

#### Comments

As the contractual parties did not nominate a governing law it is left to do so by the chosen jurisdiction. The plaintiff, the Canadian party, chose to take action in Henan Province Xinxiang Municipal Intermediate People's Court. By doing so they submitted to the conflict of law rules of the Chinese court namely as stipulated in art 126(1) of the Chinese Contract Law (1999). As the contract is only a verbal one, the Court, without noting art 96, relied on the Chinese reservation which in effect made art 11 inapplicable. This has led to a very interesting situation.

The effect was that the Court rejected the application of the CISG because the contract was orally concluded. Hence the purpose of the reservation is to allow signatories to the CISG to exclude oral formation of a contract when such a formation would be illegal in the seat. The effect is that the contract is invalid and hence unenforceable. The Court therefore had to apply Chinese domestic law to determine whether the contract was enforceable.

By applying Chinese contract law, namely art 10 of the Chinese Contract Law (1999) a problem arises. Article 10 notes that a contract can be concluded in writing, oral or other forms. This in effect replicates exactly what art 11 of the CISG notes.

This case throws up an interesting point, namely is a reservation overruled before it is withdrawn if the original reason for the reservation, namely the form of the contract, no longer exists due to legislative changes.

Looking at the prerequisite of a declaration of art 96 namely that a declaration can 'only be made by States whose legislation requires all contracts of sale governed by the Convention to be concluded in or evidenced by writing.'[1] However the prerequisite for an art 96 declaration is no longer in existence, hence arguably the CISG would still be applicable. At the time of this decision China already had adopted the 1999 Contract Law.

This problem however has been clarified that a 'Declarations that have been made under Article 96 must be observed by courts in Contracting States even if the prerequisites for such declaration were not or are no longer fulfilled, until the declaration has been withdrawn in accordance with Article 97.'[2] China's withdrawal, according to art 97(4) of the CISG took effect on 1 August 2013.

Hence the Court was correct to apply Chinese law. The contrary approach, which holds that a reservation must be considered ineffective when its conditions are not satisfied, should be disregarded by the courts[3] as it creates a significant degree of legal uncertainty and should therefore not be followed.

### Issue 1 is the Outcome Comparable to a CISG Decision?

The Court applied arts 159 and 107 of the Chinese contract law. In effect the Court acknowledged that the buyer breached the contract, as art 107 deals with the consequences of a breach of contract such as to pay compensation. Article 159 notes that the buyer is obliged to pay the price as stipulated in the contract.

---

[1] CISG Advisory Council [1].

[2] CISG Advisory Council [1].

[3] CISG Advisory Council [1].

## Reference

1. CISG Advisory Council. (2013, October 21 and 22). *CISG Advisory Council Opinion No. 15: Reservations under Articles 95 and 96 CISG*. Retrieved from http://www.cisgac.com/cisgac-opinion-no15-p3/#fn

**Professor Dr. Bruno Zeller** B.Com (University of Melbourne), B.Ed (Melb). M.Int'l.Trade Law (Deakin) PhD (Law, Melb.). He is a Professor in Transnational Commercial Law at The University of Western Australia, Perth. His teaching interests include international trade law, trade finance, conflict of laws, international arbitration and maritime law. His extensive research and publications contribute to the understanding of uniform international laws, which have been developed under the auspices of the United Nations and other international bodies. Currently the third edition of the Monograph on Damages Under the Convention on Contracts for the International Sale of Goods has been published. In addition, he has also published on alternative dispute resolution mechanisms and free trade agreements in international journals. He has supervised numerous domestic and international PhD students. Besides having taught short course at many international Universities he is also an Adjunct Professor at Murdoch University, Perth, and an Adjunct Professor the Sir Zelman Cowan Centre, Victoria University, Melbourne.

# Ri xx Development Co., Ltd. v. Hong Kong Bang xx Development Co., Ltd.

**Max Siying Wu**

## Case Information

**Case Name:** *Ri xx Development Co., Ltd. v Hong Kong Bang xx Development Co., Ltd., and Shenzhen Bang xx Factory*

**Seller:** Ri xx Development Co., Ltd.
**Place of Business:** Hong Kong

**Buyer:** Hong Kong Bang xx Development Co., Ltd.
**Place of Business:** Hong Kong

**Details of First Instance:**
**Court:** Shenzhen Bao'an District People's Court
**Date of Decision:** N/A
**Case No.:** (2008) Shen Bao Fa Min Er Chu Zi No. 1327
**Judges:** N/A

**CISG Applied:** No
**Key CISG Provisions Interpreted and Applied:** Articles 1(1), 1(1)(a)

## Case Abstract

On 26 April 2005, Seller Ri xx Development Co., Ltd. ('Ri xx Company') and buyer Hong Kong Bang xx Development Co., Ltd. ('Bang xx Company') and Shenzhen

M. S. Wu (✉)
Dacheng Law Offices, LLP, Guangzhou, China
e-mail: seawing2002@126.com

 
P. Guo et al. (eds.), *Selected Chinese Cases on the UN Sales Convention (CISG) Vol. 3*, Selected Chinese Cases on the CISG,
https://doi.org/10.1007/978-981-99-6851-0_4

Bang xx Factory ('Bang xx Factory') entered into a purchase and sale contract through a facsimile purchase order, agreeing that Ri xx Company would supply one 'ICT online detector' to Bang xx Company and Bang xx Factory at the price of HK $83,000. The delivery date was specified as 4 May 2005, and the delivery method of to be 'supplier delivery'. The settlement method was '1. Pay 50% of the price to the supplier as a deposit; 2. The remaining 50% shall be paid after the machine has been used in the factory for one month without any problems'. On 4 May 2005, Ri xx Company delivered the goods to the domicile of Bang xx Factory in Shenzhen. The next day, Bang xx Factory paid a deposit of HK $41,500 to Ri xx Company. On 17 May 2005, Bang xx Factory issued a written receipt of confirmation and signed and sealed it, however Bang xx Company and Bang xx Factory did not make the remaining payment. On 14 March 2008, Ri xx Company filed a lawsuit with the Shenzhen Bao'an District People's Court.

The Court found that Ri xx Company and Bang xx Company were both enterprises incorporated in Hong Kong. In the actual performance of this case, Ri xx Company which undertook the delivery and acceptance obligations is a company established in mainland China. The party that received the goods was Bang xx Factory, which is a 'three-plus-one' enterprise (custom manufacturing with materials, designs or samples supplied and compensation trade) established by Bang xx Company in mainland China.

The Court of First Instance held that the focus of the dispute in this case was whether the contract in the case belonged to international sale of goods, and then whether the four-year statute of limitations is applicable. Since the subject matter involved in the sales contract between Ri xx Company and Bang xx Company and Bang xx Factory was already in the territory of China when the parties signed the contract, it does not conform to the characteristics of an international sales of goods contract because there were no imported goods. Therefore, the sales contract amongst the parties was not an international contract for the sale of goods, but a general sales contract in which the subject matter of the contract, the place where the contract was signed and the place where the contract was performed are all in the territory of China. The statute of limitations in this case had expired for more than two years from the date of acceptance of the goods by Bang xx Factory (17 May 2005) to the date of Ri xx Company's lawsuit (14 March 2008), according to the Civil Law of China. There was no reason for suspension, interruption, or extension of the statute of limitations. Thus, Ri xx Company's claim was unsuccessful due to the lapse of the statute of limitations and was rejected.

The Court of Appeal further analyzed the facts and held that pursuant to art 1(1) of the CISG '[t]he Convention applies to contracts for sale of goods between parties whose places of business are in different States', because China is a Contracting State to the CISG, the 'places of business' standard apply to China. However, Hong Kong is a Special Administrative Region of China, so although China is a Contracting State, the nature of the sales contract between the parties in mainland China and in Hong Kong cannot directly apply the standard of the CISG. Moreover, even with reference to the CISG's standard for places of business, the contract in this case was a contract for the sale and purchase of goods concluded between two Hong Kong companies whose principal place of business is Hong Kong. The parties actually performing the obligation to deliver the goods are both in mainland China, which means it is not an international contract. Therefore, the basis for the appellant to identify the sales contract of this case as an international sales contract of goods with reference to the CISG and thus apply the 4-year limitation of action is not sufficient. The appeal was finally rejected, and the original judgment was upheld.

## Commentary to the Key Issues Related to the CISG

### Issues

Issue 1 Applicability of the CISG in Hong Kong-related Contracts.

### Comments

### Issue 1 Applicability of the CISG in Hong Kong-Related Contracts

#### I. Internationality and Place of Business

The CISG is a uniform law in the field of international trade in goods.[1] Before resorting to the rules of private international law to determine the applicable law, the courts of the Contracting States of the CISG should first determine the applicability of the substantive rules of the CISG. The guiding case of the Supreme People's Court in mainland China also clarified the priority application of the CISG in the mainland Chinese courts,[2] that is, the court can directly apply the CISG to deal with disputes over contracts for the international sale of goods without being guided by conflicting norms[3] as long as the applicable conditions stipulated by the CISG are met. As for judging whether a contract for the sale of goods meets the applicable conditions stipulated by the CISG and is international, the court should not rely solely on domestic laws, but should also integrate them with the provisions of the CISG.

The Court of First Instance in this case did not consider the relevant provisions of the CISG at all, but decided that the contract was not an international contract for the sale of goods on the grounds that the subject matter of the contract, the place where the contract was signed and the place where the contract was performed were all within the territory of China, and the subject matter involved in the sale did not cross the border. The Court made a judgment directly on the basis of domestic law. The judgment not only ignored the Hong Kong-related factors of the case, but also failed to make a clear explanation as to whether the Hong Kong-related contract meets the applicable conditions of the CISG. More importantly, judging whether a contract involves an international sale of goods by whether the goods cross an international

[1] Han [1], p. 218.

[2] Guidance Case No. 107: Dispute over international goods sale contract between Sinochem International (Singapore) Limited and Thyssenkrupp Materials Co., Ltd. at http://www.court.gov.cn/fabu-xiangqing-143372.html.

[3] He [2], p. 182.

border, is not conforming to the rules of the CISG, and even lacks the legal basis of domestic law. The Court gave no explanation on this, either.

The Court of Appeal corrected this problem. Firstly, it pointed out that China is a Contracting State to the CISG and the 'standard of place of business' stipulated by the CISG is applicable to China. However, the scope of application of the CISG is limited to contracts for the sale of goods between parties whose places of business are in different sovereign states. As Hong Kong is a Special Administrative Region of China, the nature of sales contracts between parties from mainland China and from Hong Kong does not necessitate the application of the CISG. Moreover, since the domestic law contains no specific rules on how to classify/identify contracts for international sale of goods, it is concluded that the parties involved in the case have their places of business in Hong Kong with reference to the provisions of the CISG. Therefore, the contract is not international and the CISG is not applicable.

Furthermore, it is worth noting that the concept of place of business is essential for determining internationality, but the Convention does not specifically define the determination of place of business in various circumstances.[4] Courts from place to place and even from case to case adopt different standards in determining the principal and most closely related place of business of the parties. In this case, the court of second instance, when determining the places of business of the parties, held that the Bang xx Factory was located in Shenzhen. It was only the processing plant and the consignee of the Bang xx Company, so it should not be determined as the place of business of the Bang xx Company. Even if Bang xx Factory was considered as the place of business because the buyer's principal contractual obligation was to pay and the buyer performed the payment obligation in Hong Kong, the place of business that is most closely related to the performance of the contract should be Hong Kong, not the place of receipt. Although the Court of Appeal made it clear that the CISG was not applicable to the contract between mainland China and Hong Kong, it still explained the parties' place of business and whether the contract was international with reference to the provisions of the CISG, which is quite applaudable.

## II. Application of the CISG Between Mainland China and Hong Kong

Courts in mainland China have always held a negative attitude towards the issue of whether the CISG can be applied to disputes between parties in Hong Kong and mainland China. It is generally believed that a contract for the sale of goods between a Hong Kong company and a party in mainland China is an interregional issue between different jurisdictions within a country. Although it may involve interregional conflicts of laws, the CISG will not be involved in general unless the parties expressly agree that the CISG is the applicable law.[5] There are two main reasons listed in the judgment of the court of mainland China. First, the court in China held that Hong Kong did not join the CISG before returning to China, and the Chinese government had not declared the Convention applicable to Hong Kong after its return. Therefore, the CISG was not applicable to Hong Kong. Second, according to art 1(1)

[4] CLOUT case No. 746 [Oberlandesgericht Graz, Austria, 29 July 2004].

[5] Han [3], p. 35.

of the CISG 'The Convention applies to contracts for sale of goods between parties whose places of business are in different States', the Convention does not apply to disputes between parties in the same sovereign country. Hong Kong and mainland China belong to the territory of China, so the CISG does not apply between mainland China and Hong Kong.

The court also held that Hong Kong is a Special Administrative Region of China, so although China is a Contracting State, the nature of the sales contract between the parties in mainland China and in Hong Kong cannot directly applies to the standard of the CISG. Even adopting the standard of the CISG, this case involved a contract for the sale of goods entered into by two companies with their principal places of business both in Hong Kong. The parties who actually fulfilled the obligation to deliver and receive goods are both in mainland China, and thus the contract is not an international one for sale of goods.

Furthermore, in the (2016) ZGFMZ No. 373 sales contract dispute case between United Sino Enterprise (Resources) Co., Ltd. And Xiamen ITG Group Corp., Ltd., heard in the Supreme People's Court of China, the Court held that 'the United Nations Convention on Contracts for the Sale of Goods applies to contracts for the sale of goods between parties whose places of business are in different states. Even taking into account the fact that the case took place before the return of the Hong Kong Special Administrative Region, the United Kingdom was not a party to the Convention, therefore the Convention should not apply to this case. If the parties agree to apply the above-mentioned Convention, the terms of the Convention shall constitute the contents of the contract between the parties.' It can be seen that the Supreme People's Court holds a negative attitude towards the application of the CISG between mainland China and Hong Kong, whether before or after the return of Hong Kong, unless the parties expressly agree to apply the CISG. Another example is (2010) ZSWZZI No.99, the dispute over the sales contract between Yingshun Development (H.K.) Limited and Zhejiang Zhongda Technical Export Co., Ltd. The Zhejiang Provincial High People's Court held that the applicability of the CISG in the dispute involving a Hong Kong business should be determined in accordance with the scope of application of the CISG. Since Hong Kong was not formally acceded to the Convention, and the Chinese government had not declared the application of the Convention to Hong Kong after its return, nor had the Chinese government made a declaration in accordance with CISG art 93(1), it cannot be considered that the CISG is applicable to Hong Kong. Moreover, Hong Kong is an administrative region of the People's Republic of China and not an independent state, so the CISG should not be applied to contracts for the sale of goods between parties whose places of business are located in Hong Kong and in mainland China.

## III. Application of the CISG Between Hong Kong and the Other Contracting States

Before Hong Kong's return to China on 1 July 1997, the UK government was responsible for deciding the conclusion and application status of the treaty in Hong Kong. Since the UK is not a Contracting State to the CISG, Hong Kong before the return did not fall within the territorial application scope of the contracting states to the CISG, and there was no dispute in this practice.

After the return of Hong Kong in 1997, the application of the CISG to Hong Kong has been unclear.

Although China is already a Contracting State to the CISG, under the framework of 'one country, two systems', international conventions concluded by the central government are not necessarily applicable to the Hong Kong Special Administrative Region. On 20 June 1997, the central government submitted a *diplomatic Note* to the Secretary-General of the United Nations. The two appendixes to the *Note* listed 214 international treaties to which China is a party that would be applied to Hong Kong after its return, but the CISG was not included in the list. The *Note* also pointed out that other treaties to which China is a party to or will become a party to that are not listed in the appendix to the *Note* will be handled separately by the Chinese government if it decides they will continue to apply to the Hong Kong Special Administrative Region. This appeared to imply that China adopted a selective and conditional position on the applicability to Hong Kong of international treaties to which it is a party.[6] Therefore, Hong Kong did not fall within the territorial scope of application of China, a Contracting State of the CISG. Under this explanation, art 1(1)(a) of the CISG is not applicable to a contract for the sale of goods between parties whose place of business is in Hong Kong and another contracting state of the CISG. As far as the constitutional basic national policy of 'one country, two systems' and the specific arrangements in the *Note* of the Chinese government are concerned, this conclusion seemed to be uncontroversial.[7]

However, there were two contrasting views on whether the *Note* can constitute a declaration under art 93 of the Convention when considering the application of the CISG to Hong Kong. Pursuant to CISG art 93(4), the CISG is to extend to all territorial units of a Contracting State unless that state declares that the CISG does not apply to a certain territorial unit. Since China has not formally declared that the CISG does not apply to Hong Kong pursuant to art 93 of the CISG, there was another interpretation that this may be explained as the CISG being applicable to Hong Kong.

For a time, the applicability of CISG in Hong Kong has become the focus of controversy among scholars, and contradictory situations also appeared in judicial practice[8] because of the contrary understanding of art 93 of the CISG and the legal effect of the diplomatic declaration of the Chinese central government at the time of the return of Hong Kong. According to some foreign courts, Hong Kong cannot be considered a party to the Convention because China did not extend the applicability of the CISG to Hong Kong. However, there were also judgments of foreign courts which had found under art 93 of the CISG that the applicability of the CISG in China included Hong Kong and thus allowed the CISG to apply, even under art 1(1)(a).

---

[6] Zeng [4], p. 86.

[7] Wang [5], p. 129.

[8] Zhang and Qi [6], p. 542.

Differing from the disputes in foreign courts, courts in mainland China have consistently refused to apply the CISG to contracts where one party's place of business is in Hong Kong and the other party's place of business is in a Contracting State. Chinese courts generally hold that the CISG cannot be applied to Hong Kong because Hong Kong was not previously a Contracting State to the CISG or was not within the territorial scope of application of China, a Contracting State to the CISG,[9] unless the parties expressly or impliedly chose the CISG.

Fortunately, the above-mentioned long-standing dispute will be resolved in a unified way. On 5 May 2022, China deposited with the Secretary-General of the United Nations a declaration to extend the territorial application of the CISG to the Hong Kong Special Administrative Region of China. According to art 97(3) of the CISG, the territorial application took effect on 1 December 2022. This means that from 1 December 2022, the CISG was officially applicable to Hong Kong, China, and the CISG will be applicable to contracts for the international sale of goods concluded between Hong Kong and other Contracting States to the CISG outside China.

### IV. Conclusion

Since the CISG governs parties to transnational trade whose places of business are in different states and Hong Kong is a Special Administrative Region of China, the CISG does not apply to the trade between parties whose places of business are in Mainland China and Hong Kong respectively unless the parties expressly agree that the CISG is the applicable law.

For contracts of international sale of goods concluded between parties from Hong Kong and from other territories outside China, the central government has made a declaration to the Secretary-General of the United Nations that the CISG applies to Hong Kong. From 1 December 2022, the territorial application of the CISG was extended to the Hong Kong Special Administrative Region of China.

However, the extended application of the CISG in Hong Kong cannot yet solve the problem of conflict of jurisdiction within the same country encountered by the contract parties in Hong Kong and in mainland China. Given the importance of the issue, it has long been suggested that the central ggovernment and the government of Hong Kong Special Administrative Region should creatively reach a special legal arrangement for the application of the rules of the CISG to the trade between mainland China and Hong Kong.[10] It is still unclear whether such arrangements will be made in near future.

## References

1. Han, S. (2016). Application of the CISG in China International Commercial Arbitration. *China Law Science*, (5), 218-238

[9] Wang [5], p. 132.

[10] Wang [5], p. 146.

2. He, H. (2019). Problems, Causes and Improvement of the Application of the CISG by Chinese Courts. *Law Science*, (4), 181-192
3. Han, S. (2021). The CISG in China: Achievements and Challenges. *People's Judicature*, 31, 31-36
4. Zeng, H. (2002). On the High Degree of Autonomy of the Hong Kong Special Administrative Region: From the Perspective of Foreign Affairs Practice. *Journal of Comparative Law*, (1), 75-91
5. Wang, Y. Z. (2013). The Application of CISG to the Hong Kong SAR -- Practice Divergence, Legal Analysis and Policy Option. *Wuhan University International Law Review*, 16(1), 127-147
6. Zhang, R. X & Qi, T. (2019). Study on the Application of CISG in Hong Kong, Macau, and Taiwan. *Macao Law*, (3), 542

**Max Siying Wu** is a senior partner in Dacheng Law Offices (Guangzhou), a PhD of International Law in Wuhan University, and was a former judge in Guangdong Provincial High People's Court hearing commercial cases involving foreign interests. He has published a personal monograph the Unification of International Commercial Contract Law: Grounds, Aims and Approaches, and also participated in several scholarly writings, eg. International Business Law. He is appointed as Executive Council Member of International Law Research Institute of Guangdong Law Society, Secretary-general of Cross-border Investment Legal Services Committee of Guangdong Lawyers Association, Member of Foreign-related Legal Services Committee of Guangzhou Lawyers Association, Mediator of Guangzhou Mediation Center for Financial Disputes, Arbitrator of eight commercial arbitration institutions in China including Guangzhou Arbitration Committee and Shenzhen Court of International Arbitration. He is also an Extramural Postgraduate Tutor of Guangdong University of Finance & Economics, and research fellow of the institute of Legal Theories & Practices of Sun Yet-sen University. He is honoured as one of the Guangdong and Guangzhou Leading Lawyers on Foreign-related Legal Services.

# U.S. Tire Imports Inc. v. Qingdao Guangming Tyre Co., Ltd.

**Jie Luo and Fang Gu**

**Case Information**

**Case Name:** *U.S. Tire Imports Inc. v. Qingdao Guangming Tyre Co., Ltd.*

**Seller:** Qingdao Guangming Tyre Co., Ltd.
**Place of Business:** China

**Buyer:** U.S. Tire Imports Inc
**Place of Business:** U.S.

**Details of First Instance:**
**Court:** Qingdao Intermediate People's Court
**Date of Decision:** 20 December 2011
**Case No.:**
**Judges:** Yuanhong Li (Presiding Judge), Huiying Xu (Acting Judge), Juan Wang (Acting Judge)

**CISG Applied:** Yes
**Key the CISG Provisions Interpreted and Applied:** Articles 11, 12, 18

**Case Abstract**

The dispute arose between the plaintiff U.S. Tire Imports Inc ('U.S. Tire') and the defendant Qingdao Guangming Tyre Co., Ltd. ('Qingdao') concerning the performance of a contract with regard to the purchase of tires.

J. Luo (✉) · F. Gu
Zhongnan University of Economics and Law, Wuhan, China
e-mail: luojie@zuel.edu.cn



P. Guo et al. (eds.), *Selected Chinese Cases on the UN Sales Convention (CISG) Vol. 3*, Selected Chinese Cases on the CISG,
https://doi.org/10.1007/978-981-99-6851-0_5

U.S. Tire claimed that on 8 April and 7 May 2009, it paid Qingdao USD $36,720 and $45,060 for the purchase of tire products produced by Qingdao. However, Qingdao did not deliver any goods to U.S. Tire and refused to refund the money paid by the plaintiff. U.S. Tire argued that Qingdao's behavior violated the contract and caused them great economic loss. U.S. Tire requested the Court to adjudicate and order Qingdao to return the payment of USD $81,780.

To prove the assertions, U.S. Tire produced evidence including the 'proforma invoice' which recorded the details of the contract including the type and form of the tires, the departure point of the goods and their destination and the method of financial transaction, and two letters of authorization for fund transfer. These two letters showed that on 8 April 2009 and 7 May 2009, U.S. Tire remitted USD $36,720 and USD $45,060 to Qingdao's accounts at Shanghai Pudong Development Bank Qingdao Branch and Huaxia Bank Qingdao Branch respectively.

Through the proforma invoice U.S. Tire aimed to prove the contract was established and valid.

Qingdao confirmed the authenticity of the evidence but called attention to the fact that although the evidence material contained the name of the defendant and the name of the defendant's original salesman, it was neither stamped, signed or authorized in any form. U.S. Tire agreed that the email was sent by Zhang Hongsen, who concluded a contract with U.S. Tire to sell the goods which were bought from Qingdao. Therefore, the email could not prove that there was a contractual relationship between the plaintiff and the defendant.

U.S. Tire submitted the above evidence to prove that it had paid the defendant USD $81,780 as agreed. Cross-examination revealed that Qingdao had no objection to the evidence itself, and the amount that had been received, but the received money was Zhang Hongsen's payment, and he had no authorized business dealings with the plaintiff.

Correspondingly, Qingdao submitted evidence including two receipt vouchers 12 sales contracts with Zhang Hongsen and an IOU, which stated 'Global Trade Service Co., Ltd. owes Qingdao Guangming Tire Co., Ltd. USD 359,787.36 for tire payment with the signature of Zhang Hongsen.

U.S. Tire believed that the 12 sales contracts submitted by Qingdao, signed with Interlink Trade and Service Co., Ltd., had nothing to do with this case. The IOU submitted by Qingdao is evidence of the legal relationship between Qingdao and Interlink Trade and Service Co., Ltd. and was not relevant to the case. The Court was of the view that the 12 sales contracts and the IOUs submitted by Qingdao directly proved that there was a sales contract legal relationship between Qingdao and parties other than U.S. Tire, and the evidence itself could not reflect relevance to this case. Whether there is a sales contract legal relationship between Qingdao and parties other than the plaintiff has no direct and inevitable connection with whether there is an international sales contract legal relationship between the parties. Therefore, the objectivity and legality of the sales contracts and IOUs submitted by Qingdao would not be given standing by the Court in this case.

The Court delivered its judgment that no contractual relationship between Qingdao and U.S. Tire could be proved. Qingdao returned USD $81,740 to U.S. Tire. within ten days of the effective date of the judgment.

## Commentary to the Key Issues Related to the CISG

### Issues

Issue 1 The Acceptance of an Offer through Conduct.

Issue 2 The Application of Art 11.

### Comments:

### Issue 1 the Acceptance of an Offer Through Conduct

It is an axiomatic assertation widely confirmed that statement of the acceptance of an offer can be demonstrated in a variety of forms.[1] A statement of acceptance may be explicit or implied. It may be made in any form (in writing, verbally, and electronically). The CISG does not restrict acceptance to the same means of communication in which the offer was made.[2] In accordance with art 18(3), the acceptance of the offer could be reflected at the moment the act is performed. This means that it is not necessary to, on any occasion, prove the explicit acceptance expressed by the offeree, however, performance still cannot be taken as assent to acceptance unless it is the way both parties realize consent without any need for explanation, which is crystallized as commercial 'usage' in the provision.[3]

The core proposition of this clause is to strike a balance between commercial efficiency and the foundation of the contract, i.e., mutual consent. Indeed, there is a waste of resources if communication and negotiation is required for the acceptance of every contract, even for quite familiar business partners. The period before the arrival of the offer could be quite long. It is more pragmatic to remove this comparatively otiose procedure and establish the contract. However, this depends on the prerequisite that both parties comprehend each other's the implicit intention. Then consensus can be reached, and the contract established, otherwise, it is neither prudent nor reasonable to validate it.

The other facet of the problem is the nature and effect of 'silence or inactivity' of art 18(1). Silence or inactivity can in principle also express an intention to accept; there is then, of course, no question of its 'reaching' the addressee. However, for such conduct to indicate assent, there must be additional factors associated with the silence or inactivity.[4] For instance, case law provides that a steady business relationship is necessary to assume that a tacit acceptance exists.[5] Practices between

[1] Schwenzer [1], p. 612.

[2] Brunner [2], p. 140.

[3] Pamboukis [3], p. 114.

[4] Supreme Court Slovak Republic [4].

[5] Arnhem [5].

the parties established through lengthy business relations will often show not only that particular conduct indicates acceptance, but also that the need for assent so expressed to reach the offeror has been waived.[6] Where there is a framework contract between the parties, it is even easier to attribute such an effect to conduct amounting to acceptance.[7]

The crux of the matter here is to prove the intention to be bound and the substantial connection to the certain offer. *In casu*, the most intractable problem lies the proof of acceptance. Indeed, in a commercial transaction, there exits all sorts of action and omissions which could convey certain information. Thus, it is necessary for the court to interpret the meaning of every action and reaction. The Court was of the view that in international trade, the factual act of payment and settlement of foreign exchange corresponds to a type of civil legal relationship, which is not unique or certain, and still needs to be proved by evidence. Combined with the facts of this case, where sending of an e-mail to the plaintiff by an outsider resulted in U.S. Tire paying Qingdao according to the instructions, and the defendant receiving the money, means that there is a legal relationship between the original party and Qingdao in the contract of international sale of goods which is still insufficient in the core element of expression of will.

**Issue 2 the Application of Art 11**

Although important legal systems maintain, *inter alia* for sales contracts, requirements as to form, or equivalent rules which must be satisfied if a contract is to be valid or its conclusion or content proved, it is recognized by many legal systems that freedom of formation shall be adopted with regard to offer and acceptance.

Hence, the Convention adopts a media-neutral approach as to form by, first, containing a principle of freedom of form and, second, understanding the notion of writing in a very open and modern sense in order to catch up with the pace of development of technology. In the contemporary era, contracts are often concluded by use of modern means such as fax, e-mail, or other forms of electronic communication.[8] Where the parties have exchanged correspondence and made oral declarations, the principle of freedom from requirements as to form contained in art 11 makes it unnecessary to differentiate clearly on grounds of form.

At the time when the dispute *in casu* occurred, China had made a reservation to art 11. In other words, China does not consider itself to be bound by art 11 as well as the provisions in the Convention relating to the content of art 11.[9] Consequently, it is reasonable for the Court in this case to refrain from further analysis of this issue. However, since 2013, China has withdrawn its reservation,[10] which demonstrates its effort to embrace the unified international standard.

---

[6] Schwenzer [1], p. 176.

[7] Ibid.

[8] Brunner [2], pp. 109–110.

[9] Ministry of Commerce of People's Republic of China [6].

[10] Yu [7].

## References


1. Schwenzer, I. (2016). *Schlechtriem & Schwenzer: Commentary on the UN Convention on the International Sale of Goods* (4th Ed.). Oxford University Press
2. Brunner, C. (2019). *Christoph Brunner & Benjamin Gottlieb: Commentary on the UN Sales Law (CISG).* Wolters Kluwer
3. 3. Pamboukis, C. (2005). The concept and function of usages in the United Nations convention on the international sale of goods. *The Journal of Law and Commerce,* 25(1), 107-131.
4. Supreme Court Slovak Republic. (2008, June 19), CISG-online 1875
5. Rechtbank Arnhem. (2007, January 17), CISG-online 1455/1476
6. People's Republic of China. (2013, January 16). Notification deposited with the Secretary-General of the United Nations. Retrieved from https://treaties.un.org/Pages/showActionDetails.aspx?objid=080000028034c1ac&clang=_en
7. Yu, M. (2022, October 16). *Application of CISG in Arbitration in China: A Case Study with CIETAC.* Retrieved from https://www.chinajusticeobserver.com/a/application-of-cisg-in-arbitration-in-china-a-case-study-with-cietac



**Jie Luo** is an associate professor of Zhongnan University of Economics and Law. She obtained a MA in Law from University of East Anglia in 2004, a Ph.D in International Law from Wuhan University in 2008 and a Ph.D in Private Law from University of Paris Sud in 2010. Her main research interests lie in international trade law. She is the principal investigator for several research projects, and she has published several articles and monographs on CISG.

**Fang Gu** Master candidate of International economic law at Law School of Zhongnan University of Economic and Law. Research Field: International Trade Law, WTO law and International Investment Arbitration.

# WuXi Hengfeng Electronic Products Co., Ltd. v. Symban Lighting Corporation

**Ye Xia**

## Case Information

**Case Name:** *WuXi Hengfeng Electronic Products Co., Ltd. v Symban Lighting Corporation*

**Seller:** WuXi Hengfeng Electronic Products Co., Ltd. ('Hengfeng Company')
**Place of Business:** China

**Buyer:** Symban Lighting Corporation ('Symban Corporation')
**Place of Business:** Canada

**Details of First Instance:**
**Court:** Wuxi Intermediate People's Court, Jiangsu
**Date of Decision:** 21 September 2010
**Case No:** (2009) Xi Min San Chu Zi No.185
**Judges:** Chao Lu (Presiding Judge), Jun Li (Acting Judge), Bei Han (Acting Judge)

**CISG Applied:** Yes
**Key CISG Provisions Interpreted and Applied:** Articles 53, 62, 78

## Case Abstract

Hengfeng Company brought a lawsuit as the plaintiff and claimed that, on 15 August 2006, Symban Corporation and Hengfeng Company signed a sales confirmation

Y. Xia (✉)
4-1004 Sanchengli, Heiniucheng Road, Tianjin, Hexi District, China
e-mail: xiayefrom022@126.com



P. Guo et al. (eds.), *Selected Chinese Cases on the UN Sales Convention (CISG) Vol. 3*, Selected Chinese Cases on the CISG,
https://doi.org/10.1007/978-981-99-6851-0_6

letter which agreed that Symban Corporation would purchase electronic ballasts from Hengfeng Company for a total cost of USD $59,361. The price terms were FOB Shanghai, the mode of transportation was sea freight, and according to a copy of the bill of lading ('B/L'), the payment terms were a 100% telegraphic transfer. Following receipt of payment, the B/L was sent by express mail or released by telex. The delivery date was stipulated as before 10 September 2006. On 6 October 2006, Hengfeng Company obtained the B/L sent from Hanghua Company as first carrier. On 24 October 24, 2006, Hengfeng Company sent the original B/L to Symban Corporation by FedEx. Since Symban Corporation failed to fulfill the agreed-upon payment, Hengfeng Company claimed for payment of the contract price and compensation for the corresponding loss of interest accrued since 2 November 2006, calculated on the daily RMB overdue loan interest rate of the People's Bank of China at 2.1/10,000 per day.

The court of first instance held that this dispute was an international commercial contract case dispute. The business places of the two parties were China and Canada. Since China and Canada are both Contracting States to the CISG, the CISG should be applied. Hengfeng Company as the plaintiff had delivered the goods under the contract and sent the bill of lading. Symban Corporation as the defendant failed to pay the price as agreed. Thus, Hengfeng Company had the right to claim compensation for the loss of interest. The plaintiff's claim was fully supported by the Court.

## Commentary to the Key Issues Related to the CISG

### Issues

Issue 1 The Applicability of the CISG.

Issue 2 Determination of the Breach of Contract.

Issue 3 Consequences of Breach.

### Comments

#### Issue 1 the Applicability of the CISG

Choosing the correct applicable law is important to protect the rights of the parties in international civil and commercial relationships. In this case, the court of first instance prioritized the resolution of the applicable law as its primary concern. This approach is consistent with the provisions of art 142(2), of the General Principles of the Civil Law[1] and art 178 of its judicial interpretation, which were the applicable laws in 2010. However, given the fact that the parties involved in this case did not expressly agree on which laws were applicable for this contract, the Court first cited

[1] Article 142(2) of General Principles of the Civil Law of the People's Republic of China: If any international treaty concluded or acceded to by the People's Republic of China contains provisions differing from those in the Civil Laws of the People's Republic of China, the provisions of the international treaty shall apply, unless the provisions are ones on which the People's Republic of China has announced reservations.

international treaty law, holding that since the places of business of the two parties were in China and Canada, both of which are Contracting States to the CISG, the CISG should be applied as the applicable law. This reason is consistent with art 1(1)(a) of the CISG. Regrettably, these provisions were omitted when citing the basis for the Court's judgment.

After the implementation of the Civil Code of the People's Republic of China, the General Principles of Civil Law was subsequently abolished. Neither the Civil Code nor the Law of the People's Republic of China on Choice of Law for Foreign-related Civil Relationships directly stipulates the manner of application for treaties. From the point of view of judicial practice, if the legal principle of art 142 of the original General Principles of Civil Law is to be followed, the court should generally choose to first begin with the direct application of international treaties, or with the application of any agreement made by the parties involved. Since China made an art 1(1)(b) reservation when adopting the CISG, the indirect application of international treaties still has certain difficulties.

**Issue 2 Determination of the Breach of Contract**

## I. On Whether the Contract for the International Sale of Goods Relationship has Been Established Between the Two Parties

For any sales contract dispute case, the establishment and effectiveness of the contract should be the cornerstone of the contract dispute judgment and is the first issue to be considered after the applicable law is determined. However, this was not discussed by the court of first instance. In accordance with CISG art 11, a contract of sale need not be concluded in or evidenced by writing and is not subject to any other requirement as to form. However, when China acceded to the Convention, it stated its reservations to these clauses. There is an argument to be made that the requirement for written form in the Contract Law of the People's Republic of China, promulgated and implemented after China's accession to the Convention, no longer meets the conditions for the reservation of art 96 of the Convention,[2] China has not explicitly stated that it has withdrawn this reservation. From the perspective of the applicable laws, the signing of the CISG should therefore also be in a written form. What is worth noting in this case is that the two parties did not form a 'sales contract' with complete form and content but confirmed the content of the contract through a written 'Sales Confirmation Letter'. The 'Sales Confirmation Letter' involved in this case includes the main content of the contract, such as the subject matter of the sale of goods, transportation method, price terms, payment method and payment terms which are included in the conditions of the offer. The buyer's confirmation of the above content legally constitutes an acceptance which meets the written form requirement for signing contracts in China. Pursuant to art 23 of the CISG, the contract is concluded when an acceptance is made in accordance with the effective provisions of the Convention. Therefore, the signing of the sales confirmation indicates the

---

[2] Yang [1], p. 307.

establishment of the CISG relationship between the two parties, and both the buyer and the seller are required to abide by the agreement in the confirmation.

**II. Analysis of the Fulfillment of the Rights and Obligations of Buyers and Sellers**

Firstly, the Court held that the buyer had fulfilled its obligation to deliver. According to CISG art 30, the seller must deliver the goods, handing over any documents relating to them and transfer the property in the goods as required by the contract and the Convention. According to art 31(a), if the seller is not bound to deliver the goods at any other particular place, his obligation to deliver is stated as 'if the contract of sale involves carriage of the goods—in handling the goods over to the first carrier for transmission to the buyer'. Under the CISG, the seller has three obligations. First, delivery of goods, second, presentation of documents and third transfer of ownership. When it comes to the transportation of goods, the place of delivery is judged to be where the goods are handed over to the first carrier. The goods in this case were transported by sea freight, and the price terms adopted were FOB Shanghai. To compare the relevant terminology utilized by the CISG and Incoterms, the provisions on delivery in the CISG tend to be more general, while Incoterms is more practical as they adhere to the International Chamber of Commerce's more operable standards. In terms of the application of the CISG and Incoterms, case analyses performed by scholars find that Incoterms, as a commercial practice, are second only to the contract agreement of the parties, and superior to the provisions of the CISG.[3] When there is no agreement between CISG and Incoterms, domestic laws can be used to fill in the gap. Judging from the handling of this case, there was no substantial difference between the CISG and FOB terms. As the case occurred in 2006, Incoterms 2000 were the applicable set of regulations to this case. In the context of Incoterms 2000, the seller in the FOB contract must 'deliver the goods on board' or 'load the ship' at the port of shipment in a timely manner. The stowage of goods in this case was the gunwale. Once the goods have passed from the gunwale at the port of destination, the seller has fulfilled its delivery obligations. The goods involved in this case can be deemed to have been delivered by the seller when the carrier issued the bill of lading on 6 October 2006.

It should also be noted that the agreed delivery date between the two parties was before 10 September 2006, and the delivery date offered by the plaintiff in this case appears to be inconsistent with the agreement. The Court did not analyse this discrepancy when the buyer did not defend the seller's breach of contract, which is consistent with the principle of 'no trial without complaint' in domestic procedural law.

Secondly, is the buyer in breach of contract? According to the agreement between the two parties, the payment terms were a 100% telegraphic transfer payment based on the copy of the bill of lading. The buyer's payment terms are fulfilled after the seller has delivered both the goods and the bill of lading. The buyer's failure to pay clearly constituted a breach of contract, which was confirmed by the Court.

[3] Zuo [2], pp. 54–59.

**Issue 3 Consequences of Breach**

In this case, the buyer and the seller were not in agreement when it came to liability for a breach of contract. How should the law be applied when the buyer breaches a contract and the seller claims compensation for incurred losses? Firstly, art 78 of the CISG provides clarification on the general obligations of both buyers and sellers in the case of a breach of contract where damages result from non-payment of the price or any other sum that is in arrears, stating that the observant party is entitled to interest on the unpaid sum. However, art 78 does not specify which interest rate shall apply. Article 78 was drafted to include provisions of official discount theory plus 1% and interest rates on unsecured short-term commercial credit. Although these rates are different, the intention of the provision has always been to apply the principle of compensation for losses caused by the loss of capital costs of the payee. Despite this topic being discussed many times by UNCITRAL, ultimately unification of interest rate standards proved to be too challenging due to the differences in interest rates across various countries' legal systems. Consequently, art 78 was adopted as current.[4]

The issue of determining the applicable interest rate ultimately depends on *lex causae* that apply in cases which CISG has not covered. Under China's private international law, the location of the seller, as the place of habitual residence of a party, is often considered to be one of the most significant relationships in a sales contract. In this case, as the seller's place of business is China, China's domestic law would be chosen as the applicable law to set the interest rate for liquidated damages. In 2012, China promulgated the Interpretation of the Supreme People's Court on Issues Concerning the Application of Law for the Trial of Cases of Disputes over Sales Contracts, with art 24 stipulating that the interest rate on an overdue payment can be referred to the issuing bank's overdue penalty interest rate. This regulation is in line with the Reply of the Supreme People's Court on Issues Concerning the Standards for the Calculation of Liquidated Damages for Overdue Payments.

It can be seen that liquidated damages in Chinese domestic law applies the principle of 'compensation based, supplied by punishment' in dealing with liquidated damages, which seems on the surface to differ from the loss compensation principle discussed in the CISG. How should this difference be viewed? To answer this, I will explore the background of the choice of the People's Bank of China's overdue loan interest rate as the standard. In domestic judicial practice, which interest rate standard of liquidated damages for overdue payment should be adopted has often been disputed between two major viewpoints: the principles of loss compensation and loss compensation plus punishment. Judges who advocate for the compensation for losses position will use bank deposit interest rates or bank loan interest rates to calculate their judgment.[5] On the other hand, judges who advocate for loss compensation

---

[4] Bai [3], pp. 105–109.

[5] The difference in the above-mentioned interest rates lies in the judges' different judgments on the scope of the loss.

plus punishment will use the bank's overdue loan interest rate in the calculation. Finally, because the parties had not agreed on the calculation standard of liquidated damages for overdue payment, the 2012 Interpretation confirmed that the principle of calculating the overdue loan based on the bank's interest rate should be adopted. The Supreme Court held that at lending or deposit rates, the defaulter's overdue payment costs would still be lower than the cost of obtaining financing through normal financing channels.[6] This is due to the fact that if commercial entities want to obtain loans from banks, they need to conduct credit investigations and provide guarantees. If, after default, liquidated damages are only calculated at the benchmark interest rate of bank loans, the price paid by the defaulting party by occupying the funds of the non-defaulting party is much smaller in comparison than if commercial loan rates are used. The overdue loan interest rate appears to be punitive to a certain extent, but the loss compensation standard is still determined by the court on the basis of commercial and judicial practice. In essence, this practice still embodies the loss compensation principle. Therefore, the calculation standard of liquidated damages for overdue payment in China's domestic law is consistent with the CISG.

Although the court of first instance in this case did not present a basis for discussion in its judgment, the afore-mentioned reply would be applicable in terms of the calculation standard for liquidated damages. It must also be pointed out that the judgment ignored recent changes in the penalty interest rate stipulated by the People's Bank of China. Since 1 January 2004, the overdue loan interest rate has been adjusted from 2.1/10,000 to an additional 30–50% on the benchmark loan interest rate. The interest rate claimed by the plaintiff was the previous standard of 2.1/10,000 per day. Although this rate was lower than the penalty interest rate at that time, it should be considered the exertion of its own rights, and the Court should confirm it. However, in the main text of the court's September 2010 judgment, describing the interest rate as the 'People's Bank of China's RMB overdue loan interest rate' would make the penalty interest rate of the ruling unknown.

## References

1. Yang, F. (2008). China's reservation to CISG and its application in CIETAC arbitration. *International Law Review of Wuhan University*, (vol 8., pp. 307). Wuhan University Press
2. Zuo, H.C. (2021). The Application of CISG and Incoterms in Risk Transfer from Neuromed case. *Journal of Henan University of Economics and Law*,1,54–59
3. Bai, L. (2014). A comparative Study of Judicial Interpretation of Sales Contracts and Intereat Reimbursement Provisions in the United Nations Convention on Contracts for the International Sales of Goods, *Application of Law*, 3, 105–109

[6] The Second Civil Division of The Supreme People's Court of P.R.C. [4].

4. The Second Civil Division of The Supreme People's Court of P.R.C. (2016). *Understanding and Application of Judicial Interpretation of Sales Contracts by the Supreme People's Court* (1st edition). People's Court Press

**Ye Xia** is a judge of the Primary People's Court of Binhai New Area of Tianjin Municipality.

# Western Mining Group (Hong Kong) Company Limited v. Hanchang Industry Co., Ltd., Shanxi Fuyuan International Commerce Co., Ltd.

**Max Siying Wu**

## Case Information

**Case Name**: *Western Mining Group (Hong Kong) Company Limited v Hanchang Industry Co., Ltd., Shanxi Fuyuan International Commerce Co., Ltd.*

**Seller**: Western Mining Group (Hong Kong) Company Limited
**Place of Business**: Hong Kong

**Buyer**: Hanchang Industry Co., Ltd.
**Place of Business**: Korea

**Details of First Instance**:
**Court**: Shanghai No. 2 Intermediate People's Court
**Date of Decision**: 21 September 2010
**Case No.**: (2007) Hu Er Zhong Min Wu (Shang) Chu Zi No 130
**Judges**: Xuejie Cui (Presiding Judge), Tianlan Han (Acting Judge), Wei Zhu (Acting Judge)

**Details of Second Instance**:
**Court**: Shanghai High People's Court
**Date of Decision**: 13 June 2011
**Case No.**: (2010) Hu Gao Min Er (Shang) Zhong Zi No 78
**Judges**: Chuan Xu (Presiding Judge), Qian Fan (Judge), Xianhua Huang (Acting Judge)

M. S. Wu (✉)
Dacheng Law Offices LLP, Guangzhou, China
e-mail: seawing2002@126.com



P. Guo et al. (eds.), *Selected Chinese Cases on the UN Sales Convention (CISG) Vol. 3*, Selected Chinese Cases on the CISG,
https://doi.org/10.1007/978-981-99-6851-0_7

**CISG Applied**: No

**Key CISG Provisions Interpreted and Applied**: N/A

**Case Abstract**

On 28 November 2006, Western Mining Group (Hong Kong) Hong Kong Company Limited ('Western Mining') and Shanxi Fuyuan International Commerce Co., Ltd. ('Fuyuan Commerce') signed a Sales Confirmation ('Sales Confirmation 1'), agreeing that Western Mining would sell 2,400 tons of zinc ingots to Fuyuan Commerce in four batches, also agreeing on the unit price and total price under the term of delivery of CIF Incheon, with the payment term by letter of credit. The Confirmation also stipulated that the goods would be shipped from Shanghai, China to Incheon, South Korea, with the shipment period from December 2006 to March 2007 at 600 tons per month with partial shipment allowed.

On the same day (28 November 2006), Fuyuan Commerce and Hanchang Industry Co., Ltd. ('Hanchang Industry') signed a Sales Confirmation ('Sales Confirmation 2') with the same number, agreeing that Fuyuan Commerce would sell 2,400 tons of zinc ingots to Hanchang Industry in four batches. The beneficiary of the letter of credit was the shipper designated by the buyer, namely Western Mining. Sales Confirmation 2 also agreed that the buyer would pay $10 off the difference between the unit price of the letter of credit and that of the Contract to the Seller on a monthly basis. Other terms of Sales Confirmation 2 were exactly the same as those in Sales Confirmation 1.

On 7 December 2006, Korean Hana Bank, upon application of Hanchang Industry, opened an irrevocable letter of credit ('ILC') in favour of Western Mining for 600 tons of zinc ingots made in India, stating that the date of shipment of the goods should not be later than 6 January 2007. Later, at the request of Western Mining, Hana Bank modified some terms of the letter of credit.

On 26 December 2006, the agent of Western Mining and the transportation company signed a Fixture Note stating that Western Mining would charter a cargo ship to deliver 660 tons of zinc ingots from Shanghai to Incheon from 1 January 2007 to 6 January 2007. Subsequently, the zinc ingots were loaded on 7 January 2007, one day after the latest shipment date agreed in the letter of credit.

On 8 January 2007, the agent of Western Mining sent a letter to Fuyuan Commerce informing it of the name, contact person, telephone, and fax numbers of the agent of the shipment. On 11 January 2007, Fuyuan Commerce sent a letter to the agent of Western Mining, indicating that Hanchang Industry had repeatedly asked for the shipment plan after issuing the letter of credit in early December, but Western Mining had not provided it. Later, Hanchang Industry contacted the shipping company and learned that the cargo ship had only left Shanghai on January 8. As a result, Hanchang Industry expressed its doubts as to whether Western Mining could strictly perform the contract. Hanchang Industry decided to cancel sales Confirmation 2 and reserve the right to further claim for the purpose of avoiding unpredictable risks to the production plan in the next few months. The agent of Western Mining sent several letters to Fuyuan Commerce expressing his regret and hoping for forgiveness. The negotiation between the parties failed, resulting in the litigation. After the goods arrived in Incheon, Western Mining shipped the cargo back to Shanghai.

In 2008 and 2009, Western Mining successively sold the zinc ingots originally planned to be sold to Hanchang Industry in separate batches.

On 3 December 2007, Western Mining filed a lawsuit against Fuyuan Commerce and Hanchang Industry, requesting the two defendants to continue to perform the contract. However, due to the fact that the two Sales Confirmations could not be actually performed, Western Mining changed its claims to request Hanchang Industry to compensate it for economic losses, specifically including the shipment and storage costs of the first batch of zinc ingots, loss of bank financing interest, loss of actual price difference, and loss of expectation benefits.

The court of first instance held that:

1. Application of the law.

Since Hanchang Industry is a legal person in South Korea and the dispute involved international trade activities, foreign factors were involved. In view of the fact that the two Sales Confirmations were signed and performed in the territory of the People's Republic of China, and Western Mining, Fuyuan Commerce and Hanchang Industry agreed in the court hearing that the laws of People's Republic of China should be applied to this case, this is what occurred.

2. Whether there is a direct trading relationship between Western Mining and Hanchang Industry.

The court of first instance held that, based on the facts of the case, Fuyuan Commerce was an intermediary and only charged Hanchang Industry intermediary fees of USD $10 per ton as agreed. Therefore, the parties to the transaction in this case were Western Mining and Hanchang Industry.

3. Whether the one-day delay in shipment constitutes a fundamental breach of contract; whether Hanchang Industry's refusal to perform constitutes a breach of contract.

The court of first instance held that pursuant to Article 94 of the Contract Law of the People's Republic of China, the parties to a contract may terminate the contract when the other party delays performance of its obligations, or breaches the contract in some other manner, rendering it impossible to achieve the purpose of the contract, that is, the breach of contract by one party has constituted a fundamental breach. In this case, the one-day delay in shipment by Western Mining did not defeat the purpose of the contract, so Western Minings behavior did not constitute a fundamental breach of contract. Therefore, Hanchang Industry can only request Western Mining to assume the liability for breach of contract for delay in performance. Hanchang Industry's refusal to accept the first batch of zinc ingots and to fulfill its duties for the last three batches of zinc ingots constituted a breach of contract.

4. Losses for which hanchang industry is liable.

The court of first instance held that the losses should include direct loss and loss of expectation benefits.

After the court of first instance delivered its judgment, Hanchang Industry filed an appeal, holding that the parties agreed to apply the laws of People's Republic of China, which did not exclude the application of international treaties and international practices, and that the United Nations Convention on Contracts for the International Sale of Goods ('CISG') should apply to the case. The delivery date agreed in Sales Confirmation 2 was the end of December 2006. The buyer unilaterally gave the shipper additional time from 1 January 2007 to 6 January 2007 by letter of credit, however the shipper still failed to deliver the goods on time. According to arts 47(1) and 49(1) of the CISG, the buyer was entitled to declare the contract avoided to the seller.

The court of second instance held that, firstly, as the parties to the case unanimously chose the laws of People's Republic of China as the applicable law in the first instance, it can be determined that the parties had agreed to exclude the application of the CISG to the case in accordance with Article 6 of the CISG. Secondly, there is no conflict between the obligations of the buyer and the seller, breach of contract, termination of contract, compensation for damages and other contents of the CISG and the Contract Law of the People's Republic of China. Therefore, pursuant to Article 142(2) of the General Principles of the Civil Law of the People's Republic of China, 'If any international treaty concluded or acceded to by the People's Republic of China contains provisions differing from those in the civil laws of the People's Republic of China, the provisions of the international treaty shall apply', there is no circumstance in the case in which CISG can be applied. The court of first instance was correct in taking the Contract Law of the People's Republic of China as the applicable law. The legal relationship and responsibility determination of all parties, and the result of judgment, were basically the same as those of the first-instance court.

## Commentary to the Key Issues Related to the CISG

### Issue 1. The Applicability of CISG

The parties to the case are located in the Chinese mainland, Hong Kong, and South Korea respectively. China and South Korea are all within the scope of contracting jurisdictions of CISG, but both courts considered that the CISG is not applicable for the following reasons. Firstly, all parties agreed to apply the laws of People's Republic of China, which was deemed as having agreed to exclude the application of the CISG. Secondly, according to Article 142(2) of the General Principles of the Civil Law, the CISG applies only when there is a conflict between the provisions of the CISG and those of the Contract Law.

The internal logic of the courts' reasoning is in fact consistent, that is, the parties agreed to apply the laws of the People's Republic of China, which means excluding the direct application of the CISG. In this case, only Article 142(2) of the General Principles of the Civil Law can be used to decide whether there is still room for application of the CISG.

With regard to this issue, the provisions of the CISG should be examined. Article 6 of the CISG stipulates 'the parties may exclude the application of this Convention', but it doesn't clearly specify whether an express exclusion is necessary or whether an implied exclusion is recognized. Regarding this, the UNCITRAL Digest of Case Law on the United Nations Convention on Contracts for the International Sale of Goods

(2016 Edition) also comments: 'According to several courts, opting out requires a clear, unequivocal, and affirmative agreement of the parties. According to one court, however, for the Convention not to apply it suffices that the 'contract contains a choice-of-law provision.'[1] In other words, the issue is divisive in different jurisdictions. Some jurisdictions explicitly recognize the possibility of an implied exclusion from the application of the Convention, but that intention must be clear and genuine. The contrary view is that only 'express' exclusion can exclude the application of the Convention in whole or in part.

There are also differences on this issue in terms of the theory and judicial practice in the Chinese mainland. There is a view that the parties' choice of applying the laws of People's Republic of China means that the application of the CISG is excluded, and only China's existing substantive law, excluding conflict law and procedural law, can be applied. Therefore, it is impossible for the court or the arbitration tribunal to apply the CISG under the guidance of the conflict rules in the laws of People's Republic of China, that is, there is no possibility of parallel application.[2] The two courts in this case also held this view. Another contrary point of view is that when the parties to the contract agree to apply the laws of People's Republic of China, it leads to the application of the CISG due to the fact that the CISG is included in the agreed civil laws.[3] That is to say, although the CISG cannot be directly applied due to the parties' autonomous choice of the laws of People's Republic of China, Article 142(2) of the General Principles of the Civil Law stipulates that 'If any international treaty concluded or acceded to by the People's Republic of China contains provisions differing from those in the civil laws of the People's Republic of China, the provisions of the international treaty shall apply'. Therefore, if there is a conflict between the laws of People's Republic of China and the CISG, the CISG shall prevail; on the contrary, the CISG cannot be applied. However, in fact, if the parties' choice of applying the specific laws of China constitutes an 'implied exclusion' of the application of the CISG, this is actually contrary to the wishes of the parties because the CISG is included in the applicable laws.

In actual fact, the above-mentioned issues have been controversial in the Chinese mainland, and scholars and judicial practice circles have different opinions on them. For parties involved in the international trade of goods, it is suggested that the applicable laws should be explicitly chosen as soon as the transaction agreement is reached, especially when the applicable law of a certain country is chosen. It should be clear whether the application of the CISG should be excluded at the same time, or whether it should be applied in parallel, so as to minimize the difficulty of dispute resolution caused by unclear application of law in the future.

### Issue 2. The Implication of Article 47(1) of CISG

Although the CISG has not been applied in this case, I would like to take the opportunity to discuss the internal meaning of Article 47(1) of the CISG proposed by the appellant, and whether the application of the CISG would have made a difference in the outcome of this case.

---

[1] UNCITRAL [1, p. 33].

[2] Chen and Wu [2, pp. 112–114].

[3] Liu [3, pp. 83–84].

Article 47(1) of the CISG provides that 'The buyer may fix an additional period of time of reasonable length for performance by the seller of his obligations.' This provision needs to be understood in conjunction with arts 45(1) and (2),[4] 46(1),[5] and 49(1).[6] According to these provisions, the 'grace period' stipulated in Article 47(1) of the CISG means that the buyer may choose to exercise the rights stipulated in the Convention in the event that the seller has breached its contractual obligations, including but not limited to continuing performance, demanding damages, granting a grace period for performance, and declaring the contract invalid. However, if the buyer has chosen to declare the contract avoided, it means that it is no longer possible to grant a grace period for performance.

Concerning the implication of the provision, the buyer can directly declare the contract avoided without using the grace period system, or it can give the seller a grace period and then terminate the contract if the seller fails to perform its obligations beyond the additional period. The significance of granting the seller a 'grace period' is to accurately determine at which point the delay in performance constitutes a fundamental breach, so as to determine the time when the non-breaching party can terminate the contract. Since there is uncertainty for the buyer as to whether the non-performance of the other party's obligations under the contract can be regarded as a fundamental breach of contract and whether it is entitled to exercise the right to terminate the contract based on this, the buyer can directly declare the contract avoided in accordance with the provisions of Article 49(2) of the Convention. If the seller still fails to perform after the buyer has given the seller a reasonable grace

---

[4] Article 45 of CISG

(1) If the seller fails to perform any of his obligations under the contract or this Convention, the buyer may:

  (a) Exercise the rights provided in articles 46 to 52;
  (b) Claim damages as provided in articles 74 to 77.

(2) The buyer is not deprived of any right he may have to claim damages by exercising his right to other remedies.

[5] Article 46 of CISG

(1) The buyer may require performance by the seller of his obligations unless the buyer has resorted to a remedy which is inconsistent with this requirement.

[6] Article 49 of CISG

(1) The buyer may declare the contract avoided:

  (a) if the failure by the seller to perform any of his obligations under the contract of this Convention amounts to a fundamental breach of contract; or
  (b) in case of non-delivery, if the seller does not deliver the goods within the additional period of time fixed by the buyer in accordance with paragraph (1) of article 47 of declares that he will not deliver within the period so fixed.

period, this will greatly reduce the risk of improper termination that the buyer may bear.

In fact, Article 94 of the Contract Law also stipulates that if the other party delayed performance of its main obligation after such performance has been demanded, and fails to perform within a reasonable period, the other party may terminate the contract, which is consistent with the internal logic stipulated in 47(1) of the CISG. The Contract Law of the PRC clearly states that the delayed performance of its 'main obligation' is the precondition, while Article 49(1)(b) of the CISG also clearly states that 'in case of non-delivery', which is also the 'main obligation' for international sales of goods. Moreover, the 'within a reasonable period' stipulated in the Contract Law and the 'fix an additional period of time of reasonable length' stipulated by the CISG also require that the grace period given must be reasonable. In case of the determination of the 'reasonable period of time', the interpretation in the UNCITRAL Digest of Case Law on the United Nations Convention on Contracts for the International Sale of Goods (2016 Edition) states that all relevant circumstances must be taken into account (including the conduct of the parties, negotiations and customary practices between the parties, as well as practice (Article 8(3)),[7] which cannot be generalized.

In this case, it is my opinion that the reason why Hanchang Industry did not choose to apply Article 94 of the Contract Law during the second instance was that, firstly, as a foreign enterprise, the familiarity and acceptance of the CISG by Hanchang Industry is definitely higher than that of the Contract Law of the PRC. Secondly, it did not explicitly demand Western Mining to deliver the goods as soon as possible in this transaction, but only re-agreed the loading period in the letter of credit after signing the Sales Confirmation 2. Under such circumstances, it is difficult to identify that it meets the requirement of the premise of 'after such performance has been demanded' as stipulated in Article 94 of the Contract Law. However, it is my belief that even if the Court approved the priority application of the CISG in this case, there is a high probability that it would not permit Hanchang Industry to appeal on the grounds of 47(1) of the CISG for declaring the contract avoided. The reason for this is the same as the aforesaid second ground. That is, Sales Confirmation 2 signed by the parties on 28 November 2006 only stipulated the shipment period from December 2006 to March 2007, while the letter of credit issued by Hanchang Industry on 7 December 2006 expressly stated that the shipment date should not be later than 6 January 2007. Neither party had specified the latest shipment date for the first batch of goods between the signing of the Sales Confirmation 2 and the issuing of the letter of credit. Additionally, Hanchang Industry did not articulate the lates date at which shipment by Western Mining should be made. The statement by Hanchang Industry that the shipment period stated in the letter of credit from 1 January 2007 to 6 January 2007 is additional time granted under Article 47(1) of the CISG was therefore untenable. In this case, the shipment period stated in the letter of credit should be deemed to be the period of performance for Western Mining as finally agreed by the parties. Therefore, as the two courts held in this case, the

[7] UNCITRAL [1, p. 225].

one-day delay in loading did not defeat the contract purpose of Hanchang Industry, so Western Mining cannot be deemed to be in fundamental breach of contract, and Hanchang Industry did not have the right to unilaterally terminate the contract.

In summary, I believe that even if the CISG was applied in this case, the result of the judgment would be no difference from that of the application of the Contract Law of the People's Republic of China.

## References

1. United Nations Commission on International Trade Law (UNCITRAL). (2016). *UNCITRAL Digest of Case Law on the United Nations Convention on Contracts for the International Sale of Goods*. https://uncitral.un.org/en/case_law/digests.
2. Chen, Z. & Wu, J. (2004). On the application of United Nations Convention on Contracts for the International Sale of Goods in China -- Concurrently Comments on the Article 142 of General Principles of Civil Law. *Law Science*, (10), 107-118
3. Liu, T. T. (2014). An Analysis of the Autonomy of Implied Exclusion in the Application of CISG -- from the Perspective of the Agreed Application of Chinese Law. *Journal of Central South University (Social Science)*, (4), 79–85

**Max Siying Wu** is a senior partner in Dacheng Law Offices (Guangzhou), a PhD of International Law in Wuhan University, and was formerly a judge in Guangdong Provincial High People's Court hearing commercial cases involving foreign interests. He has published a personal monograph the Unification of International Commercial Contract Law: Grounds, Aims and Approaches, and also participated in several scholarly writings, eg. International Business Law. He is appointed as Executive Council Member of International Law Research Institute of Guangdong Law Society, Secretary-general of Cross-border Investment Legal Services Committee of Guangdong Lawyers Association, Member of Foreign-related Legal Services Committee of Guangzhou Lawyers Association, Mediator of Guangzhou Mediation Center for Financial Disputes, Arbitrator of eight commercial arbitration institutions in China including Guangzhou Arbitration Committee and Shenzhen Court of International Arbitration. He is also an Extramural Postgraduate Tutor of Guangdong University of Finance & Economics, and research fellow of the institute of Legal Theories & Practices of Sun Yet-sen University. He is honored as one of the Guangdong and Guangzhou Leading Lawyers on Foreign-related Legal Services.

# Shanghai X Colour Printing Co., Ltd. v. Y

**Bruno Zeller**

## Case Information

**Case Name**: *Shanghai X Colour Printing Co., Ltd. v Ys*

**Seller**: Shanghai X Colour Printing Co., Ltd.
**Place of Business**: China Mainland

**Buyer**: Y
**Place of Business**: Denmark

**Details of First Instance**:
**Court**: Shanghai Pudong New District People's Court
**Date of Decision**: 23 June 2011
**Case No.**: (2010) Pu Min Er (Shang) Chu Zi No.3121
**Judges**: Li Sun, Chenglan Wang, Baoxiang Sun

**CISG Applied**: Yes

**Key CISG Provisions Interpreted and Applied**: Article 53

## Case Abstract

Shanghai X Colour Printing Co., Ltd., the seller, and Y, the buyer, had a long-term relationship regarding the purchase and supply of paper products. According

B. Zeller (✉)
University of Western Australia, Crawley, WA 6009, Australia
e-mail: bruno.zeller@uwa.edu.au



P. Guo et al. (eds.), *Selected Chinese Cases on the UN Sales Convention (CISG) Vol. 3*, Selected Chinese Cases on the CISG,
https://doi.org/10.1007/978-981-99-6851-0_8

to the seller, as of March 2010, the buyer owed the seller unpaid amounts of USD $544,623.03 under 16 orders made between Oct 2009 and March 2010, while the supplies were properly delivered. The seller brought the claim before the Shanghai Pudong New District People's Court.

The buyer disputed the jurisdiction of the Court and submitted a 'Provision of Procurement' signed by the parties in 2006, which provided that Danish law should apply in any dispute arising from a contract, and any dispute should be submitted to Vestre Landsret (High Court of Western Denmark) or ICC Arbitration. The seller denied that they had signed the Provision of Procurement with the buyer. The Court reviewed this document and rejected it due to its lack of authenticity. It was also held that the jurisdictional challenge was made after the expiration of the time limit for response and therefore could not considered by the Court.

The Court held that the dispute arose from a foreign-related contract and that the parties failed to choose the law applicable to the contract. As the places of business of the parties were in China and Denmark respectively, both of which are Contracting States to the CISG, the CISG should apply. The contract was validly formed between the parties, and the goods were properly delivered. Thus, the buyer had the obligation to pay for the goods, and the seller's claims for the payment due should be supported pursuant to Article 53 of the CISG. Also, the buyer should pay interest accordingly.

**Commentary on the Key Issues Related to the CISG**

**Issues**:

Issue 1 Contractual Issues

**Comments**:

As the seller commenced the action in China, it is the domestic law of the seat which will determine whether it has jurisdiction or not. The document in question needs to conform with domestic law not only in form but also in content. Hence the lack of authenticity is to be correctly determined correctly by Chinese law. The same argument is also valid as far as the lodgement of the jurisdictional challenge is concerned.

**Issue 1 Contractual Issues**

The first issue, namely the governing law, was correctly analysed by the Court which found that is it is a transnational contract between parties whose countries of business have both ratified the CISG. The mandate of Article 1 of the CISG was properly followed.

The real question occupying the Court was the fact that the buyer had not paid for the goods. The obligation to pay is contained in Article 53.

The Court did not go into details as to why and how the contract was validly formed. However, the question of whether the goods, and the correct goods, were delivered was a question of fact for the Court and assumedly this was not an issue between the parties. It appears that the question merely relates to the reluctance of the buyer to pay for the goods. Article 53, as noted by the Court, is the most important obligation of the buyer once the goods have been delivered pursuant to the contract. The article in brief notes that the buyer must take delivery of the goods, which is not in dispute in this case, and pay for the goods. The Court ought to have mentioned Article 78, which mandates that a party must pay interest if it fails to pay the price. The CISG is silent on question as to the rate of interest and hence as it is a gap it needs to be governed by the applicable domestic law, in this case Chinese law.[1]

## Reference

1. Liu, C. W. (2003). Recovery of Interest. *Nordic Journal of Commercial Law*, (1), 1–80.

**Professor Dr. Bruno Zeller** B.Com (University of Melbourne), B.Ed (Melb). M.Int'l.Trade Law (Deakin) Ph.D. (Law, Melb.). He is a Professor in Transnational Commercial Law at The University of Western Australia, Perth. His teaching interests include international trade law, trade finance, conflict of laws, international arbitration and maritime law. His extensive research and publications contribute to the understanding of uniform international laws, which have been developed under the auspices of the United Nations and other international bodies. Currently the third edition of the Monograph on Damages Under the Convention on Contracts for the International Sale of Goods has been published. In addition, he has also published on alternative dispute resolution mechanisms and free trade agreements in international journals. He has supervised numerous domestic and international Ph.D. students. Besides having taught short course at many international Universities he is also an Adjunct Professor at Murdoch University, Perth, and an Adjunct Professor the Sir Zelman Cowan Centre, Victoria University, Melbourne.

[1] Liu [1, pp. 30–31].

# Ningbo Bridge Import & Export Co., Ltd. v. The Money Consultants Inc.

Junmin Zhang

## Case Information

**Case Name**: *Ningbo Bridge Import & Export Co., Ltd. v The Money Consultants Inc.*.

**Seller**: Ningbo Bridge Import & Export Co., Ltd.
**Place of Business**: China

**Buyer**: The Money Consultants Inc.
**Place of Business**: United States of America

**Details of First Instance**:
**Court**: Intermediate People's Court of Ningbo City of Zhejiang Province
**Date of Decision**: 19 May 2010
**Case No.**: (2009) Zhe Yong Shang Wai Chu Zi No. 209

**Details of Second Instance**:
**Court**: High People's Court of Zhejiang Province
**Date of Decision**: 01 October 2010
**Case No.**: (2010) Zhe Shang Wai Zhong Zi No. 77
**Judges**: Qing Miao (Presiding Judge), Wei Lu (Acting Judge), Fanhong Kong (Acting Judge)

**CISG Applied**: No

J. Zhang (✉)
Shanghai Normal University, Shanghai, China
e-mail: zhangjunmin33@hotmail.com



P. Guo et al. (eds.), *Selected Chinese Cases on the UN Sales Convention (CISG) Vol. 3*, Selected Chinese Cases on the CISG,
https://doi.org/10.1007/978-981-99-6851-0_9

**Key CISG Provisions Interpreted and Applied**: N/A

## Case Abstract

This dispute was between the appellant, Ningbo Bridge Import & Export Co., Ltd. ('Ningbo Bridge'), and the appellee, The Money Consultants Inc ('Bonici Fashion') regarding a sales contract.

During the first half of 2006, Bonici Fashion ordered six models of clothes from Ningbo Bridge. On 14 June 2006, Ningbo Bridge issued a proforma invoice, itemizing each price and model: USD $7,360.50 for model BV-527, $USD 16,573 for model BV-532, USD $15,765 for model BV-528/531 and USD $15,765 for model BV-529/530. The total price was USD $55,464. The deposit was 40% of the total price, $USD 22,185.60. On 22 June 2006, Bonici Fashion paid the deposit. Later, Ningbo Bridge delivered the clothes of model BV-527. However, neither parties could not agree on matters including the delivery place. Bonici Fashion terminated the contract regarding the clothes of models BV-532, BV-528/531, and BV-529/530. Ningbo Bridge agreed with the termination, and thus did not deliver the remaining models of clothes to Bonici Fashion. Meanwhile, Ningbo Bridge agreed to compensate Bonici Fashion for the quality of the buttons in connection with 10,353 pieces of model BV-5453 of clothes at the price of USD $1 each.

Bonici Fashion applied to the Intermediate People's Court of Ningbo City of Zhejiang Province on 17 June 2009, asking Ningbo Bridge to return the deposit of USD $33,278.40 and related interest, and to compensate it for the loss of USD $10,353 due to the quality issue. Ningbo Bridge raised a counterclaim, asking Bonici Fashion to pay USD $8,931 for the model BV-527 clothes. The court of first instance held that because Bonici Fashion was registered in the United States, the case was a foreign-related commercial case. There was no prior agreement as to the applicable law. Bonici Fashion chose to apply the domestic law of China. At the same time, Ningbo Bridge argued that the applicable law should be the 1980 United Nations Convention on Contracts for the International Sale of Goods ('CISG') if the CISG conflicted with the domestic law of China. According to Article 5 of the 2007 Rules of the Supreme People's Court on the Relevant Issues concerning the Application of Law in Hearing Foreign-Related Contractual Dispute Cases in Civil and Commercial Matters, '[w]here the parties fail to choose a law governing a contractual dispute, the law of the country or region having the most significant relationship with the contract shall be the governing law'. Thus, the Intermediate People's Court of Ningbo City of Zhejiang Province decided that the applicable law should be the law of China. The court of first instance listed three points at issue in this case. The first dealt with whether the model BV-527 clothes had been successfully delivered. The second issue was concerned with the breach of contract in relation to the deposit. The third issue was whether Ningbo Bridge should compensate USD $10,353 for the buttons of the model BV-453 clothes.

After a systematic analysis, based on the 1999 Contract Law of People's republic of China, and the 2008 Provisions by the Supreme People's Court on Evidence in Civil Procedures, the court of first instance held that: (1) Ningbo Bridge must return the deposit of USD $14,825.10, and the interest based on USD $14,825.10 within 10 days of the judgment, the exact amount to be calculated from 17 June 2009 until the performance date according to the judgment, based on the ratio published by the People's Bank of China; (2) Ningbo Bridge was to compensate Bonici Fashion the loss of USD $10,353 within 10 days of the judgment for the lack of quality; (3) Bonici Fashion should pay USD $7,360.50 for the relevant products which had already been reduced from the deposit and (4) the case acceptance and administration fees should be shared by both parties.

Ningbo Bridge appealed to the High Court, arguing that: (1) the proforma invoice should be considered as a contract; (2) Bonici Fashion breached the contract, not Ningbo Bridge; (3) Bonici Fashion breached the contract fundamentally, thus Ningbo Bridge did not have an obligation to return the deposit; (4) the export quotas should be borne by Bonici Fashion and (5) as to the quality of the buttons, Ningbo Bridge had already paid the related compensation.

The High Court summarized the core issues in dispute as follows: (1) whether a deposit penalties situation existed; (2) whether Ningbo Bridge should compensate for the quality of the buttons of model BV-543 clothes and (3) which party should bear the costs of the export quotas.

As to the first issue, three orders and the proforma invoices provided by Ningbo Bridge all stated '40% deposit' or '40% prepayment'. The three proforma invoices also stated the amount of the deposit, which was 40% of the overall payment price. From the orders, proforma invoices and emails between the parties, it could be seen that both parties had reached an agreement as to the deposit clause. According to Article 120 of the 2000 Judicial Interpretation of the Supreme People's Court on Some Issues Regarding the Application of the Guarantee Law of the People's Republic of China, '[t]he penalty rule of deposit shall be applied when the purpose of the contract cannot be realized due to one party's delay in performance or other breaches of the contract, except as otherwise stipulated by law or by the parties' agreement'. That is to say, only the proof of a fundamental breach of the contract can make reference to the deposit penalties, which were not applicable in this case.

For the second issue, Ningbo Bridge argued that they had already paid compensation of USD $10,353 to a third party for the quality issue of the buttons of the model BV-543 clothes. The High Court determined that the sales contract was between Ningbo Bridge and Bonici Fashion. Assuming that the two parties had reached an agreement regarding compensation, and Bonici Fashion had transferred the debt to a willing third party, Ningbo Bridge should compensate Bonici Fashion immediately. Even though neither of these conditions could be proved by Ningbo Bridge, Bonici Fashion still has the right to ask for relative compensation.

Regarding the costs of the export quotas, Ningbo Bridge argued that both parties had confirmed by email that the export quotas would be borne by Bonici Fashion. However, Ningbo Bridge could not provide the exact dates and times of those emails. Meanwhile, the order and proforma invoices did not state whether the costs of the export quotas had been included in the payment. The High Court stated that normally the export quotas of textile products are at the exporter's expense. Thus, the High Court did not favor Ningbo Bridge's position as to the export quotas.

According to Article 153 of the 2007 Civil Procedure Law of the People's Republic of China, the High Court upheld the judgment of the Intermediate People's Court of Ningbo City of Zhejiang Province and dismissed the appeal.

**Commentary to the Key Issues Related to the CISG**

**Issues**:

Issue 1 The Domestic Law and the Application of the CISG and Existing Conflict of Law Rules.

**Comments**:

**Issue 1. The Domestic Law and the Application of the CISG and Existing Conflict of Law Rules**

Article 1(1)(a) of the CISG states that '[t]his Convention applies to contracts of sale of goods between parties whose places of business are in different States', when the States are Contracting States.[1] Meanwhile, Article 6 provides parties' freedom to exclude the application of the CISG. According to these two articles, even if the CISG 'would otherwise be applicable, courts must determine that the parties have not excluded the Convention nor derogated from its provisions, thus elevating the lack of an exclusion to an applicability requirement of the Convention'.[2] In this case, since China and the United States are Contracting States to the CISG, the parties did not exclude the application of the Convention. In this case, the CISG should be the applicable law.

However, it should be noted that in the judgments, the court of first instance referred to the 2007 Rules of the Supreme People's Court on the Relevant Issues concerning the Application of Law in Hearing Foreign-Related Contractual Dispute Cases in Civil and Commercial Matters and applied the domestic law of China by adopting the doctrine of the most significant relationship. Unfortunately, the High Court did not correct this erroneous application in the appeal. On the one hand, the 2007 Rules of the Supreme People's Court on the Relevant Issues concerning the Application of Law in Hearing Foreign-Related Contractual Dispute Cases in Civil and Commercial Matters been abrogated in the Decision of the Supreme People's Court on Abolishing Some Judicial Interpretations and Documents of a Judicial Interpretation Nature Which, was issued from 1 July 1997 to 31 December 2011. On the other hand, there exists situations where state courts mistakenly adopt domestic regulations instead of the CISG when it is applicable to international transactions.

When the CISG is consistent with domestic legislation, when determining whether the CISG should prevail, there is an inclination of Chinese courts to consider the application of domestic law 'as a preliminary step' before applying the CISG.[3] In legal practice, even if the CISG is applicable, it is common for state courts to still

[1] Article 1(1)(a), CISG.

[2] UNCITRAL [9, p. 33].

[3] Xiao and Long [11, p. 68].

refer to domestic law in international disputes. For example, in another Chinese case, *Tea Sources Europe v Xixia Huabang Food Co., Ltd.* (2012) Zheng Min San Chu Zi No. 646, the Intermediate People's Court of Zhengzhou City of Henan Province held that according to Article 41 of the 2011 Law of the People's Republic of China on Choice of Law for Foreign-related Civil Relationship, '[i]f the parties do not choose, the laws at the habitual residence of the party whose fulfillment of obligations can best reflect the characteristics of this contract or other laws which have the closest relation with this contract shall apply'. In this case, both parties were from two Contracting States to the CISG, and the parties did not exclude the application of the Convention. It reflected the fact that Chinese courts often 'neglected to seek answers from the CISG'.[4]

This phenomenon may be because state courts adopt conflict of law rules, not the direct application of the CISG. In principle, 'the application of rules on the conflict of laws is basically not allowed whenever a matter of sales law is governed by the CISG'.[5] Most commentators maintain that the CISG, 'when it applies, displaces domestic law, including local procedural doctrines that allow a court to refuse to apply the CISG'.[6] Some even argue that the judicial refusal to apply the CISG can be considered "bad policy".[7]

Article 6 clarifies that the CISG will apply unless both parties have a contrary agreement,[8] meaning that the Convention takes an opt-out approach. It reflects the principle of party autonomy, 'one of the cornerstones of contemporary conflict of laws'.[9] Additionally, Article 7(2) provides the possibility that 'domestic law determined by rules on the conflict of laws may be used to fill gaps in matters governed by the Convention'.[10] In this case, the parties did not reach agreement in excluding the application of the CISG. Ningbo Bridge expressly stated that if conflicts existed, the CISG should prevail in the choice of law. As to the legal effect of a deposit, the High Court was more accurate and readier to acknowledge it goes beyond the ambit of the CISG.[11]

There are also other possible reasons for adopting domestic law rather than the CISG when all requirements under the CISG are satisfied. For instance, non-application of the CISG under particular circumstances may be based on policy considerations.[12] Afterall, the endorsement of the CISG by state courts is not only encouraging, but also essential for the widespread application of the Convention.[13] Article 142 of the 2009 General Principles of the Civil Law of the People's Republic

[4] Liu and Ren [6, p. 898].

[5] Schwenzer [8, p. 236].

[6] Gillette and Walt [3, p. 454].

[7] Gillette and Walt [3, p. 454], CISG Advisory Council [2].

[8] Schwenzer [8, p. 331].

[9] Ragno [7, p. 245].

[10] Article 7(2), CISG; Schwenzer [8, p. 237].

[11] Liu and Ren [6, p. 898].

[12] Honnold [4, p. 41], Wethmar-Lemmer [10, p. 68].

[13] Kröll et al. [5, p. 26].

of China provides that 'if any international treaty concluded or acceded to by the People's Republic of China contains provisions differing from those in the civil laws of the People's Republic of China, the provisions of the international treaty shall apply, unless the provisions are ones on which the People's Republic of China has announced reservations'. However, the 2009 General Principles of the Civil Law of the People's Republic of China has expired, and the 2021 Civil Code of the People's Republic of China remains silent on this issue. To some extent, the choice of law rules in the area of the CISG reflects some current trends in private international law, but there are still deficiencies in Chinese statutory systems in this regard.[14]

## References


1. Chen, W. (2008). The Conflict of Laws in the Context of the CISG: A Chinese Perspective. *Pace International Law Review*, (20), 115–128.
2. CISG Advisory Council. (2014). *CISG Advisory Council Opinion No. 16, Exclusion of the CISG under Article 6*. Retrieved from https://cisgac.com/opinions/cisgac-opinion-no1-copy-copy-4-copy-copy-copy-7/.
3. Gillette, C. P. & Walt, S. D. (2017). Judicial Refusal to Apply Treaty Law: Domestic Law Limitations on the CISG's Application. *Uniform Law Review*, (22), 452–491.
4. Honnold, J. (1991), *Uniform Law for International Sales under the 1980 United Nations Convention*. Kluwer Law International.
5. Kröll, S., Mistelis, L. & Viscasillas, P. (2018). *UN Convention on Contracts for the International Sale of Goods (CISG)*. C.H. Beck Hart Nomos.
6. Liu, Q. & Ren, X. (2017). CISG in Chinese Courts: The Issue of Applicability. *American Journal of Comparative Law*, (65), 873–918.
7. Ragno, F. (2019). The CISG and the Choice of Law: Two Worlds Apart?. *Journal of Law and Commerce*, (38), 245–272.
8. Schwenzer, I. (2016). *Schlechtriem & Schwenzer: Commentary on the UN Convention on the International Sale of Goods* (4th Ed.). Oxford University Press.
9. United Nations Commission on International Trade Law (UNCITRAL). (2016). *Digest of Case Law on the United Nations Convention on Contracts for the International Sale of Goods*. Retrieved from https://uncitral.un.org/sites/uncitral.un.org/files/media-documents/uncitral/en/cisg_digest_2016.pdf.
10. Wethmar-Lemmer, M. (2016). Applying the CISG via the Rules of Private International Law: Articles 1(1)(b) and 95 of the CISG—Analysing CISG Advisory Council Opinion. *De Jure*, (49), 58–73.
11. Xiao, Y. & Long, W. (2008). Selected Topics on the Application of the CISG in China. *Pace International Law Review*, (20), 61–104.


**Dr. Junmin Zhang** Assistant Professor in Law at Shanghai Normal University. She holds a doctoral degree in law, specializing in the field of international law, from Maastricht University in the Netherlands. Dr. Zhang's research interests lie in international trade law, international commercial and investment dispute resolution. She teaches Public International Law to L.L.B. students and acts as an arbitrator in the CIETAC Cup International Commercial Arbitration Moot.

[14] Chen [1, p. 128].

# Shanghai Jiamupu Industry Co., Ltd. v. Moraglis S.A.

**Xiaojun Chen and Peng Guo**

## Case Information

**Case Name**: *Shanghai Jiamupu Industry Co., Ltd. v Moraglis S.A.*.

**Seller**: Shanghai Jiamupu Industry
**Place of Business**: China

**Buyer**: Moraglis S.A.
**Place of Business**: Greece

**Details of First Instance**:
**Court**: Shanghai First Intermediate People's Court
**Date of Decision**: 22 November 2011
**Case No.**: (2010) Hu Yi Zhong Min Wu (Shang) Chu No. 36
**Judges**: Ying Huang (Presiding Judge), Mingyan Ren (Acting Judge), Su Yang (Acting Judge)

**Details of Second Instance**:
**Court**: Shanghai High People's Court
**Date of Decision**: 28 May 2012
**Case No.**: (2012) Hu Gao Min Er (Shang) Zhong No. 4

X. Chen (✉)
Wincon Law Firm, Qingdao, China
e-mail: chenxiaojun@wincon.cn

P. Guo
Swinburne University of Technology, Melbourne, VIC 3000, Australia
e-mail: pguo@swin.edu.au



P. Guo et al. (eds.), *Selected Chinese Cases on the UN Sales Convention (CISG) Vol. 3*, Selected Chinese Cases on the CISG,
https://doi.org/10.1007/978-981-99-6851-0_10

**Judges**: Chuan Xu (Presiding Judge), Qian Fan (Judge), Xianhua Huang (Acting Judge)

**CISG Applied**: No
**Key CISG Provisions Interpreted and Applied**: Art 3(2)

**Case Abstract**

In May 2009, Moraglis S.A. ('MSA') signed a contract with Shanghai Jiamupu Industry Co., Ltd. ('JIAMUPU'), agreeing that MSA would purchase a batch of uniforms from JIAMUPU. In the contract, MSA made detailed agreements on the style, colour, specification, and colour difference of the uniforms. At the same time, the two parties also agreed in the contract that each batch of goods needed to hire SGS, an international testing and verification company, to test the specifications and quality of the goods before delivery. If the goods did not conform to the contract, JIAMUPU would bear 100% responsibility.

After the contract was signed, JIAMUPU began to produce the corresponding uniforms. However, after SGS inspected the goods, it was found that the uniforms produced by JIAMUPU had serious problems and did not meet the requirements clearly stated by MSA in the contract. Subsequently, JIAMUPU did not deliver any uniforms to MSA.

Since MSA believed that the products produced by JIAMUPU were completely inconsistent with the contract, MSA filed a lawsuit against JIAMUPU, requesting the court to terminate the contract between the two parties, and requiring JIAMUPU to return the advance payment already made to MSA.

During the first instance of this case, the Court held that the contract between MSA and JIAMUPU was a sales contract. At the same time, since both parties had not chosen the law applicable to the contract, the Court needed to first resolve which law is the applicable law of the case.

The Court held that the contract signed between the two parties in this case was a sales contract. According to Chinese law, the location of the seller in the sales contract can best reflect the characteristics of the sales contract. In this case the seller, JIAMUPU, is located in China, so Chinese law is applicable as the governing law of this case.

Ultimately, the Court held that the goods provided by JIAMUPU did not comply with the contract, and MSA had the right to terminate the contract signed between the two parties. The Court accordingly ruled that JIAMUPU should return most of the payment that MSA had already made for the goods (the Court held that a small amount of the payment made by MSA was irrelevant to the case and need not be returned).

JIAMUPU appealed to the Shanghai Higher People's Court ('SHC'). Its main point was that MSA unilaterally entrusted SGS to conduct the inspection, which did not comply with the contract between the two parties, so it cannot prove that there was a problem with the quality of the goods. Therefore, JIAMUPU requested SHC to revoke the first-instance judgment and dismiss all claims of MSA.

During the trial, SHC re-examined the nature of the contract in this case and held that the contract between the two parties was not a contract for the sale of goods. According to the contract between the two parties, MSA required JIAMUPU to produce specific uniforms. Moreover, MSA had very specific requirements on the specifications, colours, and styles of the uniforms. Therefore, what MSA needed is not the common and replaceable general goods found in the market, but specific work results. Therefore, the contract involved in this case should be a processing contract rather than a sales contract. In this case, Chinese law should still apply, and the application of the CISG is excluded.

On this basis, SHC determined that the contract between the two parties had clearly stipulated that the goods should be inspected by SGS. Therefore, although the inspection by SGS was unilaterally authorized by MSA, it still complied with the agreement between the two parties. According to the inspection by SGS, it was determined that the goods produced by JIAMUPU seriously do not conform to the contract. Therefore, MSA's contractual purpose of obtaining specific uniforms had been lost, and it had the right to terminate the contract between both parties.

Ultimately, SHC determined that although the court of first instance did make some errors, the result of the first instance judgment was correct, and it rejected JIAMUPU's appeal request.

## Commentary on the Key Issues Related to the CISG

**Issues**:

Issue 1 Why the CISG should not apply in this case.

**Comments**:

### Issue 1 Why the CISG Should Not Apply in this Case

In the judgment of the court of first instance of this case, the Court held that the contract between the two parties was an international sale of goods contract, and the court held that both parties should apply Chinese law as the applicable law. China was one of the first signatories to the CISG, which has been in force in China since 1988. Therefore, when the Court in this case determines that Chinese law is applicable as the applicable law, the court should consider whether the CISG should be applied. However, the court of first instance directly ruled out the application of the CISG without any discussion, and even did not mention the CISG at all in the judgment. Obviously, the approach of the court of first instance was wrong.

Many Chinese courts are not familiar with the CISG, so they tend to exclude its application in trials. However, the Minutes of the 'National Symposium on the Foreign-related Commercial and Maritime Trial Work of Courts promulgated by the Supreme People's Court ('SPC') in 2021 stipulates: 'Business Contracts for the international sale of goods concluded by parties located in different contracting parties to the United Nations Convention on Contracts for the International Sale of

Goods shall automatically apply the provisions of the Convention, unless the parties expressly agree to exclude the application of the Convention. The people's court shall ask the parties concerned Specific comments on the application of the Convention.[1]

Therefore, when Chinese courts hear disputes over contracts for international sales of goods after 2021, the CISG must be applied as long as the country of both parties is a contracting state of the CISG and there is no mutual agreement to exclude the application of the CISG.

During the appeal case, SHC clearly stated that the CISG should not apply to this case. The reason for this is that the contract signed by both parties in this case is not a sales contract, but a processing contract. Under the Chinese legal system, sales contracts and processing contracts are two completely different types of contracts.

The rights and obligations of the parties to these two contracts are completely different, and even the applicable laws are different. However, these two types of contracts are very similar in that one party to the contract delivers goods to the other party and receives consideration. Therefore, when trying such cases, Chinese courts usually first need to resolve the issue of which type of contract involved in the case belongs.

The key difference between a processing contract and a sales contract is that a processing contract is a contract for the purpose of completing a certain work, and the rights and obligations of both parties are mainly directed to a certain behavior; a sales contract is a contract for the purpose of transferring ownership. The object of the rights and obligations of both parties is a certainty.

It is generally held that if the goods subject to the contract have not been produced when the parties sign it, and the production process must follow the specific requirements of one of the parties (specific requirements meaning that the same finished goods cannot be purchased from the market), or if the production is under the supervision and guidance of one party and any goods purchased arbitrarily in the market do not have the specific requirements as contractually detailed, then the contract is a sales contract.

In this case, MSA purchased specific goods that had not yet been produced. Therefore, SHC believed that the contract in this case should be a processing contract rather than a sales contract. In the case of Moraglis S.A. v Qingdao Jinbei Industry and Trade Co., Ltd. (Case No.: [2017] Lu 0211 Min Chu No. 14606), MSA purchased goods from another Chinese company, and a dispute arose between them. The facts of that case are very similar to this case. During the trial, Qingdao City Huangdao District People's Court directly characterized the contract between the two parties as a processing contract. It can be seen that the nature of the contract in this case should indeed be defined as a processing contract rather than a sales contract.

It should be noted that the SHC in this case did not discuss in detail why the CISG should be excluded. It is generally believed that Article 3(2) of the CISG is the basis for excluding processing contract disputes from applying to the CISG. This clause stipulates: 'This Convention does not apply to contracts in which the preponderant part of the obligations of the party who furnishes the goods consists in

[1] SPC [1], Article 19.

the supply of labor or other services.' Chinese courts often apply this provision to exclude the application of the CISG in processing contract disputes. For example, in the case of Dou Ya Trading Co., Ltd. v Liaoning Hua Xi Group & Liaoning Hua Yi Clothing Co., Ltd. ([2011] Liao Min San Zhong No. 146), the Court held that all the raw materials of the goods were provided by the purchaser, the processor mainly providing processing services, so the application of the CISG is excluded according to the provisions of this article of the CISG.

However, it is not possible to determine whether MSA provided raw materials in the judgment of this case. Assuming that JIAMUPU purchased all or most of the raw materials in addition to providing processing services, it also seems problematic for SHC to directly exclude the application of the CISG under Article 3(2).

All in all, when Chinese courts hear similar cases, as long as the contract between the two parties is determined to be a processing contract, the application of the CISG will be excluded. This is a relatively clear conclusion.

## Reference

1. Supreme People's Court (SPC). (2021). *Minutes of the National Symposium on the Foreign-related Commercial and Maritime Trial Work of Courts*. Retrieved from https://www.pkulaw.com/en_law/bffd20e9aee35db2bdfb.html?keyword=%E4%BC%9A%E8%AE%AE%E7%BA%AA%E8%A6%81.

**Mr. Xiaojun Chen** is a partner of SHANDONG WINCON LAW FIRM. He is mainly engaged in legal services in the fields of maritime commerce, maritime affairs, international trade, cross-border investment, and corporate governance. Mr. Chen has been engaged in commercial litigation for many years, especially transnational commercial litigation and arbitration. He has represented Chinese or foreign clients for many times in transnational commercial litigation or arbitration cases in Mainland China, Hong Kong, Singapore, London, Paris and other places. He has rich practical experience in legal services such as contract disputes, corporate disputes, and maritime disputes.

**Dr. Peng Guo** is Lecturer in Law at the Swinburne University of Technology. He has worked across several Australian universities and has held visiting positions at different European universities. He has received scholarships awarded by renowned research institutions and international organisations, including the Max Planck Institute for Comparative and International Private Law, the International Institute for the Unification of Private Law (UNIDROIT), the Swiss Institute of Comparative Law, and the European Union. He specialises in the international sale of goods, international commercial arbitration, comparative contract law, and law and technology.

# GINO Co., Ltd. v. Beijing Ji Nuo Si Trading Co., Ltd.

**Xiaojun Chen and Peng Guo**

**Case Information**

**Case Name**: *Beijing Ji Nuo Si Trading Co., Ltd. v GINO Co., Ltd..*

**Seller**: GINO Co., Ltd.
**Place of Business**: Japan

**Buyer**: Beijing Jinuosi Trading Co., Ltd.
**Place of Business**: China

**Details of First Instance**:
**Court**: Beijing First Intermediate People's Court
**Judges**: N/A
**Case No.**: (2019) Yi Zhong Min Chu No. 10261

**Details of Second Instance**:
**Court**: Beijing Higher People's Court
**Date of Decision**: 20 December 2011
**Case No.**: (2011) Gao Min Zhong No. 1851
**Judges**: Bo He (Presiding Judge), Hong Rong (Judge), Xin Wei (Acting Judge)

X. Chen (✉)
Wincon Law Firm, Qingdao, China
e-mail: chenxiaojun@wincon.cn

P. Guo
Swinburne University of Technology, Melbourne, VIC 3000, Australia
e-mail: pguo@swin.edu.au



P. Guo et al. (eds.), *Selected Chinese Cases on the UN Sales Convention (CISG) Vol. 3*, Selected Chinese Cases on the CISG,
https://doi.org/10.1007/978-981-99-6851-0_11

**CISG Applied**: No
**Key CISG Provisions Interpreted and Applied**: Art 1(1)(a)

## Case Abstract

A Chinese company, Beijing Jinuosi Trading Co., Ltd. ('JINUOSI') purchased multiple batches of equipment from GINO Co., Ltd. ('GINO') in Japan. In order to comply with the special provisions of Chinese law, JINUOSI entrusted another Chinese company as its agent to purchase equipment from GINO and to pay for the goods through this agent.

Since JINUOSI did not pay for the goods after purchasing multiple batches, GINO repeatedly urged JINUOSI and the Chinese agent to pay for the goods. JINUOSI believed that GINO owed it additional money. After the two debts were offset, JINUOSI did not believe it needed to pay any fees to GINO.

After repeated urgings to no avail, GINO sued JINUOSI and demanded that JINUOSI pay for the goods and compensate GINO for legal fees and other losses incurred by the lawsuit.

During the trial, both the plaintiff and the defendant believed that the case should be resolved by Chinese law, as at that time Japan was not yet a Contracting Party to the CISG. The Court held that the case should not be governed by the CISG, but the contract law of mainland China.

Ultimately, the Court held that JINUOSI should make the confirmed payment to GINO in a timely manner and bear the legal fees paid by GINO for the case.

## Commentary on the Key Issues Related to the CISG

**Issues**:

Issue 1 Why the CISG should not be applied in this case?

**Comments**:

### Issue 1 Why the CISG Should not Be Applied in This Case?

There are two main reasons why the Court finally determined that the CISG should not be applied. The first is that Japan, where the plaintiff resides, was not a contracting state of the CISG. The second is that both the plaintiff and the defendant chose the laws of mainland China as the applicable law of the case.

The first reason is very clear and easy to accept. According to CISG Article 1(1)(a), the CISG applies to contracts for the sale of goods concluded between parties whose places of business are in different Contracting States. During the period (2005 to 2007) when the dispute arose between the parties in this case, Japan was not a party to the CISG. According to the provisions of the CISG, the Court cannot directly apply the CISG in this case.

On August 1, 2009, the CISG became effective in Japan. Therefore, if the sale in this case occurred after this date, the Court would not be able to exclude the application of the CISG on the above grounds.

The second reason is more complicated. In the 1990s and early 2000s, Chinese judges were very unfamiliar with the CISG. Although the CISG has been applicable in China since 1988, many Chinese judges did not have knowledge of the CISG at that time. The understanding of China's domestic laws, especially by judges in remote areas, required improvement. Therefore, judges could not be expected to understand and correctly apply the CISG. Additionally, most Chinese lawyers did not understand the CISG. In order to avoid the application of the CISG, judges would ask both parties which law is to be applicable during the court session. Most lawyers will choose Chinese law, and the judge will regard this choice as the exclusion of the application of the CISG. The judge made the same choice in this case.

From the beginning of the second decade of the twenty-first century, this situation has changed. Many judges no longer reject the application of the CISG, and more and more lawyers understand the CISG. Therefore, there is an increase in the number of lawsuits applying the CISG in China.

In order to standardize the application of the CISG in China, the Supreme People's Court ('SPC') released the 'Minutes of the National Court's Symposium on Foreign-related Commercial and Maritime Trials' on 31 December 2021. The SPC stipulates: 'The international sales contracts concluded by parties whose places of business are located in different contracting states of the CISG shall automatically apply the provisions of the Convention, unless the parties expressly agree to exclude the application of the Convention. The people's court shall ask the parties for specific opinions on the application of the Convention before the conclusion of the court debate'.[1]

According to the above provision, for cases that meet the application conditions of the CISG, Chinese courts will generally automatically apply the CISG. Of course, in order to ensure the correct application of the CISG and minimize the impact on those parties and lawyers who have little knowledge of the CISG, the SPC allows both parties to unanimously choose to exclude the application of the CISG. If both parties choose to exclude the application of the CISG, the Court cannot apply the CISG as the governing law.

It should be noted that although a greater number of courts have become more and more positive towards the CISG, there are still many judges who are not familiar with it. At the same time, since many Chinese lawyers do not understand the CISG, the scope of application of the CISG in Chinese courts is still somewhat limited. However, with the deepening of Chinese domestic judges' understanding of the CISG and the further development of China's cross-border trade, it is believed that progressively Chinese courts will apply the CISG at trial.

[1] SPC [1], Article 19.

## Reference

1. Supreme People's Court (SPC). (2021). *Minutes of the National Symposium on the Foreign-related Commercial and Maritime Trial Work of Courts*. Retrieved from https://www.pkulaw.com/en_law/bffd20e9aee35db2bdfb.html?keyword=%E4%BC%9A%E8%AE%AE%E7%BA%AA%E8%A6%81.

**Mr. Xiaojun Chen** is a partner of SHANDONG WINCON LAW FIRM. He is mainly engaged in legal services in the fields of maritime commerce, maritime affairs, international trade, cross-border investment, and corporate governance. Mr. Chen has been engaged in commercial litigation for many years, especially transnational commercial litigation and arbitration. He has represented Chinese or foreign clients for many times in transnational commercial litigation or arbitration cases in Mainland China, Hong Kong, Singapore, London, Paris and other places. He has rich practical experience in legal services such as contract disputes, corporate disputes, and maritime disputes.

**Dr. Peng Guo** is Lecturer in Law at the Swinburne University of Technology. He has worked across several Australian universities and has held visiting positions at different European universities. He has received scholarships awarded by renowned research institutions and international organisations, including the Max Planck Institute for Comparative and International Private Law, the International Institute for the Unification of Private Law (UNIDROIT), the Swiss Institute of Comparative Law, and the European Union. He specialises in the international sale of goods, international commercial arbitration, comparative contract law, and law and technology.

# Dou Ya Trading Co., Ltd. v. Liaoning Hua Xi Group & Liaoning Hua Yi Clothing Co., Ltd.

**Xiaojun Chen and Peng Guo**

## Case Information

**Case Name**: *Dou Ya Trading Co., Ltd. v Liaoning Hua Xi Group & Liaoning Hua Yi Clothing Co., Ltd.*

**Seller**: Liaoning Hua Xi Group
**Place of Business**: China

**Buyer**: Dou Ya Trading Co., Ltd.
**Place of Business**: N/A

**Details of First Instance**:
**Court**: Liaoning Dalian Intermediate People's Court
**Judges**: N/A
**Case No.**: (2008) Da Min Si Chu No. 116

**Details of Second Instance**:
**Court**: Liaoning Higher People's Court
**Date of Decision**: 20 December 2011
**Case No.**: (2011) Liao Min San Zhong No. 146

X. Chen (✉)
Wincon Law Firm, Qingdao, China
e-mail: chenxiaojun@wincon.cn

P. Guo
Swinburne University of Technology, Melbourne, VIC 3000, Australia
e-mail: pguo@swin.edu.au



P. Guo et al. (eds.), *Selected Chinese Cases on the UN Sales Convention (CISG) Vol. 3*, Selected Chinese Cases on the CISG,
https://doi.org/10.1007/978-981-99-6851-0_12

**Judges**: Yuefei Ma (Presiding Judge), Hongjun Chen (Acting Judge), Shanchao Liu (Acting Judge)

**CISG Applied**: No
**Key CISG Provisions Interpreted and Applied**: Art 3(2)

## Case Abstract

Dou Ya Trading Co., Ltd. ('DY') signed multiple contracts with a Chinese company, Liaoning Hua Xi Group ('LHXG'), stipulating that DY would sell raw clothing materials to LHXG. LHXG would process the raw materials into clothing and then sell the finished clothing to DY.

During performance of the contract, a dispute arose between the two parties. On 17 November 2003, DY notified LHXG that it would cancel all contracts between the two parties. After 23 November 2006, LHXG and DY sued each other respectively, demanding that the other party should bear liability for compensation.

During the court of first instance hearing, both parties agreed to choose Chinese law as the applicable law of the case. The Court held that in the contract between the two parties, all the raw materials were provided by DY, and the main contractual obligation of LHXG was to provide processing services. Therefore, the contract between the two parties was not a sales contract, but a processing contract.

According to Chinese law at that time, the statute of limitations for processing contract disputes was two years. In this case, it has been more than three years since the dispute occurred when the two parties sued each other, and this time exceeded the statute of limitations prescribed by law. Therefore, the higher court ruled to dismiss all claims of both parties.

## Commentary on the Key Issues Related to the CISG

**Issues**:

Issue 1 Why should the CISG not apply in this case?
Issue 2 Why were the claims of both parties rejected by the Court?

**Comments**:

### Issue 1 Why Should the CISG not Apply in This Case?

In this case, the Court did not apply the CISG as the applicable law. The reason for this is that according to Article 3(2) of the CISG: 'This Convention does not apply to contracts in which the preponderant part of the obligations of the party who furnishes the goods consists in the supply of labour or other services'.

The contract in this case stipulated that all the raw clothing materials were provided by DY, and the main obligation of LHXG was to process them into clothing and subsequently provide the clothing to DY.

On the face of the matter, the deal consists of two sales. First, DY sold raw materials to LHXG; secondly LHXG sold clothing to DY. However, the problem relates to the fact that almost all the raw clothing materials produced by LHXG were provided by

DY. The main obligation of LHXG was to provide workers and equipment to process the raw materials into clothing, and then sell them to DY.

Since LHXG, as the supplier of the goods, is only obliged to provide labor and sewing processing services, according to 3(2) of the CISG above, the CISG cannot be applied to the contract between the plaintiff and the defendant in this case.

A processing contract is a typical trade service contract, the key content of which is labour service. However, the CISG is an international treaty only applicable to sales contracts, with the obvious result that the CISG does not apply to this case.

**Issue 2 Why Were the Claims of Both Parties Rejected by the Court?**

The reason why the court has to determine whether the contract between the two parties is a sales contract or a contract for processing is because the result of this issue will determine whether the statute of limitations applicable to the dispute in this case is two years or four years.

The statute of limitations refers to the system in which a person knows that his rights have been violated by others, but fails to file a claim within a certain period of time, will not have support from the court. The main purpose of establishing the statute of limitations system is to promote the stability of legal relations, end the uncertain state of rights and obligations in a timely manner, stabilize the legal order, and reduce transaction costs. The statute of limitations is an important system under the civil law system, and is stipulated in the civil codes of many civil law countries. Common law countries also have similar systems. Once the statute of limitations expires, the court will no longer protect the right holder's right to win a lawsuit.

In 2006, when this case occurred, Article 135 of China's General Principles of Civil Law (repealed, and replaced by the Civil Code) stated: 'Except as otherwise stipulated by law, the limitation of action regarding applications to a people's court for protection of civil rights shall be two years'. Article 129 of the Contract Law at that time (repealed, and replaced by the Civil Code) stipulated: 'For a dispute arising from a contract for the international sale of goods or a technology import or export contract, the time limit for bringing a suit or applying for arbitration is four years, calculating from the date on which the party knows or ought to know the infringement on its rights. For a dispute arising from any other type of contract, the time limit for bringing a suit or applying for arbitration shall be governed by the relevant law.'

According to the above provisions, if the contract in this case was identified as an international sales contract, then the statute of limitations in this case is four years; if the contract in this case is identified as a processing contract, then the statute of limitations in this case is two years. In this case, DY notified the Chinese company to cancel the contract on 17 November 2003, and DY sued on 23 November 2003, while LHXG filed its lawsuit at a later date. The time when the two companies sued each other was more than two years since DY asked to terminate the contract.

If the Court believed that the contract between the two parties in this case was an international sales contract, then the two lawsuits filed by both companies did not exceed the statute of limitations. However, if the Court believed that the contract between the two parties was a processing contract, then the two lawsuits both will both be dismissed for exceeding the statute of limitations.

The Court finally held that LHXG provided processing services rather than goods, so the contract between the two parties was considered a processing contract rather than a sales contract. Finally, the Court held that the two lawsuits filed by the two companies had exceeded the statute of limitations, and dismissed all claims of the two companies accordingly.

In China's civil legal system, the trial methods for contracts of a different nature may vary greatly. When hearing different types of civil cases, the court needs to determine the nature of the contract first, and then apply the different statute of limitations regimes, allocate the burden of proof and address other issues. This is very similar to the 'preliminary issues' process in private international law. Usually, judges first need to determine the specific nature of the dispute before they can determine what legal rules need to be applied during the trial. This case is a very typical example.

**Mr. Xiaojun Chen** is a partner of SHANDONG WINCON LAW FIRM. He is mainly engaged in legal services in the fields of maritime commerce, maritime affairs, international trade, cross-border investment, and corporate governance. Mr. Chen has been engaged in commercial litigation for many years, especially transnational commercial litigation and arbitration. He has represented Chinese or foreign clients for many times in transnational commercial litigation or arbitration cases in Mainland China, Hong Kong, Singapore, London, Paris and other places. He has rich practical experience in legal services such as contract disputes, corporate disputes, and maritime disputes.

**Dr. Peng Guo** is Lecturer in Law at the Swinburne University of Technology. He has worked across several Australian universities and has held visiting positions at different European universities. He has received scholarships awarded by renowned research institutions and international organisations, including the Max Planck Institute for Comparative and International Private Law, the International Institute for the Unification of Private Law (UNIDROIT), the Swiss Institute of Comparative Law, and the European Union. He specialises in the international sale of goods, international commercial arbitration, comparative contract law, and law and technology.

# Nanjing Overseas Wood Co., Ltd. v. Trans-Pacific Trading Ltd.

**Xiaojun Chen and Peng Guo**

**Case Information**

**Case Name**: *Nanjing Overseas Wood Co., Ltd. v Trans-Pacific Trading Ltd.*

**Seller**: Trans-Pacific Trading Ltd.
**Place of Business**: N/A

**Buyer**: Nanjing Overseas Wood Co., Ltd.
**Place of Business**: China

**Details of First Instance**:
**Court**: Jiangsu Nanjing Intermediate People's Court
**Date of Decision**: 4 July 2012
**Case No.**: (2011) Ning Shang Wai Chu No. 75
**Judges**: Feng Xue (Presiding Judge), Hanqing Zhang (Acting Judge), Xin Jiang (Acting Judge)

**CISG Applied**: Yes
**Key CISG Provisions Interpreted and Applied**: Arts 35(1), 38, 50

X. Chen (✉)
Wincon Law Firm, Qingdao, China
e-mail: chenxiaojun@wincon.cn

P. Guo
Swinburne University of Technology, Melbourne, VIC 3000, Australia
e-mail: pguo@swin.edu.au



P. Guo et al. (eds.), *Selected Chinese Cases on the UN Sales Convention (CISG) Vol. 3*, Selected Chinese Cases on the CISG,
https://doi.org/10.1007/978-981-99-6851-0_13

## Case Abstract

In July 2011, the Chinese company Nanjing Overseas Wood Co., Ltd. ('NOW') signed a sales contract with a foreign company Trans-Pacific Trading Ltd. ('TPT'). The contract stipulated that NOW would purchase a batch of wooden boards from TPT, and both parties agreed on the specifications and quality standards of the goods. After NOW received the goods, it was suspected that the goods did not meet the specifications or quality standards agreed in the contract, NOW immediately hired a third party to inspect the goods.

After inspection, it was found that the batch of goods did not meet the specifications and quality standards agreed in the contract. Therefore, NOW filed a lawsuit against TPT to reduce the payment due to TPT. Since the entire payment for the goods had already been paid to TPT, NOW required TPT to return a reduced price to NOW.

During the litigation process, both the plaintiff and the defendant chose CISG as the applicable law for the trial of the case. If there is no provision in the CISG, the Chinese law would apply.

The Nanjing Intermediate People's Court found that the evidence provided by NOW proved that the quality of the goods delivered by the defendant was lower than the quality agreed in the contract. In response to the actual quality of the goods, the price of the batch of goods should be much lower than the price agreed in the contract.

The Court held that art 50 of the CISG should be applied to this case. The article states: 'If the goods do not conform with the contract and whether or not the price has already been paid, the buyer may reduce the price in the same proportion as the value that the goods actually delivered had at the time of the delivery bears to the value that conforming goods would have had at that time. However, if the seller remedies any failure to perform his obligations in accordance with article 37 or article 48 or if the buyer refuses to accept performance by the seller in accordance with those articles, the buyer may not reduce the price'. If the evidence provided by NOW can prove that the quality of the goods is lower than the quality agreed in the contract, it has the right to reduce the price.

Ultimately, after referring to the actual market price of the goods, the Court determined that the reduction in the contract price was USD $40 per cubic meter. Since the quantity of goods actually delivered by the defendant was 6998.294 $m^3$, the amount that should be returned by the defendant is USD $279931.76. Additionally, the Court ruled that TPT should bear NOW's value-added tax losses.

## Commentary on the Key Issues Related to the CISG

### Issues

Issue 1 How Chinese courts apply Article 50 of the CISG

## Comments

### Issue 1 How Chinese Courts Apply Article 50 of the CISG

In this case, the Court conducted the trial strictly in accordance with art 50 of the CISG. Article 111 of China's Contract Law (repealed and replaced by the Civil Code) and art 582 of the Civil Code include the buyer's right to demand a reduction in price if the delivered goods do not conform to the contract.

Differing from the CISG, laws such as the Civil Code of China do not stipulate how to determine how the amount of price reduction should be calculated. However, art 23 of the Interpretation of the Supreme People's Court on the Application of Law in the Trial of Sales Contract Dispute Cases promulgated by the Supreme People's Court ('SPC') on 10 May 2012 (effective on 1 July 2012) states: 'Where the quality of the subject matter does not comply with the contractual provisions, if the buyer claims a reduction of price according to Article 111 of the Contract Law, the people's court shall support such claims. Where the parties claim that the price difference is to be calculated According to the market value, at the time of delivery, of the subject matter that would comply with the contractual agreement as compared to the subject matter that was actually delivered, the people's court shall support such claims. After payment is made, where the buyer claims that the excess price after reduction should be returned, the people's court shall support such claims'.[1] After the promulgation of the Civil Code, the SPC made amendments to the above-mentioned judicial interpretation, but the basic content remained unchanged.

According to the above provisions, it can be seen that art 111 of the Contract Law or art 582 of the Civil Code and the corresponding judicial interpretations together constitute the provisions under Chinese law on the circumstances under which a party to a contract has the right to demand a reduction in price. These provisions of Chinese law are relatively similar to the provisions of art 50 of the CISG.

A major problem encountered by Chinese court judges is how to determine the amount of price reduction. In this case, NOW submitted a number of contracts for the sale of wood panels from other Canadian suppliers during the same period so that to demonstrate the market value of the wood panels at the time. In the end, the court determined the extent of the price reduction based on the evidence submitted by NOW.

However, in other cases, the plaintiff may for some reason be unable to prove the market value of the goods. For example, the plaintiff may purchase rare products, or the market stock is scarce and therefore the market value cannot be measured at all; or the market value changes so frequently it is impossible for the court to judge the accurate value. In this case, the judges of the Court can only exercise their discretionary power to judge the extent of the price reduction. In the case of Star New Energy (Beijing) Energy Conservation Technology Co., Ltd. v Guangzhou Panyu Suneng Heating and Heating Equipment Co., Ltd. heard by the Second Intermediate People's Court of Beijing (Case No.: (2022) Jing 02 Min Zhong No. 11495), the judge decided at his discretion that the defendant should return RMB 400,000 to the plaintiff with reference to the evidence submitted by both parties that could prove

[1] SPC [1], article 23.

the difference between the actual quality of the goods and the quality agreed in the contract when the market value of the goods could not be proved.

It should be noted that art 111 of the Contract Law or art 582 of the Civil Code applies not only to contracts for the sale of goods, but to any non-gratuitous contracts. In the case of Jinbi Property Co., Ltd. Yingkou Branch v Zhe Sun heard by Yingkou Intermediate People's Court, Liaoning Province (Case No.: (2022) Liao 08 Min Zhong No. 2044), the Court held that the defendant provided the property service provided by the defendant did not conform to what was stipulated in the property contract. The defendant was ordered to return 50% of the property fee to the plaintiff.

Another point to note is that most of the parties in China will stipulate a clear quality breach clause in the contract. When the quality of the goods obviously does not meet the contract, the parties are generally more inclined to ask the breaching party to pay liquidated damages or compensation for losses. Only when the contract does not stipulate liquidated damages, and the loss cannot be determined or has not yet occurred, will the parties choose to ask for a reduction in the price.

## Reference

1. Supreme People's Court (SPC). *Interpretation on the Applicable Law Issues in the Trial of Sales Contract Dispute Cases*. Retrieved from https://law.pkulaw.com/Readchinalaw/deb83c1e931b15c1bdfb.html

**Mr. Xiaojun Chen** is a partner of Shandong Wincon Law Firm. He is mainly engaged in legal services in the fields of maritime commerce, maritime affairs, international trade, cross-border investment, and corporate governance. Mr. Chen has been engaged in commercial litigation for many years, especially transnational commercial litigation and arbitration. He has represented Chinese or foreign clients for many times in transnational commercial litigation or arbitration cases in Mainland China, Hong Kong, Singapore, London, Paris and other places. He has rich practical experience in legal services such as contract disputes, corporate disputes, and maritime disputes.

**Dr. Peng Guo** is Lecturer in Law at the Swinburne University of Technology. He has worked across several Australian universities and has held visiting positions at different European universities. He has received scholarships awarded by renowned research institutions and international organisations, including the Max Planck Institute for Comparative and International Private Law, the International Institute for the Unification of Private Law (UNIDROIT), the Swiss Institute of Comparative Law, and the European Union. He specialises in the international sale of goods, international commercial arbitration, comparative contract law, and law and technology.

# A Company v. B Company

**Xiaojun Chen and Peng Guo**

**Case Information**

**Case Name**: *A Company v B Company*

**Seller**: N/A
**Place of Business**: China

**Buyer**: N/A
**Place of Business**: Japan

**Details of First Instance**:
**Court**: Shanghai Pudong District Court
**Date of Decision**: 21 May 2012
**Case No.**: (2011) Pu Min Er (Shang) Chu No. S808
**Judges**: Yuefei Ma (Presiding Judge), Hongjun Chen (Acting Judge), Shanchao Liu (Acting Judge)

**Details of Second Instance**:
**Court**: Liaoning Higher People's Court
**Date of Decision**: 20 December 2011
**Case No.**: (2011) Liao Min San Zhong No. 146

X. Chen (✉)
Wincon Law Firm, Qingdao, China
e-mail: chenxiaojun@wincon.cn

P. Guo
Swinburne University of Technology, Melbourne, VIC 3000, Australia
e-mail: pguo@swin.edu.au



P. Guo et al. (eds.), *Selected Chinese Cases on the UN Sales Convention (CISG) Vol. 3*, Selected Chinese Cases on the CISG,
https://doi.org/10.1007/978-981-99-6851-0_14

**Judges**: Li Sun (Presiding Judge), Wei Yang (Acting Judge), Yi Xing (Acting Judge)

**CISG Applied**: Yes
**Key the CISG Provisions Interpreted and Applied**: Articles 42, 71

### Case Abstract

In March 2010, Company A in China signed a sales contract with Company B in Japan, agreeing that Company B would purchase a batch of furniture from Company A. The two parties agreed in the contract that Company A should ensure that it has obtained sufficient authorization to ensure that the sale of the furniture in Japan will not infringe anyone's intellectual property rights or other rights.

After the contract was signed, Company A suddenly informed Company B that some of the furniture could not be authorized by its designer, so it might not be sold in Japan. Company B then notified Company A that it believed that Company A has breached the contract. Therefore, Company B refused to pay for the goods and demanded compensation from Company A for its losses.

Company A believed that Company B had no reason to refuse to pay for the goods, so it filed a lawsuit against Company B, requiring Company B to pay for the goods and compensate Company A for its losses.

During the first instance of this case, since both China and Japan are contracting parties to the CISG, the Court held that the CISG should apply to this case. According to the provisions of art 42 of the CISG, the goods sold by Company A should comply with the regulations of intellectual property rights in Japan and ensure that the goods it sells do not infringe anyone's intellectual property rights. However, Company A has confirmed that some of the goods it sold were not authorized by the designer, and during the trial, Company A has failed to provide proof that other goods had been authorized by the designer. Therefore, the Court held that all the furniture sold by Company A was not authorized by the designer. Therefore, according to art 42 of the CISG and art 67 of the Chinese Contract Law, the Court found that Company B did not need to pay for the goods, nor need to make any compensation to Company A.

Company A filed an appeal, and the court of second instance still held that Company A has failed to obtain the authorization of the designer of the goods it sold, and believed that the goods could not be sold in Japan because of this. On this basis, the court of second instance applied art 71 of the CISG instead of art 67 of the Chinese Contract Law, and determined that Company B did not need to pay for the goods or compensate Company A. Finally, the court of second instance rejected all the claims of Company A.

### Commentary on the Key Issues Related to the CISG

#### Issues

Issue 1 How does the Chinese court apply art 42 of the CISG?

Issue 2 How does the Chinese court apply art 71 of the CISG?

## Comments

### Issue 1 How Does the Chinese Court Apply Art 42 of the CISG?

Article 42 of CISG is a clause on the protection of intellectual property rights, which stipulates that the products sold by the seller should not infringe the intellectual property rights of others. Although the Chinese Contract Law (which has expired and has been replaced by the Civil Code) and the Civil Code have special chapters on 'sales contracts', these chapters do not specifically address the issue of intellectual property rights of goods, but generally require that the seller's goods cannot violate the legal rights of others. For example, art 612 of the Civil Code states: 'Unless otherwise provided by the law, the seller shall have the obligation to warrant that no third party has any right to the delivered subject matter'. Chinese judges believe that the 'rights' in this clause includes intellectual property rights.

If the products sold by the seller infringe any third-party intellectual property rights, Chinese courts will generally consider the seller to be in breach of the contract and require the seller to be liable for compensation to the buyer. In the case Jizhong Plumbing Sanitary Ware Store in Hanting District v Weifang Jiuyi Sanitary Ware Co., Ltd.[1] (Case No: [2022] Lu 07 Min No. 2480) heard in the Weifang City Intermediate People's Court of Shandong Province ('WFIC'), the goods sold by the seller infringed the patent rights of others, and the buyer had to compensate the intellectual property rights holder. The buyer then filed a lawsuit against the seller, demanding compensation from the seller. WFIC believed that the seller had violated the contract by selling products with intellectual property infringements to the buyer, and determined that the losses suffered by the buyer should be borne by the seller.

In fact, Chinese courts are no strangers to cases in which the seller is sued because the goods sold by the seller infringe the intellectual property rights of a third party, so they are familiar with the application of art 42 of the CISG. A typical case is *Newcore Retail (Shanghai) Co., Ltd. v Boutique Clarissa Co., Ltd.*,[2] In this case, a batch of luxury goods sold by the seller had intellectual property rights issues, and the Shanghai Minhang District People's Court applied art 42 of the CISG. The seller was ordered to return the payment already made to the buyer and compensate the seller for other losses.

### Issue 2 How Does the Chinese Court Apply Art 42 of the CISG?

Art 71 of CISG stipulates that if one party to the contract believes that the other party is likely to breach the contract, it can suspend the performance of the contract and require the possibly breaching party to provide a guarantee. Under the Chinese legal

[1] (2022) Lu 07 Min Zhong No. 2480.

[2] (2017) Hu 0112 Min Chu No. 37476.

system, this is known as the 'right to defense of uneasiness'. Arts 527 and 528 of China's Civil Code are very similar to art 71 of the CISG. Before the Civil Code took effect, arts 68 and 69 of China's Contract Law had similar provisions.

Therefore, Chinese courts are not unfamiliar with cases where art 71 of the CISG may apply. However, Chinese courts do not directly apply art 71 of the CISG to many cases since most Chinese judges and lawyers have very limited or no knowledge of the CISG.

It is worth mentioning that the court of first instance in this case did not apply art 71 of the CISG, nor arts 68 and 69 of the Contract Law (the Civil Code had not yet entered into force at the time), but instead applied art 67 of the Contract Law. Article 67 of the Contract Law stipulates: 'Where both parties have obligations toward each other and there is an order of priority in respect of the performance, and the party who is to perform first fails to perform, the party who is to perform later has the right to reject the other party's demand for performance. If the performance of the obligations of the party who is to perform first is not in conformity with the agreement, the party who is to perform later has the right to reject the other party's demand for corresponding performance.' There is an obvious difference between this clause and arts 68 and 69 of the Contract Law.

It is generally believed that the prerequisite for the application of art 67 of the Contract Law is that one party has clearly violated the contract. However, in this case, although the seller informed the buyer that some of the furniture was not authorized by the designer, there may still have been other pieces of furniture that did not infringe intellectual property rights after all. Therefore, it is not appropriate for the court of first instance to directly apply the provisions of art 67. In comparison, it is more appropriate to apply the provisions of art 71 of the CISG. The judgment of the court of second instance is more accurate than that of the court of first instance.

**Mr. Xiaojun Chen** is a partner of Shandong Wincon Law Firm. He is mainly engaged in legal services in the fields of maritime commerce, maritime affairs, international trade, cross-border investment, and corporate governance. Mr. Chen has been engaged in commercial litigation for many years, especially transnational commercial litigation and arbitration. He has represented Chinese or foreign clients for many times in transnational commercial litigation or arbitration cases in Mainland China, Hong Kong, Singapore, London, Paris and other places. He has rich practical experience in legal services such as contract disputes, corporate disputes, and maritime disputes.

**Dr. Peng Guo** is Lecturer in Law at the Swinburne University of Technology. He has worked across several Australian universities and has held visiting positions at different European universities. He has received scholarships awarded by renowned research institutions and international organisations, including the Max Planck Institute for Comparative and International Private Law, the International Institute for the Unification of Private Law (UNIDROIT), the Swiss Institute of Comparative Law, and the European Union. He specialises in the international sale of goods, international commercial arbitration, comparative contract law, and law and technology.

# A Co., Ltd. v. B Co., Ltd.

**Peng Wang and Yueshan Liu**

**Case Information**

**Case Name**: *A Co., Ltd. v B Co., Ltd.*

**Seller**: *A Co., Ltd.*
**Place of Business**: Gabon

**Buyer**: *B Co., Ltd.*
**Place of Business**: China

**Details of First Instance**:
**Court**: Pudong New Area People's Court, Shanghai
**Date of Decision**: 20 June 2012
**Case No.**: (2011) Pu Min Er (Shang) Chu Zi No S1876
**Judges**: Li Sun (Presiding Judge), Wei Yang (Acting Judge), Hongyi Zhang (Acting Judge)

**Details to Second Instance**:
**Court**: Shanghai First Intermediate People's Court
**Date of Decision**: 20 December 2012
**Case No.**: (2012) Hu Yi Zhong Min Si (Shang) Zhong Zi No S1400

P. Wang (✉) · Y. Liu
Nankai University, Tianjin, China
e-mail: wppku@163.com

Y. Liu
e-mail: liuyueshan99@yeah.net



P. Guo et al. (eds.), *Selected Chinese Cases on the UN Sales Convention (CISG) Vol. 3*, Selected Chinese Cases on the CISG,
https://doi.org/10.1007/978-981-99-6851-0_15

**Judges**: Ying Huang (Presiding Judge), Liyuan Liu (Acting Judge), Ningning Shao (Acting Judge)

**CISG Applied**: Yes
**Key CISG Provisions Interpreted**: Articles 1, 49, 74, 76

## Case Abstract

On November 8, 2010, the seller, Company A, with its place of business in China, and the buyer, Company B, with its place of business in Gabon, entered into a sales contract under which Company B purchased from Company A 2,500 $m^3$ of padouk and 1,000 $m^3$ of kevazingo for a total purchase price of EUR 1,182,000. The port of shipment was the main port of Gabon, and the port of destination was Shanghai. The price terms were cost, insurance and freight (CIF) Shanghai, with 30% of the purchase price to be paid in advance by Company B, i.e., EUR 354,600, and 70% of the purchase price to be paid by Company B by opening a letter of credit (L/C) for EUR 827,400. The sales contract was signed by Huang on behalf of the seller and stamped with the seal of Company A.

Subsequently, the parties amended the terms of the L/C agreed in the contract, and delivered the revised contract by fax. The faxed copy of the contract also bore the signature of Huang and the seal of Company A. Consequently, Company B remitted EUR 354,600 to Company A's account and opened a letter of credit in favor of Company A for the amount of EUR 827,400. From December 23, 2010, to February 10, 2011, Company A commissioned the shipping company to ship 1,399.47 $m^3$ of timber with a value of EUR 428,636.42 through 11 bills of lading. The bill of lading was a bearer bill of lading, the shipper was Company A, the notifier was Company B, and the consignee received the goods by order. The issuing bank received the documents under the above-mentioned L/C six times in succession and issued a Notice of External Payment/Acceptance to Company B. Company B paid 100% of the invoices of the 11 bills of lading to the amount of EUR 428,636.44.

On February 17, 2011, Company B applied the bank to modify some terms of the aforementioned L/C; the latest shipment deadline was changed to May 15, 2011, and the content of the goods changed to 1,000 $m^3$ of beli, 1,500 $m^3$ of padouk and 1,000 $m^3$ of kevazingo. However, Company A did not deliver the remaining timber, and Company B made repeated representations to the defendant regarding this, but Company A did not fulfill its delivery obligations. Company B appealed to the Court, requesting Company A to continue to deliver the 2,100.53 $m^3$ of timber, and filed a lawsuit for preservation.

## First Instance

The Court seized the goods under the bill of lading, and Company A requested to provide a deposit in exchange for the goods under the bill of lading that were preserved. The parties negotiated the market price of the three types of timber: beli at RMB 4,500/$m^3$, padouk at RMB 4,400/$m^3$ and kevazingo at RMB 10,000/$m^3$. Company A demanded to release the bill of lading for some of the goods according to the above unit price and post a security deposit. In the course of the first instance hearing, Company B changed its claim to require Company A to pay damages to Company B for breach of contract and refund the advance already paid by Company B.

The court of first instance held that the case was a dispute between the parties in China and Gabon over the international contract for the sale of goods, and that China and Gabon were both parties to the United Nations Convention on Contracts for the International Sale of Goods ('CISG'), so the Convention should be applied as the legal basis for the settlement of the dispute. The focus of disputes in this case are as follows: I: the authenticity of the sales contract between Company B and Company A; II: the relationship between the L/C and the sales contract in this case; and III: the loss incurred by Company B.

I. Regarding the authenticity of the sales contract, the Court confirmed the authenticity of the original sales contract and the faxed copy of the contract based on the evidence submitted by both parties. From the performance, Company B paid the advance payment and issued the L/C according to the contract, and Company A also delivered part of the goods, which confirmed the authenticity of the sales contract.
II. Regarding the relationship between the L/C and the sales contract, Company A argued that the L/C had no relationship with the sales contract. It was a L/C issued by Company B on behalf of Company D, who was not a party to the case, in order to fulfill its contribution to the cooperation contract with Company A. Company D issued a statement of circumstances to the Court, indicating that Company D and Company A had signed a cooperation agreement, according to which Company A was responsible for the sale of the timber. Later, Company A signed a foreign trade sales contract with Company B. The Court held that Company B applied for an L/C to be issued by the bank in order to fulfill its obligations under the sales contract, and that the beneficiary was Company A, not the L/C issued on behalf of Company D.
III. Regarding Company B's damages, Company A failed to deliver the goods at the time specified and, in quantity, agreed in the sales contract. Company B modified the L/C through the bank and changed the species of wood. As the modification of the L/C was the unilateral act of company B, it should not be regarded as the modification of the species of wood in the contract agreed to by both parties. Company B could receive damages including profits caused by Company A's breach of contract, but the two species of timber in the original contract shall prevail.

In accordance with arts 49, 74 and 76 of the CISG, the Court held that Company B's claim for loss of profit and return of the advance payment included the intention to declare the contract null and void (rescind the contract). The loss of profit is based on the difference between the contract price and the current price of the goods agreed between the parties when Company A requested replacement of the conserved goods with the deposit. Company B used the exchange rate between the Euro and the RMB at the time of the change of claim to calculate the difference in price, which was also reasonable. Company A no longer performed the contract, and should return the advance payment to Company B. Therefore, the Court ruled that Company A should compensate Company B for breach of contract to the amount of RMB 8,404,017.93 and return the advance payment to Company B to the amount of RMB 3,213,314.28.

### Second Instance

Company A appealed against the judgment of the first instance and requested the rejection of Company B's claim.

As to whether there is a real sales relationship between the two parties, the court of second instance held that whether the sales contract between the two parties really exists can be corroborated by the performance of the parties. Company B in the first trial provided the contract text in addition to the L/C, prepayment voucher, payment voucher under the L/C and customs declaration, and the bill of lading, which proved that the parties had partially performed the contract. There was a real contract of sale between the parties in this case. As to whether Company B's claim for damages and return of prepayment was valid, the Court held that Company B claimed the difference between the contract price and the market price of the undelivered timber, i.e., the loss of profit, and Company A should compensate Company B for the loss, including profit for the breach of contract. Considering the circumstances of the case, including the contract price of the disputed goods, the market price and the performance of the parties, the loss was determined to be RMB 3,000,000. As for the return of the advance payment, since the contract of sale and purchase in dispute did exist and the parties no longer performed, Company A should return the advance payment to Company B.

Therefore, the Court reversed the first and second items of the original judgment and ruled that Company A should pay Company B RMB 3,000,000 for its loss, and return the advance payment of RMB 3,213,314.28.

## Commentary to the Key Issues Related to the CISG

### Issues

Issue 1 The Applicability of the CISG
Issue 2 Compensation for Damages under the CISG

### Comments

### Issue 1 The Applicability of the CISG

In this case, the court of first instance held that this was a dispute between two parties, with their places of business in China and Gabon, over an international contract for the sale of goods, and that both China and Gabon were parties to the CISG, therefore the Convention should be applied as the legal basis for the settlement of the dispute. The court of second instance approved the application of the law by the court of first instance.

The CISG is a merger of the two Hague Conventions and was formally adopted at the Vienna Diplomatic Conference in March 1980 with the participation of representatives from 62 countries.[1] As of January 2023, after more than 40 years of development, the CISG has become increasingly influential in the field of international trade, with as many as 95 contracting states.[2] At present, the Chinese legal system lacks clear provisions on the status of treaties and the manner of their application. With regard to the acceptance of civil and commercial treaties in China, the academic community generally recognizes the 'ex officio incorporation theory'.[3] Prior to the promulgation of the Civil Code of the People's Republic of China ('Civil Code'), art 142 of the General Principles of the Civil Law of the People's Republic of China ('General Principles of the Civil Law') sets out the manner of application of international treaties. Although the General Principles of the Civil Law has been repealed, both the theory underlying the application of civil and commercial treaties and the specific implementation of treaties such as the CISG in China are based on this provision. Art 268 of the Maritime Law of the People's Republic of China[4] and art 9 of the Interpretation of the Law of the People's Republic of China on Choice of Law for Foreign-related Civil Relationships (1)[5] also demonstrates China's emphasis on the priority application of international treaties.

Although the General Principles of Civil Law was abolished after the implementation of the Civil Code, the application of treaties is in a situation of 'no reliance', but the long-established custom of applying 'treaty precedence' based on this provision will be continued. Specifically, this practice of application can be summarized as follows: First, civil and commercial treaties can be directly applied in Chinese courts.[6] In other words, international conventions concluded by China can be applied directly in China without prior transformation into domestic law. Second, when a civil or commercial treaty differs from the provisions of Chinese law, the treaty should be applied. One scholar has pointed out that in judicial practice, generally, if both the domestic law of the Chinese state and the international treaty have provisions, the provisions of the Chinese law shall apply; if the provisions of the Chinese law are inconsistent with the international treaty, the provisions of the international treaty

---

[1] Wang [1], p. 30.

[2] *Overview of the status of UNCITRAL Conventions and Model Laws*. Retrieved January 23, 2023 from https://uncitral.un.org/sites/uncitral.un.org/files/media-documents/uncitral/en/overview-status-table.pdf.

[3] Li [2], p. 316.

[4] Article 268: If any international treaty concluded or acceded to by the People's Republic of China contains provisions differing from those contained in this Law, the provisions of the relevant international treaty shall apply, unless the provisions are those on which the People's Republic of China has announced reservations.

[5] Article 9: If the parties invoke in the contract an international treaty that has not yet entered into force for the People's Republic of China, the People's Court may determine the rights and obligations between the parties in accordance with the content of the international treaty, except for those that violate the public interest of the People's Republic of China or the mandatory provisions of the laws and administrative regulations of the People's Republic of China.

[6] Han [3], p. 223.

shall apply, so as not to violate China's international obligations, but also to help maintain the integrity of China's domestic law.[7]

In accordance with the application of the CISG and China's judicial practice, there are three ways of application: direct application, indirect application and agreed application. This case is a direct application of the CISG. In this case, the two courts were consistent in their thinking on the application of the law. The Courts considered that the parties' places of business were located in China and Gabon respectively, both of which are parties to the CISG, and the parties did not explicitly exclude the application of the CISG, therefore the CISG was directly applied. The Courts' thinking on the trial was clear and correct.

Articles 1 to 6 of the CISG are the rules of application of the CISG, and they are in a particular order of priority. Article 1 of the CISG sets out the scope of application, arts 2 to 5 list the circumstances in which the convention cannot be applied, and art 6 sets out the circumstances in which the parties exclude the application of the CISG. As far as the direct application of the CISG is concerned, the court should first make a judgment as to whether the contract in question falls within the jurisdiction of the CISG (arts 2 to 5), followed by a judgment as to the international character of the contract in question (art 1), and whether two conditions are met. If so, the CISG can be applied directly: first, the parties' places of business are located in different countries; and second, these countries are parties to the CISG. The final determination of whether the parties have validly excluded the CISG shall be made (art 6).[8] If the parties to the contract have not excluded the application of the CISG, the CISG shall ultimately be applied. It is also important to note that direct application takes precedence over contractual application, and the court need not agree to apply the CISG by agreement based on the parties' autonomy if the CISG satisfies the prerequisites for direct application.

The direct application model requires that courts should automatically and directly apply international civil and commercial treaties.[9] Automatic application means that the court should give priority to the application of an international civil or commercial treaty if the conditions for its application are met. Direct application means that courts should apply international civil and commercial treaties as if they were domestic law, without the guidance of private international law rules. Although art 142(2) of the former General Principles of Civil Law had the role of private international law, the CISG's direct application model is sufficient to enable its direct application without the need for guidance from private international law rules.[10] In the case of *C&J Sheet Metal Co., Ltd. V. Wenzhou Chenxing Machinery Co., Ltd.*,[11] the Supreme People's Court ('SPC') corrected the errors in the application of law made by the courts of first and second instance, ruling that the places of business of the parties were located in China and the United States respectively, that both countries were parties to the

[7] Guo [4], p. 30.

[8] Zhang [5], p. 101.

[9] UNCITRAL [6], p. 5.

[10] Zhang [7], p. 112.

[11] (2014) Min Shen Zi No. 26.

CISG, and that the parties did not exclude the application of the Convention to the contract in question, which complied with the provisions of art 1(1) of the CISG on direct application, and that the CISG should be directly applied in the case. In this way, the SPC's formulation is in line with the logic of direct application and provides a case reference for the subsequent model of direct application of the Convention based on art 1(1) of the CISG.

**Issue 2 Compensation for Damages Under the CISG**

In this case, Company B initially requested Company A to continue to deliver 2,100.53 $m^3$ of timber, and later changed its claim during the trial to request Company A to pay RMB 8,504,017.93 in damages for breach of contract and refund the advance payment of RMB 3,213,341.28. The court of first instance found that it was reasonable for Company B to declare the contract null and void because Company A failed to deliver the goods in accordance with the contract and in the quantity specified. According to arts 74 and 76 of the CISG, the Court held that Company B's loss of profit should be compensated on the basis of the difference between the contract price and the current goods price agreed between the parties at the time that Company A replaced the conserved goods with the deposit, and the species of undelivered timber was subject to the two species in the contract. In the first instance, Company A was awarded RMB 8,404,017.93 as damages for breach of contract and RMB 3,213,314.28 as advance payment to Company B. The court of second instance held that the scope of damages of Company A included the loss, including profit, in addition to the contract price of the disputed goods, market price, performance of the parties. The Court reduced the loss for breach of contract to RMB 3,000,000. From the Court's decision, there are significant differences in the calculation of the amount of damages for breach of contract by different courts based on arts 74 and 76 of the CISG.

Articles 74 to 77 of the CISG provide the rules of compensation for damages, which is an important contractual remedy for breach of contract. These provisions permit one contracting party to compensate the other party for damages in accordance with the law if there is a failure by the party to perform its contractual obligations, or if the performance of that party's contractual obligations does not conform to the agreement, and also involves rules on the creation of the right of the party in default to request damages, the scope of damages and the determination of the amount of damages.

The remedies for breach of contract available to both the buyer and the seller under the CISG are mainly rescission of contract, damages, and actual performance. According to art 74 of the CISG, the scope of liability for damages includes two aspects: the actual loss and the lost benefit caused to the injured party by the breach of contract. The actual loss is the loss incurred by the injured party acting in reliance on the contract; the lost benefit is the profit that could have been made if the contract had been performed, which is generally the profit from the sale. Thus, damages under the Convention are compensatory in nature; they are intended to leave the injured party in the same financial position as it would have been in had the contract been performed. Article 74 also limits the scope of liability for damages, which may not exceed the probable loss that the party in breach of the contract foresaw, or should have foreseen, at the time of the conclusion of the contract for the breach. Some scholars have proposed a standard of proof for damages: the injured party has the burden of proving with reasonable certainty that it has suffered some loss and has the burden of proving the extent of the loss suffered, but proof of the extent of the loss does not need to be arithmetically precise.[12] In addition, the determination of the scope of liability must also take into account the so-called 'foreseeability of damages', which is a further supplement and qualification to the first half of art 74, i.e., whether actual loss or reasonably expected profit can be included is also judged according to the standard of foreseeability.

Unlike common law systems that require foreseeability on both sides of the breach and the injured party, the CISG and the General Principles of International Commercial Contracts only require foreseeability on the consequences of the breach by the breaching party. As can be seen from art 74, the Convention adopts a double standard: the objective standard is that the time for specific consideration should be the time of contract formation, examining whether the breaching party had knowledge of certain facts and circumstances and anticipated the possible damage caused by its breach; the subjective standard is to examine whether the breaching party ought to have known certain facts and circumstances and ought to have anticipated the possible damage caused by the breach. Regardless of whether it is a subjective or objective standard, the judgment is not based on the statement of the breaching party or the evidence of the damaged party but is measured by the judge according to the circumstances of the case, based on the standard foreseeable by a reasonable person. However, because each case is different, it leaves a wide range of discretion for judges and arbitrators. At this point, the principle of fair proportionality can be used as a value orientation or policy consideration to reflect its function and value in the specific arguments of judges' decisions.[13]

In this case, it was incorrect for the Court to calculate the amount of damages for Company A based on the specific amount determined by both parties at the time of the litigation preservation. Since Company B initially requested Company A to pay for the remaining timber, the market price of the timber was determined between the two parties during the trial, and only afterwards did Company B change its claim. If the claimed amount is calculated by the amount determined at the time of litigation preservation, it is against the principle of foreseeability. This is because the current price determined at the time of litigation preservation is not the price that would have arisen if the goods had been traded at the time of the original agreement. The type, quality, weight, mode of international trade and place of delivery of the goods involved in litigation preservation are different from those stipulated in the contract, which determines that the value of the goods under litigation preservation is not comparable with that of the contract goods originally stated.

Articles 75 and 76 of the CISG set out the basic method of calculating the amount of damages in the special case of avoidance of a contract by the parties, and are a

[12] Wei and He [8], p. 241.

[13] Pan [9], p. 66.

specific application of the general principle of calculating the amount of damages in art 74. The party which has been damaged is entitled to claim the difference between the contract price and the current price determined at the time and place specified in art 76 of the CISG. The time for determining the current price is the day when the contract is declared to have ceased to have effect. However, if the party which suffered damage took delivery of the goods prior to the avoidance of the contract, that earlier time shall prevail.[14] The CISG does not compel the parties to pursue all efforts to enter into a substitute transaction. If, after avoidance of the contract, the non-breaching party does not enter into a substitute transaction or enters into a substitute transaction that does not meet the requirements of art 75, any claim may be made under art 76, with the only requirement being that the goods have a current price. The current price is the general price at which goods of the same kind are sold in the market under equal conditions. The current price varies with time and the first thing to determine is which current price at the relevant point in time is to be used as the current price for calculating damages.

Section 50 (3) of the *Sale of Goods Act 1979* (UK) provides that when the seller's refusal to deliver constitutes a breach of contract, the buyer may claim damages from the seller for the difference between the contract price and the market price or current price 'at the time when the goods should have been delivered or when delivery was refused'. The Uniform Commercial Code provides that when the seller fails to deliver or breaks the contract, the buyer is entitled to claim the difference in price between the market price at the time the buyer knew of the breach and the contract price.[15] The CISG provides for two different situations for the determination of the current price: the first is when the party claiming damages declares the contract void prior to receipt of the goods, at which time it may obtain the difference between the price stipulated in the contract and the current price at the time of avoidance; the second is when the party claiming damages declares the contract void after receipt of the goods, at which time it may obtain the difference between the price stipulated in the contract and the current price at the time of receipt of the goods. This provision of the CISG is intended to prevent price speculation by the contracting party. The right to rescind the contract belongs to the defaulting party, and in general there is a period of time between the time of breach and the time of acceptance or rescission of the contract, which the defaulting party can use to observe changes in market conditions. Since the greater the price difference, the greater the damages the victim will receive, the defaulting party may wait until the price difference is maximized to declare the termination of the contract, thereby obtaining the maximum compensation amount. If the judiciary recognizes the price at the time of avoidance as the current price, it will put the defaulting party in an obviously unfair position and disrupt the normal order of international trade transactions.

Company A argued that Company B did not prove the existence of the actual loss, only claiming that there was an alleged difference in price in order to make a claim without legal basis. Company A argued that Company B needed to provide the

---

[14] UNCITRAL [6], p. 353.

[15] Yu [10], p. 112.

Court with the contract and invoice for the wood that had been received and actually resold to a third party to substantiate the price difference, and that if no profit was made, there was no basis for Company B's claim. According to art 76 of the CISG, Company B did not have to actually engage in a substitute transaction to seek lost profits from Company A. As for the determination of the current price, Company B had already received part of the goods (1,399.47 $m^3$), and Company B's request for Company A to continue to deliver 2,100.53 $m^3$ of timber proved that it had already accepted part of the goods. Therefore, the current price should be based on the price at the location where the goods should have been delivered. Since Company B declared the contract void after taking delivery of part of the goods, the current price at the time of taking delivery of the goods should be applied, not the current price at the time of declaring the contract void.

According to the timeline of the case, Company B appealed to the court on June 16, 2011, to request Company A to deliver the remaining timber. On September 27, 2011, the market price of the timber was negotiated between the two parties, and only on April 17, 2012, did Company B change its claim to request Company A to pay for the breach of contract and refund the advance payment. The Court regarded Company B's change of claim to return the advance payment as a declaration of nullity of the contract. If the Court arbitrarily applied the current price at the time of avoidance, it would lead to speculative behavior by the parties. The price of timber had increased during the course of the trial. Company B determined that the difference in price obtained by voiding the contract would be more than the expected profit from the delivery of the remaining timber, and then declared the contract invalid. This behavior by Company B could not protect the reliance interests of Company A. The loss of profit should not be based on the difference between the contract price and the current price of the goods at the time of deposit but should be determined by the current price at the time of receipt of the goods.

In the first trial, Company A argued in its reply brief that Chinese law only supports actual damages. Although the damages in this case can be directly applied to the CISG, Company A's claim can also show that Chinese Civil Code needs further improvement in the system of compensation for damages.

Art 577 and art 583 of the Civil Code indirectly provide for the injured party's right to claim damages for breach of contract, but the provisions on the scope of damages for breach of contract are not sufficiently clear, and the principle of full compensation is not clearly stipulated. Art 584 of the Civil Code provides that the injured party shall receive damages in an amount equal to the loss caused by the breach of contract, including the benefits that can be obtained after the performance of the contract. This provision is positive regulation of the scope of damages, but it is insufficiently clear. As a rule, international legal texts expressly refer to the principle of full indemnity as the basic principle for determining the scope of damages. The principle of full indemnity is an effective measure to achieve comprehensive and adequate protection of the interests of the injured party and is the guiding principle of damages for breach of contract. Therefore, the Civil Code should make it clear that damages for breach of contract to which the injured party is entitled to compensation include both any loss suffered by the injured party and any gain deprived by it.

Art 75 of the CISG stipulates the method of calculating damages in case of substitute transaction and Article 76 stipulates the method of calculating damages based on the current price in cases which do not engage in substitute transaction. Although this is not explicitly stated in the Civil Code, Zhang believed that art 113(1) of the Chinese Contract Law (art 584(1) of the Civil Code) is based on the general provisions on expectancy benefit and recognizes the rule of substitute transaction as a method of calculating expectancy benefit at the interpretive level and develops and improves it with the help of relevant practical applications and theoretical discussions.[16]

In the process of calculating damages for breach of contract, it is necessary to determine the time standard, place standard and monetary standard for calculating damages. If there is a special law or regulation that specifies this, it will be applied.[17] In the absence of special laws and regulations, the time standard for calculating damages should be determined according to the principle of full compensation in the light of the specific circumstances of the case, rather than adopting a uniform time standard from various judgments for breach of contract. Secondly, in the process of calculating damages, the location standard is also a factor to be considered. The location criteria for calculating damages are mainly the place where the contract is concluded, the place where the contract is performed, the place where the subject matter is accepted, and the place where the parties to the contract are domiciled. In addition to strict compliance with the above rules, there is a need to properly address some specific issues, such as the inclusion in the Civil Code of relevant provisions on price reduction and how to determine the standard of interest.

## References


1. Wang, C. L. (2015). *International Economic Law* (Fifth Edition). China University of Political Science and Law Press
2. Li, H. P. (2003). *Introduction to the Law of Treaties*. Law Press
3. Han, S. Y. (2016). Application of the CISG in International Commercial Arbitration in China. *China Legal Science*, 5, 218–238
4. Guo, Y. (2005). *The Spirit of the Maritime Law: Practice and Theory in China*. Peking University Press
5. Zhang, P. (2022). The Application of CISG in Chinese Courts: Also on the Application of Treaties After the Implementation of the Civil Code. *Journal of Northeastern University (Social Science)*, 24(04), 100–108
6. UNCITRAL. (2016). *Digest of Case Law on the United Nations Convention on Contracts for the International Sale of Goods* (Chinese version). Publications and Libraries Section, United Nations Office at Vienna
7. Zhang, P. (2022). The Applicability and Application Modes of International Civil and Commercial Treaties in Chinese Courts. *Journal of Henan University of Economics and Law*, 37(01), 105–116
8. Wei, J. J. & He, D. N. (2008). Advisory Council Opinions V and VI of the United Nations Convention on Contracts for the International Sale of Goods. *Collection of International Commercial Law*, 9(00), 238–287


[16] Zhang [11], p. 134.

[17] Mo [12], p. 107.

9. Pan, W. L. (2017). To Construct Uniform Foreseeability Rule in the Law of Compensation for Damages. *The Jurist*, 163(04): 58–66+176–177
10. Yu, W. R. (2007). Damage-measuring according to the United Nations Convention on the International Sale of Goods (CISG) — Taking CISG as the Example. *Journal of South-Central Minzu University (Humanities and Social Sciences)*, 152(03):111–114
11. Zhang, J. H. (2017). On Alternative Transaction Rules as a Method of Calculating Damages for Breach of Contract. *Law Science*, 430(09):133–144
12. Mo, W. Y. (2014). The System of Damages for Breach of Contract in International Legal Texts and Use for Reference. *Presentday Law Science*, 12(02): 103–108

**Peng Wang** the associate professor of Nankai University Law School. He graduated from Peking University with a doctor of Law degree in 2003. His main areas of research include Public International Law, International Economic Law and Legal Professional Ethics. Professor Wang has published one monograph On the Nature of International Mixed Arbitration in 2007. He participated in the National Social Science Foundation's project, Research on the Development of Human Rights with Chinese Characteristics in 2012. He is a director of Tianjin Sports Law Society and a director of Tianjin International Economic Law Society.

**Yueshan Liu** graduated from Nankai University with a master of International Law degree in 2023. Prior to that, she graduated from Nankai University with a bachelor of Law degree in 2021, double-majoring in Business Management in Tianjin University. Her research interests lie in Public International Law and International Economic Law.

# Bongsan Stone v. Fujian Nan'an Lianfengmei Stone Co., Ltd. and Xiamen Yuxin Xingye Import and Export Trade Co., Ltd.

**Wenjing An**

## Case Information

**Case Name**: *Bongsan Stone v Fujian Nan'an Lianfengmei Stone Co., Ltd. and Xiamen Yuxin Xingye Import and Export Trade Co., Ltd.*

**Seller**: Fujian Nan'an Lianfengmei Stone Co., Ltd.
**Place of Business**: China

**Buyer**: Bongsan Stone
**Place of Business**: Korea

**Details of First Instance**:
**Court**: Intermediate People's Court of Xiamen City of Fujian Province
**Date of Decision**: 25 August 2011
**Case No.**: (2011) Xia Min Chu Zi No. 179
**Judges**: Fagui Cao (Presiding Judge), Lulu Chen (Acting Judge), Peihua Hong (Acting Judge)

**CISG Applied**: Yes
**Key CISG Provisions Interpreted and Applied**: Articles 1, 25, 38

W. An (✉)
North China Electric Power University, Baoding, China
e-mail: awj012@126.com



P. Guo et al. (eds.), *Selected Chinese Cases on the UN Sales Convention (CISG) Vol. 3*, Selected Chinese Cases on the CISG,
https://doi.org/10.1007/978-981-99-6851-0_16

## Case Abstract

On 20 December 2008, the Korean company Bongsan Stone ('Bongsan Company') signed a sales contract for Italian wood grain stone slabs with Lianfengmei Stone Co., Ltd. in Nan'an City, Fujian Province, China ('Lianfengmei Company'). Due to the fact that Lianfengmei Company had no import and export operation rights, Yuxin Xingye Import and Export Trading Co., Ltd. in Xiamen, Fujian, China ('Yuxin Company') exported to Bongsan Company as a foreign trade agent. The contract stipulated that the seller would deliver two containers of goods on 8 January 2009, and the delivery would be completed on 22 January. Lianfengmei Company sent the first batch of goods on 17 January 2009, and the second batch of goods on 31 January 2009. The delivery location was at the seller's factory, and Wen Chunshi, an employee of the buyer, Bongsan Company, signed the outbound delivery list after testing the goods. When the buyer, Bongsan Company, picked up the goods in South Korea, they found quality issues with them and sent a fax to Lianfengmei Company to raise the quality issues and request termination of the contract. On 14 February 2009, Lianfengmei Company sent the third batch of goods, but did not complete the handover procedures at the seller's factory, and Bongsan Company's employee did not sign the outbound delivery list. The goods were directly consigned by Yuxin Company and delivered to Dayu Construction Company ('Dayu Company') after being received by Ridge P and C Co., Ltd. ('Ridge Company'), the next customer of Bongsan Company. Ridge Company later filed a claim against Bongsan Company due to stone quality issues. Bongsan Company sued Lianfengmei Company and Yuxin Company for the quality of the goods and delayed performance which constituted a fundamental breach of contract, demanding that the defendant should compensate Bongsan Company for its economic losses.

The Intermediate People's Court of Xiamen City, Fujian Province held that the two parties did not agree on the issue of the applicable law in the contract. As China and South Korea are both Contracting States to the CISG, disputes arising from the contract between Bongsan Company and Lianfengmei Company should be governed by the provisions of art 142(2) of the General Principles of the Civil Law of the People's Republic of China. Article 142(2) stipulates that if there are different provisions between the CISG and the civil laws of China, the provisions of the Convention shall apply, except for the provisions on which China has declared reservations. For matters not stipulated in the Convention, or where both provisions are consistent, the laws of China shall apply.

For the first two batches of goods delivered by Lianfengmei Company, as the employee of Bongsan Company had already inspected the goods at the seller's factory and signed the outbound delivery list, it should be considered that the buyer had exercised the right to inspect the goods, and no quality issues had been raised at this time. After the goods arrived in Korea, the buyer claimed that there was a quality issue with the goods. The court found that there was no legal basis for the buyer to claim compensation for the quality issue at this time.

For the third batch of goods, according to the contract there was already a delay in delivery. Bongsan Company did not inspect the goods at the seller's factory, but instead directly picked up the goods by its next customer, Ridge Company, as the bill of lading notifier. Ridge Company did not exercise the right to inspect the goods and directly delivered them to Dayu Company. After discovering quality issues, Ridge Company filed a claim against Bongsan Company. The Court held that the buyer's failure to exercise the right to inspect the goods resulted in the failure to detect defects in the goods in a timely manner. In the event of the seller's delay in performance, the buyer's customer received the goods, which should be considered as the buyer's acceptance of the goods. If the buyer fails to reject, deposit or return the goods, the seller's delay in performance shall not constitute a fundamental breach of contract. The buyer's acceptance of the goods shall be deemed to agree to the seller's continued performance of the contract, and therefore the buyer has no right to demand termination of the contract on the grounds of fundamental breach of contract. However, the seller may be required to bear the liability for breach of contract for delayed performance.

## Commentary to the Key Issues Related to the CISG

### Issues

Issue 1 The Applicability of the CISG
Issue 2 Determination of Fundamental Breach of Contract
Issue 3 The Issue of Inspection Time

### Comments

### Issue 1 The Applicability of the CISG

In 2011, the Intermediate People's Court of Xiamen City, Fujian Province, tried the case of a dispute over the sale contract of stone slabs between the South Korean Bongsan Company and the Chinese Lianfengmei Company ('the Bongsan Case'). The Court in this case, by citing art 142(2) of the General Principles of the Civil Law of the People's Republic of China, ultimately determined that the CISG should be applied in this case. When there are no provisions in the Convention, or the content of Chinese law is consistent with the CISG, Chinese law should be applied. Prior to the expiration of the General Principles of the Civil Law, some courts also adopted views similar to those in the Bongsan Case. To understand this approach, it is necessary to analyze it in conjunction with art 142(2) of the General Principles of the Civil Law.

#### I. Analysis of Article 142(2) of the General Principles of the Civil Law of China

The General Principles of the Civil Law came into effect on 1 January 1987, and was repealed after the Civil Code of the People's Republic of China became effective on 1 January 2021. During the 34 years since the implementation of the General Principles of the Civil Law, scholars have exhibited different understandings of the rationale of art 142(2).

Art 142(2) of the General Principles of the Civil Law stipulated as follows: If an international treaty concluded or participated in by the People's Republic of China has different provisions from the civil laws of the People's Republic of China, the provisions of the international treaty shall apply, except for the provisions on which the People's Republic of China has declared reservations.

On the one hand, scholars have affirmed the principle of priority of international treaties proposed in this provision, but on the other hand, some scholars believe that it only stipulates that when Chinese law and international treaties have different provisions, international treaties can be applied first. When Chinese law and international treaties are the same, should international treaties or Chinese law be applied? Furthermore, what are the criteria for determining whether international treaties are the same as Chinese law?[1] According to the literal meaning of this art 142(2), if the provisions of international treaties are the same as those of Chinese law, Chinese law will apply, which is contrary to the goal of promoting the unification of rules for international contracts for the sale of goods pursued by international treaties such as the CISG. The author believes that when it comes to the application of civil and commercial treaties such as the CISG, there is no need to compare their content with domestic law. If the conditions for the application of the Convention are met, the Convention can be applied first without considering the provisions of domestic law. Even if domestic law is the same as the content of the Convention, the provisions of the Convention should still apply.

Due to the controversy surrounding this provision, scholars have varying opinions on the retention of this provision in the subsequent process of formulating the Civil Code. The Law of the People's Republic of China on Choice of Law for Foreign-related Civil Relationships passed in 2010 absorbed the provisions of art 142(1) of the General Principles of the Civil Law, but there is no provision for art 142(2). In 2012, art 4 of the Interpretations of the Supreme People's Court on Several Issues Concerning Application of the Law of the People's Republic of China on Choice of Law for Foreign-Related Civil Relationships (I) quoted that art 142(2) of the General Principles of the Civil Law. However, after the promulgation of the Civil Code, the Supreme People's Court revised its judicial interpretation and deleted the provisions of art 4. In addition, in June 2016, when the Standing Committee of the National People's Congress reviewed the draft of the General Provisions of the Civil Law, some scholars also proposed that the General Provisions of the Civil Law omitted provisions on international treaties concluded or participated in by China, and suggested retaining the provisions of art 142(2) of the General Principles of the Civil Law applicable to international treaties.[2] Some scholars suggested that this issue could be included in the applicable part of foreign-related civil legal relations in the Civil Code. However, in the end, the Civil Code did not include the application of foreign-related civil legal relations as an independent part, resulting in the repeal of art 142(2) of the General Principles of the Civil Law due to the promulgation of the Civil Code, and there were no corresponding provisions in the Civil Code. Some scholars suggest

[1] Chen and Wu [1], p. 114.

[2] Liang [2], p. 10.

that the effectiveness relationship between international law and domestic law can be clearly defined in the Constitution or Legislative Law.[3] Others also suggested that the issue could be clarified by formulating the judicial interpretation of the Civil Code.[4] Due to the different nature of international instruments, different types of conventions may have different methods for their domestic application. For civil and commercial treaties, the fundamental principle is that international law is superior to domestic law.

### II. Analysis of the Application of the Convention in the Bongsan Case

Before the repeal of the General Principles of the Civil Law, the court was affected by art 142(2) when determining the application of law. Therefore, the Court in this case, by citing this provision, held that if the provisions of Chinese law and the CISG were different, the CISG should be applied, and if the content was the same, the provisions of Chinese law should be applied. In this case, when it comes to specific contract disputes, the Court analyzed the issues involved by applying the provisions of arts 25, 38, and 75 of the CISG. It can be seen that the Court still applied the provisions of the Convention in substance and did not invoke the provisions of Chinese domestic law: the Court still prioritized the application of the provisions of the Convention. The Court did not mention the issue of whether Chinese domestic law is consistent with the content of the Convention in its judgment. This issue mainly arises from art 142(2) of the General Principles of the Civil Law. After the repeal of the General Principles of the Civil Law, such issues were resolved due to the lack of legal provisions. In the judicial practice of applying the CISG in China, the current common practice is not to compare whether the content of domestic law and the CISG is consistent. If the application conditions stipulated in the Convention are met, the Convention can be applied.

## Issue 2 Determination of Fundamental Breach of Contract

In this case, the buyer believed that the seller, Lianfengmei Company, delayed delivery and provided substandard products, directly causing the buyer to fail to achieve the purpose of signing the sales contract. Therefore, the buyer believed that the seller's behavior constituted a fundamental breach of contract and requested the termination of the contract. This case involves two types of breach of contract, namely delayed performance and defective performance. Whether the two can meet the standard of fundamental breach of contract requires a specific analysis based on the circumstances of the case.

### I. Does the Delay in Performance in This Case Constitute a Fundamental Breach of Contract?

In a fundamental breach of contract caused by delayed performance, the importance of time is usually clearly stated in the contract terms. This means that failure to deliver on time will have a serious impact on the achievement of the contract's

---

[3] Wan [3], p. 482.

[4] Wang [4], p. 209.

purpose. If both parties have not agreed on the importance of time, and delay in performance does not seriously deprive the buyer of the contract's expectations, then in judicial practice, a judge will not easily determine that delay in delivery constitutes a fundamental breach of contract. In many cases, judges believe that even if the parties agree on a delivery date, and the seller delays delivery for one or two days[5] but the value of the goods has not been reduced, the buyer has not been substantially deprived of their contractual expectations. Therefore, delayed delivery does not constitute a fundamental breach of contract. In one case, a dispute between a German seller and a Finnish buyer over animal feed, heard by the Court of Appeal in Turku, Finland on 18 February 1997,[6] the seller delayed delivery for six weeks. The Court held that the delay could not be relied on solely to determine whether the damage caused by the delay had substantially deprived the buyer of their expectations. Taking into account the quality of the goods and the fact that the buyer was a company engaged in wholesale business, it cannot be stated that the buyer would suffer significant damage due to the seller's delay in delivery. Therefore, the seller's delay in delivery does not constitute a fundamental breach of contract.

In addition, if the buyer accepts the delayed delivery, it indicates that time is not important to the buyer and therefore does not constitute a fundamental breach of contract. This is the case in the Bongsan Case. The contract stipulated that the delivery would be completed on 22 January, and the seller shipped the third batch of goods on 14 February. The buyer did not inspect the goods according to the agreement, but instead received the goods directly from the buyer's customer. The Court believed that since the buyer has received the third batch of goods delivered by the seller, the seller's delayed performance breach would not constitute a fundamental breach under art 25 of the Convention, and the author agrees with this viewpoint. If time is crucial for the buyer, the buyer will take corresponding measures after the seller delays performance, such as purchasing substitute goods or not accepting the goods delivered by the seller. In this case, although the buyer claimed that they urgently purchased substitute goods, they still received the goods delayed by the seller through the buyer's customer, indicating that the delayed performance did not cause the buyer

[5] For example, in the case of a clothing dispute between a French seller and a German buyer heard by the Stuttgart District Court on August 13, 1991, the seller delayed delivery by two days. This precedent is detailed in https://iicl.law.pace.edu/cisg/case/germany-lg-aachen-lg-landgericht-district-court-german-case-citations-do-not-identify-197; The case of clothing dispute between the Italian seller and the German buyer heard by the Oldenburg District Court on March 27, 1996, in which the seller delayed delivery for one day, is detailed in the case in https://iicl.law.pace.edu/cisg/case/germany-lg-aachen-lg-landgericht-district-court-german-case-citations-do-not-identify-172; The case of a dispute between a Finnish seller and a US buyer over naphthopyrone role was heard by the Federal District Court of New Jersey on April 4, 2006, where the seller delayed delivery by two days. The case is detailed in https://iicl.law.pace.edu/cisg/case/united-states-state-minnesota-county-hennepin-district-court-fourth-judicial-district-53; As well as the small bus dispute between the Dutch seller and the German buyer heard by the Arnhem District Court on July 29, 2009, the seller delayed delivery for two days. See the case for details in https://iicl.law.pace.edu/cisg/case/netherlands-july-29-2009-rechtbank-district-court-x-v-omnibus-trading-bv.

[6] This precedent is detailed in https://iicl.law.pace.edu/cisg/case/germany-february-28-1997-oberlandesgericht-court-appeal-german-case-citations-do-not.

to lose its contractual expectations. Therefore, the delayed performance in this case does not constitute a fundamental breach of contract. In practice, the determination of fundamental breach of contract should be strictly limited, as it can lead to the termination of the contract, seriously affecting the realization of the contractual interests of both parties. Therefore, most judges adopt a cautious attitude towards this.

### II. Does the Defective Performance in This Case Constitute a Fundamental Breach of Contract?

In this case, in addition to delayed performance, the buyer believed that the seller still had a problem of defective performance. The buyer claimed that the first two batches of goods delivered by the seller did not match the contract, but the buyer claimed that the quality did not match when they received the goods. The buyer had already sent an employee to inspect the seller's goods when they were shipped out, and the employee signed the delivery note for confirmation. Therefore, the Court held that the quality of the goods delivered by the seller had been confirmed by the buyer, so there was no issue of breach of contract.

For the third batch of goods, the buyer's employee did not sign and confirm the delivery note. The goods were directly received by the buyer's customer, Ridge Company, but the buyer's customer did not inspect the goods at the time of receipt. When the buyer's customer Ridge Company delivered the goods to the next customer, Dayu Company raised the issue of quality defects, and the evidence provided by the buyer did not prove that the goods did indeed have quality problems. Therefore, the Court did not support the buyer's claim that the third batch of goods had quality defects.

It can be seen that whether the buyer inspects the goods within the specified time and raises objections is an important criterion for determining whether there has been defective performance. After receiving the goods, if the buyer fails to inspect them within a reasonable time, and the buyer's customer raises quality defects after use, it is obvious that they will not receive the support of the court. Regarding whether defective performance constitutes a fundamental breach, similar to the judgment of delayed performance, it is not easy to determine whether it does so, and it needs to be judged whether it seriously affects the realization of the parties' contractual expectations. In this case, the buyer actually received the goods but did not raise quality defects issues within a reasonable time and did not notify the seller in a timely manner, thus losing the right to claim that the goods did not comply with the contract in accordance with art 39 of the Convention.

### Issue 3 The Issue of Inspection Time

The time for inspecting goods is stipulated in art 38 of the Convention. The buyer must inspect the goods within as short a period as is practicable in the circumstances. If transportation is involved, the inspection can be postponed until the goods arrive at the destination. According to art 39 of the Convention, if the buyer fails to notify the seller within a reasonable period of time after he has discovered, or ought to have discovered, that the goods do not conform to the contract and explain the situation of non-compliance, the buyer will lose the right to claim that the goods do not conform to the contract. In this case, it is necessary to determine whether the buyer inspected the goods within the shortest practical time, and whether they notified the seller within a reasonable time.

In this case, both the first two batches of goods were inspected and signed off by the employee sent by the buyer upon the seller's delivery of the goods. The buyer's first two inspection times met the practical and feasible minimum time requirements. During this period, the buyer's employees did not raise any quality issues relating to the goods, which also constitutes proof that the goods submitted by the seller did not have quality defects. The third batch of goods was not inspected by the buyer's employee when they were shipped out of the warehouse. After being transported to the destination, the goods were directly collected by the buyer's customer, and the buyer did not entrust the customer to inspect the goods. Instead, the customer directly handed over the goods to their next construction company for use. This shows that the buyer did not complete the inspection as soon as possible after receiving the goods. The objection was not raised until the buyer's client's next client, the construction company, used the goods. The buyer had full opportunity to send employees or entrust their customers to conduct inspections before delivering the goods to the construction company, but they did not take action. The defect in the goods was raised by the construction company when the buyer's customer delivered the goods to the construction company. The buyer, Bongsan Stone, proved the existence of quality defects in the goods provided by the seller based on the materials claimed between Ridge Company and Dayu Company. The Court found that there was no correlation between the two. At this point, notifying the seller again no longer meets the condition of 'notifying the seller within a reasonable time after discovering discrepancies in the goods' as stipulated in art 39 of the Convention. Therefore, the Court did not agree with the buyer's claim that the goods had quality defects. The author agrees with the Court's view that the buyer neglected to exercise their rights and did not inspect the goods, thus losing the right to claim that the goods did not comply with the contract.

## References


1. Chen, Z. D. & Wu J. H. (2004). On the Application of the United Nations Convention on Contracts for the International Sale of Goods in China-Comment on Article 142 of the General Principles of the Civil Law of China. *Law*, 10, 107–118
2. Liang, H. X. (2016). Draft Civil Code of the People's Republic of China: Interpretation, Review and Suggestion. *ECUPL Journal*, 5, 5–25
3. Wan, E. X. (2011). *Research on the Relationship between International Law and Domestic Law*. Peking University Press
4. Wang, M. L. (2021). Legislation Form of International Treaty Status in the Era of Civil Code. *Modern Law Science*, 1, 199–209

**Dr. Wenjing An** is graduated from the Law School of Nankai University in 2017, the research direction is international economic law. The title of graduation thesis is "Study on the Determination of Fundamental Breach in the International Commercial Contracts". Since 2008, she has served as a Lecturer in Law in the Department of Law and Political Science of North China Electric Power University, teaching International Economic Law and International Law courses for undergraduates and postgraduates. She published the following papers: "The Analysis of Decision-Making Mechanism of Multilateral Development Banks and the Inspiration for the Asian Infrastructure Investment Banks", Social Sciences in Chinese Higher Education Institutions, Issue 4, 2015; "Theoretical and Empirical Study on the Foreseeability Standard of CISG Fundamental Breach", Hebei Law Science, Issue 1, 2019.

# Rubberflex Sdn Bhd Co., Ltd. v. Fujian Agricultural Materials Group Xiamen Import and Export Co.

**Xu Yan**

**Case Information**

**Case Name**: *Rubberflex Sdn Bhd Co., Ltd. v Fujian Agricultural Materials Group Xiamen Import and Export Co.,*

**Seller**: Rubberflex Sdn Bhd Co., Ltd.
**Place of Business**: Malaysia

**Buyer**: Fujian Agricultural Materials Group Xiamen Import and Export Co.,
**Place of Business**: China

**Details of First Instance**:
**Court**: Xiamen Intermediate People's Court, Fujian
**Date of Decision**: 28 May 2013
**Case No.**: (2011) Xia Min Chu Zi No. 575
**Judges**: Jinqing Chen (Judge), Lin Chen (Judge), Peihua Hong (Judge)

**CISG Applied**: No
**Key CISG Provisions Interpreted and Applied**: Articles1(1), 34, 66

**Case Abstract**

The plaintiff, Rubberflex Sdn Bhd Co., Ltd. ('Rubberflex Sdn'), is a Malaysia corporation, and the defendant, Fujian Agricultural Materials Group Xiamen Import and

---

X. Yan (✉)
General Times Center, No. 1 Xiying Street, Fengtai District, Beijing, China
e-mail: yanxu6789@hotmail.com



P. Guo et al. (eds.), *Selected Chinese Cases on the UN Sales Convention (CISG) Vol. 3*, Selected Chinese Cases on the CISG,
https://doi.org/10.1007/978-981-99-6851-0_17

Export Co., ('Fujian Agricultural Company') is incorporated China. On 7 August 2008, Rubberflex Sdn, and Fujian Agricultural Company entered into a contract under which Rubberflex Sdn would supply to Fujian Agricultural Company rubber thread. The price clause was CIF Hongkong, with a total value of USD $865,076.25. On 12 August 2008, Fujian Agricultural Company opened an irrevocable letter of credit of USD $865,076.25 from Xiamen Zhongxin Bank with Rubberflex Sdn as the beneficiary.

Rubberflex Sdn divided the rubber thread under contract into three orders, and for all orders the carrier was On Time International Logistics Ltd. The first cargo was valued at USD $251,940, and the carrier issued the bill of lading on 4 August 2008. The second cargo was valued at USD $524,475, and the carrier issued the bill of lading on 16 August 2008. The third cargo was valued at USD $88,661.25, and the carrier issued the bill of lading on 24 August 2008.

On 20 August 2008, Xiamen Zhongxin Bank (the issuing bank) notified Rubberflex Sdn that the advising bank found the documents submitted non-compliant and refused to pay under the letter of credit valued at USD $524,475.

On 6 September 2008, Fujian Agricultural Company requested Xiamen Maritime Court to refuse the bank payment of USD $865,076.25, the total value of the contract, as they claimed that they failed to get in touch with Nobel Shipping Agency Ltd. (the consignee) stated on the bill of lading. After Xiamen Maritime Court refused the payment, Xiamen Zhongxin Bank appealed to Fujian High People's Court. However, the Fujian High People's Court set aside this judgement and on this basis Xiamen Zhongxin Bank paid USD $251,940 and USD $88,661.25 for the first cargo and third cargo respectively.

On 13 October 2011, Rubberflex Sdn brought an action against Fujian Agricultural Company, alleging that Fujian Agricultural Company had failed to pay Rubberflex Sdn a total of USD $524,475 (the value of second cargo). However, Fujian Agricultural Company argued that Rubberflex Sdn failed to fulfil its obligation of delivery pursuant to the parties' purchase-and-sale agreement, as the designated contact of delivery was fraudulent, and they could not contact it. According to INCOTERMS 2000, the term CIF indicates the transformation of risk on the costs of any loss or damage to the product, rather than the transformation of ownership of the goods. The seller has the obligation to provide qualified documents. Also, according to art 133 of the Chinese Contract Law, the ownership over a targeted matter is transferred upon the delivery of the targeted matter or the delivery of the documents of the targeted matter. Thus, before the acquisition of documents, the ownership over the targeted matter could not be transferred to the buyer. The issuing bank refused payment of the letter of credit due to document non-compliance is in accordance with the UCP600 Uniform Rules for Documentary Credits. The plaintiff sued the carrier in a Malaysian court, and the subject matter included the payment in this case, which means the plaintiff acknowledged the failure to fulfil the obligation of delivery.

The Court held that, the *lex causae* has not been chosen by the parties, and Malaysia is not a Contracting State to the CISG, so the CISG should not be applied in this case. According to the most significant relationship principle, this case should apply Chinese law as Fujian Agricultural Company had already fulfilled its obligation to

Rubberflex Sdn. Even though Xiamen Zhongxin Bank refused the bill of credit, it does not mean there is a violation of basic contract. The buyer still has the obligation to pay for the cargo they purchased. Regarding the fraudulent documentation claimed by Fujian Agricultural Company, the Court stated that false information was not enough to influence the effect of the bill of lading. From several transactions completed by the parties, it could be presumed that there was a possibility the goods had been collected by the designated consignee. Thus, failure to make payment by the buyer constituted a breach of contract.

## Commentary to the Key Issues Related to the CISG

### Issues

Issue 1 Why was the CISG not Applied in this Case?
Issue 2 Whether the Refusal of the Letter of Credit would Result in Breach of the Basic Contract
Issue 3 Whether the Seller has Accomplished the Obligation of Delivering

### Comments

### Issue 1 Why Was the CISG not Applied in This Case?

In this case, the Court first recognized the foreign-related aspect of the business, and the issue that arises regarding whether the Court should apply the CISG to the purported contract.

Article 1(1) of the CISG stipulates that 'this Convention applies to contracts of sale of goods between parties whose places of business are in different States: (a) when the States are Contracting States; or (b) when the rules of private international law lead to the application of the law of a Contracting States.' China is a Contracting State of the CISG; however, China made an art 95 declaration, stating that China was relieved of its duty to apply the CISG via art 1(1)(b). This means that China agrees to apply the CISG only when both parties' places of business are in Contracting States to the CISG. The business places of the buyer and the seller are in China and Malaysia, and Malaysia is not a signatory to the CISG. Therefore, the CISG is not applicable to this case. In addition, it should be noted that, even though the CISG cannot be directly applied when one of the parties is a non-contracting State, it can be applied based on the principle of party autonomy.

Because the two parties failed to stipulate the applicable law, according to art 41 of the Law of the Application of Law for Foreign-related Civil Relations of the People's Republic of China, the law of the country which has the closest connection to the contract should be applied. Thus, in this case, the Court applied Chinese law.

## Issue 2 Whether the Refusal of the Letter of Credit Would Result in Breach of the Basic Contract

### I. The Independence Between the Letter of Credit and the Basic Contract

The unique legal structure of a letter of credit makes it a versatile financial instrument, especially because of the 'independence principle' that governs it. It would not be an exaggeration to say that without the independence principle, the letter of credit would cease to be a useful payment mechanism and as a result would soon cease to be.[1] According to the independence principle, letters of credit should be kept separate from, and independent of, the other contracts and agreements which generated them. Consequently, the undertaking of a bank to pay the letter of credit is not subject to claims or defenses by the applicant resulting from his relationships with the issuing bank or the beneficiary.

### II. The Refusal of a Letter of Credit Does Not Result in the Breach of Basic Contract

In this case, the issuing bank refused the payment of the letter of credit due to discrepancy with the documents. According to the independence principle, the obligation of a letter of credit issuer is separate from the other contracts and arrangements out of which the letter of credit arises. On the basis of this, the Court stated that the refusal of payment by the issuing bank neither indicated any breach of the basic contract, nor did it absolve the buyer from the obligation to pay for the cargo. The refusal notice is unconnected with the problem of whether there is a breach of the basic contract. Therefore, after refusal from the issuing bank, the seller is entitled to request payment from the buyer.

## Issue 3 Whether the Seller Has Accomplished the Obligation of Delivering

In this case, Fujian Agricultural Company argued that Rubberflex Sdn failed to fulfil its obligation of delivery pursuant to the parties' purchase-and-sale agreement as the designated contact of delivery was fraudulent and they could not contact it. One of the focuses of dispute in this case is whether the seller had accomplished the obligation of delivering. As Fujian Agricultural Company emphasized the error existing on the bill of lading, the Court moved the focus to whether the error was severe enough to affect the function of the bill of lading.

From the evidence provided by Rubberflex Sdn, the address stated on the bill of lading was 'Nobel Shipping Agency Limited', and the company registration information indicated the company address is 'Noble Shipping Agency Limited'. By comparing two names, it was found that the difference only exists in the first five letters of the alphabet: the former 'Nobel' and the latter is 'Noble'. The Court stated that Rubberflex Sdn's argument has credibility based on the statement that the address on the bill of lading was a written mistake.

---

[1] McLaughlin [1], p. 503.

Additionally, in order to clarify the issue, the Court referred to the previous transactions that took place between the plaintiff and defendant. From the previous 29 bills of lading between the plaintiff and defendant, the 'contact information' were all the same as the bill of lading at issue in this case.

A bill of lading serves as a shipment receipt when the carrier delivers the goods at a predetermined destination. The bill of lading enables the buyer or his agent to obtain actual delivery of the goods on their arrival at the port of destination. Thus, the Court made the findings of fact based upon the evidence adduced at the hearing and stated that even if some error existed in the bill of lading, it was not enough to effect the bill of lading's main function, and there was a great possibility that the defendant had already collected the cargo. Thus, the defendant bears the obligation to make the payment, the lack of which would make it breach the contract.

## Reference

1. McLaughlin, G. T. (2002). Exploring boundaries: legal and structural analysis of the independence principle of letter of credit law. *Banking Law Journal*, 119(6), 501–565

**Dr. Xu Yan** is an in-house attorney in China National Instruments Import & Export Group Corporation. Prior to that she got her doctoral degree from Nankai University. She has received scholarships awarded by China Scholarship Council to hold joint PhD. position at University College Dublin. She got her LLM from Durham University and University of Strathclyde. Her research interests include international economic law, international commercial law, as well as dispute resolution and international arbitration.

# Tradeways S.R.L Co., Ltd. v. Xuchang Foreign Trading Co., Ltd.

**Xu Yan**

**Case Information**

**Case Name**: *Tradeways S.R.L Co., Ltd. v Xuchang Foreign Trading Co., Ltd.*

**Seller**: Xuchang Foreign Trading Co., Ltd.
**Place of Business**: China

**Buyer**: Tradeways S.R.L Co., Ltd.
**Place of Business**: Italy

**Details of First Instance**:
**Court**: People's Court of Huangpu, Guangzhou
**Date of Decision**: N/A
**Case No.**: (2009) Huang Min Si Chu Zi No. 2
**Judges**: N/A

X. Yan (✉)
General Times Center, No. 1 Xiying Street, Fengtai District, Beijing, China
e-mail: yanxu6789@hotmail.com



P. Guo et al. (eds.), *Selected Chinese Cases on the UN Sales Convention (CISG) Vol. 3*, Selected Chinese Cases on the CISG,
https://doi.org/10.1007/978-981-99-6851-0_18

**Details of Second Instance**:
**Court**: Guangzhou Intermediate People's Court, Guangdong
**Date of Decision**: 17 October 2011
**Case No.**: (2011) Hui Zhong Fa Min Si Zhong Zi No. 71
**Judges**: Junmei Yu, Runzhi Guan, Mingyan Zhang

**CISG Applied**: Yes
**Key the CISG Provisions Interpreted and Applied**: Articles 1, 25, 38, 49, 74

## Case Abstract

The plaintiff, Tradeways S.R.L Co., Ltd. ('Tradeways Company'), is the buyer with its place of business located in Italy. The defendant, Xuchang Foreign Trading Co., Ltd. ('Xuchang Company') is the seller, and its place of business is in China. They concluded two contracts for the purchase of oxalic acid. According to the contract, Xuchang Company would provide 210 tons of oxalic acid for USD $153,426, with the trade term CIF Genoa. The minimum purity of the oxalic acid should not be below 99.6%. During the performance of the contracts, disputes arose between the parties regarding the quality of oxalic acid.

On the 23 August 2007, the first cargo, containing two containers (CCLU2799834 and CCLU2912827) arrived at Genoa, however Italian customs detained the cargo due to the certificate of analysis and the requirement for laboratory tests. On the 30 August 2007, the second cargo, containing five containers, arrived at Genoa. Tradeways Company cleared three containers (CSLU1032031, TGHU0388295, TGHU2260025), and the other four containers were cleared by a client of Tradeways Company.

After the clearance of the cargo, Tradeways Company commissioned Analytical Company to conduct a test on oxalic acid. Some of the oxalic acid had been on-sold to P.A.G S.R.L. Company, and this company entrusted a test institution (IREOS) to provide an additional examination report. Both reports showed that the minimum purity of the oxalic acid did not meet the requirement of the contract.

Due to failure of negotiations, in April and August of 2008 Tradeways Company returned all seven containers to a port in Xuchang Company's country of business. After the transshipment, all the goods concerned were placed into new containers. Tradeways Company had destroyed all the goods after evidence preservation through notarization and sent the preserved sample to CCIC Guandong Company (a test authority) for it to be tested. This report also showed that the quality of the oxalic acid did not meet the requirement of the contract.

On the 24 April 2009, Tradeways Company litigated in the People's Court of Huangpu, alleging the oxalic acid provided by seller did not conform to the quality standards of the contract. With regard to the applicable law, the court of first instance ascertained that this is an international sale of goods and both parties agreed to apply Chinese law to settle the dispute. The seller's place of business and the origin of the shipment was China, thus the Court decided to apply Chinese law to the dispute. The regulations relating to international treaties is contained in art 142 of the General

Principles of Civil Law of the People's Republic of China is applicable to this case. The court of second instance upheld the judgment in this matter.

The court of first instance held that, under the term CIF, the obligation to inspect the cargo belongs to the buyer. The buyer also bears the burden of proof to substantiate the product has quality defects. Regarding the evidence, the buyer provided three survey reports. However, two survey reports from IREOS and CCIC Guangdong Company were inadmissible, and it was difficult to prove the test sample was identical to the product concerned. Even though the report from Analytical Company contained some flaws, it could be served as prima facie evidence to prove the quality of the oxalic acid did not meet the requirement of contract. Xuchang Company, the seller, did not provide any evidence on the issue during the hearing. Based on this, the Court ruled that the quality of the product could not meet the requirement of the contract, and as the seller had breached the contract, it should bear compensation liability. Accordingly, the Court of first instance held that the Xuchang Company should return the payment of USD $101,561.25 to Tradeways Company, as well as losses of the import tariff of €2098.12. Considering Tradeways Company exhibited some faults in the course of trade, return expenses, appraisal costs and the expected profit were dismissed.

Neither party accepted the judgement of the court of first instance and appealed to Guangzhou Intermediate People's Court. Tradeways Company argued that the appraisal costs, return expenses and the expected profit should be compensated for by Xuchang Company. Xuchang Company claimed Tradeways Company did not have substantive evidence to prove the quality defects of the goods. Without the fact and legal foundation of contract breach, Xuchang Company argued it should not bear liability for compensation. Finally, the court of second instance upheld the judgment reached by the court of the first instance.

## Commentary to the Key Issues Related to the CISG

### Issues

Issue 1 The Applicability of the CISG

Issue 2 The Efficacy of the Inspection Report

Issue 3 Compensation for Damages

### Comments

### Issue 1 The Applicability of the CISG

In this case, with regard to the applicable law, the Court stated that the trade between the plaintiff and the defendant concerned the international sale of goods. Both parties agreed to apply Chinese law to settle the dispute. The seller's place of business and the origin of shipment are in China, thus the Court decided to apply Chinese law to this dispute. The Court added that art 142(2) and (3) of the General Principles of Civil Law of the People's Republic of China are applicable to this case, specifically the regulation on the applicability of international treaties and international practices. Therefore, the CISG is also applicable. The appeal court affirmed this conclusion. Unfortunately, there is an error in relation to the applicable law. In this case, the CISG should be directly applied as *lex causae*, rather than the Chinese law.

Before the enactment of the Chinese Civil Law Code, in most cases Chinese courts interpreted *lex causae* in reference to art 142(2) of the General Principles of Civil Law, which provides that 'if any international treaty concluded or acceded to by the People's Republic of China, the provisions of the international treaty shall apply, unless the provisions are one on which the People's Republic of China has announced reservations'. In theory, once international civil and commercial treaties, such as the CISG, are incorporated into China's legal system, they constitute part of Chinese domestic law, and should be directly applied. However, in practice, regarding the sequence of the applicability of international treaties, the Court developed a chaotic situation.

Before the CISG came into force in China, the Supreme People's Court of China transmitted a document in order to stress the priority of the CISG. It provided that, 'According to the provision of art 1(1) of the Convention, from January 1, 1988, the contracts for the sale of goods reached between the Chinese companies and the companies in the aforementioned countries (except Hungary) will automatically apply to the provisions of the Convention and the disputes or litigation arisen should be also settled under the Convention, unless otherwise agreed.'[1]

It should be noted that, based on art 142 of the General Principles of Civil Law, to sequence the applicable law is not to conform to the applicable method of the CISG. As China accepts the CISG as part of its domestic law, courts should adopt the applicable method of the CISG. According to art 1(1)(a) of the CISG, when parties whose places of business are in different Contracting States, the CISG is directly or autonomously applicable. This is called 'direct applicability' or 'autonomous applicability.'[2] Therefore, in this case, the CISG should be applied directly, rather than Chinese law.

### Issue 2 The Efficacy of the Inspection Report

The focus of dispute is whether the quality of oxalic acid meets the requirements set in the contract. Regarding the international sale of goods, unless otherwise agreed, the quality of the goods cannot be solely drawn from the test reports from the seller, which may result in adverse outcomes where the unfaithful seller has an opportunity to cheat on the buyer. Under the term CIF, the seller is responsible for the cost and freight of bringing the goods to the port of destination specified by the buyer, and risk transfer takes place when the merchandise passes the ship's rail at the designated loading port. The appellate court held that, under the term CIF Genoa, the buyer should bear

[1] *Circular of the Supreme People's Court on Transmitting Certain Issues of the Ministry of Foreign Trade and Economic Cooperation in Connection with the Implementation of United Nations Convention on Contracts for the International Sale of Goods*. (Promulgated by the Sup. People's Ct., Oct. 10, 1987, Effective Oct. 10, 1987), Fa [Jing] Fa (1987) No. 34.

[2] UNCITRAL [1], p. 5, paras 9–13.

the obligation to examine the goods. In this case, there are three inspection reports which were provided by the buyer, and all the reports showed that the minimum content of the oxalic acid did not meet the requirement of the contract. In order to clarify the quality issue, it is important to distinguish the efficacy of the test reports, and whether these test reports are legally acceptable.

A month after the clearance of the cargo, Tradeways Company commissioned Analytical Company to conduct a test on oxalic acid. Xuchang Company argued that, according to art 38(2) of the CISG, the examination should take place in Genoa port, rather than after the cargo had departed from the port. In practice, art 38(2) is applied in a broad sense; the examination place is not limited to the customs area or the port, especially in regard to goods re-dispatched to a new destination, the situation involved in art 38(3). In Egypt, the Court of Cassation stated that 'if delivery is made in instances where it is not suitable to examine the goods except by the time of arrival (i.e., at the customs), it is permitted to examine the goods at the point of arrival, even if delivery was made to the buyer and goods were delivered to the first shipper as per article 31(1) of the CISG.'[3] The inspection in this case was been a month after clearance of the cargo, which does not conform to the requirement stated in art 38(1). Article 38(1) states that the examination should take place 'within as short a period as is practicable in the circumstances'. The court of first instance held that even though the inspection report had some obscurities, it did not affect its efficacy to estimate the quality of cargo. The appellate court upheld this opinion.

Some of the oxalic acid has been sold to the China System Company, and was then on-sold to P.A.G S.R.L. Company, which entrusted a test institution (IREOS) to provide an examination report. The defendant argued that the bill of lading number showing on the invoice which Tradeways Company issued to China System Company was not the same number on the invoice which Xuchang Company issued to Tradeways Company. Thus, the defendant challenged the validity of the inspection report for the reason that the existing evidence could not prove the test sample was identical to the original product. Finally, on the basis of this reason, the Court dismissed this inspection report.

Even if the bill of lading number was the same on the two invoices, this inspection report still presents difficulty for acceptance by the Court. According to art 38(3) of the CISG, 'if the goods are redirected in transit or re-dispatched by the buyer without a reasonable opportunity for examination by him and at the time of the conclusion of the contract the seller knew or ought to have known of the possibility of such redirection or redispatch, examination may be deferred until after the goods have arrived at the new destination.' On the basis of art 38(3), it is reasonable to have an inspection after the goods are re-dispatched to a new destination. However, it should be noted 're-dispatched' means the buyer has accepted the cargo in the original destination and then re-dispatched it to other places in the buyer's own name.[4] In this case,

[3] *The Australian Wheat Board (AWB) v. General Company for Silos & Storage SAE*, (2020) 2490 of Judicial Year No. 81, Court of Cassation, Egypt, 23 June 2020.

[4] The Official Records of United Nations Conference on the Contract for International Sale of Goods, Paragraph 18, p. 320.

the cargo arrived at the original port and was accepted by the Tradeways Company. Later the cargo was sold to China System Company, which sold it to P.A.G S.R.L. Company. Considering the inspection report was issued to P.A.G S.R.L. Company, it is an inspection that took place above the legal time limits of the original buyer. Even though the original buyer could use this inspection as auxiliary evidence, there is reasonable suspicion that the inspection sample was not identical to the original product. It is not difficult to perceive why the Court dismissed this inspection report.

**Issue 3 Compensation for Damages**

In this case, the seller breached the contract by providing an unqualified product, and the goods were returned to China without agreement being reached between the parties. The issue of compensation for damages is controversial, especially regarding the loss arising from the return of the goods.

The court of first instance held that, as the transactions had been completed, and the product no longer exists, it is inappropriate to annul the contract. The Xuchang Company should return the payment of USD $101,561.25 to Tradeways Company, in addition to the loss of the import tariff of €2098.12. Considering that Tradeways Company returned the goods without consultation with Xuchang Company, and in the absence of any customs evidence showing that the returned goods were the same as the original, it is outrageous that the freight arising from returning the goods was far more expensive than the price of the goods. Thus, the Court dismissed Tradeways Company's claims, including return expenses, appraisal costs and the expectation profit, on the reasoning that these costs are all extended loss, and an unexpected loss when parties entered into the contract.

In the appeal case, Tradeways Company argued that the court of first instance conflated the actual loss with foreseeable loss. The costs of preservation of the goods, the cost arising from their return, the expense of storage and container detention charges incurred after the goods returned to seller, are all actual expenses. The loss of profits is a foreseeable loss, which should be compensated for by Xuchang Company.

The appellate court held that the contract is the true meaning of expression, and the content is lawful and valid, so parties should perform it. In regard to the appraisal cost, CIF directs inspect obligation to the buyer, thus the relevant inspection will be at the buyer's expense. In the absence of notarization, the buyer's claim on storage and transportation expenses incurred inside Italy were dismissed. Regarding the loss arising from the return of the goods, the Court determined that the goods were returned to China without the consent of the seller, and Tradeways Company could not prove that returning goods was more reasonable than destroying the goods in Italy. Thus, the Court upheld the judgment of the court of first instance, disregarding the returning expense claim of the buyer.

In this case, the court of first instance and the court of second instance both issued a compensation judgement before they ascertained the validity of the contract and confirmed that Xuchang Company should bear the responsibility for the breach of contract and refund the price. Both courts had the awareness to apply the CISG, but in analysing the compensation issue, both courts did not refer to the CISG. In regard to the controversy on the buyer's foreseeable loss, CISG art 74 has a relatively clear approach on compensation, especially on loss of profit. Also, there is ample case law on the application of art 74 of the CISG, but unfortunately the Court neglected it.

The buyer could have claimed the seller's fundamental breach of the contract and declared the contract avoided in order to get adequate relief, or at least gain a legal basis for returning goods and claiming compensation for relevant losses. A breach of contract in accordance with art 25 of the CISG exists when a breach of any contractual obligation has occurred, irrespective of whether it has been specifically laid down in the sales contract or arises from the Convention's residuary rules.[5] In this case, the required quality standard of the goods was specifically set down in the contract. Xuchang Company stated that, 'from the emails between two parties, it was clearly informed that the oxalic acid was for medical purposes'. Thus, the seller failed to provide oxalic acid with the minimum purity not below 99.6%, depriving the buyer of what he is entitled to expect under the contract. This consists of a fundamental breach of contract. After Tradeways Company knew, or ought to have known, of the breach, according to art 49(2) of the CISG, it should have declared the contract avoided within a reasonable time. However, in this case, Tradeways Company held the inspection after one month of clearance, which means it did not inspect the goods within as short a time period as is practicable in the circumstances. Due to its indolence in inspecting the goods and declaring the contract avoided, the buyer missed the opportunity to claim the contract avoided. The absence of a legal basis for returning the goods resulted in failure to gain compensation for the expense of returning the goods.

## References

1. United Nations Commission on International Trade Law (UNCITRAL). (2016). *UNCITRAL Digest of case law on the United Nations conventions on contracts for the international sale of goods*. Retrieved from https://uncitral.un.org/en/case_law/digests
2. Schwenzer, I. (2016). *Schlechtriem & Schwenzer: Commentary on the UN Convention on the International Sale of Goods* (4th Ed.). Oxford University Press

**Dr. Xu Yan** is an in-house attorney in China National Instruments Import & Export Group Corporation. Prior to that she got her doctoral degree from Nankai University. She has received scholarships awarded by China Scholarship Council to hold joint PhD. position at University College Dublin. She got her LLM from Durham University and University of Strathclyde. Her research interests include international economic law, international commercial law, as well as dispute resolution and international arbitration.

[5] Schwenzer [2], p. 741.

# YT Tech Corporation v. Yantai Haiwan Plastic Products Co., Ltd

**Charles Caishun Guo, Wenjing Lin, and Charlie Xiao-chuan Weng**

**Case Information**

**Case Name:** *YT Tech Corporation v Yantai Haiwan Plastic Products Co., Ltd.*

**Seller:** Yantai Haiwan Plastic Products Co., Ltd.
**Place of Business:** China

**Buyer:** YT Tech Corporation
**Place of Business:** The United States of America

**Details of First Instance:**
**Court:** Yantai Intermediate People's Court of Shandong Province
**Date of Decision:** 6 April 2012
**Case No.:** (2011) Yan Min San Chu Zi No. 5
**Judges:** Xu Chengfeng (Presiding Judge), Ren Guangke (Judge), Yang Xia (Acting Judge)

**CISG Applied:** No
**Key CISG Provisions Interpreted and Applied:** Articles 38, 50, 74

C. C. Guo (✉)
Fujian High People's Court, Fuzhou, China
e-mail: charlesguo@u.nus.edu

W. Lin
Shishi Primary People's Court of Fujian Province, Quanzhou, China

C. X. Weng
University of New South Wales, Sydney, Australia
e-mail: xiaochuan.weng@unsw.edu.au



P. Guo et al. (eds.), *Selected Chinese Cases on the UN Sales Convention (CISG) Vol. 3*, Selected Chinese Cases on the CISG,
https://doi.org/10.1007/978-981-99-6851-0_19

## Case Abstract

*YT Tech Corporation v Yantai Haiwan Plastic Products Co., Ltd.* is an international sale of goods contract dispute, in which the plaintiff, YT Tech Corporation ('YT Tech'), claimed that it had a sales relationship with the defendant, Yantai Haiwan Plastic Products Co., Ltd. ('YTHW'). From September 2007 to September 2008, YT Tech ordered 18 shipping containers of container bags from YTHW. YT Tech sold the container bags to its clients at a discount. In late September 2009, a client returned 10,170 container bags due to quality issues, requesting a refund. YT Tech reached an agreement with its client, refunding a payment of USD $81,733.40. YT Tech immediately contacted YTHW, which admitted that its products had quality problems and agreed that it should bear all losses. However, by the end of September 2009, YTHW had neither proposed any specific measures to cover YT Tech's losses nor accepted the return of the goods.

Because the quality of YTHW's products failed to conform with what was agreed to in the contract, and the product quality problems could not be remedied in time, this resulted in the return of goods from YT Tech client and the loss of clients of YT Tech. Consequently YT Tech sued for payment from YTHW, being: 1. YT Tech's direct loss of USD $81,773.40 caused by YTHW's breach of contract (equivalent to RMB 559,056.45, calculated at 1:6.84); 2. YT Tech's indirect loss of USD $51,272.21 from 2008 to 2009 (equivalent to RMB 350,701.91, calculated at 1:6.84); 3. litigation costs of RMB 60,000; 4. storage expenses of USD $4,800.00; 5. travel expenses of USD $572.21 to the client's office for inspection and discussion on return of the goods. YT Tech withdrew the fifth claim during the trial.

YTHW argued that:

1. According to privity of contract, the contractual relationship in this case exists between YT Tech and YTHW, and the quality problem of goods raised by a third party had nothing to do with YTHW.
2. It was agreed in the order that the samples confirmed by YT Tech should be the quality standards, and YT Tech should have inspected the goods on receipt. However, YT Tech did not raise any objection to the quality of the goods provided by YTHW after receiving them, and proceeded to store them, which should be deemed that the goods provided by YTHW met the agreement.
3. The quality objection raised by YT Tech's client could not be the basis for YT Tech to claim against YTHW that the goods did not meet the quality standard.

In the two exchanges of evidence, YT Tech did not provide sufficient evidence to prove that the goods it provided to its client were the goods provided by YTHW, nor did it provide sufficient evidence to prove that the goods with quality problems raised by YT Tech were related to the goods provided by YTHW. In addition, YT Tech did not provide evidence to prove the quality standards agreed between YT Tech and its client were consistent with the goods standards agreed between the two parties in this case.

4. According to the agreement between the two parties in this case, the quality guarantee period for the goods was one year, starting from the date of production of

the finished products. The quality objections raised by YT Tech's client at the end of September 2009 exceeded the agreed quality guarantee date between the two parties.

Yantai Intermediate People's Court found that.

1. In respect of the contract signed by the two parties

On 25 October 25, 2007, YT Tech and YTHW signed a payment agreement, stipulating that, at the request of YTHW, YT Tech agreed to pay 20% of the order payment in advance before product processing. Upon receipt of the payment, YTHW should commence production immediately. The remaining 80% of the payment should be paid after the products have been shipped. YT Tech should remit the payment by telegraphic transfer immediately after YTHW faxing or emailing the copy of invoice, packing list and bill of lading. The quality of the goods transported should be in conformity with the samples provided by YTHW and confirmed by YT Tech, or in conformity with the specification sheet provided by YT Tech. Otherwise, YTHW should replace the goods or compensate YT Tech through negotiation between both parties.

2. In respect of the content and execution of three orders that YT Tech claimed had quality problems

The content of the order 251-102,841: FOB, Qingdao Port, date: 2008-1-28, to Omaha, NE68137; Project number, TSYTTECH0001, '40 × 40 × 47' U shape; 7600 items, USD $5.93 each, USD $45,068.00 total; Terms and conditions: (a). Date of shipment: 26 March 2008; (b). Container bags must be of the same quality as the bags of Order No. 251-102,691 and 251-102,692; (c). The price cannot be changed once it is fixed; (d). All bags must be shipped on pallets with 150 bags per pallet; (e). Please write the order number on all invoices.

The contents of the order 251-102,842 were consistent with those of order 251-102,841.

The content of the order 251-103,143: FOB, Qingdao Port, date: 2008-7-31, to Omaha, NE68137; Project number, TSYTTECH0005, '40 × 40 × 47', the number of TS21655-1 was 7600, USD $8.21 each, USD $62,396.00 total. Terms and conditions: (a). Date of shipment: as soon as possible; (b). Bags must be made according to each detail list; (c). The price cannot be changed once it is fixed; (d). All bags must be shipped on pallets; (e). Please write the order number on all invoices.

Three commercial invoices issued by YTHW to YT Tech: (1). Invoice number xxx-102841 was for USD $47,509 being for a quantity of 7600 pieces with a unit price of USD $5.93 plus additional costs of USD $2,441. The accompanying bill of lading number was APLU063195637, and the date of departure was 19 March 2008. (2). Invoice number xxx-102842 was for USD $47,209 for the same quantity and unit price as the first invoice, plus additional costs of USD $2,141. The bill of lading number was OOLU3032301320, and the date of departure was 27 March 2008. (3). Invoice number xxx-103143 was for USD $67,126 being for a quantity of 7,600 pieces with a unit price of USD $8.21 plus additional costs of USD $4,730. The bill of lading number was OOLU3038293520, and the date of departure was 17 September 2008.

During the trial it was acknowledged that YT Tech had designed the product before issuing the order, and that YTHW produced samples according to the design and sent the samples to YT Tech. YT Tech, after confirming the samples then instructed YTHW to produce according to the samples. YT Tech was unable to produce the sample as evidence as it had given the sample to its client and failed to retrieve it.

3. In respect of the evidence on quality problems and statements of both parties on quality problems during the trial

Sun Lirong, YTHW's agent, and Yang Jitan, YT Tech's legal representative, communicated about the goods via email and telephone. YT Tech claimed that the contents of email and telephone recordings indicated that YTHW had agreed to return the goods, but YTHW disputed this.

YT Tech claimed that there were about 20 orders between the two parties, among which eight containers contained products with quality problems. Through consultation with its client, most of the products with quality problems were sold, leaving only one and a half containers of goods. Later, the client ordered that the remaining goods be returned. This consisted of some 10,170 bags from the three orders (102,841, 102,842, 103,143).

YTHW claimed that the two parties did not agree on the weight of the bag lining, but the goods were only produced by sample. YTHW would carry out production if YT Tech C confirmed YTHW's samples were qualified. Therefore, YTHW claimed that the weight of the bag lining should not be considered as a quality problem.

4. In respect of the basis of YT Tech's claim for the amount of damages

Both parties acknowledged that there was no agreed time limit for raising quality objections. YT Tech claimed that a reasonable time limit should be two years, while YTHW claimed it should be one year from the date of production, and that YT Tech should reject the products if the goods failed to meet the agreed quality standards after acceptance.

On 16 June 2011, YT Tech mailed a letter to YTHW. As YTHW had moved its business address, the express mail letter was returned. On 4 July 2011, YT Tech mailed a letter to YTHW's legal representative, advising that YT Tech was unable to pay for the increasingly high warehousing fees of the container bags in the United States sold by YTHW. If YTHW agreed to the return of the container bags, it must immediately find a shipping company, arrange the freight collect, refund the full amount of the payment for the container bags to YT Tech and pay the related indirect losses. Otherwise, YT Tech would no longer have custody of the goods. The time limit for YTHW to reply was before 6 July 2011.

The direct losses claimed by YT Tech were the payment refunded by YT Tech to its client for 10,170 container bags. The indirect losses were the profits calculated based on the difference in product price between YT Tech and its client and YTHW respectively, the agreed annual supply quantity, and the early termination period (one year and three months) of the contract between YT Tech and its client. The warehousing fees were calculated at USD $300 per month. At the same time, YT

Tech claimed that, due to YT Tech's inability to pay the warehousing fees, it had to abandon the remaining container bags and it was unclear how its client had dealt with them.

Pursuant to the provisions of arts 38, 50 and 74 of the CISG, arts 2 and 11 of *Several Provisions of the Supreme People's Court on Evidence on Civil Procedures*, Yantai Intermediate People's Court dismissed YT Tech's claim. The case acceptance fee of RMB 13,265 was to be borne by YT Tech.

## Commentary to the Key Issues Related to the CISG

### Issues

Issue 1 Whether the CISG is Applied
Issue 2 Whether the Quality of the Container Bags Met the Requirements Set by YT Tech
Issue 3 Whether the Loss Claimed by the Plaintiff has Factual and Legal Basis

### Comments

#### Issue 1 Whether the CISG is Applied

The goal of the United Nations Convention on Contracts for the International Sale of Goods ('CISG') is to 'contribute to the removal of legal barriers in international trade and promote the development of international trade'.[1] The CISG has been ratified by 94 States.[2]

The case was a dispute over the international sale of goods between two parties whose places of business are China and U.S.A. respectively. Both China and U.S.A. are Contracting States to the CISG.[3] Pursuant to art 1(1) (a), the CISG applies to contracts of sale of goods between parties whose places of business are in different States when the States are Contracting States. However, according to the principle of party autonomy, art 6[4] allows the parties to exclude the application of the CISG (the so-called 'opt-out'). In this case, given that neither party chose the governing law in the process of the agreement being made, nor specifically excluded the application of the CISG prior to the dispute, the dispute arising between the parties should be resolved by applying the CISG as a matter of priority. If there is no specific agreement

[1] See the Preamble of the CISG.

[2] *Status: United Nations Convention on Contracts for the International Sale of Goods (Vienna, 1980) (CISG)*. UNCITRAL. Retrieved 10 December 2022, from https://uncitral.un.org/en/texts/salegoods/conventions/sale_of_goods/cisg/status.

[3] Ibid.

[4] Article 6 of the CISG: The parties may exclude the application of this Convention or, subject to article 12, derogate from or vary the effect of any of its provisions.

on the CISG, the law of the People's Republic of China should be applied to resolve the dispute according to the choice of law of the parties in the litigation. Therefore, the CISG is the applicable law in this case.

**Issue 2 Whether the Quality of the Container Bags Met the Requirements Set by YT Tech**

The plaintiff and the defendant disputed the quality of the container bags delivered by the defendant under orders 251-103,143, 251-102,841 and 251-102,842. From the payment agreement, the order form and the statements of the plaintiff and the defendant at the trial, it is known that the parties used samples to determine the quality of the products. The plaintiff claimed that the products delivered by the defendant did not conform to the agreement pertaining to the samples, which should be proved by submitting evidence. First, the plaintiff claimed that the quality of the defendant's products did not meet the agreement between the two sides. The quality problems were: 1, the weight of the bag liner should be 5 oz, while the defendant produced a 4-oz liner. 2, the shape of the liner should be square, while the defendant produced a round liner. 3, the bag was supposed to be filled with beans, however, the bottom bag cracked when stacked in three layers of full bags, with some bags breaking and beans leaking out due to impact when bagging. However, as the plaintiff failed to provide samples, it is not possible to determine whether the plaintiff's claim is substantiated. Secondly, from the evidence provided by the plaintiff, although the defendant admitted in the Email that the quality of the product was unstable, the product quality problems claimed by the plaintiff were not recognized. As the plaintiff failed to provide the defendant's products, the Court could not determine whether the products delivered by the defendant had the quality problems claimed by the plaintiff. Thirdly, art 38(1) and (2) of the CISG stipulates that the buyer must examine the goods or have them examined by another person within the shortest time practicable according to the circumstances.[5] If the contract involves the carriage of the goods, the examination may be postponed until the goods have arrived at their destination. From the plaintiff's statement, it appears that the plaintiff did not inspect the goods in accordance with the above provision. In summary, according to the evidence provided by the plaintiff, there is insufficient proof to support the quality problems claimed by the plaintiff.

**Issue 3 Whether the Loss Claimed by the Plaintiff Has Factual and Legal Basis**

I. **Loss of Value of Goods Due to Defendant's Quality Problems**

[5] Article 38(1) and (2) of the CISG:

(1) The buyer must examine the goods, or cause them to be examined, within as short a period as is practicable in the circumstances;

(2) If the contract involves carriage of the goods, examination may be deferred until after the goods have arrived at their destination.

Article 50 of the CISG[6] provides that if the goods do not conform to the contract, whether or not the price has been paid, the buyer may reduce the price by the proportion between the value of the goods actually delivered at the time of delivery and the value of the goods conforming to the contract at that time. The plaintiff who requested the defendant to bear the loss of the value of the products with quality problems, should prove the number of products with quality problems. However, from the admissible evidence adduced by the plaintiff, it was not possible to determine the number of products with quality problems, and thus the value of the goods lost by the plaintiff due to the quality problems of the defendant's products.

## II. Loss of Expected Benefits by the Plaintiff

Article 74 of the CISG[7] provides that the amount of damages payable by one party for breach of contract shall be equal to the amount of loss, including profit, suffered by the other party as a result of his breach of contract. Such damages shall not exceed the probable loss which the party in breach of contract foresaw, or ought to have foreseen, at the time of the conclusion of the contract in accordance with the facts and circumstances which he knew, or ought to have known, at that time in respect of the breach. As the plaintiff can neither prove that the defendant's products have quality problems, nor prove that it had signed a contract with clients which was subsequently terminated because of quality problems resulting in the loss of expected available benefits, the loss claimed by the plaintiff cannot be supported by the Court.

In this case, the defendant objected to the authenticity of Exhibit 9- Testimony of Witness, claiming that it was unable to confirm witness Zhao Xingxing as the employee of Grefer, the plaintiff's customer. In order to prove that he was an employee of Grefer, the witness, Zhao Xingxing, submitted a letter issued by Grefer to him (which was extraterritorial evidence and neither notarized by a public notary nor authenticated by a consular) and his business card. His testimony was not accepted by the Court due to a lack of due notarization and authentication of the letter.

In foreign-related litigation cases, it is difficult for the courts to determine the authenticity of evidence formed outside the jurisdiction due to the limitations of jurisdiction. In order to enhance the authenticity of extraterritorial evidence as evidence, most national laws have made special provisions for the use of extraterritorial evidence. The relevant judicial interpretations in China also provide that

[6] Article 50 of the CISG: If the goods do not conform with the contract and whether or not the price has already been paid, the buyer may reduce the price in the same proportion as the value that the goods actually delivered had at the time of the delivery bears to the value that conforming goods would have had at that time. However, if the seller remedies any failure to perform his obligations in accordance with article 37 or article 48 or if the buyer refuses to accept performance by the seller in accordance with those articles, the buyer may not reduce the price.

[7] Article 74 of the CISG: Damages for breach of contract by one party consist of a sum equal to the loss, including loss of profit, suffered by the other party as a consequence of the breach. Such damages may not exceed the loss which the party in breach foresaw or ought to have foreseen at the time of the conclusion of the contract, in the light of the facts and matters of which he then knew or ought to have known, as a possible consequence of the breach of contract.

evidence formed abroad needs to be notarized by the notary public in the country where it is formed and authenticated by the Chinese embassy or consulate in that country. Notarial authentication refers to the authentication of a notarial certificate, which is the activity of a diplomatic or consular authority to certify that the last signature or seal of a notary or certifying authority (including diplomatic or consular authorities of the country or foreign country) is genuine on a document certified by a public notary. In practice, two types of notarial authentication are widely used, namely 'diplomatic authentication' and 'consular authentication'. The purpose of notarial authentication is to give the document extraterritorial legal effect. Therefore, notarization and authentication of extraterritorial evidence is deemed to play an essential role in foreign-related cases.

III. **Storage Costs**

As to storage costs claimed by the plaintiff, the plaintiff also failed to provide evidence to prove the fact that it had paid storage costs. Consequently, the Court could not support the claim.

In conclusion, the loss claimed by the plaintiff does not have factual and legal basis.

## Closing Remark

Whether in civil law jurisdiction or common law jurisdiction, the system of 'Examination of Goods and Notice of Non-conformity' is important in the sales of goods. The CISG regards the examination of goods as an important responsibility that the buyer should perform.[8] This system requires the buyer to promptly examine the goods after receiving them. If the buyer discovers that the subject matter does not comply with the contract, it must notify the seller within the statutory or agreed time limit or within a reasonable period of time. Once the time limit expires, the quantity and quality of the subject matter will be deemed to comply with the contract.

The main purposes of the system of 'Examination of Goods and Notice of Non-conformity' can be summarized as the following three aspects[9]:

Firstly, to stabilize the trading order. Timely examination of the subject matter can quickly determine the quality status of the subject matter, clarify responsibilities, and resolve disputes in a timely manner, which is conducive to accelerating the circulation of goods.[10] Secondly, to protect bona fide sellers. In most cases, the seller does not have any malice on the non-conformity of the subject matter. For example, in the transaction of coal, steel, sand and chemical products, it is normal to have a certain weight difference or natural loss in transit. The seller's timely awareness of the breach of contract related to quality and quantity can help the buyer investigate and take remedial measures as soon as possible. Thirdly, to secure the evidence in a timely manner. In judicial practice, such provisions are also conducive to urging the buyer to promptly fulfill its examination obligations.

[8] Zhang [1], p. 251.

[9] Jiang and Xia [2], p. 399.

[10] Hu [3], p. 265.

## References

1. Zhang, Y. (2009). *Uniform Law on the International Sale of Goods: Interpretation of the CISG.* China Commercial Press
2. Jiang, B. & Xia., D. (2020). *Detailed Explanation of Key Articles and Practices of the Civil Code of the People's Republic of China (Part 1).* People's Court Press
3. Hu, K. (2012). *Interpretation of the Contract Law of the People's Republic of China.* Law Publisher.

**Charles Caishun Guo** is a Judge Assistant at the Fujian High People's Court (currently on a secondment to the Supreme People's Court of China). He is also a Ph.D. candidate at University of Cologne. He was a Visiting Scholar at Emory University School of Law in 2019 while he was pursuing his second LL.M. in Common Law at City University of Hong Kong (Chinese Judges Programme). Prior to that, he earned his first LL.M. in International Business Law from National University of Singapore in 2010. He obtained his LL.B. from Fujian Agriculture and Forestry University, China in 2008.

**Wenjing Lin** is a Judge Assistant of the Primary People's Court of Shishi City of Fujian Province. She earned her LL.M. in Intellectual Property Law and LL.B. in Law from Renmin University of China.

**Charlie Xiao-chuan Weng** joined the UNSW Law faculty in 2015 as an Associate Professor. Previously, he was Eastern Scholar Chair Professor of Law and Assistant Dean at the KoGuan Law School of Shanghai Jiao Tong University (SJTU, China). He also taught at Nagoya University Graduate School of Law (Japan) as Designated Associate Professor. He studied law at East China University of Political Science and Law (ECUPL) before completing his LLM at the National University of Singapore (NUS). After working for ECUPL for five years, he went to the University of Pennsylvania School of Law for his LLM and SJD in corporate law, followed by an appointment as a Robert S. McNamara Fellow at the Yale Law School Center for the Study of Corporate Law. In 2012, he was recruited by SJTU as a Research Professor. He also held fellow/ visiting professor positions in many leading research institutions, such as Stanford Law School and Cambridge University.

# Hangzhou X Insulation Materials Co., Ltd. v. Y Electric Wire Industrial Co., Ltd.

**Edgardo Muñoz**

## Case Information

**Case Name:** *Hangzhou X Insulation Materials Co., Ltd. v Y Electric Wire Industrial Co., Ltd.*

**Seller:** Hangzhou X Insulation Materials Co., Ltd.
**Place of Business:** China

**Buyer:** Y Electric Wire Industrial Co., Ltd.
**Place of Business:** (not indicated, possibly Korea)

**Details of First Instance:**
**Court:** Hangzhou Intermediate People's Court
**Date of Decision:** 17 October 2012
**Case No.:** (2011) Zhe Hang Shang Wai Chu Zi No.36
**Judges:** Fei Shen, Mian Zhang, Guihua Chen

**CISG Applied:** Yes
**Key CISG Provisions Interpreted and Applied:** Articles 30, 31, 53, 74, 78

## Case Abstract

On 14 September 2010, the buyer, *Y Electric Wire Industrial Co., Ltd.*, signed a contract for the sale of double-sided and single-sided aluminum products with the

---

E. Muñoz (✉)
School of Law, Universidad Panamericana, Calzada Alvaro del Portillo 49, 45010 Guadalajara, Jalisco, Mexico
e-mail: edgardo.munoz@up.edu.mx; emunoz@up.edu.mx

 
P. Guo et al. (eds.), *Selected Chinese Cases on the UN Sales Convention (CISG) Vol. 3*, Selected Chinese Cases on the CISG,
https://doi.org/10.1007/978-981-99-6851-0_20

seller, *Hangzhou X Insulation Materials Co., Ltd.* The seller issued an invoice of USD $33,608.80 on 27 September 2010. The goods were shipped from Qingdao, China, on 3 October 2010. The amount, however, was never paid by the buyer. The seller brought claims for the unpaid amount, as well as interest incurred and losses due to the exchange rate, against the buyer before the Hangzhou Intermediate People's Court.

The Court held that this dispute was a foreign-related one, and it had the jurisdiction to hear this case because the contract was concluded in Hangzhou on the basis of Article 241 of the Chinese Civil Procedure Law. The Court further determined the applicable law by referring to Article 145 of the Chinese General Principles of Civil Law, which states:

> Parties of a foreign-related contract can choose the law applicable to the contract unless the law provides otherwise. In the absence of such choice, the law of the State having the closest connection with the contract shall apply.

As this is a dispute concerning contracts for international sales of goods, and both China and Korea are Contracting States of the CISG, the CISG shall apply. For issues not governed by the CISG, the applicable law should be the law of the place having the closest connection to the contract, which should be the place of the performance of the contract, so Chinese law shall apply.

The Court held that:

- the contract was formed;
- the seller performed its contractual obligations to pass the goods and invoices to the buyer;
- the buyer failed to fulfil its contractual obligation to pay and therefore breached the contract.

The court further held that:

- Pursuant to Article 78 of the CISG, the buyer shall bear the interest incurred from the day the payment was due to the day when this judgment takes effect, calculated on the basis of the base loan interest rate of the Chinese People's Bank for the corresponding term;
- As admitted by the seller, the contract was concluded and performed based in USD, so the losses caused by the fluctuation of the exchange rate between USD and RMB were not supported.

The Court ruled that the buyer should pay for:

- The unpaid amount of USD $33,608.80.
- the interest incurred from 3 November to the day the judgment takes effect.

### Commentary to the Key Issues Related to the CISG

### Comments

The abstract above does not confirm whether the seller had its place of business in South Korea or in North Korea. The buyer probably had its place of business in South Korea since North Korea only adopted CISG Contracting State status in 2020.[1] Hangzhou Intermediate People's Court's decision to apply the CISG to a case where the seller has its place of business in China and the buyer has its place of business in either *South* Korea *or North* Korea is correct. However, the reasons given for such a decision are not. The application of the CISG must result, first, from its own scope of application rules in Articles 1 – 6 of the CISG. Article 1 of the CISG contains an autonomous conflict of laws rule that is binding on the judicial courts of any Contracting State.[2] This provision takes priority over other conflict of laws rules of the forum; forum rules, such as Article 145 of the Chinese General Principles of Civil Law, only apply to CISG Contracts by the express provision in the CISG (see, for instance, Article 1(1)(b) subject to any reservations pursuant to Article 95).[3]

Article 1(1)(a) of the CISG states that the Convention applies to contracts of sale of goods between parties whose places of business are in different Contracting States.[4] China is a Contracting State of the CISG as are the Koreas. If the buyer in this dispute had indeed had its place of business in *South* Korea, the CISG would have directly applied to this case in the absence of any choice of law clause in the contract.[5] Reliance on Article 145 of the Chinese General Principles of Civil Law was, thus, unnecessary.

Hangzhou Intermediate People's Court's decision that a contract of sale existed is correct. Under Article 11 of the CISG, a contract of sale need not be concluded in or evidenced by writing and is not subject to any other requirement as to form.[6] It may be proved by any means, including witnesses. Assuming for a moment that the buyer had its place of business in North Korea, this country made a reservation under arts 12 and 96 of the CISG (stating that any provision of art 11 of the CISG that allowed a contract of sale to be made in any form other than in writing would not apply where any party had its place of business in North Korean territory). However, such a reservation would not apply here for two reasons. First, the invoice sent by the seller may be considered sufficient proof of a contract made in *writing* (if it was followed by the buyer's conduct of acceptance, for instance, by taking delivery of the goods). Even if these two elements would be considered insufficient evidence of a contract in writing, the reservation made by the State where one of the parties has

---

[1] *Status: United Nations Convention on Contracts for the International Sale of Goods (Vienna, 1980) (CISG).* United Nations. Retrieved May 30, 2023, from https://uncitral.un.org/en/texts/salegoods/conventions/sale_of_goods/cisg/status.

[2] Manner and Schmitt [1], p. 19; Gillette and Steven [2], p. 1.

[3] Brunner and Balogh [3], pp. 21–22; Gillette and Steven [2], pp. 38–39.

[4] Art. 1(1)(a) CISG states: (1) This Convention applies to contracts of sale of goods between parties whose places of business are in different States: (a) when the States are Contracting States.

[5] Schwenzer and Hachem [4], p. 108.

[6] Brunner and Balogh [5], p. 104; Schwenzer and Schmidt-Kessel [6], p. 205.

its place of business only applies to that country's courts, in this instance, to North Korean courts. In other words, Chinese courts would not be bound to follow such a reservation. In essence, the seller's invoice sent to the buyer coupled with conduct of the buyer showing acceptance of the terms of the offer, is sufficient to conclude a contract of sales under arts 14–24 of the CISG.[7]

The main obligations of the seller under the CISG are to deliver the goods, their property, and the documents relating to them (CISG art 30).[8] The equivalent obligations for the buyer are to pay the purchase price and take delivery of the goods (CISG art 53).[9] From the above abstract, it is not clear whether the buyer refused to take delivery of the goods. The Court found that the seller performed its contractual obligations to pass the goods and invoices to the buyer. It also concluded that the buyer failed to fulfil its contractual obligation to pay, and therefore breached the contract. In view of this, it is most likely that the buyer actually took delivery of the goods as the seller has claimed for the full contract price (plus interest) before the Court.

Under the CISG, the seller who suffers a breach of contract is entitled to the remedies introduced by art 61 of the CISG, which include: the requests to order the buyer to pay price, take delivery of the goods or perform its other obligations (CISG art 62),[10] the right to fix an additional period of time for the buyer to perform its obligations (CISG art 63),[11] the right to declare the contract avoided (CISG art 64)[12] and the right to claim compensation for the loss caused by the breach (CISG arts 74–77).[13] The Hangzhou Intermediate People's Court was therefore correct in ordering the seller to pay the outstanding amount of USD $33,608.80 for the goods delivered by the seller as a remedy under art 62 of the Convention.

The Hangzhou Intermediate People's Court was also correct in ordering the seller to pay interest on the unpaid amount of USD $33,608.80 from the date such amount was due (3 November 2010 according to the above abstract). Interestingly, the Court fixed the end-date for the obligation to pay interest "to the day the judgment takes effect". The author of the abstract ignores whether such a decision derives from mandatory law of the judge that could displace the principle of full compensation under the CISG (reflected in CISG art 74). Under such a principle, "interest ceases to accrue when the obligation to pay is extinguished."[14]

Hangzhou Intermediate People's Court is also correct when determining that the interest rate owed to the seller must be calculated on the basis of the base loan interest rate of the Chinese People's Bank for the corresponding term. Article 78 of the CISG

[7] Brunner et al. [7], p. 113; Schroeter [8], p. 224.

[8] Brunner and Dimsey [9], p. 198; Schwenzer and Widmer [10], p. 514.

[9] Brunner and Lerch [11], p. 393; Mohs [12], p. 821.

[10] Mohs [13], p. 906.

[11] Mohs [14], pp. 915, 917.

[12] Brunner and Mosimann [15], pp. 432, 437, 441; Mohs [16], p. 925.

[13] Schwenzer [17], pp. 1060–1061.

[14] CISG Advisory Council [18], paras. 3.49 and 3.40.

does not explicitly state what rate must be applied to calculate interest.[15] However, the full compensation principle in the CISG should also be considered when determining interest claims and the focus should be on the creditor and compensating its losses.[16] Accordingly, absent an agreement on this issue, the applicable rate of interest is the rate which the court at the creditor's place of business [in this case the seller] would grant in a similar contract of sale not governed by the CISG.[17]

Finally, the Court was correct in dismissing the seller's claim for compensation for losses caused by the fluctuation of the exchange rate between USD and RMB. Since the contract price was agreed in USD, the risk of RMB devaluation was not assigned to the buyer. The buyer is bound to pay the price in the currency stated in the contract as such an agreement is recognized and enforceable under art 6 of the CISG.[18]

## References


1. Manner, S. & Schmitt, M. (2019). Art.1, in Brunner, C & Gottlieb, B. (Eds.), *Commentary on the UN Sales Law (CISG)* (1st Ed.). Kluwer Law International.
2. Gillette, C. & Steven, W. (2016). *The UN Convention Contracts for the International Sale of Goods* (2nd Ed.). Cambridge University Press.
3. Brunner, C. & Balogh, K. (2019). Art. 1, in Brunner, C & Gottlieb, B. (Eds.), *Commentary on the UN Sales Law (CISG)* (1st Ed.). Kluwer Law International.
4. Schwenzer, I. & Hachem P. (2016). Art. 6, in Schwenzer, I. (Eds.), *Schlechtriem & Schwenzer: Commentary on the UN Convention on International Sale of Goods* (4th Ed.). Oxford University Press.
5. Brunner, C. & Balogh, K. (2019). Art. 11, in Brunner, C & Gottlieb, B. (Eds.), *Commentary on the UN Sales Law (CISG)* (1st Ed.). Kluwer Law International.
6. Schwenzer, I. & Schmidt-Kessel M. (2016). Art. 11, in Schwenzer, I. (Ed.), *Schlechtriem & Schwenzer: Commentary on the UN Convention on International Sale of Goods* (4th Ed.). Oxford University Press.
7. Brunner, C., Pfisterer, S., & Köster, P. (2019). Arts. 14–24, in Brunner, C & Gottlieb, B. (Eds.), *Commentary on the UN Sales Law (CISG)* (1st Ed.). Kluwer Law International.
8. Schroeter, U. (2016). Arts. 14–24, in Schwenzer, I. (Ed.), *Schlechtriem & Schwenzer: Commentary on the UN Convention on International Sale of Goods* (4th Ed.). Oxford University Press.
9. Brunner, C. & Dimsey, M. (2019). Art. 30, in Brunner, C & Gottlieb, B. (Eds.), *Commentary on the UN Sales Law (CISG)* (1st Ed.). Kluwer Law International.
10. Schwenzer, I. & Widmer, C. (2016). Art. 30, in Schwenzer, I. (Ed.), *Schlechtriem & Schwenzer: Commentary on the UN Convention on International Sale of Goods* (4th Ed.). Oxford University Press.
11. Brunner, C. & Lerch, M. (2019). Art. 53, in Brunner, C & Gottlieb, B. (Eds.), *Commentary on the UN Sales Law (CISG)* (1st Ed.). Kluwer Law International.
12. Mohs, F. (2016). Art. 53, in Schwenzer, I. (Ed.), *Schlechtriem & Schwenzer: Commentary on the UN Convention on International Sale of Goods* (4th Ed.). Oxford University Press.


[15] Brunner and Feit [19], p. 554; Bacher (2020), p. 1112.

[16] CISG Advisory Council [18], paras. 3.35.

[17] CISG Advisory Council [18], Rule 9.

[18] Mohs [12], p. 823.

13. Mohs, F. (2016). Art. 62, in Schwenzer, I. (Ed.), *Schlechtriem & Schwenzer: Commentary on the UN Convention on International Sale of Goods* (4th Ed.). Oxford University Press.
14. Mohs, F. (2016). Art. 63, in Schwenzer, I. (Ed.), *Schlechtriem & Schwenzer: Commentary on the UN Convention on International Sale of Goods* (4th Ed.). Oxford University Press.
15. Brunner, C. & Mosimann, O. (2019). Arts. 61–64, in Brunner, C & Gottlieb, B. (Eds.), *Commentary on the UN Sales Law (CISG)* (1st Ed.). Kluwer Law International.
16. Mohs, F. (2016). Art. 64, in Schwenzer, I. (Ed.), *Schlechtriem & Schwenzer: Commentary on the UN Convention on International Sale of Goods* (4th Ed.). Oxford University Press.
17. Schwenzer I. (2016). Arts. 74–77, in Schwenzer, I. (Ed.), *Schlechtriem & Schwenzer: Commentary on the UN Convention on International Sale of Goods* (4th Ed.). Oxford University Press.
18. CISG Advisory Council, *Opinion No. 14: Interest Under Article 78 CISG*. CISG Advisory Council. Retrieved May 30, 2023, from https://cisgac.com/opinions/cisgac-opinion-no1-copy-copy-4-copy-copy-copy-5/.
19. Brunner, C. & Feit, M. (2019). Art. 78, in Brunner, C & Gottlieb, B. (Eds.), *Commentary on the UN Sales Law (CISG)* (1st Ed.). Kluwer Law International.

**Dr. Edgardo Muñoz** is Professor of Law at Universidad Panamericana. He is a Member of the CISG Advisory Council since 2020. After completing his law studies in Mexico and France, Dr. Muñoz obtained a Master of Laws (LL.M.) degree from the University of Liverpool, in the United Kingdom, a second Master of Laws (LL.M.) degree from the University of California Berkeley, in the United States, and a Doctor of Laws (Ph.D.) degree, summa cum laude, from Basel University, in Switzerland. He has been Visiting Scholar at Columbia University Law School, New York, McGill University School of Law and Montreal University School of Law, in Canada.

# Balance Industry Co., Ltd. v. Cixi Chenyang Packaging Co., Ltd.

**Benjamin Hayward**

**Case Information**

**Case name**: *Balance Industry Co., Ltd. v Cixi Chenyang Packaging Co., Ltd.*

**Seller (Plaintiff)**: Balance Industry Co., Ltd.
**Place of Business**: Korea

**Buyer (Defendant)**: Cixi Chenyang Packaging Co., Ltd.
**Place of Business**: China

**Details of First Instance**:
**Court**: Ningbo Intermediate People's Court
**Date of Decision**: /
**Case No.**: (2009) Zhe Yong Shang Wai Chu Zi No. 296 (judgment not available)

**Details of Second Instance:**
**Court**: Zhejiang High People's Court
**Date of Decision**: 18 April 2011
**Case No.**: (2011) Zhe Shang Wai Zhong Zi No.11
**Judges**: Qing Miao, Jianxia Guo, Yihan Sun

**CISG Applied**: Yes
**Key CISG Provisions Interpreted and Applied**: Article 71

B. Hayward (✉)
Monash Business School, Department of Business Law and Taxation, VIC, Level 4, Building S, 900 Dandenong Road, Caulfield East 3145, Australia
e-mail: Benjamin.Hayward@monash.edu



P. Guo et al. (eds.), *Selected Chinese Cases on the UN Sales Convention (CISG) Vol. 3*, Selected Chinese Cases on the CISG,
https://doi.org/10.1007/978-981-99-6851-0_21

**Case Abstract**

On 28 February 2008, the buyer Cixi Chenyang Packaging Co., Ltd. ('Chenyang') signed the following contracts with the seller Balance Industry Co., Ltd. ('Balance') regarding the purchase of wastepaper:

- Contract No. xxx-0802-28-No. 3, for the purchase of 1,000 tons (±10%) of No. 3 Korean-standard wastepaper, at the price of USD $215/ton ('the first contract'); and
- Contract No. xxx-0802-28-OCC, for the purchase of 10,000 tons (±10%) of OCC 11 Korean-standard wastepaper, at the price of USD $223/ton ('the second contract').

Both contracts provided for:

- the Korean standard of wastepaper applying to the quality of the goods;
- water content of no more than 12%;
- impurities of no more than 1%;
- substandard goods less than 0.3%;
- weighing error less than 1%;
- payment being made via an irrevocable letter of credit (90 days); and
- delivery being able to be made by instalments.

Chenyang received goods under the two contracts above between April and May 2008.

During the performance of the first two contracts, the parties also concluded the third contract on 3 April 2008:

- Contract No.xxx-0804-03-OCC, for the purchase of 10,000 tons (±10%) of OCC 11 Korean-standard wastepaper ('the third contract').

This contract provided for:

- the Korean standard of wastepaper applying to the quality of the goods;
- water content of no more than 12%;
- impurities of no more than 1%;
- OCC no less than 90%;
- weighing error less than 1%;
- payment being made via an irrevocable letter of credit (90 days), and Chenyang should guarantee that the letter of credit should be issued before 16 April 2008;
- the final due date of shipment being 20 June 2008;
- the goods to be accompanied by an inspection report issued in Korea by the China Certification & Inspection (Group) Co., Ltd. ('CCIC') or Japan China Commodity Inspection Co., Ltd. ('JCIC'); and
- Chenyang being entitled to bring claims relating to quality issues within 20 days after the goods arrived at the destination port.

After signing the third contract, Chenyang received several instalments of goods under the second contract and revealed that the goods were defective. In the faxed communication from Balance to Chenyang on 16 April 2008, Balance acknowledged the complaint, confirmed that they had performed the contract and that they would compensate the buyer if the quality issues existed, and demanded the letter of credit for the third contract, as they had prepared about 4,000 tons of goods under the third contract.

In further faxed communication on 22 April 2008, Balance acknowledged that the quality of the goods was not totally satisfactory and demanded further comments from the buyer. In response, Chenyang faxed Balance on the same day stating that the first 2,000 tons of wastepaper under the second contract generally met the quality requirement stated in the contract, whilst the further 5,000 tons of goods contained 37.4% water content, as well as a much higher rate of impurities than agreed in the contract. Balance faxed its response on the same day that they did not challenge the results (37.4% water content) provided by Chenyang but would expect them to take into account that other goods were "extremely dry" and provided further explanation on issues such as pulp yield and impurities.

Balance also sent their legal representatives to visit Chenyang to solve the quality issues and sent their written report on the solution to Chenyang by 12 May 2008. In this report Balance stated that they agreed to deduct 156.26 tons of goods, equivalent to USD $34,845.98 in value, from the contract.

On 13 May 2008, Balance faxed Chenyang to apologise for the quality issues arising under both the first and second contracts but expressed concerns about the claim for damages raised by Chenyang. Balance also argued that they endured losses for dealing with the approximately 4,000 tons of goods under the third contract and proposed a price cut (USD $215 instead of USD $233) for approximately 6,000 tons of goods subject to the second agreement which had not yet been accepted by Chenyang.

On 15 May 2008, Chenyang faxed Balance to reject its proposals and demand further solutions.

On 22 May 2008, Balance faxed Chenyang, stating that Chenyang had committed a fundamental breach under the third contract for failing to obtain the letter of credit as agreed, and claimed damages.

On 23 May 2008, Chenyang replied to Balance by fax, stating that:

- Chenyang did not get a reasonable solution for the serious quality issues of goods subject to the earlier contracts and suffered significantly from Balance's breach. Thus, they doubted Balance's ability to perform their duties under the third contract and suspended the issuance of the letter of credit. Chenyang had provided notice to Balance that they intended to suspend performance, which was accepted by Balance.
- Chenyang still appreciated the 10,000 tons of goods under the third contract and would obtain the letter of credit on the condition that Balance could guarantee the quality of goods and provide Chenyang with evidence that it had the ability to perform the third contract.
- Chenyang disagreed with the description of the dispute in Balance's letter of 22 May 2008 and required Balance to take further steps to solve the quality issues

under the second contract and compensate Chenyang for the losses caused by the quality issues.

On 26 May 2008, Balance replied by fax rejecting Chenyang's comments in their letter dated 23 May 2008.

On 2 June 2008, Balance proposed the following solution for the performance of the third contract:

- if the water content and impurities in the goods exceeded the amount required by the contract, then an amount calculated fairly and reasonably by both parties could be deducted from the total amount; and
- if the goods were rejected by Chenyang, Balance would dispose of the goods and bear all the delivery costs except the costs between the ports and Chenyang's address (those costs to be borne by Chenyang).

On 3 June 2008, Chenyang informed Balance that the goods subject to the second contract were under the inspection of CCIC and proposed that the goods subject to the third contract should be inspected by CCIC before shipment.

On 3 June 2008, CCIC produced a report on the quality of the goods supplied by Balance under both the first and second contracts. It stated that the water content in four samples were: 34, 71.8, 56.9 and 64.6%.

On 5 June 2008, Balance further demanded Chenyang's performance of the third contract by fax.

On 6 June 2008, Chenyang sent Balance the 3 June report issued by CCIC and demanded a solution; it also demanded that Balance should obtain CCIC's report before shipment of the goods subject to the third contract.

On 7 June 2008, Balance replied that the compensation under the second contract must be negotiated with both parties present at the port where the goods were located and rejected Chenyang's proposal relating to the third contract.

The parties failed to negotiate on the quality of goods under the first two contracts. On 27 August 2008, Chenyang brought the case to CIETAC Shanghai for arbitration. An award was made on 16 July 2009, confirming the quality issue relating to the goods (that the water content in the disputed goods was at least 34%), with damages of USD $471,599.95 to be paid to Chenyang by Balance.

The third contract was not performed. Balance brought the case to the Ningbo IPC, claiming damages of USD $744,746.35 and litigation costs on the basis of Chenyang's fundamental breach of the third contract.

The Ningbo IPC made the following findings and reasoning in the case at first instance.

- It had jurisdiction to hear the case. Balance was a Korean enterprise, so jurisdiction should be determined on the basis that this is a foreign-related civil dispute. According to art 22(2) of the Chinese Civil Procedure Law, the place of domicile of Chenyang was in Cixi, which was within the jurisdiction of the Ningbo IPC.
- The CISG and Chinese law apply to this case. The parties' places of business were located in different States, and both States became Contracting States to the CISG before the conclusion of this sale of goods contract. The parties did not exclude

the application of the CISG in their contract. Thus, the CISG should apply. In addition, both parties chose to apply the CISG and the Chinese law during the hearing, so any issues not regulated by the CISG will be solved by the Chinese law.

- Chenyang could, and actually did, suspend the performance of the contract anticipating the other party's breach. Art 71(1) of the CISG allows a party to suspend performance if "it becomes apparent that the other party will not perform a substantial part of his obligations as a result of: (a) a serious deficiency in his ability to perform or in his creditworthiness; or (b) his conduct in preparing to perform or in performing the contract". Art 68 of the Chinese Contract Law has a similar rule.

According to the above facts, the water and impurities contained in the goods supplied by Balance in performing the first and second contracts significantly exceeded the limit specified in the contracts. This caused significant losses to Chenyang, as confirmed by the CIETAC Shanghai award. Taking into account the consequence of the quality issues arising from the performance of the first and second contracts, it was reasonable for Chenyang to doubt Balance's credibility and anticipate the losses it would suffer and the difficulties to obtaining compensation in the cross-border transaction should they pay through the letter of credit, and should similar quality issues again arise in the goods supplied by Balance under the third contract. Thus, Chenyang was entitled to suspend the performance of its obligations under the third contract.

Art 71(3) of the CISG requires the party suspending performance to "immediately give notice of the suspension to the other party and must continue with performance if the other party provides adequate assurance of his performance". A similar rule is provided by art 69 of the Chinese Contract Law.

Balance argued that they had never received any written notice of suspension of performance from Chenyang. The court held that the required notice can be made in ways other than in writing. It can be inferred from the contents of the faxed communication dated 16 April 2008 by Balance that Chenyang had complained about the quality issues before. The court also held that Chenyang's intention to suspend performance could be identified from various facts, including Chenyang's complaints before 16 April 2008, its reluctance to obtain the letter of credit by 16 April 2008, the subsequent negotiations on the quality issues, solutions proposed by Balance on 12 May 2008, Chenyang's demand for guarantees relating to the quality of goods, etc. Further, Chenyang required Balance to provide a guarantee for the quality of goods under the third contract and required them to take measures such as obtaining reports from institutions such as CCIC before shipments, which were never accepted by Balance. On the basis of the above facts, the court held that Chenyang was entitled to, and actually did, suspend their performance which led to the termination of the performance of the contract.

On that basis, the Ningbo IPC ruled in favour of Chenyang and rejected all claims brought by Balance.

Balance then appealed to the Zhejiang HPC, claiming:

1. that Chenyang was not entitled to suspend its performance under the third contract. It claimed that:
   - Chenyang could not use the quality issues arising from the first two contracts as the basis for suspending their performance under the third contract;
   - Chenyang failed to prove any legitimate ground for suspension before 16 April 2008 (when they should have performed their obligation to obtain the letter of credit), as the formal complaint about the quality issues was made on 22 April 2008, the CCIC report was made on 3 June 2008, and the CIETAC Shanghai award was rendered on 16 July 2009;
   - the court should not rely on the test report used in the arbitration proceeding to determine the quality issue in this case; and
   - according to the CIETAC Shanghai award, the goods with quality issues only amounted to 10% of the total value of goods, which did not provide sufficient grounds for Chenyang to doubt Balance's ability to perform.
2. that timely notice to suspend performance was never given by Chenyang. The express statement of suspension of performance was only made on 23 May 2008. Thus, Chenyang should bear the loss caused by the delay in giving notice.

Chenyang's response to the appeal included the following points:

1. that Chenyang had legitimate reasons to doubt Balance's ability to perform and their credibility in complying with the contractual obligations;
2. that Chenyang had given timely notice regarding the quality issues and communicated their intention to suspend their performance; and
3. that Balance continued to procure wastepaper after receiving Chenyang's notice to suspend its performance, and failed to mitigate their own losses.

The Zhejiang HPC made the following determinations:

1. The Ningbo IPC's determinations on jurisdiction and applicable law are correct and are not disputed by the parties in the appeal. Thus, these decisions are upheld.
2. The parties concluded multiple contracts for the sale of wastepaper. The goods subject to those contracts were measured by similar standards. It was proved by facts submitted to the court and via the CIETAC Shanghai award that the quality issue widely existed in goods subject to the first two contracts. According to art 71(1) of the CISG, it is reasonable and legitimate for Chenyang to believe, on the basis of the performance of the first two contracts, that Balance might have serious deficiency in its ability to perform its main obligation, namely, to provide conforming goods under the third contract. Chenyang should be entitled to suspend the performance of their own contractual obligations until Balance restored its ability to perform or provided adequate assurance of their performance. Balance's first claim in the appeal failed.
3. Further, Chenyang gave timely notice to Balance regarding their suspension of performance. It could be inferred from Balance's message on 16 April 2008 that Chenyang had already communicated with them the quality issues arising from the goods before that date. Balance also admitted in the hearing of the appeal that

Chenyang notified them on 22 April 2008 that they would not obtain the letter of credit and started to resell their goods from 25 April 2008 to mitigate their losses. Balance's second claim in the appeal failed.

4. The court further held that Balance failed to provide the CCIC report or other adequate assurance regarding their ability to perform the third contract, and thus had no ground to require Chenyang to resume their performance. Thus, the contract had been terminated.

The court upheld the judgment made by the Ningbo IPC and rejected all claims raised by Balance in the appeal. This judgment was final and binding.

## Commentary on the Key Issues Related to the CISG

### Issues

Issue 1 The Applicability of the CISG
Issue 2 The Courts' Examination of the Parties' Communications
Issue 3 Suspension of Performance, Termination of the Contract, and Other Notes on the Parties' Obligations and Remedies

### Comments

### Issue 1 The Applicability of the CISG

The application of the CISG to this dispute, when assessed from the perspective of international understanding of the convention's applicability, is both correct and uncontroversial. However, in contrast to the reasoning given by both the Ningbo IPC and the Zhejiang HPC, it is possible to explain how and why the CISG applies in this case in greater detail, with more specific reference to the CISG's internal rules of applicability. Those rules contain the legal standards that determine whether the CISG applies in any particular case, including this case, as a matter of law.

The parties to this dispute initially brought their case before the Ningbo IPC, and then later the Zhejiang HPC, having their places of business in Korea (in the case of the seller)[1] and in China (in the case of the buyer). As each court noted, both Korea and China are Contracting States to the CISG: Korea having had the convention come into force locally on 1 March 2005, and China on 1 January 1988.[2] The fact that both parties in this dispute had their places of business in Contracting States, and that no issues arose as to the CISG's temporal application under CISG art 100, leads to the

[1] For the purposes of this Comment, Korea is used as a shorthand reference to the Republic of Korea, commonly known as South Korea. This clarification is necessary as the Democratic People's Republic of Korea, commonly known as North Korea, is also a CISG Contracting State, though has no relationship to this dispute. The convention came into force in North Korea on 1 April 2020. See UNCITRAL [1].

[2] UNCITRAL [1].

treaty's application via CISG art 1(1)(a). This is a provision that has been described in the literature as embodying 'a unilateral conflict norm'.[3]

In the Chinese context, application of the CISG via art 1(1)(a) (as opposed to CISG art 1(1)(b)) is necessary as the People's Republic of China has made a declaration under art 95 of the CISG that it will not be bound by art 1(1)(b),[4] the latter being an alternative private international law-based trigger for the CISG's application. The Ningbo IPC's observation that both Korea and China had become Contracting States to the CISG prior to the conclusion of the parties' third contract is relevant for the purposes of the treaty's temporal application rule contained in CISG art 100, as referred to above, but is also relevant to the CISG's application via art 1(1)(a) CISG as compared to art 1(1)(b). If (hypothetically) Chinese law had applied in this case, and Korea had not yet become a Contracting State at the relevant time, CISG art 1(1)(b) would have been the only avenue for the convention's application.[5] That the CISG was not excluded, as the court also observed, is relevant for the purposes of the party autonomy rule contained in CISG art 6: whereby '[t]he parties may exclude the application of this Convention or, subject to article 12, derogate from or vary the effect of any of its provisions'. These powers had not been exercised by the parties in this case, which provides part of the legal underpinning for the CISG's application here.

In addition to the CISG's default application, the parties to this dispute reached agreement to apply the CISG and Chinese law during the proceedings themselves. Chinese courts respect specific party choice of (i.e., opting into) the CISG, even where the convention would not have applied on its own terms.[6] This is interesting from a private international law perspective, as there are different ways in which the act of choosing the CISG in and of itself can be understood. Unlike cases where the CISG has default application because it is 'part of' the relevant governing law,[7] the CISG might be understood as being comprised of non-national rules when it is chosen in the abstract.[8] If one takes this view, the question of whether nor not party choice of the CISG in the abstract is valid would depend upon whether or not the relevant State rules of private international law permit the choice of non-national law: noting that many private international law systems do not permit such a choice.[9] Alternatively, choosing the CISG in the abstract might be interpreted as an incorporation of its provisions into the parties' contract by reference: in which

---

[3] Jayme [2], p. 28.

[4] UNCITRAL [1].

[5] See e.g., *Playcorp Pty Ltd. v Taiyo Kogyo Ltd.* [2003] VSC 108, [237]: where Australia had adopted the CISG at the relevant time, but Japan had not.

[6] Wang et al. [3], p. 5–6: There, the CISG was chosen (and was thus applied) in relation to a contract of sale between parties whose places of business were in Mainland China and the Hong Kong Special Administrative Region of the People's Republic of China, respectively: a contract which would not otherwise have satisfied Art. 1(1) CISG's internationality rules.

[7] See, e.g., *Roder Zelt-und Hallenkonstruktionen GmbH v Rosedown Park Pty Ltd.* (1995) 57 FCR 216, 222.

[8] Marshall [4], p. 180.

[9] Marshall [4], p. 175–7.

case the CISG's provisions would have contractual, rather than legal, force pursuant to that choice.[10] Finally, choice of the CISG in the abstract might still be considered a choice of law—rather than a choice of non-national rules—and then given effect on that basis. It appears that Chinese courts take this latter approach.

The parties' agreement in this case, reached during the proceedings, coupled their choice of the CISG with a choice of Chinese law. Even if choosing the CISG in the abstract would be considered an impermissible choice of non-national rules, in this context, it might be easier to interpret the parties' choice of the CISG as a choice of hard law: that is, it is arguable that the CISG was chosen as part of Chinese law in this case. The choice of law agreement in this case is arguably no different to a choice of just Chinese law, which (given China's status as a CISG Contracting State, and given the satisfaction of the CISG's application criteria) would bring the CISG's application along with it in any event. Such an interpretation would overcome any potential problems with the CISG—in the complete abstract—being understood as non-national law.

The Ningbo IPC held that, pursuant to the parties' choice of law, issues not regulated by the CISG were to be dealt with by Chinese law. This view is a correct application of the parties' choice and correctly understands the convention's limited subject-matter scope, which is set out in art 4 of the CISG. Any issues not falling within art 4's subject-matter scope (i.e., any legal issues that are not related to contract formation or party rights/obligations) necessarily fall to be determined in accordance with an otherwise-applicable law.[11] Chinese law would perform that supplementary role in this case, in accordance with the parties' choice of law.

The Ningbo IPC referred to art 68 of the Chinese Contract Law as being similar to CISG art 71(1), and also referred to art 69 of the Chinese Contract Law as being similar to art 71(3) of the CISG in this case. Strictly speaking, application of the CISG is supposed to displace local law (including these provisions, in this case) to the extent of its CISG art 4 subject-matter scope. In addition, CISG art 7(1) requires the treaty's provisions to be given an autonomous interpretation: that is, 'an interpretation free from domestic preconceptions'.[12]

Nevertheless, there is an important difference between referring to local law for comparative purposes (an exercise that is permissible), and equating the CISG with local law (a type of analysis that is not permissible, on the basis of art 7(1) of the CISG's autonomous interpretation rule). Some Australian courts have, for example, equated aspects of the CISG with local sales law,[13] and have been rightly criticized for doing so.[14] On the former approach, however, as Professor Franco Ferrari has

---

[10] *ICC Case No 7585/1992* (1995) 6(2) ICC Bull 60, 61. Since the CISG also applied on its own terms in that case, it had both contractual force and a 'statutory character'.

[11] Schlechtriem [5], p.784.

[12] Schwenzer and Schroeter [6], p. 137.

[13] *Playcorp Pty Ltd. v Taiyo Kogyo Ltd.* [2003] VSC 108, [235], [245]; *Castel Electronics Pty Ltd. v Toshiba Singapore Pte Ltd.* [2010] FCA 1028, [123]; *Castel Electronics Pty Ltd. v Toshiba Singapore Pte Ltd.* (2011) 192 FCR 445, 460 [89]; *Fryer Holdings Pty Ltd. (in liq) v Liaoning MEC Group Co., Ltd.* [2012] NSWSC 18, [16], [19].

[14] Zeller and Andersen [7], p. 15–16.

observed: 'I'm not saying a judge should not somehow find inspiration by domestic case law on how to approach a given issue ... Obviously you will, you do that as a judge'.[15] It appears that the Chinese Contract law was being referred to in this case for purely comparative purposes. Although the Zhejiang HPC's judgment indicates that the seller's appeal to that court actually cited arts 68–69 of the Chinese Contract Law (rather than the CISG's corresponding provisions) as its basis, the court itself grounded the reasoning in the CISG, which is the correct applicable law.

Whilst it is always desirable for courts to be rigorous in explaining the basis for their application of the CISG,[16] the Ningbo IPC's brevity at first instance (and the Zhejiang HPC's equal brevity on appeal) likely reflects the practicalities of this dispute and the issues it raised. Save as to the Zhejiang HPC appeal being incorrectly based upon the Chinese Contract Law, it does not appear that the CISG's applicability was directly in dispute in the case at hand.

**Issue 2 The Courts' Examination of the Parties' Communications**

This case is particularly noteworthy for the significant extent to which the courts at both first instance and on appeal examined and interpreted the parties' communications. Those communications had legal significance as, in order to justify its suspension of performance, the buyer needed to establish that immediate notice of that suspension had been given (CISG art 71(3)). The giving of this immediate notice was disputed by the seller.

The Ningbo IPC held that the notice required in this case could be given otherwise than by writing. This view is consistent with both the text of the CISG (that text being the convention's key interpretative starting point),[17] and also with the CISG's general principle of freedom of form.[18] That general principle is evidenced in art 11 of the CISG, although that provision does not (by its own terms) apply to notices.

The Ningbo IPC and the Zhejiang HPC both identified numerous aspects of the parties' communications which they found evidenced, via inference, the notice required by CISG art 71(3). The earliest communication in time (noting that CISG art 71(3) requires that immediate notice be given) was a 16 April 2008 fax. Still, the contents of that communication went on to evidence the fact that prior complaints about quality issues had also been raised.

The courts at both first instance and on appeal referred to a range of communications, occurring over a period of time, as evidencing the notice that was required by art 71(3) of the CISG. On one view, this might be seen as problematic, in the sense that art 71(3) imposes a requirement of immediate notice. That the notice must be immediate might suggest that a single notice, completely sufficient in itself, needs to be provided at the earliest opportunity. If notice must be immediate, it is arguable that earlier notices that are not sufficient in themselves cannot be aggregated with later (and, by definition, non-immediate) notices. So far as art 71(3)'s application to

[15] FGV [8], 00:17:44–00:17:58.

[16] Wang et al. [9], p. 29.

[17] Schwenzer and Schroeter [6], p. 145.

[18] Schwenzer and Schroeter [6], p. 151.

the facts of this dispute is concerned, however, even if this is the correct reading of art 71(3), reliance on the parties' earliest quality-related communications might have sufficed. Perhaps the courts' references to the pattern of communications between the parties as a whole reflects the seller's argument that notice of the buyer's *suspension of performance* (as opposed to notice of quality issues per se) had not been given. These communications taken as a whole seem to have been understood by the courts at both first instance and on appeal as evidence of that required notice of *suspension.*

In order to assist the Ningbo IPC and the Zhejiang HPC in understanding whether the communications between the parties actually constituted the required notice of suspension of performance, both courts could have sought assistance from the interpretative rules set out in CISG art 8: though neither did so in this dispute. Those rules are commonly applied in the contractual interpretation context.[19] However, their application extends beyond contractual interpretation per se. Art. 8's rules assist in interpreting any 'statements made by and other conduct of a party'. Since the provision of notice can constitute either a statement or a form of conduct, art 8 could have been used by the Ningbo IPC and/or the Zhejiang HPC to identify whether the seller would have understood the buyer's communications as constituting the required notice of suspension of performance.[20] Since neither court did so, they appear to have instead resorted to interpreting the parties' communications at face value, without the assistance of a legal interpretative standard.

The primary rule contained in art 8 of the CISG—primary in the sense that it is the first rule to be considered—is the subjective intent rule in CISG art 8(1). According to this provision, 'statements made by, and other conduct of a party are to be interpreted according to [their] intent where the other party knew or could not have been unaware what that intent was.' The objective intent rule, whereby 'statements made by, and other conduct of a party are to be interpreted according to the understanding that a reasonable person of the same kind as the other party would have had in the same circumstances', applies where the requirements of the subjective intent rule are not satisfied: CISG art 8(2). Since there are strict conditions placed upon the application of the subjective intent rule, it is likely that the subsidiary objective intent rule will apply in most cases.[21] That would most likely have been the case in relation to this dispute.

Whilst the seller argued that no notice of suspension of performance had been given, an application of CISG art 8(2)'s objective interpretation rule would have supported the view that the seller should (objectively) have understood the buyer's communications as evidencing notice of their suspension of performance. This is particularly so given that CISG art 8(3) requires that 'due consideration is to be given to all relevant circumstances of the case including the negotiations, any practices which the parties have established between themselves, usages and any subsequent conduct of the parties'. Of particular importance here is the parties' negotiation history and their subsequent conduct, where a quality guarantee was sought,

[19] Schwenzer and Schroeter [10], pp. 160–161.

[20] Schwenzer and Schroeter [10], p. 162.

[21] Farnsworth [11], p. 99.

and where notice was given that the issuance of the required letter of credit had been suspended. These factors in particular, amongst all the circumstances of the case, should have demonstrated to a reasonable party in the seller's position that performance was in fact being suspended.

Otherwise, as to the requirement of the notice's immediacy, there is a view in the literature that 'a failure to give notice under Art. 71(3) CISG does not affect the actual right to suspend, but can only make the suspending party liable for damages.'[22] This view was actually reflected in the arguments that were made in this case. On this view, the fact that a combination of communications was relied upon by the Ningbo IPC and by the Zhejiang HPC to evidence the required notice would not disqualify that composite notice from being effective, on the basis of a lack of immediacy, for the purposes of art 71 of the CISG.

**Issue 3 Suspension of Performance, Termination of the Contract, and Other Notes on the Parties' Obligations and Remedies**

The key substantive issues arising in relation to this dispute were the buyer's claim to suspension of performance, and the parties' subsequent termination of the contract. The key provision at issue here, in relation to suspension of performance, is CISG art 71. The requirements of art 71 have already been partly addressed in relation to Issue 2's discussion of the interpretation of the parties' communications.

CISG art 71(1) allows for suspension of performance where, 'after the conclusion of the contract, it becomes apparent that the other party will not perform a substantial part of [their] obligations as a result of (a) a serious deficiency in [their] ability to perform or in [their] creditworthiness; or (b) [their] conduct in preparing to perform or in performing the contract'. Art 71 of the CISG is thus different in its focus to CISG art 79(1), which provides for the suspension of liability 'for a failure to perform any ... obligations ... due to an impediment beyond [a party's] control'. Art 79 of the CISG is concerned with impediments affecting performance that are external to the parties,[23] whilst art 71 of the CISG addresses performance issues relating to the parties themselves.[24] It is the latter form of suspension that was relevant in this case.

Though the Ningbo IPC addressed the requirements of arts 71(1) and (3) of the CISG, it noted that the contract was thereby terminated, without any other reference to the CISG's text. The relevant provision that would have justified termination in this case is actually art 72(1) of the CISG[25]—addressing the concept of anticipatory breach—whereby '[i]f prior to the date for performance of the contract it is clear that one of the parties will commit a fundamental breach of contract, the other party may declare the contract avoided'. It is evident that two relevant requirements of art 72(1) of the CISG were not explored by the Court: whether or not it was clear that there would be a fundamental breach, and whether or not a declaration of avoidance had been made by the buyer. The judgment's original text suggests that this might be

[22] Huber and Mullis [12], p. 343.

[23] Huber and Mullis [12], pp. 257–258.

[24] Huber and Mullis [12], p. 340.

[25] Huber and Mullis [12], p. 342.

a result of the parties themselves agreeing that the contract was in fact terminated: thus, the termination issue did not appear to be a live issue requiring either court's determination. Nevertheless, it is still useful for the purposes of this Comment to consider whether it was clear that there would be a fundamental breach, and whether there was a relevant declaration of avoidance, to determine whether the parties' agreement had a correct basis in law.

Fundamental breach is defined in CISG art 25: being a breach that 'results in such detriment to the other party as substantially to deprive [them] of what [they are] entitled to expect under the contract, unless the party in breach did not foresee and a reasonable person of the same kind in the same circumstances would not have foreseen such a result'. The CISG adopts a high threshold for fundamental breach, given that it constitutes a trigger for termination, and given that unwinding international sales contracts is more expensive and time consuming as compared to unwinding purely domestic transactions.[26] Was it clear that the buyer was going to commit a fundamental breach here? There appear to be good grounds to think so. The CIETAC Shanghai award addressing the parties' previous contracts found that the water content in the disputed goods there was at least 34%, when the parties' third contract (yet to be performed) required a water content of no more than 12%. The Ningbo IPC described this as significantly exceeding the requirements on those previous occasions, concerning the first contract and the second contract. It stands to reason that the same water content, if present in the goods delivered under the third contract, would be a similarly significant breach of that third contract. To adapt the words of art 25, the detriment caused by this likely breach would substantially deprive the buyer of what they were entitled to expect in relation to their purchase.

Whether or not the buyer gave an effective declaration of avoidance can also be tested by assessing the parties' communications in light of the CISG's interpretative rules contained in art 8:[27] specifically, the objective intent rule contained in art 8(2). The buyer's communications would probably communicate an intention to avoid, here, for the same reasons that they also communicated an intention to suspend performance, as discussed in relation to Issue 2.

As noted in relation to Issue 1, upon appeal to the Zhejiang HPC, the seller's arguments addressed arts 68–69 of the Chinese Contract Law, rather than art 71 of the CISG. Despite the seller's appeal being framed in this way, the Zhejiang HPC correctly went on to apply art 71 instead to resolve the appeal. This reasoning correctly prioritized the CISG's application over the application of non-harmonized Chinese law, to the extent of the convention's art 4 CISG subject-matter scope.

This case involved the buyer alleging a likelihood of breach before performance of the contract had fallen due. As a result, CISG art 35—the CISG's key provision dealing with the seller's conformity obligations—was not directly at issue. However, for the purposes of this Comment's completeness, it can be noted that the parties' contractual specifications regarding the requirements of the goods (for example, the parties' agreement upon the application of the Korean standard for wastepaper,

[26] Schwenzer [13], p.799.

[27] Schwenzer and Schroeter [10], p. 161.

and their agreements concerning water content, impurities, and OOC requirements) would have constituted contractual conformity stipulations for the purpose of CISG art 35(1). They may also have replaced some of the default conformity obligations that are set out in CISG art 35(2). The latter applies '[e]xcept where the parties have agreed otherwise', which effectively constitutes a restatement of the party autonomy principle that would otherwise have applied, even without this qualification, as set out in CISG art 6. In addressing anticipatory breach, the courts at first instance and also on appeal thus correctly deferred to the parties' own agreement concerning the expected characteristics of the goods.

## References


1. United Nations Commission on International Trade Law (2022). *Status: United Nations Convention on Contracts for the International Sale of Goods (Vienna, 1980) (CISG).* Retrieved November 30, 2022, from https://uncitral.un.org/en/texts/salegoods/conventions/sale_of_goods/cisg/status
2. Jayme, E. (1987). Article 1, in Bianca, C. M. & Bonell, M. J. (Eds.), *Commentary on the International Sales Law.* Giuffrè
3. Wang, G., Zhang, S. & Guo, P. (2022). Novelact (Resources) Limited v Xiamen Special Economic Zone International Trade Trust Company, in Guo, P., Zuo H. & Zhang, S. (Eds.), *Selected Chinese Cases on the UN Sales Convention (CISG) Vol 1* (pp. 1–11). Springer
4. Marshall, B. (2018). The Hague Choice of Law Principles, CISG, and PICC: A Hard Look at a Choice of Soft Law. *American Journal of Comparative Law*, 66(1), 175–217
5. Schlechtriem, P. (2005). Requirements of Application and Sphere of Applicability of the CISG. *Victoria University of Wellington Law Review*, 36(4), 781–794
6. Schwenzer, I. & Schroeter, U. (2022). Article 7, in Schwenzer, I. & Schroeter, U. (Eds.), *Schlechtriem & Schwenzer: Commentary on the UN Convention on the International Sale of Goods* (5th ed., pp.135–158). Oxford University Press
7. Zeller, B. & Andersen, C. (2019). The Transnational Dimension of Statutory Interpretation: Tragically Overlooked in a Global Commercial Environment. *Nordic Journal of Commercial Law*, 2019(1), 5–19
8. FGV (2012, December 21). *The United Nations Convention on Contracts for the International Sale of Goods* (Part 3). Retrieved November 30, 2022, from https://www.youtube.com/watch?v=Tt8ZY2zFhbM
9. Wang, G., Zhang, S. & Guo, P. (2022). Skandinaviska Metemo AB v Hunan Co. For International Economy and Trade, in Guo, P., Zuo H. & Zhang, S. (Eds.), *Selected Chinese Cases on the UN Sales Convention (CISG) Vol 1* (pp. 27–34). Springer
10. Schwenzer, I. & Schroeter, U. (2022). Article 8, in Schwenzer, I. & Schroeter, U. (Eds.), *Schlechtriem & Schwenzer: Commentary on the UN Convention on the International Sale of Goods* (5th ed., pp.159–199). Oxford University Press
11. Farnsworth, E. A. (1987). Article 8, in Bianca, C. M. & Bonell, M. J. (Eds.), *Commentary on the International Sales Law* (pp.95–102). Giuffrè
12. Huber, P. & Mullis, A. (2007). *The CISG: A New Textbook for Students and Practitioners.* Sellier European Law Publishers
13. Schwenzer, I. (2005). The Danger of Domestic Pre-Conceived Views with Respect to the Uniform Interpretation of the CISG: The Question of Avoidance in the Case of Non-Conforming Goods and Documents. *Victoria University of Wellington Law Review*, 36(4), 795–807

**Dr. Benjamin Hayward** is an Associate Professor in the Department of Business Law and Taxation at the Monash Business School, Monash University. His research expertise spans international sales law, international commercial arbitration law, and private international law, as well as Australian contract, commercial, and consumer law topics. Dr Hayward's PhD thesis addressed arbitrators' identification of the governing substantive law (including the CISG) in international commercial arbitration, and was published in 2017 by Oxford University Press as Conflict of laws and Arbitral Discretion: The Closest Connection Test. Dr Hayward has otherwise published widely in Australian and international law journals, regularly presents his research to local and international audiences, and communicates his research to wider professional and public audiences via blogs, interviews, and podcasts.

# Daewon GSI Co., Ltd. v. Zhejiang Wuyi Tea Industry Co., Ltd.

**Charles Caishun Guo, Wenjing Lin, and Charlie Xiao-chuan Weng**

## Case Information

**Case Name:** *Daewon GSI Co., Ltd. v Zhejiang Wuyi Tea Industry Co., Ltd.*

**Seller**: Daewon GSI Co., Ltd.
**Place of Business:** Korea

**Buyer:** Zhejiang Wuyi Tea Industry Co., Ltd.
**Place of Business:** China

**Details of First Instance:**
**Court:** Zhejiang Jinhua Intermediate People's Court
**Date of Decision:** 2 December 2010
**Case No.:** (2010) Zhejiang Jin Shang Wai Chu Zi No. 16
**Judges:** Liu Junhua (Presiding Judge), Liu Jing (Acting Judge), Shen Qiang (Acting Judge)

**Details of Second Instance:**

C. C. Guo (✉)
Quanzhou Intermediate People's Court, Quanzhou, China
e-mail: charlesguo@u.nus.edu

W. Lin
The Primary People's Court of Shishi City of Fujian Province, Shishi, Japan
e-mail: 819722979@qq.com

C. X. Weng
University of New South Wales, Sydney, Australia
e-mail: xiaochuan.weng@unsw.edu.au



P. Guo et al. (eds.), *Selected Chinese Cases on the UN Sales Convention (CISG) Vol. 3*, Selected Chinese Cases on the CISG,
https://doi.org/10.1007/978-981-99-6851-0_22

**Court:** Zhejiang High People's Court
**Date of Decision:** 26 August 2011
**Case No.:** (2011) Zhe Shang Wai Zhong Zi No. 16
**Judges:** Zheng Juhong (Presiding Judge), Dong Guoqing (Acting Judge), Wang Jianfang (Acting Judge)

**CISG Applied:** Yes
**Key CISG Provisions Interpreted and Applied:** Article 50

## Case Abstract

*Daewon GSI Co., Ltd. v Zhejiang Wuyi Tea Industry Co., Ltd.* is an international sale of goods contract dispute, in which the seller, Daewon GSI Co., Ltd. ('Daewon') and the buyer, Zhejiang Wuyi Tea Industry Co., Ltd. ('Zhejiang Wuyi') both refused to accept the civil judgment (2010) Zhejiang Jin Shang Wai Chu Zi No. 16 of the Zhejiang Jinhua Intermediate People's Court and appealed to Zhejiang High People's Court.

The court of first instance, Zhejiang Jinhua Intermediate People's Court, found that on 6 March 2008, Daewon and Zhejiang Wuyi signed Contract of Sale, which principally including the following content: 1. Zhejiang Wuyi purchased from Daewon a 'Daewon' brand PUBU-15 color sorting machine at the price of RMB 861,000; 2. The payment method was payment of a deposit of RMB 50,000 at the time of signing the contract, and payment of RMB 350,000 after customs declaration at Shanghai Port. The balance should be paid before 20 June 2009; 3. 20 days after the arrival of the machine, if the buyer was not satisfied with the quality, the goods should be unconditionally returned to the seller; 4.The quality should be subject to the technical parameters of the seller's technical specification; 5. The seller entrusted Dalian Daewon Grain Machinery International Industry and Trade Co., Ltd. ('Daewon Grain Machinery') with full authority to handle the relevant matters under the contract.

Zhejiang Wuyi's legal representative and Daewon's agent, Kong Qingshuai, signed and sealed the Contract of Sale. On the day of signing the contract, Zhejiang Wuyi paid a deposit of RMB 50,000. On May 5, 2008, Zhejiang Wuyi made another payment of RMB 350,000. After the machine was installed, Zhejiang Wuyi advised Kong Qingshuai that the machine had quality problems. On 20 May 2008, Kong Qingshuai stated on the Contract of Sale kept by Zhejiang Wuyi: 'The color sorting machine has some problems such as slow flashing frequency, which will affect the tea color sorting. Our company will arrange personnel to deal with it as soon as possible.' On 15 October 2008, Zhejiang Wuyi put forward a written notice to Kong Qingshuai, requiring Daewon Grain Machinery to return the goods and refund the payment. On the same day, Kong Qingshuai replied on the notice: 'I promise to report this problem to our company as soon as possible. I hope to solve it through negotiation and try not to return the goods.' Due to failure of negotiation, Zhejiang Wuyi neither returned the PUBU-15 color sorting machine nor paid the balance of RMB 461,000.

After repeated requests, Daewon sued for payment of the balance plus interest, totaling RMB 461,000. Zhejiang Wuyi filed a counterclaim, suing for the return of the PUBU-15 color sorting machine, together with a refund of RMB 400,000.

Pursuant to provisions of arts 5, 112, 159 and 161 of the *Contract Law of the People's Republic of China* and art 2 of *Several Provisions of the Supreme People's Court on Evidence on Civil Procedures*, the court of first instance held that:

1. Zhejiang Wuyi shall pay Daewon the payment of RMB 261,000.
2. Other litigation claims by Daewon are dismissed.
3. The counterclaim of Zhejiang Wuyi is dismissed.

The case acceptance fee of RMB 8215 and the counterclaim acceptance fee of RMB 7300, totaling RMB 15,515 shall be borne by Daewon (RMB 3564) and Zhejiang Wuyi (RMB 11,951).

After the first instance judgment was made, both Daewon and Zhejiang Wuyi refused to accept it and appealed to the Zhejiang High People's Court. The Zhejiang High People's court held that the goods sold by Daewon did not conform to the standard set by the Contract of Sale, and that Daewon should assume the responsibility for breach of contract through goods return or price reduction. Considering that the color sorting machine did have quality defects while Zhejiang Wuyi was still using the machine, the judgement of the court of first instance is not improper. The facts found in the first instance case are clear, and the substantial matters were dealt with properly, but the failure to apply the CISG is inappropriate and should be corrected.

Pursuant to provisions of art 50 of the CISG and art 153(1)(1) of the *Civil Procedure Law of the People's Republic of China* the court of second instance held that the appeal should be dismissed, and the judgment made in the court of first instance should be sustained.

The case acceptance fee should be borne by Daewon for RMB 8215 and by Zhejiang Wuyi for RMB 7300.

## Commentary to the Key Issues Related to the CISG

### Issues

Issue 1 Whether CISG is Applied
Issue 2 Whether Kong Qingshuai Enjoyed Daewon's Agency Right
Issue 3 Whether Zhejiang Wuyi was Entitled to Claim Return of Goods and Refund from Daewon DAEWON

### Comments

#### Issue 1 Whether CISG is Applied

The case concerned is a dispute over a contract for the international sale of goods between two parties from China and South Korea, both of which are Contracting

States to the CISG. Pursuant to art 1(1)(a)[1] of the CISG, the Convention applies to contracts for the sale of goods between parties whose places of business are in different Contracting States. Since its application was not specifically excluded, the CISG should be applied to this case.

**Issue 2 Whether Kong Qingshuai Enjoyed Daewon's Agency Right**

According to art 14(1) of the Contract of Sale, Daewon Grain Machinery had the right to handle relevant matters under the Contract of Sale, including, but not limited to, delivery, maintenance, payment collection and dispute settlement. Kong Qingshuai was a salesperson of Daewon Grain Machinery. In this case, he signed a contract with Zhejiang Wuyi by holding a standard-form-contract stamped with the seals of both Daewon and Daewon Grain Machinery in which he was stated to be responsible for transaction, commissioning, maintenance and other relevant sales matters. Daewon was unable to provide evidence to deny the authenticity of Kong Qingshuai's signature, nor did it successfully prove that Kong Qingshuai colluded with Zhejiang Wuyi to add the statement to the contract at a later date. Therefore, it can be concluded that Kong Qingshuai had the agency right with Daewon. His statement on the contract could be regarded that he was, in fact, acting as the agent of Daewon and recognized the fact that Zhejiang Wuyi had raised an objection to the quality within 20 days after the arrival of the goods.

**Issue 3 Whether Zhejiang Wuyi Was Entitled to Claim Return of Goods and Refund from Daewon**

**I. Whether DAEWON Should Bear Liability for Breach of Contract**

It was agreed in the Contract of Sale that if the buyer is not satisfied with the quality within 20 days after the arrival of the machine, it could return the machine unconditionally to the seller. This agreement is the true intention of both parties, and the content does not violate the mandatory provision of laws and administrative regulations, which should be recognized as legal and effective. The statement made on 20 May 2008 by Kong Qingshuai, the agent of Daewon, indicated that Daewon had confirmed the fact that its color sorting machine failed to satisfy Zhejiang Wuyi's requirements, and that Zhejiang Wuyi had raised an objection to the machine's quality effect within 20 days after its arrival. Therefore, Daewon had breached the contract and should bear liability for breach of contract.

---

[1] Article 1 of the CISG:

(1) This Convention applies to contracts of sale of goods between parties whose places of business are in different States:

(a) when the States are Contracting States; or

(b) when the rules of private international law lead to the application of the law of a Contracting State.

## II. Whether Zhejiang Wuyi Can Return the Machine and Claim the Refund from Daewon at the Same Time

Art 50 of the CISG[2] states 'if the goods do not conform with the contract and whether or not the price has already been paid, the buyer may reduce the price in the same proportion as the value that the goods actually delivered had at the time of the delivery bears to the value that conforming goods would have had at that time'. Therefore, Zhejiang Wuyi has the right to claim return of goods or reduction of price. However, since Zhejiang Wuyi continued to use the machine after proposing to return it in October 2008, and based on the principle of fairness, it is more reasonable to reject the claim for both returning the goods and claiming a refund. It would be more appropriate to demand Daewon reduce the payment for the goods.

## Closing Remarks

Schwenzer and Hachem's *Commentary* on art 50 of the CISG provides an in-depth analysis of the provision and its interpretation by courts and scholars.

Article 50 of the CISG addresses the buyer's obligation to examine the goods upon their delivery. Specifically, art 50 provides that the buyer must examine the goods, or have them examined, within as short a time period as is practicable in the circumstances. The purpose of art 50 is to ensure that the buyer inspects the goods promptly upon their arrival and notifies the seller of any defects or non-conformities as soon as possible. This allows the seller to remedy any defects or non-conformities in a timely manner and minimizes the risk of disputes between the parties.

The examination must be carried out in a manner consistent with the nature of the goods and must include checking for quantity, quality and specifications as specified in the contract of sale. If the buyer discovers any lack of conformity, they must give notice to the seller within a reasonable time after discovering the lack of conformity. The buyer may exercise the right to reduce the price regardless of whether the price has already been paid, and that the reduction must be proportional to the difference in value between the non-conforming goods and conforming goods at the time of delivery.[3]

It is important to note that failure to examine the goods or give notice of any lack of conformity within the prescribed time limits may result in the loss of the buyer's right to rely on such lack of conformity. Therefore, buyers should take care to comply with the requirements of art 50 in a timely and thorough manner to protect their rights under the contract of sale. In this case, the buyer did not fail to notify the seller within a reasonable time after discovering the non-conformity, which ensures

[2] Article 50 of CISG:

If the goods do not conform with the contract and whether or not the price has already been paid, the buyer may reduce the price in the same proportion as the value that the goods actually delivered had at the time of the delivery bears to the value that conforming goods would have had at that time. However, if the seller remedies any failure to perform his obligations in accordance with article 37 or article 48 or if the buyer refuses to accept performance by the seller in accordance with those articles, the buyer may not reduce the price.

[3] Schwenzer and Hachem [1], pp. 726–754.

its right to claim the price reduction proportional to the difference in value between the non-conforming goods and conforming goods at the time of delivery. However, considering its continuous use of the machine in dispute, the buyer finally lost the right to claim for return of the goods or claim for refund.

## Reference

1. Schwenzer, I. & Hachem, P. (2020). Article 50, in Schwenzer I. (Eds.), *Schlechtriem & Schwenzer: Commentary on the UN Convention on the International Sale of Goods* (4th ed., pp.726–754). Oxford University Press

**Charles Caishun Guo** is a Judge Assistant at the Fujian High People's Court (currently on a secondment to the Supreme People's Court of China). He is also a Ph.D. candidate at University of Cologne. He was a Visiting Scholar at Emory University School of Law in 2019 while he was pursuing his second LL.M. in Common Law at City University of Hong Kong (Chinese Judges Programme). Prior to that, he earned his first LL.M. in International Business Law from National University of Singapore in 2010. He obtained his LL.B. from Fujian Agriculture and Forestry University, China in 2008.

**Wenjing Lin** is a Judge Assistant of the Primary People's Court of Shishi City of Fujian Province. She earned her LL.M. in Intellectual Property Law and LL.B. in Law from Renmin University of China.

**Charlie Xiao-chuan Weng** joined the UNSW Law faculty in 2015 as an Associate Professor. Previously, he was Eastern Scholar Chair Professor of Law and Assistant Dean at the KoGuan Law School of Shanghai Jiao Tong University (SJTU, China). He also taught at Nagoya University Graduate School of Law (Japan) as Designated Associate Professor. He studied law at East China University of Political Science and Law (ECUPL) before completing his LLM at the National University of Singapore (NUS). After working for ECUPL for five years, he went to the University of Pennsylvania School of Law for his LLM and SJD in corporate law, followed by an appointment as a Robert S. McNamara Fellow at the Yale Law School Center for the Study of Corporate Law. In 2012, he was recruited by SJTU as a Research Professor. He also held fellow/visiting professor positions in many leading research institutions, such as Stanford Law School and Cambridge University.

# Hangzhou Thousand-Island Lake Tiantu Needlework Co., Ltd. v. Huatai Group of America, Inc. and Wenzhou Gongmei International Trade Co., Ltd.

**Chaolin Zhang, Junkai Fan, and Peng Guo**

## Case Information

**Case name:** *Hangzhou Thousand-Island Lake Tiantu Needlework Co., Ltd. v Huatai Group of America, Inc. and Wenzhou Gongmei International Trade Co., Ltd.*

**Seller:** Hangzhou Thousand-Island Lake Tiantu Needlework Co., Ltd.
**Place of Business:** China

**Buyer:** Huatai Group of America, Inc.
**Place of Business:** USA

**Buyer's Agent:** Wenzhou Gongmei International Trade Co., Ltd.
**Place of Business:** China

**Details of First Instance:**
**Court:** Wenzhou Intermediate People's Court of Zhejiang Province
**Date of Decision:** July 2014
**Case No:** (2011) Zhe Wen Shang Wai Chu Zi No.73

C. Zhang (✉)
Qufu Normal University, Rizhao, Shandong, China
e-mail: zhang_chaolin@163.com

J. Fan
Qingdao Maritime Court, Qingdao, Shandong, China

P. Guo
Swinburne University of Technology, Melbourne, VIC 3000, Australia
e-mail: pguo@swin.edu.au



P. Guo et al. (eds.), *Selected Chinese Cases on the UN Sales Convention (CISG) Vol. 3*, Selected Chinese Cases on the CISG,
https://doi.org/10.1007/978-981-99-6851-0_23

**Judges:** Qingqing Lin (Presiding Judge), Xinxin Cao (Judge), Zhuosen Cai (Judge)

**CISG Applied:** Yes
**Key CISG Provisions Interpreted and Applied:** Articles 33, 35, 39, 58(1), 61(1)(b), 74

### Case Abstract

Hangzhou Thousand Island Lake Tiantu Needlework Co., Ltd. ('Tiantu') is a legal person registered under the laws of China, whose business scope is the processing and sale of knitted textiles. The company was the seller of the contract in question and the plaintiff in this case. Huatai Group of America, Inc. ('Huatai'), the buyer and defendant in this case, is a corporation incorporated in the State of New York. Although Huatai was dissolved on October 17, 2013, it is allowed to participate in the litigation under art 10, s1006 of the New York State Business Corporation Law, which has been recognized by Chinese courts. In addition, another defendant in this case, Wenzhou Gongmei International Trade Co., Ltd. ('Gongmei'), also a Chinese company, whose business scope is import and export of goods and technology, is the agent of the buyer in this case.

In 2006, Huatai and Gongmei signed the 'Agency Export Agreement', in which the parties agreed on the minimum amount of goods to be purchased by Huatai in China and the resulting, graded agency export service fee that Gongmei could obtain. The agreement was valid from August 2, 2006, to August 1, 2016. According to the agreement: (1) Huatai shall bear all costs and responsibilities arising from purchasing goods in China; (2) Gongmei shall check the goods together with Huatai, be responsible for the booking of goods, production of export documents, customs declaration of goods, verification of tax refund and other export matters and bear the costs; (3) Huatai shall sign a separate agency purchase contract or agreement with the factory, affirming that the obligation of payment of goods shall be borne by Huatai, and Gongmei shall only be responsible for the export procedures and payment of goods on behalf of the company.

From April 2007 to April 2010, Huatai and Tiantu signed several contracts for the sale and purchase of various types of scarves and shawls. The parties agreed on the following contents in the contracts: (1) the item number, color and specification of the scarves and shawls, (2) the price and purchase quantity of the scarves and shawls, (3) the delivery time.

After the above contract was concluded, Tiantu delivered the goods progressively and provided the corresponding packing list. Accordingly, Gongmei's salesmen sent faxes to Tiantu in 2007, 2008 and 2009, requesting Tiantu to ship Huatai's goods to the designated place at the designated time in a consolidated container.

From 2007 to September 2010, the value of scarves and shawls delivered by Tiantu totaled RMB 6,189,175.99. Until December 2010, Huatai paid a total of RMB 3,865,755.98 for part of the goods through Gongmei, leaving a balance of RMB 2,323,420.01 unpaid. In addition, Tiantu had issued VAT invoices and

Gongmei had gone through export tax refund procedures for the goods valued at RMB 5,569,348.99; however, for the goods valued at RMB 619,827, Tiantu had not issued VAT invoices and there was no evidence to prove that Gongmei had undertaken export procedures for them.

On October 27, 2011, Tiantu filed a lawsuit with the Wenzhou Intermediate People's Court, requesting an order that: (1) Huatai and Gongmei immediately pay the remaining payment for goods of RMB 2,323,420.01. (2) To pay the late payment liquidated damages of RMB 153,206.3, the amount of which is calculated as follows: 2.1 percent per day from December 16, 2010, to October 26, 2011; the late payment liquidated damages up to the date of performance of the judgment are calculated separately. (3) The costs of this case shall be borne by Huatai and Gongmei.

In response, Huatai argued that: (1) there was a delay in the delivery of goods by Tiantu. (2) The goods supplied by Tiantu had serious quality problems. (3) Some of the goods in question were exported by other companies entrusted by Huatai, which had nothing to do with Gongmei Company. (4) There was no basis for Tiantu to claim liquidated damages for late payment.

In response, Gongmei argued that: (1) Gongmei is not the buyer in the sale contract in question, and only acts as an agent to handle the relevant export procedures, so it should not assume the payment obligation of the sale contract. (2) The goods exported by Gongmei only include the part worth RMB 5,569,348.99 for which Tiantu has issued a VAT invoice; the goods worth RMB 619,827 claimed by Tiantu have nothing to do with Gongmei. (3) There is no basis in law for Tiantu to claim liquidated damages.

After the trial, the Wenzhou Intermediate People's Court made the following verdict as: (1) The defendant, Huatai, shall pay the plaintiff Tiantu RMB 2,323,420.01 for the goods within ten days from the effective date of the judgment. (2) The defendant, Huatai, shall pay the amount of damages. The specific amount shall be calculated from December 16, 2010, at the rate of 2.1 ten thousandths per day to the date of payment determined by the judgment; if the performance is late, the interest on the debt during the period of late performance shall be doubled. (3) The other claims of the plaintiff, Tiantu, were rejected.

## Commentary to the Key Issues Related to the CISG

### Issues

Issue 1 The Application of the CISG
Issue 2 Change of Delivery Date
Issue 3 Time Limit for Notification of Cargo Discrepancies
Issue 4 Liquidated Damages for Late Payment

### Comments

In this case, the parties' dispute focused on the following three substantive issues: (1) Was a sales contract relationship established between Tiantu and Gongmei? (2)

Was there any delay in the delivery of goods by Tiantu? (3) Was there a delay in the delivery of the goods by Tiantu, and was there a quality problem with the goods supplied by Tiantu? (4) Should the liquidated damages for late payment claimed by Tiantu be supported by the Court? The latter two of these issues are set forth in the CISG, and the relevant provisions of the CISG have been substantially invoked by the Court in this case to resolve the dispute. Therefore, after analyzing the applicability of the CISG, this commentary will focus on the latter two substantive issues.

**Issue 1 The Application of the CISG**

According to the information provided in the judgment, it is clear that the parties did not agree to apply the CISG or to exclude the Convention, which the Chinese court applied ex officio and on its own initiative.

In this case, the places of business of the parties to the contract of seller and buyer were in China and the United States, both of which are Contracting States to the CISG. The Wenzhou Intermediate People's Court held that 'if the parties to an international contract for the sale of goods have their places of business in different contracting states of the CISG, even if the parties have not expressly agreed on the application of the CISG, the provisions of the CISG shall automatically apply to the contract of sale between the parties and shall take precedence over domestic law, unless the parties expressly exclude the application of the CISG'.

The above interpretation of the application of the Convention by the Wenzhou Intermediate People's Court in this case has the following three implications. First, if the parties agree to exclude the application of the Convention, this exclusion agreement has priority in effect, and the courts of the Contracting States will respect this expression of party autonomy and no longer apply the CISG. The status of party autonomy is most directly and clearly confirmed in art 6[1] of the Convention.[2] By allowing the parties to exclude the Convention or derogate from its provisions, the drafters affirmed the principle that the primary source of rules for international sales contracts is party autonomy.[3] Thus the drafters clearly acknowledged the Convention's non-mandatory nature and the central role that party autonomy plays in international commerce—specifically, in international sales.[4] Party autonomy dominates not only the determination of contractual rights and obligations, but also the identification of applicable laws for a contract.[5]

Second, when the parties are silent on the use of the CISG, the parties have not agreed to apply or not to apply, the treaty will be activated and applied through

[1] The CISG, Article 6: "The parties may exclude the application of this Convention or, subject to article 12, derogate from or vary the effect of any of its provisions."

[2] Liu and Ren (Liu and Ren [1], p. 901.

[3] UNCITRAL United Nations Commission on International Trade Law (United Nations Commission on International Trade Law (UNCITRAL) [2], p. 33, para. 3.

[4] UNCITRAL United Nations Commission on International Trade Law (United Nations Commission on International Trade Law (UNCITRAL) [2], p. 33, para. 3.

[5] Liu and Ren [1], p. 901.

the mechanism of automatic application. In other words, the CISG is to be applied 'directly' or 'automatically'.[6]

Third, where the CISG can be applied, the effect will prevail over domestic law. This is relevant to the issue of the CISG's direct/automatic application, which is analysed below in conjunction with the actual circumstances of this case. From the basic information of the case provided in the adjudication documents, it is known that the Wenzhou Intermediate People's Court handled this case between 2011 and 2014, so, the *Law of the People's Republic of China on Choice of Law for Foreign-related Civil Relationships (2011)* should be applied to the issue of the application of law.

The foreign-related sales contract between Tiantu and Huatai was signed from April 2007 to April 2010. According to the provisions of this Law and the judicial interpretation[7] in force at that time, in handling relevant disputes, the Court shall apply *the General Principles of the Civil Law of the People's Republic of China (2009 Amendment)*, art 142. Especially, art 142(2) provides that: 'If any international treaty concluded or acceded to by the People's Republic of China contains provisions differing from those in the civil Laws of the People's Republic of China, the provisions of the international treaty shall apply, unless the provisions are ones on which the People's Republic of China has announced reservations'. In this regard, Professor Haicong Zuo argues that this expression in fact implicitly presupposes that China adopts treaties directly into domestic law, because otherwise there would be no way to speak of treaty precedence in case of conflict. He therefore concludes that it clearly indicates that if a treaty conflicts with domestic law the treaty takes precedence.[8] Further, Professor Zuo suggests that China's treaty application clause is in fact a one-step solution to the three issues of acceptance of treaties into domestic law, direct application of treaties, and priority in case of conflict between treaties and domestic law, i.e., through the above-mentioned direct application clause. This clause has become a fixed model; it simultaneously indicates three levels of meaning: these treaties have been adopted as part of Chinese law, they are directly applicable by courts or/and administrative organs, and they take precedence in case of conflict with relevant domestic law.[9]

---

[6] Liu and Ren [1], p. 898.

[7] *Interpretations of the Supreme People's Court on Several Issues Concerning Application of the Law of the People's Republic of China on Choice of Law for Foreign-Related Civil Relationships (I)*, Interpretation No. 24 [2012] of the Supreme People's Court, Article 2: "For any foreign-related civil relationship happening before the implementation of the Law on Choice of Law for Foreign-Related Civil Relationships, the people's courts shall determine the applicable laws in accordance with relevant laws and regulations at the time of the occurrence of such foreign-related civil relationship." At present, this judicial interpretation has been amended in 2020, and the revised version does not make any changes to this article. See *Interpretations of the Supreme People's Court on Several Issues Concerning Application of the Law of the People's Republic of China on Choice of Law for Foreign-Related Civil Relationships (I) (2020 Amendment)*, Interpretation No. 18 [2020] of the Supreme People's Court, Article 2.

[8] Zuo [ 3], p. 94.

[9] Zuo [3], p. 94.

**Issue 2 Change of Delivery Date**

In this case, Huatai and Tiantu had already agreed on the delivery date in the initial contract. Subsequently, the buyer's agent, Gongmei, notified the seller by fax to deliver the goods on a specific delivery date. Tiantu actually delivered goods worth RMB 6,189,175.99, and Huatai confirmed receipt of the goods. However, Huatai claimed that Tiantu did not deliver the goods on time and there was a delay in delivery.

With respect to the seller's obligation to deliver on time, art 33 of the CISG stipulates: The seller must deliver the goods: (a) if a date is fixed by or determinable from the contract, on that date; (b) if a period of time is fixed by or determinable from the contract, at any time within that period unless circumstances indicate that the buyer is to choose a date; or (c) in any other case, within a reasonable time after the conclusion of the contract. This article specifies the time at or within which the seller must deliver the goods: (1) In accordance with the general principle of party autonomy proposed in the Convention, arts 33(a) and (b) states that the time of delivery is first determined by the terms of the contract; (2) Article 33(c) stipulates a default rule requiring delivery 'within a reasonable time after the conclusion of the contract' if no delivery date or delivery period can be deduced from the contract.[10]

The judgment does not show whether the delivery date in the original contract and the faxed delivery date are the same, but it is reasonable to assume from the Court's applicable reasoning section in art 33 that there is a difference between the two. The Court held that although the delivery date was agreed in the contract in question, the fax sent by Gongmei as Huatai's agent to Tiantu indicated that as the buyer requested Tiantu to deliver the goods to the specified place at the specified time, therefore, the Court ruled that Tiantu's delivery according to this instruction was in accordance with the buyer's request. According to the judgment, it is not difficult to restore the fact by speculation that Tiantu completed the delivery according to the second delivery date requested by fax, and not according to the first delivery date agreed in the initial contract. In other words, the Court recognized the validity of the agreement on the second delivery date.

In essence, the Court recognized the change in the time of delivery between the parties. After the buyer's agent requested the change, the seller also made the delivery in accordance with his request. Therefore, the Court found that the fax from the buyer's agent, and the seller's delivery of goods in accordance with the faxed instructions, were changes to the original contract between the parties. For changes to the contract, art 29(2) of the CISG is relevant, which provides: '(1) A contract may be modified or terminated by the mere agreement of the parties. (2) A contract in writing which contains a provision requiring any modification or termination by agreement to be in writing may not be otherwise modified or terminated by agreement. However, a party may be precluded by his conduct from asserting such a provision to the extent that the other party has relied on that conduct.' Under the above provisions, unless additional requirements are imposed on the form, the contract may be modified or

[10] UNCITRAL United Nations Commission on International Trade Law (United Nations Commission on International Trade Law (UNCITRAL) [2], p. 133, para.1.

terminated by mutual consent of the parties.[11] China did not make a reservation on this clause; it could not be found from the judgment that the parties had specifically provided for it. More importantly, after the buyer's agent made a claim for a change in the delivery time, the seller actually performed its delivery obligation, and the buyer accepted the goods. Therefore, it is clear that the parties have agreed to replace the contractual first delivery date with the second delivery date agreed by fax.

In consequence, with no other conditions to add, and with the known information, it can be argued that the buyer's claim that the seller delayed delivery may have been a litigation tactic and that the Court's failure to uphold the claim was appropriate both in law and in fact.

**Issue 3 Time Limit for Notification of Cargo Discrepancies**

Wenzhou Intermediate People's Court held that the goods in question were delivered at the end of 2010 at the latest, and Huatai only raised the claim that the goods did not conform after the occurrence of the present lawsuit when it submitted its defense in 2012, which was not in line with the provisions of the Convention.

This is related to art 39 of the CISG, which stipulates that if the buyer claims that the goods delivered do not conform to the contract, he is obliged to notify the seller of the non-conformity.[12] CISG art 39 provides: '(1) The buyer loses the right to rely on a lack of conformity of the goods if he does not give notice to the seller specifying the nature of the lack of conformity within a reasonable time after he has discovered it or ought to have discovered it. (2) In any event, the buyer loses the right to rely on a lack of conformity of the goods if he does not give the seller notice thereof at the latest within a period of two years from the date on which the goods were actually handed over to the buyer, unless this time limit is inconsistent with a contractual period of guarantee'.

For the purposes of this case, two aspects of this provision are important. The first is the consequences of failure to give notice. Both paragraphs of this article of the Convention provide that if the buyer fails to give the required notice, he loses the right to claim that the goods do not conform. This appears to mean that the buyer loses the right to any remedy for the non-conformity, including, for example, the right to require the seller to repair the goods, the right to claim damages, the right to reduce the price, and the right to avoid the contract.[13] In this case, the Court held that the buyer had not fulfilled its obligation to give notice in accordance with the time required by the Convention and, on that basis, discontinued the buyer's claim that the goods did not conform to the contract.

The second and more important point for this case is that art 39 provides for the time of notice. This article is divided into two paragraphs, providing for two different

[11] UNCITRAL United Nations Commission on International Trade Law (United Nations Commission on International Trade Law (UNCITRAL) [2], p. 123, para.1.

[12] UNCITRAL United Nations Commission on International Trade Law (United Nations Commission on International Trade Law (UNCITRAL) [2], p. 171, para.1.

[13] UNCITRAL United Nations Commission on International Trade Law (United Nations Commission on International Trade Law (UNCITRAL) [2], p. 171, para.3.

situations and their different time limits. Paragraph (1) provides for timely notice in the general sense and under ordinary circumstances, which is generally understood to mean that the buyer should give notice within a generally reasonable time after discovering or reasonably discovering that the goods do not conform to the same.[14] Paragraph (2) supplements the 'reasonable time' standard in paragraph (1) with an 'absolute cut-off'—a maximum time period after which a CISG buyer is barred from asserting a claim in respect to any non-conformity.[15] In addition, according to art 6 of the Convention, the contract between the parties always prevails over the supplementary rules of the Convention, and if the contract expressly and validly provides for a shorter or longer deadline, then the aforementioned limitations made by the Convention no longer apply.[16]

In this case, if the parties had agreed on a maximum period of notice, it would have been easy for the Court to base its decision on the contractual agreement, but apparently such an agreement did not exist, as the Court's judgment indicates that the judge applied the provisions of art 39(2) to the issue. However, as the judgment maintains the characteristics of the earlier judgment documents, which were 'evidence-based, judgment-oriented, and light on reasoning', it is silent on specific details, which makes it impossible to obtain some specific factual information from the judgment document.

It is known from the judgment that the Court judged the two-year period to be from the end of 2010, the 'latest date for delivery' of the goods in this case. This method is not entirely consistent with the 'date of actual receipt of the goods' required by art 39(2) of the Convention, because the Court seems to take the time of delivery of the goods from the seller's point of view as the starting date, while the Convention requires the time of receipt of the goods from the buyer's point of view. The purpose of this method of calculation is easy to understand: the buyer can only 'take over' the goods and actually discover, or have the possibility of discovering, that the goods are defective if he has actually taken delivery of them.[17] However, the judgment does not state how the 'date of delivery' is to be understood in this case, and whether this date corresponds to the actual date of acceptance. In addition, the Court's explanation of how to calculate the deadline is also ambiguous. Huatai's claim that the goods do not meet the same point in time is '2012 when the reply was submitted', but the judgment also does not specify the specific date. Since the parties did not appeal, it can be reasonably inferred that the Court's practice did not deviate from the parties' reasonable expectations, and its practice should be consistent with the general treatment.

The distinctive features of Chinese courts' decision reasoning are the result of a combination of Chinese legal traditions, the professional standards of judges, and the judicial system features, and have their reasons and necessities. However, Chinese

---

[14] UNCITRAL United Nations Commission on International Trade Law (United Nations Commission on International Trade Law (UNCITRAL) [2], p. 176, para.19.

[15] Lookofsky [4], p. 98.

[16] Lookofsky [4], p. 99.

[17] Gillette and Walt [5], p. 178.

courts have not ignored their shortcomings in reasoning, and reasoning reform is considered an important aspect of the judicial reform list and has been called a 'hard nut to crack'.[18] The Supreme People's Court has repeatedly emphasized the enhancement of the reasoning of judgment documents and has called for the improvement of the quality of the judgment documents. This is provided for in *the 1st Five-Year Outline of the Program for Reform of People's Courts (1999–2003), The 4th Five-Year Outline of the Program for Reform of People's Courts (2014–2018)* published by the Court. It also specifically introduced the *Notice of the Supreme People's Court on Issuing the Guiding Opinions on Strengthening and Standardizing the Analysis and Reasoning in Adjudicative Instruments* (No. 10 [2018] of the Supreme People's Court).[19]

### Issue 4: Liquidated Damages for Late Payment

In this case, the plaintiff Tiantu requested Huatai and Gongmei to make the outstanding payment of RMB 2,323,420.01 yuan, and requested the two companies to pay the liquidated damages of RMB 153,206.3 for late payment. Both Huatai and Gongmei suggested that this claim by Tiantu lacked foundation. The Wenzhou Intermediate People's Court cited arts 58(1),[20] 61(1)(b)[21] and 74[22] of the CISG to address this issue.

It is clear from the judgement of this case that the contract in question did not make any agreement on the time of payment. Article 58 defines the time when the price becomes due in the absence of any particular contractual stipulation on the matter.[23] In addition, art 58(1) further establishes a default rule of simultaneous handover of the goods (or of documents controlling their disposition) and payment of the price: the buyer must pay the price when the seller places either the goods or documents controlling their disposition at its disposal.[24] In this case, Huatai had actually received the goods and, as mentioned earlier, Huatai's claim that Tiantu had failed to perform the seller's obligations and constituted a breach of contract was not

---

[18] Wang [6], pp. 89–90.

[19] Wang [6], pp. 90.

[20] Article 58: (1) If the buyer is not bound to pay the price at any other specific time, he must pay it when the seller places either the goods or documents controlling their disposition at the buyer's disposal in accordance with the contract and this Convention. The seller may make such payment a condition for handing over the goods or documents.

[21] Article 61: (1) If the buyer fails to perform any of his obligations under the contract or this Convention, the seller may: ...... (b) claim damages as provided in articles 74–77.

[22] Article 74: Damages for breach of contract by one party consist of a sum equal to the loss, including loss of profit, suffered by the other party as a consequence of the breach. Such damages may not exceed the loss which the party in breach foresaw or ought to have foreseen at the time of the conclusion of the contract, in the light of the facts and matters of which he then knew or ought to have known, as a possible consequence of the breach of contract.

[23] UNCITRAL United Nations Commission on International Trade Law (United Nations Commission on International Trade Law (UNCITRAL) [12], p. 271, para.1.

[24] UNCITRAL United Nations Commission on International Trade Law (United Nations Commission on International Trade Law (UNCITRAL) [2], p. 271, para.2.

established. Accordingly, the Court correctly supported Tiantu's request and held that Huatai should pay the remaining purchase price in accordance with the contract.

In dealing with Tiantu's claim for damages for breach of contract, the Court applied arts 61(1)(b) and 74. Article 61(1) generally describes the remedies available to the seller in the event of the buyer's failure to perform its obligations (such as the breach of art 58 in this case), and its paragraph (1)(b) provides a legal basis for the seller's right to claim damages for losses suffered, as provided in arts 74–77.[25] Article 74 sets out the general method for calculating damages under the Convention. The first sentence of art 74 provides for the recovery of all losses, including loss of profits, suffered by the aggrieved party as a result of the other party's breach. The second sentence limits recovery to those losses that the breaching party foresaw or could have foreseen at the time the contract was concluded.[26]

The plaintiff's claim was for 'liquidated damages' based on late payment, and the Court used the phrase 'damages' in the results section, which shows that the Court used the terms 'liquidated damages' and 'damages' in the same way during the trial. In the context of Chinese law, 'liquidated damages' is a concept in *the Contract Law of the People's Republic of China* in effect at the time of trial.[27] In fact, the CISG's abandonment of the concept of 'liquidated damages' is a deliberate move, as the CISG has abandoned uniformity on this issue because of the wide variation in national laws regarding liquidated damages provisions, leaving domestic law as the governing law.[28] The key question for this case is what is the relationship between 'liquidated damages' in the context of Chinese law and 'damages' in the context of the CISG?

Although the Convention provides for damages for breach of contract, it does not specify in more detail in art 74 what specific types of damages are compensable, other than the explicit inclusion of lost profits.[29] According to the usual view, recoverability has to be determined in accordance with the overall objective of the CISG to achieve full compensation in view of the particular purpose of the contract.[30] For the CISG,

---

[25] UNCITRAL United Nations Commission on International Trade Law (United Nations Commission on International Trade Law (UNCITRAL) [2], p. 284, para.1.

[26] UNCITRAL United Nations Commission on International Trade Law (United Nations Commission on International Trade Law (UNCITRAL) [2], p. 334, para.1.

[27] *Contract Law of the People's Republic of China*, Article 114: The parties may agree that if one party breaches the contract, it shall pay a certain sum of liquidated damages to the other party in light of the circumstances of the breach, and may also agree on a method for the calculation of the amount of compensation for the damages incurred as a result of the breach. Where the amount of liquidated damages agreed upon is lower than the damages incurred, a party may petition the People's Court or an arbitration institution to make an increase; where the amount of liquidated damages agreed upon are significantly higher than the damages incurred, a party may petition the People's Court or an arbitration institution to make an appropriate reduction. Where the parties agree upon breach of contract damages in respect to the delay in performance, the party in breach shall perform the obligations after paying the breach of contract damages.

[28] Zuo and Yang [7], p. 160.

[29] UNCITRAL United Nations Commission on International Trade Law (United Nations Commission on International Trade Law (UNCITRAL) [2], p.335, para.16.

[30] Schwenzer [8], p. 1063.

as Professor Ingeborg Schwenzer says, the main focus must lie on the performance principle—i.e. the purpose of the damages provisions to protect the promisee in obtaining performance as required by the contract.[31] Specifically, cross-border sales contracts usually serve a commercial purpose, so the liability for damages under the CISG is conditional on the other party to the contract suffering damages for breach of contract.[32] In other words, the CISG only allows for damages, and obviously cannot award purely punitive damages.[33] Regarding the function and nature of 'liquidated damages', the Chinese academic community usually adheres to the fundamental principle of 'prohibited interests' in Chinese laws, and it is thought that the parties included a provision for liquidated damages in the contract to put pressure on the other party to urge it to fulfill the contract; Liquidated damages can be paid to cover losses when the goal of contract performance cannot be attained, so the liquidated damages is in principle for damages liquidated damages.[34] In a general sense, the basic idea of the concept of liquidated damages under Chinese law and the concept of damages in the CISG is the same, and the courts' practice of using the two concepts interchangeably does not create new problems if other more subtle distinctions and more complicated situations are not involved. This is also confirmed in academic studies, where some scholars have used liquidated damages as an expression when discussing the issue of damages covered by art 74 in general.[35]

The last issue is the calculation of liquidated damages. In this case, art 114 of the *Contract Law of the People's Republic of China* and the relevant judicial interpretation[36] should be applied.According to the provisions, the overdue liquidated damages are generally agreed by the parties in the contract. If there is no agreement, the Court may calculate the liquidated damages for overdue payment with reference to the standard of overdue loan interest charged by financial institutions as stipulated by the People's Bank of China. Article 3 of the *Notice of the People's Bank of China on Some Issues concerning Renminbi Loan Interest Rates (2003)* further provides, 'On the issue of penalty interest rate. The current method of calculating the interest for overdue loans (i.e., the loans which the borrower has failed to return on the date stipulated in the contract) with the penalty interest rate at two point one ten-thousandth (0.021%) per day, shall be changed into a method in which an additional amount of 30–50% is added on the basis of the loan interest rate stated in the loan contract'. In this case, the buyer and seller did not agree on the specific method of calculating the late liquidated damages. With reference to the aforementioned provisions, the Court's calculation of 2.1‰ per day as liquidated damages for late payment is accurate.

---

[31] Schwenzer [8], pp.1063–1064.

[32] Wang [9], p. 29.

[33] Schwenzer [8], p. 1064.

[34] Wang [ 10], p. 115.

[35] Han [11], p. 34.

[36] *The reply of the Supreme People's Court on the amendment of the Reply of the Supreme People's Court on the Question of the Standard for the calculation of Liquidated Damages for Overdue Payment*, Fa Shi [2000] No.34.

## References


1. Liu, Q., & Ren, X. (2017). CISG in Chinese Courts: The Issue of Applicability. *The American Journal of Comparative Law*, 65, 873–918.
2. United Nations Commission on International Trade Law (UNCITRAL). (2016). *UNCITRAL Digest of Case Law on the United Nations Convention on Contracts for the International Sale of Goods*. Retrieved from https://uncitral.un.org/sites/uncitral.un.org/files/media-documents/uncitral/en/cisg_digest_2016.pdf.
3. Zuo, H. C. (2008). Research on Direct Application of Treaties. *Chinese Journal of Law*, 3, 88–97.
4. Lookofsky, J. (2017). *Understanding the CISG: A Compact Guide to the 1980 United Nations Convention on Contracts for the International Sale of Goods* (5th ed.). Publishers, Kluwer Law International B.V.
5. Gillette, C. P. & Walt, S. D. (2016). *The UN Convention on Contracts for the International Sale of Goods: Theory and Practice* (2nd ed.). Cambridge University Press.
6. Wang, C. (2019). The Modeling and Limitation of the Rhetoric Style of Judicial Judgment Reasoning in China: An Empirical Analysis Based on Relevant Judgments. *Law and Social Development*, 25(03), 89-105.
7. Zuo, H. C. & Yang, M. S. (2016). Study on Interpretive and Supplementary Functions of PICC to CISG——Taking the Damages System as Examples. *Journal of Comparative Law*, (01), 149-161.
8. Schwenzer, I. (2016). Article 74, in: Schwenzer, I. (eds), *Schlechtriem & Schwenzer: commentary on the UN convention on the international sale of goods* (4th ed., pp. 1057–1085). Oxford University Press.
9. Wang, C. J. (2021). Application of the United Nations Convention on Contracts for the International Sale of Goods in CIETAC Arbitration. *People's Judicature*, (31), 26–30.
10. Wang, H. L. (2014). Reflections on the Functions of Penalty Clause in Civil Contract. *Science of Law (Journal of Northwest University of Political Science and Law)*, (02), 115–125.
11. Han, S. Y. (2021). CISG in China: Achievements and Challenges. *People's Judicature*, (31), 31–36.



**Dr. Chaolin Zhang** is a Lecturer in Law at the Qufu Normal University. She obtained a Ph.D. in International Law from Nankai University, China. Prior to that, she obtained an LLM in International Economic Law from the School of Law at the City University of Hong Kong, China. Her research interests lie in international trade law, data law, and law and technology.

**Mr. Junkai Fan** is a judge assistant at Qingdao Maritime Court. He hears cases on admiralty law, maritime law and international trade law. He also served as an executive officer and is familiar with the mechanism of the enforcement of ship arrest and auction as well as the protection of international seafarers' rights and interests. His cases were selected as the Top Ten Typical Cases of National Admiralty & Maritime in 2020. He holds an LLM by research from Tongji University.

**Dr. Peng Guo** is Lecturer in Law at the Swinburne University of Technology. He has worked across several Australian universities and has held visiting positions at different European universities. He has received scholarships awarded by renowned research institutions and international organisations, including the Max Planck Institute for Comparative and International Private Law, the International Institute for the Unification of Private Law (UNIDROIT), the Swiss Institute of Comparative Law, and the European Union. He specialises in the international sale of goods, international commercial arbitration, comparative contract law, and law and technology.

# Choi Wonkyu v. Xu Chunhua

**Sarah Xiao Xun, Charles Caishun Guo, and Wenjing Lin**

## Case Information

**Case Name:** *Choi Wonkyu v Xu Chunhua*

**Seller**: Xu Chunhua
**Place of Business:** China

**Buyer:** Choi Wonkyu
**Place of Business:** Korea

**Details of First Instance:**
**Court:** Dalian Intermediate People's Court of Liaoning Province
**Date of Decision:** 29 May 2013
**Case No.:** (2012) Da Min Si Chu Zi No. 111
**Judges:** Xue Hui (Presiding Judge), Jia Chunyu (Acting Judge), Wang Zhu (Acting Judge)

S. X. Xun (✉)
Guanghua Law School, Zhejiang University, Office 1-113, Zhijiang CampusZhejiang Province, Hangzhou, China
e-mail: sarahxun@163.com

C. C. Guo
Quanzhou Intermediate People's Court, Quanzhou, China
e-mail: charlesguo@u.nus.edu

W. Lin
The Primary People's Court of Shishi City of Fujian Province, Shishi, Japan
e-mail: 819722979@qq.com



P. Guo et al. (eds.), *Selected Chinese Cases on the UN Sales Convention (CISG) Vol. 3*, Selected Chinese Cases on the CISG,
https://doi.org/10.1007/978-981-99-6851-0_24

**CISG Applied**: Yes
**Key CISG Provisions Interpreted and Applied:** Articles 1, 14(1), 15(1), 23

### Case Abstract

*Choi Wonkyu v Xu Chunhua* is an international sale of goods contract dispute, in which the plaintiff, Choi Wonkyu, claimed he reached an oral agreement on the purchase of mushroom spawns with the defendant, Xu Chunhua. The oral agreement obliged Xu Chunhua to deliver the goods after receiving advance payment, with the delivery period between September and November 2011. From January 2011 to June 2011, Choi Wonkyu paid RMB 58,200 in four instalments to Xu Chunhua. However, Xu Chunhua failed to fulfill the delivery obligation and refused to return the advance payment despite repeated reminders. Choi Wonkyu then sued for return of the advance payment of RMB 58,200 for the purchase of the mushroom spawns.

The defendant, Xu Chunhua, admitted that he and Choi Wonkyu had agreed on the sale of mushroom spawns, and that he had received the advance payment from Choi Wonkyu. However, Xu Chunhua argued that delivery of all the mushroom spawns had been made to Choi Wonkyu through a freight forwarder.

The court of first instance, Dalian Intermediate People's Court of Liaoning Province found that:

1. Choi Wonkyu serves as the president of Hwasung Supply and is the legal representative of this company. Xu Chunhua is the legal representative of Donggang Anhua Edible Fungus Service Professional Cooperative ('Anhua Cooperative').
2. On 21 March 2010, Choi Wonkyu, on behalf of Hwasung Supply, signed a contract with Anhua Cooperative. In the contract at the place of 'seller' was affixed the official seal of Anhua Cooperative, and Choi Wonkyu and Xu Chunhua signed the contract at the place of 'each party's representative'.
3. It was agreed in the contract that Hwasung Supply would purchase Xiangyang No. 2 mushroom spawns from Anhua Cooperative. The farm loading price was RMB 7.5 per stick, and the quantity was approximately 21,000 sticks. The mushroom spawns would be delivered in three batches. The first and second batches would be delivered in September 2010, and the third batch would be delivered in early October 2010.
4. Payment method of the contract:

Deposit: The unit price of each mushroom spawn stick was RMB 3.5, and the quantity was approximately 21,000 sticks, equivalent to RMB 73,500. The buyer should pay the seller a deposit of RMB 24,500 upon the signing date of the contract, and the balance of RMB 49,000 shall be payable on 19 March 2010. The remittance voucher shall be taken as evidence and the goods will not be produced until remittance reaches the account.

Balance settlement method: the balance of the mushroom spawns other than the deposit was RMB 84,000, excluding agency fee, ocean freight and short-distance transportation fee. The payment should be made one day in advance of delivery, and the payment for each container/batch shall be RMB 28,000.

1. In the trial, Choi Wonkyu admitted that it was orally agreed by the two parties that the agency fee, ocean freight and short-distance transportation fee should be borne by himself. The contract did not specify the applicable law for dispute settlement.
2. From August 2010 to June 2011, Choi Wonkyu made seven remittances by transfer (totaling USD $37,455.62) and two cash payments (totaling RMB 25,000) to Xu Chunhua. The timing and the amounts were not in dispute.
3. On 20 October 2010 and 22 April 2011, Xu Chunhua entrusted an agent to export 7,100 and 14,000 mushroom spawns respectively to Hwasung Supply. On 24 April 2011, Xu Chunhua entrusted another agent to export 12,000 mushroom spawn sticks to Hwasung Supply. Choi Wonkyu admitted that he had received all the above-mentioned mushroom spawn, totaling 33,100 sticks.

According to the customs declaration, the unit price of 14,000 mushroom spawn sticks was USD $0.3 (FOB), the unit price of 7,100 mushroom spawn sticks was USD $0.4 (FOB), and the unit price of 12,000 mushroom spawn sticks was USD$ 0.7 (CIF). Xu Chunhua argued that the actual unit price of 7,100 sticks and 12,000 sticks should be RMB 7.5, and the unit price of 14,000 sticks should be RMB 6. The unit price on the customs declaration was filled in at the request of Choi Wonkyu in order to pay less import duties, which was lower than the actual price, and the certificate of its agent was submitted as evidence.

Pursuant to provisions of arts 142.1 and 142.2 of the *General Principles of the Civil law of the People's Republic of China*, art 41 of the *Law of the Application of Law for Foreign-related Civil Relations of the People's Republic of China*, arts 1, 14(1), 15(1) and 23 of the CISG, art 136 of the *Contract Law of the People's Republic of China*, art 7 of the *Supreme People's Court Interpretation on the Law Application in the Trial of Disputes over Sales Contracts* and arts 2, 5.1 and 64 of *Several Provisions of the Supreme People's Court on Evidence on Civil Procedures*, Dalian Intermediate People's Court dismissed Choi Wonkyu's claim. The case acceptance fee of RMB 1255 shall be borne by Choi Wonkyu.

## Commentary to the Key Issues Related to the CISG

### Issues

Issue 1 Who are the Proper Plaintiff and Defendant?
Issue 2 Whether the CISG is Applied
Issue 3 Whether the Plaintiff's Claim can be Supported

### Comments

#### Issue 1 Who Are the Proper Plaintiff and Defendant?

Unlike the common law dispute cases of international sale of goods contracts in which both parties are usually legal persons, the parties in this case are both natural persons. However, the contract was signed in the name of two companies, whose legal representatives are the plaintiff and the defendant. So, the question is, why did the counterparties of the contract change from legal persons to natural persons? The key point is that the court should respect both parties' choice of the counterparty of the contract. In this case, both parties agreed that the contract was actually an individual act, and had no objection to the capacity of the counterparty to sue and respond to the lawsuit in their own name. Moreover, Hwasung Supply issued evidence to prove that the money involved in the case was the advance payment of the plaintiff, Choi Wonkyu, and the defendant, Xu Chunhua, also promised that he would bear the responsibility of Anhua Cooperative. All the above facts indicate that the actual performers of the contract, and the subjects liable for breach of contract, should be Choi Wonkyu and Xu Chunhua. Therefore, it can be confirmed that Choi Wonkyu and Xu Chunhua are the proper plaintiff and defendant in this case.

**Issue 2 Whether the CISG is Applied**

### I. The Application of the CISG to a Natural Person.

There is no provision in the CISG indicating that the Convention can merely be applied to legal person rather than natural person. Pursuant to the *Foreign Trade Law of the People's Republic of China*, once having handled industrial and commercial registration or other formalities for business operation, any legal person, whether organization or individual, is eligible to be a foreign business operator. With the development of electronic cross-border trade, international commercial trades between natural persons or between a natural person and a legal person have come more frequent. Thus, there appears to be no reason to exclude a natural person as the subject of the application of the Convention. However, a further question is how to define the 'internationality' in the sale of goods where natural persons are the subject.

### II. The Standard of Internationality: Nationality or Place of Business?

The difference between contracts for the international sale of goods and for domestic sale of goods is that the former is of international application or 'involving foreign interests'. What is considered international can be determined by a number of criteria, such as the nationality of the parties, the place of business of the parties, the place where behaviour occurs, or whether the goods cross the border.[1] The standard under the Convention is the place of business of the parties. Pursuant to art 1 of the CISG, the Convention applies to contracts for the sale of goods between parties whose places of business are in different States, and neither the nationality of the parties nor the civil or commercial character of the parties, or of the contract, is to be taken into consideration in determining the application of the Convention. The plaintiff in this case, Choi Wonkyu, is of Korean nationality, and the dispute between him and Xu Chunhua over the contract for sale and purchase is a foreign-related commercial case. Therefore, the relevant provisions of foreign-related civil litigation shall apply, however he nationality of the parties concerned cannot lead to the application of

[1] Yu and Wu [1], p.73.

the Convention. Therefore, the place of business of both parties needs to be further analysed.

The Convention does not adopt the standard of 'nationality' and 'civil or commercial character of the parties or of the contract because these terms can be too confusing and complex, which is not conducive to the uniform and global application of the Convention.[2] By contrast, the place of business of both parties can be more stable and easier to define. Thus, when considering whether a contract is international, the Convention takes the 'place of business' of the parties as the judgment standard. However, the definition of 'place of business' in the Convention is not clear,[3] which, in practice, should be determined by the arbitration institution or the court accepting the case according to the specific situation. The main problem encountered is that, if a party has several connected places of business, which one should be selected as the 'place of business' to determine whether the relevant transaction is 'international'?

## III. How to Determine the Place of Business of a Natural Person.

As discussed above, the 'place of business' is significant to determine the 'internationality' of the contract for the sale of goods, but the Convention has not given a precise definition of 'place of business' but rather has defined the 'place of business' in several aspects.

For legal persons, art 10 (a) stipulates that if a party has more than one place of business, the 'place of business' is that which has the closest relationship to the contract and its performance, having regard to the circumstances known to, or contemplated by, the parties at any time before or at the conclusion of the contract. What is 'closest relationship to the contract and its performance' still needs further explanation. Due to the lack of clear provisions, the standards of judicial practice concerning the definition of 'place of business' varies from country to country. For example, some courts hold that the 'place of business' should be the location of an institution that has been established for a long time and has a certain degree of autonomy and is actually engaged in production and operation. While the 'place where goods are stored only' nor the 'temporary booth' can be defined as the 'place of business' under the Convention,[4] some courts also exclude the 'liaison office' from the 'place of business'.[5] In addition, there are also precedents stating that 'merely the place of signing and the place of negotiation" cannot be regarded as "the place of business'.[6]

For natural persons, art 10(b) stipulates that if a party does not have a place of business, reference is to be made to their habitual residence. Considering that in judicial practice the legal person has the place of business, and the natural person has habitual

---

[2] CIETAC Hong Kong Arbitration Center [2].

[3] Xu [3].

[4] Oberlandesgericht Stuttgart, Germany, 28 February 2000, *Internationales Handelsrecht*, 2001, 66; CLOUT case No. 608 [Trib. Rimini, Italy, 26 November 2002].

[5] UNCITRAL Compendium of case law on the United Nations Convention on Contracts for the International Sale of Goods, [4], p. 5.

[6] Xu [3] p.

residence, it can be concluded that the 'place of business' of a natural person is their habitual residence. Given that, for the purposes of the Convention, stability is the value pursuit when choosing reference of 'internationality', and habitual residence is more stable than nationality, this provision holds that habitual residence is suitable as the reference for a natural person in jurisprudence related to the Convention.

In this case, however, the situation is slightly different in that both parties involved are actually the legal representatives of the legal person who signed the contract. Although both parties agreed to undertake contractual obligations in their own name, the signing and performance of the contract are inextricably linked with the two companies with Choi Wonkyu and Xu Chunhua as their legal representatives respectively. Therefore, the situation is more similar to the cases in which both parties are legal persons. Considering all of this, it is submitted that, on the whole, the 'place of business' of a natural person should be regarded as the natural person's habitual residence. However, this case should be considered as a special situation in which both parties are actually the legal representatives of the contracted companies, and needs to follow the standard of legal person when choosing reference to 'place of business'.

In conclusion, in view of the fact that the dispute in question was a dispute over an international contract for the sale of goods, and that the places of business of the parties to the case, i.e. China and Korea, are both Contracting States to the Convention, and that the parties did not exclude the application of the Convention in the contract, the Convention should be the governing law for dealing with the dispute. For matters not expressly provided for in the Convention, the law of the party's habitual residence or other law most closely connected with the contract shall apply according to the provisions of art 41 of the *Law of the People's Republic of China on the Application of Law to Foreign-related Civil Relations*, which best characterizes the performance of the contract. The relevant provisions of the laws of the People's Republic of China should apply.

**Issue 3 Whether the Plaintiff's Claim Can Be Supported**

The plaintiff, Choi Wonkyu, claimed that after the signing of the contract, the two parties did not strictly perform according to the contract. The defendant shipped 33,100 mushroom spawn sticks in three batches, which had nothing to do with this case. The previous transactions between the two parties had been settled. The plaintiff's claim was based on an oral agreement separately agreed upon by both parties. The agreement stated that the plaintiff paid for four advance payments totalling RMB 58,200. The plaintiff claimed to have paid the defendant RMB 8,000 in cash on the same day, but failed to submit evidence to support this claim. The defendant failed to deliver the goods as agreed. The defendant denied receiving RMB 8,000 but had no objection to other payments. However, the defendant argued that the three payments (equivalent to RMB 50,200) were the final payments for the 33,100 mushroom spawn sticks, and the plaintiff still owed some money which has not been paid.

The plaintiff has the burden of proof that a contract of sale was concluded in accordance with the provisions of the CISG. However, the plaintiff failed to justify its claim and convince the Court of what he claimed. The defendant admitted that he had received a total of more than RMB 270,000 from the plaintiff. After deducting the agency fees, ocean freight, and short-distance transportation fees that should be borne by the plaintiff, the remaining amount of money is basically consistent with the price of the three batches of mushroom spawn sticks. Therefore, the defendant's defence is more logical and reasonable.

In summary, the plaintiff, Choi Wonkyu, failed to provide sufficient factual evidence and lacked a legal basis to prove that he had reached an oral agreement with the defendant who would return the advance payment of RMB 58,200. The Court therefore did not support his claim.

**Closing Remarks**

Article 2 of the *Provisions by the Supreme People's Court on Evidence in Civil Procedures*[7] provides that 'the party has the burden of proof to prove the facts on which it bases its claim or to refute the facts on which the other party bases its claim. If there is no evidence or if the evidence is insufficient to prove the party's factual claims, the party with the burden of proof shall bear the adverse consequences.'

Article 5 of *Provisions by the Supreme People's Court on Evidence in Civil Procedures*[8] provides guidance on the burden of proof in different types of contractual disputes.

Firstly, in a contractual dispute where one party claims that the contract has been established and has taken effect, that party bears the burden of proving that the contract has been concluded and has taken effect. On the other hand, if one party claims that the contract has been altered, dissolved, terminated, or canceled, that party has the burden of proving such changes to the contract. Secondly, in a dispute over the performance of a contract, the party that is obligated to perform the contract has the burden of proving that they have fulfilled their obligations under the contract. Lastly, in a dispute over the power of agency, the party that claims the existence of such power has the burden of proving it.

These guidelines help ensure that the party with the best access to information and evidence bears the burden of proving their claims. It also promotes fairness and efficiency in resolving contractual disputes, as each party is responsible for providing evidence to support their claims.

## References

1. Yu, J. S. & Wu, Z. P. (2014). *International Economic Law* (4th ed.). Peking University Press
2. CIETAC Hong Kong Arbitration Center. (2022). *"Place of business" under the CISG: how to determine it?*. Retrieved 2023 March 22 from https://mp.weixin.qq.com/s/T4ASZv9KTwPg yTE008oXTg

[7] SPC [5].

[8] SPC [5].

3. Xu, S. Q. (2022, Sep 30). *Discussion on Issues Related to the Extension of CISG to Hong Kong*. Beijing Jingtian & Gongcheng Law Firm. Retrieved 2023 March 22, from: https://mp.weixin.qq.com/s/aPRnepKVbQ6O0SUytttzSg
4. UNCITRAL. (2008). *Compendium of case law on the United Nations Convention on Contracts for the International Sale of Goods*. Retrieved from https://uncitral.un.org/sites/uncitral.un.org/files/media-documents/uncitral/zh/second_edition_chinese.pdf
5. The Supreme People's Court of the People's Republic of China (SPC). (2019). *Several Provisions of the Supreme People's Court Concerning Evidence in Civil Procedures*. Retrieved from https://www.court.gov.cn/zixun-xiangqing-212721.html

**Sarah Xiao Xun** is a post-doctoral fellow at Guanghua Law School, Zhejiang University. She specializes in company law, corporate governance, and interdisciplinary studies. She obtained her PhD from Erasmus University Rotterdam in the Netherlands and presented her works at academic conferences across Europe and the United States. She received the degrees of LLM and LLB from China University of Political Science and Law. In addition to her academic experience, she has been practicing law at Beijing De Heng Law office in cross-border transactions, including takeovers and bank loans. She is also a visiting fellow at the University of New South Wales.

**Charles Caishun Guo** is a Judge Assistant at the High People's Court of Fujian Province (currently on a secondment to the Supreme People's Court of China). He is also a Ph.D. candidate at University of Cologne. He was a Visiting Scholar at Emory University School of Law in 2019 while he was pursuing his second LL.M. in Common Law at City University of Hong Kong (Chinese Judges Programme). Prior to that, he earned his first LL.M. in International Business Law from National University of Singapore in 2010. He obtained his LL.B. from Fujian Agriculture and Forestry University, China in 2008.

**Wenjing Lin** The Primary People's Court of Shishi City of Fujian Province

# Tong v. Kaiping X Stainless Steel Products Ltd.

**Benjamin Hayward**

## Case Information

**Case name:** *Tong v Kaiping X Stainless Steel Products Ltd.*

**Seller**: Kaiping X Stainless Steel Products Ltd.
**Place of Business:** China

**Buyer:** Y Trading Company
**Place of Business:** not stated

**Details of First Instance:**
**Court**: Kaiping People's Court
**Date of Decision**:
**Case No.**: (2008) Kai Fa Min Si Chu Zi No.3 (judgment not available)

**Details of Second Instance:**
**Court**: Jiangmen Intermediate People's Court
**Date of Decision**: 19 November 2013
**Case No.**: (2012) Jiang Zhong Fa Min Si Zhong Zi No.18
**Judge**: Jianwen Ma

**CISG Applied**: No
**Key CISG Provisions Interpreted and Applied**: N/A

B. Hayward (✉)
Department of Business Law and Taxation, Monash Business School, Level 4, Building S, 900 Dandenong Road, Caulfield East, VIC 3145, Australia
e-mail: Benjamin.Hayward@monash.edu

 
P. Guo et al. (eds.), *Selected Chinese Cases on the UN Sales Convention (CISG) Vol. 3*, Selected Chinese Cases on the CISG,
https://doi.org/10.1007/978-981-99-6851-0_25

## Case Abstract

On 1 November 2004, the buyer, Y Trading Company ('Y'), signed a contract for the sale of stainless-steel kitchenware products with the seller Kaiping X Stainless Steel Products Ltd. ('X'). Y paid for the goods and received delivery. They considered the goods to be non-conforming and having significant quality issues. Tong, Y's shareholder, brought a claim against X before the Kaiping People's Court.

The Kaiping People's Court found that Y was incorporated in Hong Kong, and that its shareholder, Tong, was a Hong Kong resident. The contract was performed within China. Art 145 of the Chinese General Principles of Civil Law (GPCL) states:

> Parties of a foreign-related contract can choose the law applicable to the contract unless the law provides otherwise. In the absence of such choice, the law of the State having the closest connection with the contract shall apply.

Thus, in this case, Chinese law applied. The court proceeded to reject the claims made by Tong on the basis of a lack of sufficient evidence as to the goods' non-compliance, without reference to any particular rules of contract law. The decision was instead based upon an application of the rules concerning burden of proof.

Tong brought an appeal before the Jiangmen Intermediate People's Court. In response to the appellant (Tong's) claim that losses had been suffered due to X's provision of non-conforming goods, X argued, among other reasons, that the losses listed by Tong were not supported by art 119 of the Chinese Contract Law, art 114 of the GPCL, as well as art 77 of the CISG. It was argued that the goods in dispute had passed the compulsory inspection of the Chinese customs and quality-control authorities for exported goods, and that the subsequent issues reported by Tong arising after that compulsory inspection, even if proven, should not be the responsibility of X. The mitigation of damages provisions cited by X were argued to be relevant because if the goods had passed their compulsory inspections, it must be the case that the losses were the result of the buyer's own actions, which should not then be compensated.

The Jiangmen IPC found that the dispute was a foreign-related dispute due to Tong's Hong Kong residency. Thus, the applicable law was to be determined pursuant to art 145 of the GPCL (quoted above), and art 41 of the Chinese Law on the Application of Law in Foreign-Related Civil Relationships (the Law Application Law), which similarly provides:

> The parties of a contract can choose the law applicable to the contract. In the absence of such choice, the law applicable to the contract should be the law of the usual residence of the party whose performance better reflects the feature of contract, or other law that is most closely connected to the contract.

In this dispute, the purchase was between X and Y, and the goods were shipped by X from Mainland China to South Africa. Both the domicile of X and the performance of the contract were in Mainland China. As a result, the law applicable to the contract was Chinese Law, as held by the Kaiping People's Court.

The court further agreed with the Kaiping People's Court that the evidence submitted by Tong was insufficient to support the claims made. It rejected Tong's attempt to rely upon new evidence for civil procedure reasons and rejected the appeal.

## Commentary on the Key Issues Related to the CISG

### Issues

Issue 1 The Applicability of the CISG, in General

Issue 2 The Applicability of the CISG to Mainland China/Hong Kong Transactions

Issue 3 The Use of the CISG as a Supplementary Source of Law

Issue 4 Damages Under the CISG

### Comments

### Issue 1 The Applicability of the CISG, in General

As this dispute involved parties incorporated in Mainland China and in Hong Kong, this case raises interesting issues as to the applicability of the CISG to such 'intra-China' transactions. These issues are addressed as Issue 2. First, however, it is necessary to address other issues raised by this case as to the CISG's application criteria, in general.

CISG art 1(1) provides that '[t]his Convention applies to contracts of sale of goods between parties whose places of business are in different States'. From the outset, it can be observed that this case only found that Y Trading Company, the buyer in the dispute, was incorporated in Hong Kong, with Tong—Y Trading Company's shareholder—also being a Hong Kong resident. Neither Y Trading Company's place of incorporation, nor Tong's place of residence, are strictly relevant for the purposes of art 1(1)'s internationality criterion, which is defined in terms of the parties' places of business. In addition, it can be noted that art 1(1)'s internationality criterion looks to the places of business *of the parties*. For this reason, in assessing the CISG's potential applicability, it is the place of business of Y Trading Company (the buyer) and not Tong (Y Trading Company's shareholder) that needs to be determined.

Art 10 of the CISG provides assistance in identifying a party's place of business where it has more than one place of business, and that provision further refers to a party's habitual residence only where a party does not have a place of business. This might have conceivably been relevant to Tong, though once again, Tong was not a party to the relevant sales contract, so their own habitual residence was not relevant for CISG purposes. In general terms, a place of business exists where 'a party uses it openly to participate in trade and if it displays a certain degree of duration, stability, and independence'.[1] A company's place of incorporation is itself not definitive, though it may be the case that a company's 'place of its administrative center' is its place of business too.[2]

This case is not unique amongst Chinese CISG decisions in relation to its failure to clearly identify and apply CISG art 1(1)'s place of business criterion in assessing

[1] Schwenzer and Schroeter [1], p. 36.

[2] Schwenzer and Schroeter [1], p. 36; Jayme [2], p. 30.

the CISG's potential application.[3] The failure of the Kaiping People's Court and the Jiangmen IPC to do so in this case, however, most likely reflects the fact that it was non-harmonized Chinese law that was ultimately applied. The CISG, although referred to by X, was not directly applied by either court. Instead, the CISG's relevance here arose as a result of X referring to CISG art 77 CISG, alongside art 119 of the Chinese Contract Law and art 114 of the Chinese General Principles of Civil Law, on appeal to the Jiangmen IPC. CISG art 77 CISG addresses the issue of mitigation of damages.[4] Mitigation of damages is also the legal subject-matter of art 119 of the Chinese Contract Law and art 114 of the Chinese General Principles of Civil Law.

If the CISG did (hypothetically) directly apply in this case, it would not have been possible (as X sought to do) to rely upon this combination of provisions. Instead, CISG art 77 (and all other CISG provisions, to the extent of the treaty's subject-matter scope as set out in CISG art 4) would have applied to the exclusion of corresponding rules contained in non-harmonized Chinese law.[5]

**Issue 2 The Applicability of the CISG to Mainland China/Hong Kong Transactions**

Putting these general issues concerning CISG art 1(1)'s application criteria to one side, this case also raises interesting issues as to the relevance of the CISG to intra-China transactions carried out between parties having their places of business in Mainland China and in the Hong Kong Special Administrative Region of the People's Republic of China, respectively. These issues intersect with law reform considerations that are ongoing at the time of writing this Comment.

Prior to 1 December 2022, there was some uncertainty as to whether the CISG's adoption by the People's Republic of China extended also to the Hong Kong Special Administrative Region, following Hong Kong's return to the People's Republic of China as of 1 July 1997. This uncertainty at least existed so far as the CISG might apply to trade between Hong Kong parties and non-Chinese parties.[6] What was clear, all along, was that the CISG did not (according to its own terms) govern intra-China trade between parties with places of business in Mainland China and in Hong Kong.[7] This follows from an aspect of CISG art 1(1)'s application test that is additional to those already considered with respect to Issue 1 above: '[t]his Convention applies to contracts of sale of goods between parties whose places of business are in *different States*' (emphasis added).

Whilst it is possible for the CISG to apply in different territorial units of a single Contracting State,[8] as is the case in Australia where the treaty applies in each internal

---

3 Wang et al. [3], p. 29; Wang et al. [4], pp. 89–91; An [5], p. 174; Li [6], p. 209; Shang [7], p. 238; Wang [8], p. 266; Zhang et al. [9], pp. 326–327; Li [10], p. 332.

4 Knapp [11].

5 Khoo [12], p. 46.

6 Schroeter [13], p. 309.

7 Schroeter [13], pp. 329–330.

8 Art. 93(1) CISG; Jayme [2], p. 30.

state and territory[9] as well as in the external territory of Norfolk Island,[10] the CISG still cannot—on its own terms—apply to intra-State trade between such places. Although Hong Kong is a Special Administrative Region of the People's Republic of China, with its own Legislative Council, it is not a 'different State [...]' to the People's Republic of China for the purposes of CISG art 1(1). This is confirmed by the 'one country, two systems' principle which underpins the relationship between the People's Republic of China as a whole, and the Hong Kong Special Administrative Region in particular. Thus, regardless of whether the CISG applies in Hong Kong, it cannot govern intra-China trade according to its own terms, just as it could not (hypothetically) govern contracts between English and Scottish parties, if the UK were to accede to the treaty in the future.[11]

Uncertainty as to the CISG's extension to the Hong Kong Special Administrative Region was resolved, as of 1 December 2022, via the Hong Kong Legislative Council's enactment of (and the coming into force of) the *Sale of Goods (United Nations Convention) Ordinance* (Hong Kong) cap 641. Strictly speaking, it is not quite correct to state (as the relevant United Nations press release does) that '[t]he territorial application will take effect on 1 December 2022':[12] since there is still a view (even if this is not a view shared by Hong Kong and the People's Republic of China) that the CISG did apply in the Hong Kong Special Administrative Region before 1 December 2022, independently of that fact's recent legislative confirmation. Still, as explained above, the resolution of this uncertainty does not address the separate issue as to the CISG's application to intra-Chinese trade.

CISG art 1(1)'s application criteria thus preclude the CISG's application to intra-Chinese trade on the treaty's own terms. It is nevertheless still possible for Mainland China and the Hong Kong Special Administrative Region to arrange for the CISG's application to intra-China trade, as between themselves. If such an arrangement were concluded that arrangement would overcome the limitations of art 1(1), for the specific purposes of the relationship between Mainland China and the Hong Kong Special Administrative Region of the People's Republic of China. At the same time, CISG Contracting States' public international law obligations to implement the CISG according to its terms would remain unchanged.[13]

There is precedent for concluding such reciprocal arrangements, in the related international commercial arbitration arena. The Convention on the Recognition and Enforcement of Foreign Arbitral Awards,[14] a treaty dealing with the cross-border enforceability of arbitration agreements and arbitral awards, does not (on its own

---

[9] *Sale of Goods (Vienna Convention) Act 1987* (ACT); *Sale of Goods (Vienna Convention) Act 1986* (NSW); *Sale of Goods (Vienna Convention) Act 1987* (NT); *Sale of Goods (Vienna Convention) Act 1986* (Qld); *Sale of Goods (Vienna Convention) Act 1986* (SA); *Sale of Goods (Vienna Convention) Act 1987* (Tas); *Goods Act 1958* (Vic) pt IV (formerly *Sale of Goods (Vienna Convention) Act 1987* (Vic)); *Sale of Goods (Vienna Convention) Act 1986* (WA).

[10] *Sale of Goods (Vienna Convention) Act 1987* (NI).

[11] Jayme [2], p. 30.

[12] United Nations Information Service [14].

[13] Köhler [15], pp. 20, 25.

[14] Opened for signature 10 June 1958, 330 UNTS 3 (entered into force 7 June 1959).

terms) govern intra-State award enforcement. However, enforcement as between Mainland China and Hong Kong has been provided for independently of that treaty's own text by way of a reciprocal arrangement between the two entities.[15] A similar arrangement concerning the enforcement of arbitral awards also exists as between the Hong Kong Special Administrative Region and the Macao Special Administrative Region of the People's Republic of China.[16]

In the CISG's case, the Department of Justice of Hong Kong's initial draft consultation Bill—which was distributed (for feedback purposes) with the Department's CISG consultation materials—originally included the following clause:

> 4. Convention has the force of law in Hong Kong ...
>
> (b) Despite Hong Kong being a territorial unit of China, the provisions of the Convention as it has effect under this Ordinance apply between the Mainland and Hong Kong as if the Mainland and Hong Kong were 2 different states and 2 different Contracting States.[17]

This proposal to extend the CISG's application to intra-Chinese trade was, according to the Department of Justice's consultation paper, intended to reflect 'the close economic ties between Mainland China and Hong Kong', and was thus intended 'to facilitate sale of goods between businesses in the two places.'[18]

Despite this admirable intention, it is possible that this clause as originally drafted could have precipitated unintended consequences. Had it been implemented as part of Hong Kong law, this clause would have required Hong Kong's courts to apply the CISG to intra-Chinese trade. However, without a corresponding provision implemented, at the same time, under Mainland Chinese law, the CISG would not have been applied where intra-China sales law disputes were heard by Mainland courts. This problem could have incentivized forum shopping, given that a plaintiff's choice of court (Hong Kong or Mainland China) would have affected the law applied to the merits.[19] This risk was identified by respondents to the Department of Justice of Hong Kong's CISG consultation.[20] Upon further reflection, the clause as originally drafted might have carried additional risks too: where the CISG's application would have depended upon whether Hong Kong or Mainland courts ultimately heard a dispute, parties might also have faced uncertainty in identifying the law governing the performance of their contracts outside of formal dispute resolution.[21] The Bill

[15] Department of Justice of Hong Kong [16]. See *Arbitration Ordinance* (Hong Kong) cap 609, ss 92–98.

[16] Department of Justice of Hong Kong [17]. See *Arbitration Ordinance* (Hong Kong) cap 609, ss 98A-98D.

[17] Consultation Draft of Sale of Goods (United Nations Convention) Bill (Hong Kong) cl 4(b). See Department of Justice of Hong Kong [18], pp. 176–178.

[18] Department of Justice of Hong Kong [18], p. 79.

[19] Juenger [19], p. 554.

[20] Department of Justice of Hong Kong [20], p. 6.

[21] Hayward [21], pp. 34–35.

that was introduced to the Legislative Council of Hong Kong[22]—and the Ordinance that was eventually passed[23]—thus omitted this initially-proposed clause.

As the Department of Justice has explained, however, the idea of applying the CISG to intra-China trade has not been abandoned.[24] Instead, it is currently proposed that the CISG may still be applied in this way, in the future, via a reciprocal arrangement.[25] Concluding such an arrangement would avoid the forum shopping problems implicated in the original proposed clause.

Concluding, as a matter of law, that the CISG itself does not govern intra-China trade involves a relatively simple analysis of CISG art 1(1). That any change to this position requires future law reform in Hong Kong and in the People's Republic of China is equally clear. Nevertheless, the points addressed here have significant practical importance. Chinese courts currently respect party choice of the CISG in the context of Mainland China / Hong Kong transactions,[26] notwithstanding the requirements of CISG art 1(1). This is itself interesting, given that it involves applying the CISG beyond the parameters of its own terms.[27] Still, on the present state of the law, the CISG cannot apply to intra-Chinese trade as a default law, in the absence of party choice. International commercial contracts not infrequently omit choice of law clauses.[28] Case law evidencing the CISG's application to intra-Chinese trade via party choice suggests that appetite might also exist for the convention's default application in this context. If the CISG is to be given such default application in the future, as explained with respect to Issue 1, it will displace non-harmonized Chinese law to the extent of the treaty's art 4 CISG subject-matter scope. The CISG's potential default application to intra-China trade will therefore affect the identity, and possibly also the contents, of the legal rules applied to any particular sales law dispute.

Finally, with respect to Issue 2, it can be noted that the differing reservation profiles adopted by the People's Republic of China and the Hong Kong Special Administrative Region will not affect the CISG's future application to intra-Chinese trade. The People's Republic of China has made an art 95 CISG reservation in relation to CISG art 1(1)(b), though that reservation has not been extended to the Hong Kong Special Administrative Region.[29] CISG art 1(1)(b), which can be applied in Hong Kong but which does not apply in Mainland China, is a means by which the treaty's application can be extended beyond situations where both parties have their places of business in Contracting States. Pursuant to art 1(1)(b), the convention can apply if only one (or indeed none) of the parties have their places of business in Contracting States, if a contract's governing law (identified by virtue of either party choice of law or the

[22] Sale of Goods (United Nations Convention) Bill (Hong Kong).

[23] *Sale of Goods (United Nations Convention) Ordinance* (Hong Kong) cap 641.

[24] Department of Justice of Hong Kong [20], pp. 6–7.

[25] Department of Justice of Hong Kong [20], p. 7.

[26] Wang et al. [3], pp. 5–6.

[27] Cf *Quarella SpA v Scelta Marble Australia Pty Ltd.* [2012] 4 SLR 1057, 1061–1062.

[28] Hayward [21], pp. 19–25.

[29] United Nations Information Service [14].

application of conflict of laws rules) is a Contracting State's law.[30] Application of the CISG via art 1(1)(b), as compared to the treaty's application via CISG art 1(1)(a), reduces in importance as more States join the CISG family.[31] Should the CISG's application be extended to intra-China trade, the different reservation profiles of the People's Republic of China and the Hong Kong Special Administrative Region would not affect that application: both Mainland China and Hong Kong would be territories where the CISG is in force, and the requirements of art 1(1)(a) would therefore be deemed satisfied. It is thus not necessary, as the Department of Justice of Hong Kong initially suggested, for Hong Kong to 'mirror [...] the reservations and declarations that have been made by China' so as 'to prevent confusion in application of the CISG between Mainland China and Hong Kong'.[32]

**Issue 3 The Use of the CISG as a Supplementary Source of Law**

As noted with respect to Issue 1, the CISG was not directly invoked or applied in this case. Instead, CISG art 77 (the treaty's mitigation of damages rule) was referred to by X alongside Chinese Contract Law art 119 and Chinese General Principles of Civil Law art 114, in an effort to explain why Tong's damages claim was unsustainable. In this context, it appears that the CISG was referred to merely as a supplementary source of law.

It is not preferred, as has happened in some Australian cases,[33] for parties to argue indiscriminately on the basis of both the CISG and non-harmonized local law, where it must actually be the case that either one or the other (but not both) apply. Still, it is not objectionable to refer to the CISG as a supplementary source of law intended to assist local courts in understanding and applying local non-harmonized law. This is the context in which the CISG appears to have been invoked before the Jiangmen IPC. Such use of the CISG in other jurisdictions has not been controversial.[34] Indeed, the CISG has actually inspired domestic contract law reform in many jurisdictions,[35] and was also identified from the time of its initial entry into force as potentially supplying 'a subsidiary solution for cases in which the applicable foreign law cannot be ascertained'.[36]

Seeking assistance from the CISG's mitigation of damages provision when applying non-harmonized law also addressing mitigation might be legitimate for an additional reason in China: the CISG inspired the 1999 iteration of the Chinese Contract Law,[37] which was in force at the time of this dispute. Just as the UNIDROIT

---

30 Jayme [2], pp. 31–32.

31 Schwenzer and Schroeter [1], p. 29.

32 Department of Justice of Hong Kong [18], p. 79.

33 *NT Beverages Group Pty Ltd. v PT Bromo Tirta Lestari* [2017] FCA 775, [38]; *Playcorp Pty Ltd. v Taiyo Kogyo Ltd.* [2003] VSC 108, [199].

34 *Yoshimoto v Canterbury Golf International Ltd.* [2001] 1 NZLR 523, 547–548 [88]–[90]; *Renard Constructions (ME) Pty Ltd. v Minister for Public Works* (1992) 26 NSWLR 234, 264.

35 Andersen [22], pp. 147–149.

36 Jayme [2], p. 33.

37 Andersen [22], p. 148.

Principles of International Commercial Contracts might be referred to as a persuasive source in understanding the CISG,[38] the CISG might in turn be a useful persuasive source in understanding how certain provisions of the Chinese Contract Law are intended to apply.

As the original judgment text confirms, both the Kaiping People's Court and the Jiangmen IPC resolved this dispute by applying burden of proof rules, and other civil procedure rules, rather than substantive contract law. Chinese courts have also taken this kind of evidentiary approach in other CISG-related cases.[39] It is thus not evident that the Jiangmen IPC actually needed to consider X's arguments that were based upon CISG art 77, in any detail. In principle, however, the Jiangmen IPC might have done so had the need actually arisen.

**Issue 4 Damages Under the CISG**

Finally, it can be noted that CISG art 77 sits amongst the convention's provisions addressing damages: contained across CISG arts 74–77. CISG art 77 itself is a qualification placed upon the treaty's other damages rules: where a party relying on a breach of contract fails to take 'such measures as are reasonable in the circumstances to mitigate [their] loss', the party in breach 'may claim a reduction in the damages in the amount by which the loss should have been mitigated'. Whilst authorities often speak of a 'duty to mitigate',[40] CISG art 77 does not impose a duty in the sense of a legal obligation the breach of which triggers a right to compensation.[41] Instead, Art 77 provides a means by which recoverable damages can be reduced. In this sense, its function in limiting recovery is similar to the foreseeability limitations contained in CISG art 74, being the treaty's primary damages rule.[42] This explains why X sought to invoke the principles reflected in CISG art 77 in particular in this case. Since the goods had passed their relevant certifications, X argued that responsibility for the losses must lie with Y, reflecting a failure to mitigate that would have rendered those losses irrecoverable.

Again, as noted with respect to Issue 1, CISG art 77 was not directly applied in this case. However, if the Jiangmen IPC were to have relied upon the provision as a supplementary source of law, the provision would need to be understood in its proper context.

---

38 Schwenzer and Schroeter [23], pp. 147–148.

39 Kolieb [24], p. 371.

40 Huber and Mullis [25], p. 274.

41 Huber and Mullis [25], p. 289.

42 Knapp [26], pp. 539–543.

## References


1. Schwenzer, I. and Schroeter, U. (2022). Article 1, in Schwenzer, I. & Schroeter, U. (Eds.), *Schlechtriem & Schwenzer: Commentary on the UN Convention on the International Sale of Goods* (5th edition, pp.26–46). Oxford University Press
2. Jayme, E. (1987). Article 1, in Bianca, C. M. & Bonell, M. J. (Eds.), *Commentary on the International Sales Law* (pp.27-33). Giuffrè
3. Wang, G., Zhang, S. & Guo, P. (2022). Skandinaviska Metemo AB v Hunan Co. for International Economy and Trade, in Guo, P., Zuo, H. & Zhang, S. (Eds.), *Selected Chinese Cases on the UN Sales Convention (CISG) Vol 1* (pp.27–34). Springer
4. Wang, G., Guo, P. & Zhang, S. (2022). Lianhe Enterprise (US) Ltd. v Yantai Branch of Shandong Foreign Trade Co, in Guo, P., Zuo H. & Zhang, S. (Eds.), *Selected Chinese Cases on the UN Sales Convention (CISG) Vol 1* (pp.87–94). Springer
5. An, W. (2022). Japanese Xinsheng Trade Company v Ningxia Hui Autonomous Region Nihong Metallurgic Product Company, in Guo, P., Zuo, H. & Zhang, S. (Eds.), *Selected Chinese Cases on the UN Sales Convention (CISG) Vol 1* (pp.171-181). Springer
6. Li, L. (2022). Resource Engineering Co., Ltd. v Qing Li, Ming Sun and Shanghai Donglin International Trade Co., Ltd., in Guo, P., Zuo, H. & Zhang, S. (Eds.), *Selected Chinese Cases on the UN Sales Convention (CISG) Vol 1* (pp.207–210). Springer
7. Shang, Y. (2022). Wang Ruixiang Fashion Co., Ltd. v Trend Co., Ltd. and Shanghai Silk (Group) Co., Ltd., in Guo, P., Zuo, H. & Zhang, S. (Eds), *Selected Chinese Cases on the UN Sales Convention (CISG) Vol 1* (pp.235–238). Springer
8. Wang, S. (2022). Sinochem Shanghai Co., v Kolorit TM Co., Ltd., in Guo, P., Zuo, H. & Zhang, S. (Eds.), *Selected Chinese Cases on the UN Sales Convention (CISG) Vol 1* (pp.263–268). Springer
9. Zhang, C., Zhang, S. & Guo, P. (2022). China Changzhou Kairui Weaving and Printing Company v Taiwan Junlong Machinery Company, in Guo, P., Zuo, H. & Zhang, S. (Eds.), *Selected Chinese Cases on the UN Sales Convention (CISG) Vol 1* (pp.319-330). Springer
10. Li, L. (2022). Qingdao Benefim Trading Co., Ltd. v Sinochem International FZE, in Guo, P., Zuo, H. & Zhang, S. (Eds), *Selected Chinese Cases on the UN Sales Convention (CISG) Vol 1* (pp.331–333). Springer
11. Knapp, V. (1987). Article 77, in Bianca, C. M. & Bonell, M. J. (Eds.), *Commentary on the International Sales Law* (pp.559-567). Giuffrè
12. Khoo, W. (1987). Article 4, in Bianca, C. M. & Bonell, M. J. (Eds.), *Commentary on the International Sales Law* (pp.44-48). Giuffrè
13. Schroeter, U. (2004). The Status of Hong Kong and Macao Under the United Nations Convention on Contracts for the International Sale of Goods. *Pace International Law Review*, 16(2), 307-332
14. United Nations Information Service. (2022, 6 May). *China Deposits Declaration of Territorial Application of the United Nations Convention on Contracts for the International Sale of Goods to Hong Kong SAR.* Retrieved November 30, 2022, from https://unis.unvienna.org/unis/en/pressrels/2022/unisl327.html
15. Köhler, B. (2021). For an Independent Development of the CISG Beyond Article 7(2): A Stocktake and a Proposal, in Meškić, Z. et al (Eds.), *Balkan Yearbook of European and International Law 2020* (pp.3-39). Springer
16. Department of Justice of Hong Kong. (2013, 7 January: signed; 2013, 16 December: entered into force). *Arrangement Concerning Mutual Enforcement of Arbitral Awards Between the Mainland and the Hong Kong Special Administrative Region.* Retrieved November 30, 2022, from https://www.doj.gov.hk/en/legal_dispute/pdf/mainlandmutual2e.pdf.
17. Department of Justice of Hong Kong. (1999, 12 June: signed; 2000, 1 February: entered into force). *Arrangement Concerning Reciprocal Recognition and Enforcement of Arbitral Awards Between the Hong Kong Special Administrative Region and the Macao Special Administrative Region.* Retrieved November 30, 2022, from https://www.doj.gov.hk/en/mainland_and_macao/pdf/macaoe.pdf.

18. Department of Justice of Hong Kong. (2020). *Consultation Paper on the Proposed Application of the United Nations Convention on Contracts for the International Sale of Goods to the Hong Kong Special Administrative Region.* Retrieved November 30, 2022, from https://www.doj.gov.hk/en/featured/pdf/CISG_Consultation_Paper_PDF.pdf.
19. Juenger, F. K. (1989). Forum Shopping, Domestic and International. *Tulane Law Review*, 63(3), 553-574
20. Department of Justice of Hong Kong. (2021, March). *Legislative Council Panel on Administration of Justice and Legal Services: Proposed Application of the United Nations Convention on Contracts for the International Sale of Goods to the Hong Kong Special Administrative Region, Paper CB (4)648/20–21(03).* Retrieved November 30, 2022, from https://www.legco.gov.hk/yr20-21/english/panels/ajls/papers/ajls20210322cb4-648-3-e.pdf.
21. Hayward, B. (2017). *Conflict of Laws and Arbitral Discretion: The Closest Connection Test.* Oxford University Press
22. Andersen, C. B. (2012). Breaking the Mould of Scope: Unusual Usage of the CISG. *Vindobona Journal of International Commercial Law and Arbitration*, 16(2), 145-162
23. Schwenzer, I. & Schroeter, U. (2022). Article 7, in Schwenzer, I. & Schroeter, U. (Eds.), *Schlechtriem & Schwenzer: Commentary on the UN Convention on the International Sale of Goods* (5th edition, pp.135–158). Oxford University Press
24. Kolieb, J. (2022). Skalli Corporation v Shanghai Tongya Liquor Co., Ltd. – Dispute Arising from a Sale of Goods Contract, in Guo, P., Zuo, H. & Zhang, S. (Eds.), *Selected Chinese Cases on the UN Sales Convention (CISG) Vol 1* (pp.369–376). Springer.
25. Huber, P. and Mullis, A. (2007). *The CISG: A New Textbook for Students and Practitioners.* Sellier European Law Publishers
26. Knapp, V. (1987). Article 74, in Bianca, C. M. & Bonell, M. J. (Eds.), *Commentary on the International Sales Law* (pp.538-548). Giuffrè

**Dr. Benjamin Hayward** is an Associate Professor in the Department of Business Law and Taxation at the Monash Business School, Monash University. His research expertise spans international sales law, international commercial arbitration law, and private international law, as well as Australian contract, commercial, and consumer law topics. Dr Hayward's PhD thesis addressed arbitrators' identification of the governing substantive law (including the CISG) in international commercial arbitration, and was published in 2017 by Oxford University Press as Conflict of Laws and Arbitral Discretion: The Closest Connection Test. Dr Hayward has otherwise published widely in Australian and international law journals, regularly presents his research to local and international audiences, and communicates his research to wider professional and public audiences via blogs, interviews, and podcasts.

# Knoles & Carter La Piel, Inc. v. Richina Leather Industrial Co., Ltd.

**Shao Long and Sichen Lu**

**Case Information**

**Case Name:** *Knoles & Carter La Piel, Inc. v. Richina Leather Industrial Co., Ltd.*

**Seller:** Richina Leather Industrial Co., Ltd.
**Place of Business**: China

**Buyer:** Knoles & Carter La Piel, Inc.
**Place of Business**: USA

**Details of First Instance:**
**Court:** First Intermediate People's Court of Tianjin Municipality
**Date of Decision:** N/A
**Case No.:** (2010) Yi Zhong Min Wu Chu Zi No.42
**Judges:** N/A

**Details of Second Instance:**
**Court:** Tianjin High People's Court
**Date of Decision:** 18 June 2012
**Case No.:** (2012) Jin Gao Min Si Zhong Zi No.128
**Judges:** Geng Xiaoning (Presiding Judge), Li Tong (Assistant Judge), Tang Na (Assistant Judge)

**CISG Applied:** Yes
**Key CISG Provisions Interpreted and Applied:** Articles 1, 6, 9, 30, 53

S. Long (✉) · S. Lu
University Hunan University, Changsha, Hunan, China
e-mail: longshao@hnu.edu.cn

 
P. Guo et al. (eds.), *Selected Chinese Cases on the UN Sales Convention (CISG) Vol. 3*, Selected Chinese Cases on the CISG,
https://doi.org/10.1007/978-981-99-6851-0_26

## Case Abstract

Knoles & Carter La Piel, Inc. ('Piel'), a US company, entered into three contracts with Richina Leather Industrial Co., Ltd. ('Richina'), a Chinese company, to buy batches of lambskin. The contracts were concluded on 27 February and 6 March 2009, with a total price of USD $636,734.66, employing a trade term of CNF Tianjin. Piel agreed to prepay 30% of the total price before Richina dispatched the goods, and pay the remainder in 45 days after Richina issued the invoices. The goods would be delivered to Tianjin, 28 days after which Richina would accept no return of goods or damages claims.

On 19 March 19, Richina received USD $47,020.40 as the 30% advance payment for part of the goods. The seller issued four invoices on 23 and 24 March 2009, and delivered 266 cases of goods (with a combined worth of USD $156,734.66) to Tianjin FNB Leather Apparel Co., Ltd. ('FNB') according to Piel's demand. Since the USD $109,714.26 balance had so far not been paid by Piel, Richina did not dispatch any further goods. The court of first instance additionally found that, in the other two contracts fulfilled by Richina and Piel, both consignees were FNB, and Richina had invoiced FNB.

Richina brought this case before the court of first instance with the request to compel Piel to immediately pay the balance of USD $109,714.26 and overdue interest calculated from 6 June 2009 till the effective date of the judgment, and bear the $95 service fee. The court of first instance reasoned that since the place of signing and performing the contract was China, Chinese law should be applied as the law of the closest connection. The contract signed by the parties represented their true intention, and the content did not violate any law or regulation, and therefore should be deemed valid. Because Piel did not pay the price as agreed in the contract, constituting a breach of contract, it should pay the balance and overdue interest calculated from 6 June 2009 to the effective date of the judgment according to the Chinese People's Bank's USD deposit rate for the same period. Piel argued that since Richina invoiced FNB, it could not pay the balance in the absence of the invoices. The court of first instance reasoned that invoicing to FNB was a business practice between the parties, in light of the fact that in the other two performed and undisputed contracts, the consignee and invoice/receiver was also FNB, and the place of delivery was Tianjin. Piel's claim was therefore unfounded and not supported. Piel's other claim, which concerned the inconformity of the goods and the parties' agreement on the return of them, was also dismissed by the court. Three emails provided by Piel to prove its claim were evidence generated abroad and were neither notarized nor authenticated, so the Court rendered them inadmissible. The court of first instance thus ruled in favour of Richina based on Chinese Contract Law.

Piel appealed, requesting the court of appeal to revoke the judgment of the court of first instance, dismiss Richina's claims, and make Richina undertake all the litigation costs. It pointed out that the court of first instance was wrong to apply Chinese law and its understanding of the facts was not precise. The court of appeal confirmed the facts found in the previous instance but held that the CISG should be applied. The parties' places of business were the United States and China respectively, both of which are

Contracting States to the CISG, and they did not agree to exclude the Convention. Therefore, the CISG should be applied. According to arts 61(1)(a) and 62 of the CISG, Richina's request for arrears should be supported. Its claim for overdue interest was reasonable under art 78. The court of appeal ruled that Piel should pay the balance to Richina in light of the business practice between them. Richina had dispatched the goods to FNB, a company which process materials provided by Piel in Tianjin, as agreed. It had invoiced FNB since it is the receiver of the goods specified in the customs declaration form for imported goods. This is the usual pattern of processing trade between the parties. In the two undisputed and performed contracts, the same route was followed and Piel made payments after receipt of the invoices. The court of appeal additionally confirmed the rejection of the three emails by the court of first instance. They were neither notarized nor authenticated. Moreover, Piel did not return the goods. In general, though a different governing law was applied, the final judgment of the first trial was upheld.

## Commentary to the Key Issues Related to the CISG

### Issues

Issue 1 The Applicability of the CISG

Issue 2 The Application of Business Practices under the CISG

Issue 3 The Plaintiff's Claim for the Price and the Calculation of Interest

### Comments

### Issue 1 the Applicability of the CISG

### I. Convention Prevails Over Recourse to Private International Law

Traditionally, when a situation is international, courts resort to private international law rules in force in their country to determine which substantive rules to apply. However, when there are international uniform substantive rules in force, such as those set forth by the Convention, courts must determine whether those international uniform substantive rules apply before resorting to private international law rules at all. Regarding the CISG, it is *lex specialis* against the general domestic rules on conflict of laws.[1] This can also be justified since the Convention, as a set of uniform substantive law rules, is more specific because its sphere of application is more limited and leads directly to a substantive solution, whereas adopting private international law requires a two-step approach— that is, the identification of the applicable law and the application thereof.[2] As the Convention becomes part of the domestic law of a country, once that country has become a Contracting State to the CISG, judges must

[1] CLOUT case No. 1908, INTRAVAL S.L. v. ECOM Industries GmbH, Supreme Court (Civil Division), Spain, 06/07/2020; CLOUT case No. 867, Mitias v. Solidea S.r.L, Tribunale di Forlì, Italy, 9/12/2008; UNCITRAL [1], p.4.

[2] CLOUT case No. 608, Al Palazzo S.r.1.v. Bernardaud s.a., Tribunale di Rimini, Italy, 26/11/2002.

examine whether the CISG is applicable to any given issue.[3] If the requirements for its application are met, the CISG applies. That is to say, art 1(1)(a) sets 'autonomous' requirements for the application of the Convention.[4]

Following this reasoning, and since China is a Contracting State to the CISG, the courts hearing this case should firstly determine the Convention's applicability. Therefore, the court of appeal was correct to start with determining the applicability of the Convention in this case, while the court of first instance mistakenly resorted to private international rules.

### II. The Autonomous Application of the CISG

Pursuant to art 1(1)(a), the CISG is a self-executing treaty, which means that it governs its own sphere of application.[5] To be more specific, if the parties conclude a contract of sale, and the parties' places of business are in different Contracting States, then the CISG should be automatically applied, unless the parties have designated a given law with the intention to exclude the Convention (art 6).[6] In the case at hand, the parties made no indication regarding the applicable law of the contracts, and their places of business are in different Contracting States. The parties' places of business are China and US respectively, which are both CISG Contracting States, the criterion of internationality is met.

The substantive requirements for the application of the Convention were met (arts 2 and 3). Firstly, the goods involved in the case was lambskin, which does not belong to the exceptions enumerated in art 2. Moreover, art 3 specifies mixed contracts which involve the buyer's obligation to supply materials for the production or manufacture of the goods concerned. Since the disputed contracts involved no service provided by the parties, they are not 'mixed contracts'[7] in the sense of art 3.

Therefore, the court of appeal was justified in applying the CISG directly, which also corrected the mistake made by the court of first instance.

## Issue 2 the Application of Business Practices Under the CISG

Article 9 of the CISG differentiates between usages to which the parties have agreed or practices which they have established between themselves on the one hand (art 9(1)), and, on the other hand, usages which apply by virtue of their prevalence and their recognition, regardless of whether the parties have agreed on them or

[3] CLOUT case No. 999, Construction Acton Vale Lteé v. KVM Industrimaskiner A/S, Ad hoc Arbitral Tribunal, Denmark, 10/11/2000; CLOUT case No. 1105, CIETAC, China, 06/11/2000; Hachem [2], p. 32.

[4] CLOUT case No. 1765, Oy Pokostore Systems Ltd. v. TP-Konepajat Polska Sp.z o.o, Turun hovioikeus, Finland, 18/12/2013; CLOUT case No. 650, Kling & Freitag Gmbh s.r.l. vs Società Reference Laboratory s.r.l., Corte Suprema di Cassazione, Sezioni Unite, Italy, 20/09/2004; Schwenzer and Hachem [3] p. 38; Spagnolo [4], p. 10.

[5] Hachem [2], p. 32.

[6] CLOUT case No. 1149, Višje sodišče v Celju, Slovenia, 08/06/2011; CLOUT case No. 1187, Mazzetta Company, llc. V. Dégust-Mer Inc., Quebec Court of Appeal, Canada, 12/04/2011; UNCITRAL [1], p. 5; Ferrari [5], p. 60.

[7] CISG Advisory Council [6].

not (art 9(2)).[8] In these terminologies are significant yet subtle differences. It is commonly acknowledged that, in international sales, a 'practice' is unique to the relationship between two particular parties, which is a subjective notion, while a 'usage' is generally accepted by all actors within the particular trade or industry.[9] In the case at hand, the court of appeal held that there was a practice between the parties. However, the CISG does not define the length or intensity that a particular behavior must satisfy in order to fall within the definition of a 'practice established between the parties', nor did the court of appeal in this case make any indication thereof.

## I. The Existence of a Binding Practice

'[The] consideration of usages and practices under paragraph 1 occurs on the basis of the intent of the parties, determined under Article 8'.[10] Although whether the parties have established a practice between themselves must be determined on a case-by-case basis,[11] some general guidelines are common among legal systems both at the domestic as well as at the international level. A practice can be established by reference to the frequency with which it is adopted, the duration over which it occurs and the accuracy with which the parties adhere to the same conduct.[12] Generally, a uniform notion of practices will emerge progressively from the international application of the CISG,[13] but there are currently more controversies than consensus in relevant court rulings and arbitral awards.

Various courts and tribunals had expressed their view regarding the criterion of 'practice' under art 9 of the CISG. Some courts attach great importance to the number of times a particular behavior has been practiced by the parties. A Spanish court confirmed the existence of a practice between the parties by observing '[the] numerous, repeated e-mails exchanged between the parties and the attitude of the parties to those e-mails'.[14] An Austrian court rendered a practice existed because '[the] forms had been used several times before' between the parties, and under art 9, '[such] practices could be behavior patterns frequently upheld during a certain period and in a way that parties in good faith can rely on the fact that the practices will be followed in future occasions again'.[15] A French court considered a practice existed because the 'same procedure … had been followed before' by the parties.[16]

---

[8] Schwenzer and Fountoulakis [7], p. 93.

[9] Schwenzer et al. [8], §27.02–27.03.

[10] Schmidt-Kessel [9], p. 181.

[11] Graffi [10].

[12] Ferrari [11], p.196.

[13] Pamboukis [12].

[14] CLOUT case No. 1495, Productos Solubles, S.A. v. Krüger GMBH & Co.,K.G, Palencia Provincial High Court, Spain, 09/09/2014.

[15] CLOUT case No. 750, Oberster Gerichtshof, Austria, 31/08/2005.

[16] CLOUT case No. 490, Société H GmbH & Co., v. SARL M, Cour d'appel de Paris, France, 10/09/2003.

However, judges and arbitrators tend to differ from each other on the exact number of repetitions required for a practice to form. For instance, a Hungarian court believed that a sales contract that had previously been concluded between the parties could be used as a practice between the parties to the price of the goods and the other elements of the disputed contract.[17] A German court ruled to the contrary.[18] Further, a Swiss court ruled that since the buyer had on two occasions cancelled or modified orders without the seller objecting to such behavior, there was a valid practice established between the parties under art 9(1) of the CISG.[19] However, other courts have ruled that two previous repetitions in a long business relationship could not amount to established practices, and behaviors of a certain duration and frequency relating to the length of the business transaction involved is required.[20]

Other courts emphasize the duration of a particular behavior has lasted between the parties. A Swiss court, although without clear reasoning, considered a practice existed due to '[a] business relationship of several years' standing' between the parties,[21] while a court in the Netherlands found that the parties had established a practice in their '[long-standing] business relationship for over 30 years'.[22] A French court considered 'a number of months' as the basis of 'long-standing practices'.[23] An Austrian court took the seller's '[length], intensity and economic importance of the business relationship with the buyer' into consideration when ascertaining the existence of a practice.[24] On the contrary, a court in the Netherlands held that '[even] if the one between parties was a long-term business relationship, it was neither certain nor proven that the retention of title amounted to a usage or practice between them'.[25]

By all accounts, we may safely conclude from the above-mentioned case law that, for an alleged practice to be established, the parties' relationship must have lasted for some time and must have led to the conclusion of various contracts.[26] Consequently, one or two previously concluded contracts among many other contracts between the parties will typically not be sufficient to establish a practice. As presented in CLOUT case No. 360,[27] what determines the existence of a practice is not the number of times that the behavior has been performed, but the ratio of such repetitions among all their transactions. In this case, both courts ruled that there was a practice established

[17] CISG-online No. 61, Adamfi Video Production GmbH v. Alkotók Studiósa Kisszövetkezet, Fővárosi Bíróság, Hungary, 24/03/1992.

[18] CISG-online 519, Landgericht Zwickau, Germany, case no. 3 HK O 67/98, 19/03/1999.

[19] CISG-online 329, Handelsgericht Aargau, Switzerland, 26/09/1997.

[20] CLOUT case No. 360, Amtsgericht Duisburg, Germany, 13/04/2000; CISG-online 346, Zivilgericht Kanton Basel-Stadt, Switzerland, 03/12/1997.

[21] CLOUT case No. 889, Handelsgericht des Kantons Zürich, Switzerland, 24/10/2003.

[22] V. Geitonas and Co., Ltd. v. Palinghandel BV, Rechtbank, Noord-Nederland, Netherlands, 05/01/2022.

[23] CLOUT case No. 202, Société française de Factoring international Factor France v. Roger Caiato, Court of Appeal of Grenoble, France, 13/07/1995.

[24] CISG-online 1093, Oberster Gerichtshof, Austria, 31/08/2005.

[25] CISG-online 1550, Gerechtshof's Hertogenbosch, Netherlands, 29/05/2007.

[26] Ferrari [13].

[27] CLOUT case No. 360, Amtsgericht Duisburg, Germany, 13/04/2000.

by the parties on the basis of two other performed undisputed contracts and the similar wording in the disputed contracts. Such reasoning was legitimate, since the consignee and place of delivery remained the same throughout all the transactions. Therefore, it was reasonable for the seller to believe that it should also invoice to the same company. Moreover, the fact that parties are bound by those practices that have originated between them in the course of extended business relations is in keeping with the general principles of good faith underlying the CISG, as well as the prohibition of *venire contra factum proprium.*[28] The seller in the current case was justified to assume in good faith that the practice will be observed again in a similar instance, without being otherwise indicated by the buyer.

In most cases, the party claiming a practice bears the burden of proving its prerequisites.[29] They should submit sufficient evidence with regard to the terms of the other transactions successfully concluded with the other party.[30] This is because, according to the prevailing view, the party benefiting from a provision must prove the prerequisites set out by that provision.[31] The seller in the current dispute provided sufficient evidence in this regard.

## II. The Binding Effect of Established Practices

Established practices between the parties includes the quality, quantity and price of the goods,[32] delivery of spare parts,[33] the tolerances of unilaterally cancelling or changing orders,[34] inclusion of standard terms,[35] and take back defective goods amongst others.[36] The value of the practices and usages is normative as they are considered to be sources of the contract by express or implied agreement.[37] Therefore, it is generally agreed that there is a hierarchy of rules. Above all, the agreement of the parties (arts 6 and 9(1)) have priority over the provisions of the CISG.[38] Next in the hierarchy, importance is placed on the usages of trade (art 9(2)), and at the

---

[28] Bridge [14], §10.62.

[29] Schmidt-Kessel [9], p.186.

[30] CISG-online 1782, Hannaford v. Australian Farmlink Pty Ltd., Federal Court of Australia, Australia, 24/10/2008; CISG-online 440, Calzaturificio Claudia s.n.c. v. Olivieri Footwear Ltd., U.S. District Court, S.D., New York, USA, case no. 96 Civ. 8052 (HB)(THK), 06/04/1998.

[31] Ferrari [11], p. 205.

[32] CISG-online 236, ICC Court of Arbitration, Paris, 23/01/1997.

[33] CISG-online 61, Adamfi Video Production GmbH v. Alkotók Studiósa Kisszövetkezet, Fővárosi Bíróság, Hungary, 24/03/1992.

[34] CISG-online 329, Handelsgericht Aargau, Switzerland, 26/09/1997.

[35] CISG-online 660, Court of Appeal of Turku, Finland, 12/04/2022.

[36] CLOUT case No. 889, Handelsgericht des Kantons Zürich, Switzerland, 24/10/2003.

[37] Viscasillas [15], p. 163.

[38] CLOUT case No. 313, Société Calzados Magnanni v. SARL Shoes General International (SGI), Court of Appeal of Grenoble, France, 21/10/1999. A highly criticized ruling is CLOUT case No. 644, in which the court stated that "[The] practice may simply be the consequence of a mere tolerance by the seller and, as such, unable to establish a place of performance different from the legal one".

lowest level, the rules of the Convention.[39] Consequently, the courts were correct to recognize the established practice between the parties, and such practice has a priority over rules of the Convention.

**Issue 3 the Plaintiff's Claim for the Price and the Calculation of Interest**

As analyzed above, since Richina had delivered the goods and invoiced FNB according to the practice between the parties, it had fulfilled its obligations under the contracts under art 30 of the CISG. Therefore, Piel should pay the price as agreed in the contracts under art 53 of the CISG. According to art 62, the seller may require the buyer to pay the purchase price, take delivery or perform its other obligations. Thus, the court was correct to order Piel to pay the price. According to art 78, the seller has the right to claim interest based upon the arrears, but the article is silent on the issue of interest rate and the time when interests accrue.[40] As provided in art 9 of CISG-AC Opinion No. 14, the domestic law of the creditor's place of business should be applied to decide the interest rate. Therefore, the court of appeal was correct to uphold the decision, in which the court of first instance applied Chinese law, domestic law of the creditor's place of business, to determine the interest in this case. Additionally, the CISG Advisory Council deems that interest begins to accrue as soon as the payment is in arrears, such as when the payment of the purchase price ought to have been made.[41] Since the parties had agreed that Piel should pay the price in 45 days upon receipt of the invoice, interest should be calculated from that date. Therefore, the results of the decision of the first instance were correct, though it applied the law inaccurately.

## References

1. United Nations Commission on International Trade Law (UNCITRAL) (2016). *UNCITRAL digest of case law on the United Nations convention on contracts for the international sale of goods*. https://uncitral.un.org/en/case_law/digests.
2. Hachem, P. (2014). Applicability of the CISG – Articles 1 and 6, in Schwenzer, I., Atamer, Y. M. & Butler P. (Eds.), *Current Issues in the CISG and Arbitration* (p. 32). Eleven International Publishing.
3. Schwenzer, I. & Hachem, P. (2016). Ch.I Sphere of Application, Article 1, in Schwenzer, I. (Ed.), *Schlechtriem & Schwenzer: Commentary on the UN Convention on the International Sale of Goods* (4th Edition, p. 38). Oxford University Press.
4. Spagnolo, L. (2014). CISG Exclusion and Legal Efficiency (1st ed.). Kluwer Law International.
5. Ferrari, F. (2012). *Contracts for the International Sale of Goods: Applicability and Applications of the 1980 United Nations Sales Convention*. Koninklijke Brill NV.
6. CISG Advisory Council. (24 October 2004). *Opinion No. 4, Contracts for the Sale of Goods to Be Manufactured or Produced and Mixed Contracts (Article 3 CISG)*. CISGAC. Retrieved June 20, 2023, from https://cisgac.com/opinions/cisgac-opinion-no1-copy-copy/.
7. Schwenzer, I. & Fountoulakis, C. (2007). *International Sales Law*. Routledge-Cavendish.

[39] CLOUT case No. 425, Oberster Gerichtshof, Austria, 21/03/2000.

[40] Eiselen [16], p. 231.

[41] CISG Advisory Council [17], article 3(a).

8. Schwenzer, I., Hachem, P. & Kee, C. (2012). *Global Sales and Contract Law*. Oxford University Press.
9. Schmidt-Kessel, M. (2016). Part I Sphere of Application and General Provisions, Ch.II General Provisions, Article 9, in Schwenzer, I. (Ed.), *Schlechtriem & Schwenzer: Commentary on the UN Convention on the International Sale of Goods* (4th Ed. p. 181). Oxford University Press.
10. Graffi, L. (2011). Remarks on Trade Usages and Business Practices in International Sales Law. *Journal of Law and Commerce*, 29, 273–295.
11. Ferrari, F. (2004). Trade usage and practices established between the parties: Article 9, in Ferrari, F., Flechtner, H. & Brand, A. R. (Eds.), *The Draft UNCITRAL Digest and Beyond: Cases, Analysis and Unresolved Issues in the U.N. Sales Convention* (1st ed., p. 196). Sellier. European Law Publishers.
12. Pamboukis, C. (2005–06). The Concept and Function of Usages in the United Nations Convention on International Sale of Goods. *Journal of Law and Commerce*, 27, 107–131.
13. Ferrari, F. (2003). Trade usage and practices established between the parties under the CISG. *International Business Law Journal*, 2003(5), 571–580.
14. Bridge, M. (2017). *The International Sale of Goods* (4th ed.). Oxford University Press.
15. Viscasillas, P. (2018). Article 9, in Kröll, S., Mistelis, L. & Viscasillas, P. (Eds.), *UN Convention on Contracts for the International Sale of Goods (CISG): A Commentary* (2nd ed). Verlag C. H. Beck oHG.
16. Eiselen, S. (2007). Interest on sums in arrears: Remarks on the manner in which the UNIDROIT Principles of International Commercial Contracts may be used to interpret or supplement Article 78 of the CISG, in Felemegas, J. (ed.), *An International Approach to the Interpretation of the United Nations Convention on Contracts for the International Sale of Goods (1980) as Uniform Sales Law* (1st ed.). Cambridge University Press.
17. CISG Advisory Council. (21 and 22 October 2013). *Opinion No. 14, Interest under Article78 CISG*. CISGAC. Retrieved June 20, 2023, from https://cisgac.com/opinions/cisgac-opinion-no1-copy-copy-4-copy-copy-copy-5/.

**Dr. Shao Long** is an Assistant Professor in Law at Hunan University. She holds a doctoral degree in law, specialising in the field of international law, from Vienna University. Dr. Long's research interests lie in international trade law, WTO law, and international commercial arbitration. She teaches International Economic Law to LLB students and acts as the coach of HNU CIETAC Cup (pre-vis) moot team.

**Lu Sichen** LLB (Hunan University). The author majors in private international law; participated in the 19th annual CIETAC Cup International Commercial Arbitration Moot and helped the team to win the Best Memo Award.

# Castronics Precision Metals (Tianjin) Co., Ltd. v. Boram Hi-Tek Co.,

**Hongzhi Hu**

## Case Information

**Case Name:** *Castronics Precision Metals (Tianjin) Co., Ltd. v Boram Hi-Tek Co.,*

**Seller:** Boram Hi-Tek Co.,
**Place of Business**: South Korea

**Buyer:** Castronics Precision Metals (Tianjin) Co., Ltd.
**Place of Business:** China

**Details of First Instance:**
**Court:** Tianjin First Intermediate People's Court
**Case No:** (2012) Yi Zhong Min Wu Chu Zi No 39 Civil Judgment

**Details of Second Instance:**
**Court:** Tianjin High People's Court
**Date of Decision:** 9 October 2012
**Case No:** (2012) Jin Gao Min Si Zhong Zi No 149 Civil Judgment
**Judges:** Zhai Hong (Presiding Judge), Zhao Qingquan (Judge), Li Tong (Acting Judge)

**CISG Applied:** Yes
**Key the CISG Provisions Interpreted and Applied:** Arts 1(1)(a), 4, 6, 53, 59, 61, 62

H. Hu (✉)
Nankai University, Tianjin, China
e-mail: hongzhihu@126.com



P. Guo et al. (eds.), *Selected Chinese Cases on the UN Sales Convention (CISG) Vol. 3*, Selected Chinese Cases on the CISG,
https://doi.org/10.1007/978-981-99-6851-0_27

### Case Abstract

The seller, Boram Hi-Tek Co, with its place of business in South Korea, agreed to sell a batch of mold to the buyer, Castronics Precision Metals (Tianjin) Co., Ltd. ('Castronics Company'), with its place of business in Tianjin, China. A dispute arose when the seller stated the buyer did not pay the price as required by the contract. However, the buyer alleged that the 'Supply Contract' concluded by Boram Hi-Tek Co., and Castronics Company was not valid. This is because when the contract was concluded, Kim Kwang-seok, the legal representative of Boram Hi-Tek Co, also served as the vice chairman of Castronics Company. Jin Guangshi, the CEO of Boram Hi-Tek Co, violated his duty of loyalty to Castronics Company, and the concluding of the 'Supply Contract' in this case was an act of 'self-dealing'. As to the applicable law, in the first instance, Tianjin First Intermediate People's Court held that the parties did not agree on the law applicable to the settlement of contractual disputes in the sales contract. According to the principle of closest connection, the law of the People's Republic of China is applicable to this case. In the second instance case, the Tianjin High People's Court held that the case was a dispute over an international sale of goods contract. The business places of the buyer and the seller are located in South Korea and the People's Republic of China. Both countries are Contracting Parties to the CISG, and the parties had not agreed to exclude the Convention in the contract. Therefore, this case should apply the CISG.

With respect to the buyer's contractual obligations, the Court stated that the contract was legal and valid and legally binding on the parties. Thus, the parties should perform their obligations in accordance with the agreement. The seller delivered the goods and handed over documents within the time limit agreed in the contract and performed its contractual obligations. After the buyer had taken delivery of all the goods, they should pay the agreed amount. The failure to pay constituted a breach of contract, and the buyer should bear breach of contract liability. The buyer must continue with performance. Thus, the Court rejected the buyer's argument.

### Commentary to the Key Issues Related to the CISG

### Issues

Issue 1 CISG Pre-empts the Application of Conflict of Laws

Issue 2 Direct Application of the Convention

Issue 3 Chinese Law as Supplementary Law

Issue 4 The Validity of the Contract

Issue 5 Determination of the Buyer's Breach of Contract

### Comments

### Issue 1 CISG Pre-empts the Application of Conflict of Laws

Traditionally, international civil and commercial activities have been mainly governed by the conflict of laws. Although the objects of conflict of laws are foreign-related and cross-border, private international law is mainly domestic law, not international law, because it is mainly formulated by individual countries.[1] The role of private international law is to solve the problem of the application of law, that is, from the laws of several countries related to a legal relationship, determine one of them to apply to the legal relationship. Relying on private international law avoids conflicts of law.[2] Thus, under the conflict of laws paradigm, international civil and commercial legal relations are essentially governed by the domestic laws of different countries. International civil and commercial relations are under the jurisdiction of the domestic laws of sovereign countries, which are flawed and lack the certainty and predictability that the law should have.

However, International Uniform Substantive Law directly governs international civil and commercial behaviour by placing the same legal relationship under a common and unified legal norm. Compared with the conflict of laws, it is more in line with the essential requirements of international civil and commercial relations. This is because a single legal regime will be known and understood by each of the parties and will ensure a minimum of security for the transactions involved.[3]

International uniform substantive rules only partly avoid the uncertainty in applicable law created by conflicts rules. This is because it does not entirely displace them.[4] The CISG is concerned with certain rules only. Within its scope, International Uniform Substantive Law displaces and pre-empts the application of conflict of laws and domestic law.

Therefore, where international uniform substantive rules, such as the CISG, are in force, courts must determine whether those international uniform substantive rules apply before resorting to private international law rules. In other words, international uniform substantive rules prevail over recourse to the forum's private international law rules.[5] However, from a practical point of view, some courts have ignored the pre-emption application of the Convention. The law applicable to the case is determined directly in accordance with the conflict of laws rules.

In the first instance of this case, Tianjin First Intermediate People's Court held that the parties did not agree on the law applicable to the settlement of contractual disputes in the sales contract. According to the principle of closest connection, the law of the People's Republic of China is applicable to this case.[6] The parties failed to realize that the CISG should be applied in this case instead of the law of the People's Republic of China. In the second instance case, the parties also did not object to the erroneous application of the law. Fortunately, such errors in the application of the law can often be corrected on appeal. In the appellate trial, the Tianjin High People's

---

[1] Li [1], p. 3; Wang [2], p. 44.

[2] Li [3], p. 8.

[3] See A/CN.9/L.19 - Progressive codification of the law of international trade: note by the secretariat of the International Institute for the Unification of Private Law (UNIDROIT), Yearbook of the United Nations Commission on International Trade Law, 1970, Volume I, p. 285.

[4] Gillette & Walt [4], p. 25.

[5] UNCITRAL [5], p. 4.

[6] (2012) Yi Zhong Min Wu Chu Zi No 39 Civil Judgment.

Court held that this case was a dispute over an international sale of goods contract. The business places of the buyer and the seller are located in the South Korea and the People's Republic of China. Both countries are Contracting Parties to the CISG, and the parties have not agreed to exclude the Convention in the contract. Therefore, this case should apply the CISG. The Court held that the first instance court erred in the application of the law, and this Court corrected it.[7]

This indicates that some courts do not have an accurate understanding of the relationship between the International Uniform Law Convention and the conflict of laws. For instance, in *Knoles & Carter Lapiel Inc. v Fuguo Leather Industry Co., Ltd.*, Tianjin First Intermediate People's Court also held that this was a dispute over an international sale of goods contract, the place of signing and performance of the contract was within the territory of the People's Republic of China, and the law of the country most closely related to the contract should apply. Therefore, this case should be governed by the laws of the People's Republic of China. Fortunately, in the appellate trial, the Tianjin High People's Court corrected errors in the application of the law.[8]

In *Exportaciones Tierra Del Fuego SPA v Lianyungang Jinchuan Seaweed Co., Ltd.*,[9] Exportaciones Tierra Del Fuego SPA is a corporate entity organized and existing under the laws of Chile. Lianyungang Jinchuan Seaweed Co., Ltd. is a corporate entity organized and existing under the laws of the People's Republic of China. Both the People's Republic of China and the Republic of Chile are Contracting States to the CISG. The parties did not agree on the law applicable to the settlement of contractual disputes in the sales contract. During the trial, the plaintiff (Exportaciones Tierra Del Fuego SPA) agreed that the 'agreement shall be governed by the laws of the People's Republic of China'. The defendant (Lianyungang Jinchuan Seaweed Co., Ltd.) did not appear in court to participate in the proceedings and did not expressly choose the applicable law. Even though the parties agreed that the 'agreement shall be governed by the laws of the People's Republic of China', a reference to a national law does not suffice to exclude the application of the Convention. The CISG shall pre-empt in this case. However, Lianyungang Intermediate People's Court held that in accordance with the provisions of arts 3 and 41 of the Law of the People's Republic of China on the Application of Laws to Foreign-Related Civil Relations, the laws of the People's Republic of China shall apply to this case.

However, in China's judicial practice, most courts have accurately applied the Convention.[10]For instance, in *Jinan Mingquan Pen Industry Co., Ltd. v Senator GmbH &Co., KGaA*,[11] in determining the governing law, Shandong High People's Court held that this case was a foreign-related commercial case and a dispute over an international sale of goods contract. The business places of the buyer and the

[7] (2012) Jin Gao Min Si Zhong Zi No 149 Civil Judgment.

[8] (2012) Jin Gao Min Si Zhong Zi No. 128 Civil Judgment.

[9] (2015) Lian Shang Wai Chu Zi No. 0004 Civil Judgment.

[10] He [6], p. 181; Liu [7], pp. 191–201.

[11] (2014) Lu Min Si Zhong Zi No. 80 Civil Judgment.

seller are located in Germany and the People's Republic of China. Both countries are contracting parties to the CISG. Thus, the CISG shall pre-empt in this case.

**Issue 2 Direct Application of the Convention**

The applicability of the CISG is addressed in Chap. 1 of the CISG. According to art 1(1)(a) and art 6 of the CISG, when parties whose places of business are in different Contracting States, the contract is silent as to the applicable law, or the parties have not designated a given law with the intention to exclude the Convention, the Convention is 'directly' or 'autonomously' applicable. For matters not clearly provided for in the Convention, the relevant provisions of the laws of a Contracting State agreed by the parties shall apply.

In other words, according to the arts 1(1)(a), 2, 3, 4 and 5, when parties whose places of business are in different Contracting States, and all the CISG's requirements of applicability are met, the CISG does not necessarily apply. This is because freedom of contract, as a basic principle in the context of international trade, has been recognized by the drafters of the CISG. According to art 6 of CISG, the parties may exclude the application of the Convention. Thus, subject to the conditions of application of the Convention, the court must look into whether the CISG has been excluded by the parties.[12] If the Convention is not excluded, the Convention will automatically or directly apply. If the Convention has been excluded, the agreement shall be governed by the laws chosen by the parties.

In this case, Boram Hi-Tek Co., is a corporate entity organized and existing under the laws of the South Korea. Castronics Company is a corporate entity organized and existing under the laws of the People's Republic of China. Thus, the dispute is a foreign-related commercial case, and the relevant provisions on foreign-related civil litigation shall apply. The Tianjin High People's Court concluded that the parties had not designated a given law with the intention to exclude the Convention, and the parties' contract was governed by the Convention because the parties had their places of business in two different Contracting States (South Korea and China) pursuant to art 1(1)(a) of the CISG.

From the perspective of judicial practice, the Supreme People's Court held that the Convention has automatic and direct applicability when the conditions for the application of the Convention are met. For instance, in *American United Enterprise Co., Ltd. v Yantai Company, Shandong Foreign Trade Corporation, China,*[13] the Supreme People's Court found that the parties did not agree on the law applicable to the settlement of the contract disputes in this case. Since American United Enterprise Co., is a corporate entity organized and existing under the laws of the United States, and China and the United States are both Contracting States to the CISG, the relevant provisions of the Convention should be applied to this case. In *Thyssen Krupp Metallurgical Products GmbH v. Sinochem International (Overseas) Pte Ltd.*, the Supreme People's Court found that the buyer, a Singaporean corporation, and the seller, a German corporation, are parties whose places of business are in different

---

[12] Ferrari [8], p.15.

[13] (1998) Jing Zhong Zi No. 358 Civil Judgment.

Contracting States. Although the parties agreed that their agreement shall be governed by the laws of the United States, Singapore, Germany and the United States are all Contracting States to the CISG, and the parties did not exclude the application of the Convention. Thus, the CISG should first be applied to the trial of this case.[14]

The Supreme People's Court's Model Cases provide guidance for lower courts to accurately apply the Convention. In China, although the Supreme People's Court's case law is not binding, lower courts follow the Supreme People's Court's case law given the authority of the Supreme People's Court. Even if the first-instance court erred in the application of the law, the second-instance court is often able to correct the error.

**Issue 3 Chinese Law as Supplementary Law**

The Convention is concerned with certain rules only. Within its scope, CISG preempts the application of conflict of laws and domestic law. However, the application of the Convention does not make national law irrelevant. The indication of the law of a Contracting State must be interpreted as both making the CISG applicable (as part of the chosen law) and as determining the law applicable to the issues not governed by the CISG (to the extent to which the parties are allowed to make a choice in respect of those issues), such as issues relating to validity, thus avoiding to have to resort to the complex rules of private international law in order to determine the law applicable to the issues not governed by the CISG.[15] In other words, beyond the scope of the CISG, some issues can be solved by the national law the parties agree to choose.

In this case, Castronics Company claimed that the contract is invalid. Pursuant to art 4 of the CISG, 'this Convention governs only the formation of the contract of sale and the rights and obligations of the seller and the buyer arising from such a contract. In particular, except as otherwise expressly provided in this Convention, it is not concerned with the validity of the contract or of any of its provisions or of any usage.'

In this regard, the parties agree to apply the Company Law of the People's Republic of China to determine the validity of the contract. The validity of the contract is detailed in the following analysis.

**Issue 4 the Validity of the Contract**

In October 2010, the seller, Boram Hi-Tek Co, and the buyer, Castronics Company, concluded a contract for the purchase of mold. Boram performed its obligations of delivery of the goods and handing over of documents, however Castronics Company did not pay the price for the goods. When the contract was concluded, Kim Kwang-seok, the legal representative of Boram Hi-Tek Co, also served as the vice chairman of Castronics Company. Castronics Company claims that Jin Guangshi violated his duty of loyalty to Castronics Company, and the concluding of the 'Supply Contract'

[14] (2013) Min Si Zhong Zi No. 35 Civil Judgment.

[15] Ferrari [8], p. 27.

involved in this case was an act of self-dealing which falls under art 149(1.4) of the Company Law of the People's Republic of China. Thus, the contract is invalid.

According to CISG art 4, the Convention governs only the formation of the contract of sale and the rights and obligations of the seller and the buyer arising from such a contract. In particular, it is not concerned with the validity of the contract. On this issue, Boram Hi-Tek Co., and Castronics Company agreed that their agreement shall be governed by the laws of the People's Republic of China.

Tianjin High People's Court held that according to art 149(1.4) of the Company Law of the People's Republic of China, directors and senior managers shall not violate the provisions of the company's articles of association or enter into contracts with the company without the consent of the shareholders' meeting.

This clause refers to prohibiting the directors and managers of the company as a party from entering into contracts or transactions with the company unless permitted by the company's articles of association or approved by the shareholders' meeting. This is because directors and senior managers are responsible for the company's business decision-making and business execution. When they enter into contracts or other transactions with the company they work for as the counterparty to the contract, they will inevitably sacrifice the company's interests for their personal benefits. Therefore, the Company Law of the People's Republic of China provides restrictive provisions on this.

In this case, when the contract was concluded, Kim Kwang-seok, the legal representative of Boram Hi-Tek Co, also served as the vice chairman of Castronics Company. However, the parties to the contract are Boram Hi-Tek Co., and Castronics Company, not a transaction between Kim Kwang-seok and Castronics Company, and the recipient is also Castronics Company. Therefore, this does not belong to the situation stipulated in art 149(1.4) of the Company Law of the People's Republic of China.

Therefore, the Court refused the claim of Castronics Company on the grounds that the 'Supply Contract' concluded by Boram Hi-Tek Co., and Castronics Company is legal and valid, it is legally binding on the parties, and the parties should perform their obligations in accordance with the agreement.

**Issue 5 Determination of the Buyer's Breach of Contract**

The core issue in this case is whether the buyer breached the contract during the performance of the contract and failing to pay the full price.

Paying the price for the goods is an important obligation of the buyer. According to CISG art 53, 'the buyer must pay the price for the goods and take delivery of them as required by the contract and this Convention.' The buyer must also, pursuant to art 59, 'pay the price on the date fixed by or determinable from the contract and this Convention without the need for any request or compliance with any formality on the part of the seller.' According to the above analysis, the contract concluded by Boram Hi-Tek Co., and Castronics Company is valid. The agreement between the two parties in the 'Supply Contract' provides that Castronics Company should pay the price of the goods to Boram in the form of wire transfer after the contract was concluded. Boram delivered the goods to Castronics Company. However, after taking delivery, Castronics Company failed to pay the price for the goods as agreed in the contract. Therefore, Castronics Company is in breach of this important obligation.

The CISG provides specific performance as a remedy in case a breach of contract occurs.

According to art 61(1)(a) of the CISG, 'if the buyer fails to perform any of his obligations under the contract or this Convention, the seller may exercise the rights provided in articles 62 to 65.' According to art 62 of the CISG, 'the seller may require the buyer to pay the price, take delivery or perform his other obligations, unless the seller has resorted to a remedy which is inconsistent with this requirement.' In accordance with arts 61 and 62 of the CISG, where the buyer fails to fulfil any of its obligations under a contract, the seller shall be entitled to demand the payment of the price from the buyer.

As a result of Castronics Company's material breaches of its contractual obligations, Boram Hi-Tek Co., is entitled to demand the payment of the price of the goods from the buyer. Therefore, Tianjin High People's Court upheld the request of Boram Hi-Tek Co., to ask Castronics Company to pay USD $26,858.

## References


1. Li, H. (1994). *The concept and legal sources of international law*. Guizhou People's Press
2. Wang, T. (1998). *Introduction to International Law*. Peking University Press
3. Li, W. (2011). *Conflict of Laws*. Law Press
4. Gillette, C. & Walt, S. (2016). *The UN Convention on Contracts for the International Sale of Goods: Theory and Practice* (2nd Ed.). Cambridge University Press
5. United Nations Commission on International Trade Law (UNCITRAL) (2016). *UNCITRAL Digest of Case Law on the United Nations Convention on Contracts for the International Sale of Goods*. https://uncitral.un.org/en/case_law/digests
6. He H. (2019). Problem of CISG Application by Chinese Courts, its Causes and How to Improve. *Law Science*, 4, 181–192
7. Liu, Y. (2019). Application of CISG by Domestic Courts of Contracting States. *Science of Law*, 3, 191–201
8. Ferrari, F. (2005). Remarks on the UNCITRAL Digest's Comments on Article 6 CISG. *Journal of Law and Commerce*, 6, 13–37


**Dr. Hongzhi Hu** holds a LL.B. (U. Nankai), LL.M (U. Nankai), and Dr. iur. (U. Nankai). His research focuses on the CISG, International Financial Law. He has published "China-EU Monetary Cooperation in the process of RMB Internationalization: Motivations and Prospects" 7 Intertrade (2020); "International Legal Basis and Obligations of RMB Internationalization: From the Perspective of the International Monetary Fund Legal System" 5 Legal Forum (2020); and "On the Developments and Influence of the Currency Provisions of the United States-Mexico-Canada Agreement (USMCA)" 4 Social Sciences in Chinese Higher Education Institutions (2020).

# Castronics Precision Metal (Tianjin) Co., Ltd. v. Boram Hi-Tek Co., Ltd.

**Junmin Zhang**

**Case Information**

**Case Name:** *Castronics Precision Metal (Tianjin) Co., Ltd. v Boram Hi-Tek Co., Ltd.*

**Seller:** Boram Hi-Tek Co., Ltd.
**Place of Business:** South Korea

**Buyer:** Castronics Precision Metal (Tianjin) Co., Ltd.
**Place of Business:** China

**Details of First Instance:**
**Court**: First Intermediate People's Court of Tianjin Municipality
**Date of Decision:** 2012
**Case No.:** (2012) Yi Zhong Min Wu Chu Zi No. 43

**Details of Second Instance:**
**Court**: High People's Court of Tianjin Municipality
**Date of Decision:** 9 October 2012
**Case No.:** (2012) Jin Gao Min Si Zhong Zi No. 153
**Judges:** Hong Zhai (Presiding Judge), Qingquan Zhao (Judge), Tong Li (Acting Judge)

**CISG Applied:** Yes
**Key CISG Provisions Interpreted and Applied:** Articles 4, 61(1)(a), 62-65

J. Zhang (✉)
Shanghai Normal University, Shanghai, China
e-mail: zhangjunmin33@hotmail.com

 
P. Guo et al. (eds.), *Selected Chinese Cases on the UN Sales Convention (CISG) Vol. 3*, Selected Chinese Cases on the CISG,
https://doi.org/10.1007/978-981-99-6851-0_28

## Case Abstract

Castronics Precision Metal (Tianjin) Co., Ltd. ('Castronics') and Boram Hi-Tek Co., Ltd. ('Boram') signed a supply contract ('the Contract') in February 2010, stating that Boram would sell Castronics three types of tools, Sharp-A, Sharp-B, and Sharp-E, with a total price of USD $14,800. According to the Contract, Boram was to ship the products, and then Castronics would pay by telegraphic transfer. The Contract also included a dispute resolution clause, providing that any disputes should be resolved by the court located at the place of business of Castronics. Boram performed accordingly, while Castronics did not fulfill the payment obligation. Thus, Boram applied to the First Intermediate People's Court of Tianjin Municipality, asking Castronics to pay USD $14,800 and bear the cost of the dispute.

The First Intermediate People's Court of Tianjin Municipality held that this case was an international sales dispute. Based on the Contract and the principle of the most connected or significant relationship, since the two parties did not choose the applicable law governing the Contract, the applicable law should be the domestic law of the People's Republic of China.

During the appeal, the High People's Court of Tianjin Municipality ('High Court') determined that both China and South Korea are Contracting States to the 1980 United Nations Convention on Contracts for the International Sale of Goods ( 'CISG'), and both parties did not exclude the application of the CISG. Thus, the CISG was the proper applicable law governing this dispute raised from an international sales contract, not the domestic law of China.

Castronics argued that Kim Kwang Suk, the chairman of the board of Boram, had violated the duty of loyalty through self-dealing, which led the Contract to be void according to art 149 of the 2005 Contract Law of the People's Republic of China. The High Court referred to art 4 of the CISG, which does not regulate the validity of contracts. Both parties agreed to refer to the Contract Law of the People's Republic of. China as applicable law for this issue. According to art 149 of the 2005 Contact Law of the People's Republic of China, no director or senior manager may affect '[e]ntering a contract or trading with this company by violating the bylaw or without consent of the shareholders' meeting or shareholders' assembly'. In this case, even though Kim Kwang Suk was the vice chairman of the board of Castronics at the time of signing, the Contract's parties were Boram and Castronics, not Kim Kwang Suk himself and Castronics. This situation was inconsistent with the prohibition under art 149 of the 2005 Contact Law of the People's Republic of China.

According to art 61(1)(a) of the CISG, if the buyer fails to perform the obligations under the CISG, the seller may exercise the rights provided in arts 62 to 65. Article 62 of the CISG provides that '[t]he seller may require the buyer to pay the price, take delivery or perform his other obligations, unless the seller has resorted to a remedy which is inconsistent with this requirement'. Based on these provisions, the High Court held that Castronics should pay USD $14,800 to Boram for the products under the Contract. Therefore, the High Court dismissed the appeal and upheld the previous judgment by the First Intermediate People's Court of Tianjin Municipality. It was also ruled that Castronics had to pay RMB 3,737 for the litigation fee.

## Commentary to the Key Issues Related to the CISG

### Issues

Issue 1 The Application of the CISG

Issue 2 The Validity of Contracts under the CISG

Issue 3 The Payment Obligation of the Buyer under the CISG

### Comments

### Issue 1 the Application of the CISG

Article 1(1)(a) of the CISG states that '[t]his Convention applies to contracts of sale of goods between parties whose places of business are in different States', when the States are Contracting States.[1] The nationality of the parties, or their professional qualification, do not influence the application of the CISG.[2] In this case, the parties did not choose the applicable law. The First Intermediate People's Court of Tianjin Municipality adopted the doctrine of the most significant relationship and determined that the domestic law of China be applicable. Unlike the judgment in *Ningbo Bridge Import & Export Co., Ltd. v The Money Consultants Inc.* (2010) Zhe Shang Wai Zhong Zi No. 77, the High Court, in this case, corrected the mistaken application of domestic laws by adopting the CISG.

From this correction, it has been seen that understanding regarding the application of the CISG in more recent Chinese cases is improving and correct. A statement made in 1987 by the Ministry of Foreign Economic Relations and Trade[3] makes it clear that an automatic application of the CISG displaces the conflict of law rules. It does not obviate the effect of a voluntary choice of law by parties given by the Convention.[4] For example, in the retrial judgment, *C&J Sheet Metal, Co., v Wenzhou Chenxing Machinery, Co.,* (2014) Min Shen Zi No. 266, the Supreme Court of the People's Republic of China held that that the place of business of the two parties were in the United States and China respectively. Both parties in this international contract for the sales of goods did not exclude the application of the CISG. In this case, the application of the CISG by lower courts was proper and correct.

### Issue 2 the Validity of Contracts Under the CISG

The CISG is 'not a comprehensive code' regulating all issues related to its application.[5] Article 4(a) of the CISG states that '[t]his Convention governs only the formation of the contract of sale and the rights and obligations of the seller and the buyer arising from such a contract', excluding the validity of the contract. Generally,

---

[1] Article 1(1)(a), CISG.

[2] Schlechtriem [1], p. 782.

[3] Now it is the Ministry of Commerce of P. R. China.

[4] Liu and Ren [2], p. 899.

[5] Kröll et al. [3], p. 64.

the Convention leaves the validity of contracts as the issue by which 'the domestic law would render the contract void, voidable, unenforceable' to the applicable national law.[6] As a matter that the CISG does not govern, the validity of contacts should be dealt with 'either domestic law or other uniform sets of rules in force which address the matter at issue'.[7] The determination of which domestic law is in accordance with the applicable conflict of laws rules of the forum.[8]

To explore the issue of validity, it is necessary to determine the definition of 'validity', which is currently controversial.[9] Interestingly, there was a lack of debate regarding the meaning of 'validity' in the Convention. The drafters of the CISG did not agreed on, or even discuss in detail, the exact meaning of 'validity'.[10] There is a strong argument that 'the drafters mainly had in mind mandatory rules that involve an element of public policy'.[11] This exception has even been described as a 'potential black hole that removes the issues from the Convention's universe'.[12] In adopting the doctrine of substance over form, the exclusion covers a wide range of issues.[13] The validity issue may include legal capacity, consent of the parties, individual clauses and standard terms, usages, and domestic or international regulations prohibitions.[14] This list is not exhaustive.[15] In this case, the validity issue related to fraud. Case law and commentary has shown that where the contract is concluded by fraud, such an issue of validity is not governed by the CISG and needs to refer to domestic law.[16] Some claims may also concur with remedies under the CISG for breach of contract when applicable domestic law so decides.[17]

The co-existence of domestic law and the CISG reduces the need for judges to progressively interpret the Convention because they can turn to the assistance of domestic law.[18] However, the Preamble of the Convention should be borne in mind. The Preamble insists that 'the adoption of uniform rules which govern contracts for the international sale of goods and take into account the different social, economic and legal systems would contribute to the removal of legal barriers in international trade and promote the development of international trade'.[19] Being the 'external

[6] UNCITRAL [4], p. 25.
[7] Schwenzer [5], p. 297, see also DiMatteo et al. [6], p. 64.
[8] Schwenzer [5], p. 297.
[9] Bridge [7], p. 23.
[10] Hartnell [8], p. 20.
[11] Leyens [9], p. 23.
[12] Koneru [10], p. 145; Winship [11], p. 636.
[13] Schlechtriem [1], p. 788.
[14] Schwenzer [5], pp. 306–310.
[15] Kröll et al. [3], p. 69.
[16] Kröll et al. [3], p. 74.
[17] Schwenzer [5], p. 308.
[18] Meyer [12], p. 321.
[19] Recital 3 of the Preamble, CISG.

gap' that the CISG is not concerned with, the validity issue acts as 'a source of uncertainty'.[20]

When considering the goal of uniformity, the exclusion of validity issue has faced some fundamental criticism in several aspects.[21] Most of the validity issues are not covered by the CISG, some of which arise owing to certain types of trade, or political questions.[22] Governing those issues by domestic laws may lead to non-unification in international trade law. For the continuous success of the CISG, with more practical experience and joint efforts by Contracting States, it is possible to find a uniform approach to fill in the glaring gap regarding the validity issue in the upcoming future.[23]

**Issue 3 the Payment Obligation of the Buyer Under the CISG**

Article 61(1) summarizes the possible remedies for breach of contract by the buyer in arts 62 to 65, irrespective of the nature of the breach.[24] It states that if the buyer fails to perform his obligations under the contract or the CISG, the seller may exercise the rights provided in art 62.[25] According to art 62 of the CISG, the seller is entitled to require the buyer to 'pay the price, take delivery or perform his other obligations, unless the seller has resorted to a remedy which is inconsistent with this requirement'.[26] In this case, the High Court supported the claims of Boram, requiring Castronics to pay the price of USD $14,800 according to the Contract.

It should be noted that art 61(1) only provides the principal remedies available to the seller. Other additional remedies can be found in arts 71, 72, 73, 78, and 88 of the CISG. Civil and common law show differences regarding the availability of the remedy of specific performance. In common law jurisdictions, contrary to civil law jurisdictions, damages related to specific performance is not usually seen as a remedy for breach of contract.[27] From the expression of art 62, in principle, specific performance is available.

## References


1. Schlechtriem, P. (2005). Requirements of Application and Sphere of Applicability of the CISG. *Victoria University of Wellington Law Review* (36), 781–794
2. Liu, Q. & Ren, X. (2017). CISG in Chinese Courts: The Issue of Applicability. *American Journal of Comparative Law* (65), 873–918
3. Kröll, S., Mistelis, L. & Viscasillas, P. (2018). *UN Convention on Contracts for the International Sale of Goods (CISG).* C.H. Beck Hart Nomos


[20] Schroeter [13], p. 50.

[21] Meyer [12], p. 321; Schwenzer [14], p. 472.

[22] Schroeter [13], p. 70.

[23] Drobnig [15], p. 643; see also Lopez [16], p. 136.

[24] Schwenzer [5], p. 1354; see also Kröll et al. [3], p. 827; UNCITRAL [4], p. 284.

[25] Article 61(1)(a), CISG.

[26] Article 62, CISG.

[27] Kröll et al. [3], p. 831.

4. UNCITRAL. (2016). *Digest of Case Law on the United Nations Convention on Contracts for the International Sale of Goods*. Retrieved from https://uncitral.un.org/sites/uncitral.un.org/files/media-documents/uncitral/en/cisg_digest_2016.pdf
5. Schwenzer, I. (2016). *Schlechtriem & Schwenzer: Commentary on the UN Convention on the International Sale of Goods* (4th Ed.). Oxford University Press
6. DiMatteo, L., Dhooge, L. J., Greene, S., Maurer, V. G. & Pagnattaro, M. (2005). *International Sales Law—A Critical Analysis of CISG Jurisprudence*. Cambridge University Press
7. Bridge, M. (2007). A Law for International Sales. *Hong Kong Law Review* (37), 17–40
8. Hartnell, H. (1993). Rousing the Sleeping Dog: The Validity Exception to the Convention on the Contracts for the International Sale of Goods. *Yale Journal of International Law* (18), 1–94
9. Leyens, P. C. (2005). CISG and Mistake: Uniform Law vs. Domestic Law—The Interpretative Challenge of Mistake and the Validity Loophole, in Pace International Law Review (Ed.), *Review on the Convention for the International Sale of Goods 2002–2003* (pp. 3–52), Sellier European Law Publishers
10. Koneru, P. (1997). The International Interpretation of the UN Convention on Contracts for the International Sale of Goods: An Approach Based on General Principles. *Minnesota Journal of International Law*, (6), 105–152
11. Winship, P. (1988). Commentary on Professor Kastely's Rhetorical Analysis Symposium: Reflections on the International Unification of Sales Law. *Northwestern Journal of International Law & Business*, (8), 623–639
12. Meyer, O. (2009). Constructive Interpretation Applying the CISG in the 21st Century, in Janssen, A. & Meyer, O. (Eds.), *CISG Methodology* (pp. 319–342). Sellier European Law Publishers
13. Schroeter, U. G. (2017). Contract Validity and the CISG. *Uniform Law Review* (22), 47–71
14. Schwenzer, I. (2009). The CISG—Successes and Pitfalls. *American Journal of Comparative Law* (57), 457–478
15. Drobnig, U. (1992). Substantive Validity. *American Journal of Comparative Law* (40), 635–644
16. Lopez, M. B. (2010). Resurrecting the Public Good: Amending the Validity Exception in the United Nations Convention on Contracts for the International Sale of Goods for the 21st Century. *Journal of Business and Securities Law* (10), 133–172

**Dr. Junmin Zhang** , Assistant Professor in Law at Shanghai Normal University. She holds a doctoral degree in law, specializing in the field of international law, from Maastricht University in the Netherlands. Dr. Zhang's research interests lie in international trade law, international commercial and investment dispute resolution. She teaches Public International Law to L.L.B. students and acts as an arbitrator in the CIETAC Cup International Commercial Arbitration Moot.

# Nanjing Dingfu Toys & Gifts Co., Ltd. v. Michyvic S.L., Yu Hai

**Sarah Xiao Xun, Charles Caishun Guo, and Wenjing Lin**

**Case Information**

**Case name:** *Nanjing Dingfu Toys & Gifts Co., Ltd. v. Michyvic S.L., Yu Hai*

**Seller:** Nanjing Dingfu Toys & Gifts Co., Ltd.
**Place of Business:** China

**Buyer:** Michyvic S.L.
**Place of Business:** Spain

**Details of First Instance:**
**Court:** Nanjing Intermediate People's Court of Jiangsu Province
**Date of Decision:** 18 November 2014
**Case No.:** (2012) Ning Shang Wai Chu Zi No. 46
**Judges:** Zhang Han Qing (Presiding Judge), Jiang Xin (Judge), Lu Hongxia (Acting Judge)

**CISG Applied:** Yes
**Key CISG Provisions Interpreted and Applied:** Articles 1, 8, 33, 45, 53

S. X. Xun (✉)
Office 1-113, Zhijiang Campus, Guanghua Law School, Zhejiang University, Zhejiang Province, Hangzhou, China
e-mail: sarahxun@163.com

C. C. Guo
Quanzhou Intermediate People's Court, Quanzhou, China
e-mail: Charlesguo@u.nus.edu

W. Lin
The Primary People's Court of Shishi City of Fujian Province, Shishi, China



P. Guo et al. (eds.), *Selected Chinese Cases on the UN Sales Convention (CISG) Vol. 3*, Selected Chinese Cases on the CISG,
https://doi.org/10.1007/978-981-99-6851-0_29

**Case Abstract**

*Nanjing Dingfu Toys & Gifts Co., Ltd. v. Michyvic S.L., Yu Hai* is an international sale of goods contract dispute in which the plaintiff, Nanjing Dingfu Toys & Gifts Co., Ltd. ('Dingfu') claimed that it had a sales relationship with the defendant Michyvic S.L. ('Michyvic').

On 11 December 2007, Dingfu signed a contract for the sale of goods with Michyvic, agreeing that Dingfu would sell nine kinds of stuffed toys to Michyvic, CIF Valencia, with the settlement currency in USD and a total value of USD $19,225. After the contract was signed, Dingfu delivered the goods from Shanghai Port to Valencia, Spain. Once the goods arrived at the port of destination, Dingfu repeatedly demanded payment from Michyvic, but Michyvic refused to pay for the goods. Dingfu then sued for payment of USD $19,225 (equivalent to RMB 120,231.39) and case acceptance fee borne by the defendant. At the same time, Dingfu claimed that Michyvic and Yu Hai were joint buyers of the goods and should bear joint liability. At the trial, Dingfu acknowledged that it had agreed to a 50% reduction due to Dingfu's delayed delivery.

The defendant, Michyvic did not plead contest.

The defendant, Yu Hai argued that the contract for the sale of goods in this case was signed between Dingfu and Michyvic. Although Yu Hai, an employee of Michyvic, handled the transaction, no contract was signed with Dingfu in his name.

The court of first instance, Nanjing Intermediate People's Court, found that:

1. On 11 December 2007, Dingfu and Michyvic signed a 'Sales Confirmation' via email, which agreed that Dingfu would sell 10,700 stuffed toys to Michyvic, at the price of CIF Valencia USD $19,225, with the shipment date of 30 December 2007 with a payment period of D/A 90 days. During the contract negotiation, the email contact at Michyvic was Yu Hai, but Yu Hai did not negotiate in his name in the email.
2. On 4 January 2008, Dingfu delivered the goods agreed to in the contract to the carrier, Jiangsu Zhonghai Container Transportation Co., Ltd., and emailed the bill of lading, packing list, and invoice to Yu Hai at Michyvic. The bill of lading indicated that the consignee was Yu Hai of Michyvic, and the packing list and invoice indicated that the purchaser was Michyvic. On 18 February 2008, Zhonghai Container Transportation (Shanghai) Co., Ltd. sent a letter to Dingfu, stating that 'Due to the adjustment of the route, the original mother ship of container 8NKGVLC3A33821 * 20GP, which your company distributed to us cannot take cargo, and now it is changed to transit by ship XINOUZHOU0003W from Shekou on February 9'. On 26 February 2008, the goods arrived at the port of Valencia, Spain.
3. On 24 February 2008, Yu Hai sent an email to Gong Weiwan of Dingfu, indicating that the partners of Michyvic agreed to purchase only the goods involved in this case at 50% of the original price. A statement issued by Jiangsu Zhonghai Container Transportation (Shanghai) Co., Ltd. to Dingfu, stated that the goods in dispute had been picked up.

4. On 26 December 2010, Gong Weiwan, on behalf of Dingfu, sent an email to Yu Hai requesting payment of the goods under the contract. On 30 December 2010, Yu Hai replied in an email stating that 'Because your goods did not arrive within the agreed time, which delayed our normal sales, we paid a lot of liquidated damages. At that time, for the sake of relatives, we took delivery of this batch of goods to reduce the loss for you. Otherwise, I could return them directly'.
5. The suffix 'S.L.' in Michyvic's company name means 'limited liability company'.

Pursuant to art 142 of the *General Principles of the Civil law of the People's Republic of China*, arts 1, 8, 33, 45, and 53 of the CISG and arts 142 and 144 of the *Civil Procedure Law of the People's Republic of China*, the court of first instance held the following:

1. Michyvic S.L. shall pay Nanjing Dingfu Toys & Gifts Co., Ltd. the payment of goods to the value of USD $9612.5 within ten days from the effective date of the judgment;
2. Dismissal of the rest claims of Nanjing Dingfu Toys & Gifts Co., Ltd.

The case acceptance fee of RMB 2400 and announcement fee of RMB 800, totalling RMB 3200, shall be borne by Nanjing Dingfu Toys & Gifts Co., Ltd. and Michyvic S.L., with each bearing RMB 1600 respectively.

**Commentary to the Key Issues Related to the CISG**

**Issues**:

Issue 1 Whether the CISG is Applied

Issue 2 Whether the Defendant Michyvic S.L. Should Pay for the Goods and to what Extent it Should Pay

Issue 3 Whether the Defendant Yu Hai Should Bear Joint Liability

**Comments**:

**Issue 1 Whether the CISG is Applied**

This case is an international sale of goods contract dispute. The place of business of the plaintiff is China and the place of business of the defendant is Spain. China and Spain are both Contracting States to the CISG (United Nations Convention on Contracts for the International Sale of Goods, also called the 'Vienna Sales Convention'), which governs more than 80-90 % of worldwide trade and regulates sales contracts without expressly defining the term. Pursuant to art 1(1)(a) of the CISG, the CISG applies to contracts of sale of goods between parties whose places of business are in different States when the States are contracting members. Given that both parties did not agree to exclude the application of the CISG expressly, which is stipulated in art 6 of the CISG as an 'opt-out' clause, the CISG should be applied in this case.

**Issue 2 Whether the Defendant Michyvic S.L. Should Pay for the Goods and to what Extent it Should Pay**

**I. Seller's and Buyer's Contractual Obligations under the CISG**

*A. Seller's Contractual Obligations under the CISG*

According to the provisions of the CISG, the seller's main obligation is to deliver the goods as agreed in the contract signed by the parties. The seller shall then bear the following four main obligations in the process of performing the delivery obligation: (1) deliver the goods at the time and place agreed in the contract; (2) hand over documents relating to the goods; (3) carry out a guarantee of quality for the goods; and (4) carry out a guarantee of right for goods. In this case, the main obligation relating to the seller is the delivery of goods as the contract stipulated.

If the time and place of delivery are clearly specified in the contract for the sale of goods, the seller shall deliver the goods at the time and place specified in the contract. However, if the contract does not stipulate the time and place of delivery, the seller shall perform its obligation in accordance with the law applicable to the contract, which, in this case, is the CISG. Articles 31 to 33 of the CISG specify the time and place for the seller to perform the delivery obligation. Article 33 stipulates that the seller must deliver the goods: (a) if a date is fixed by or determinable from the contract, on that date; (b) if a period of time is fixed by or determinable from the contract, at any time within that period unless circumstances indicate that the buyer has the right to choose a date (for example, if the parties agreed in the contract that the delivery period is from January to March, and there is no other terms indicating the buyer is to choose the date, then the seller has the right to choose any time between 1 January and 31 March to perform the delivery; or (c) in any other case, within a reasonable time after the conclusion of the contract. As for what is a reasonable time, it should be determined according to the specific situation of the transaction.

*B. Buyer's Contractual Obligations under the CISG*

Pursuant to art 53 of the CISG, there are two main obligations of the buyer: one is to pay the price for the goods; the second is to take delivery of the goods as required by the contract and the CISG. Special provisions are made in the first section of Chapter III in the third part of the CISG regarding the obligation to pay the price for the goods. There are a number of obligations, such as performing the necessary payment procedures, reasonably determining the price of goods, and determining the time and place of payment. For these issues, the provisions of the CISG are more detailed and specific than the domestic laws of many countries.

**II. Breach of Contract by the Seller and the Remedies under the CISG**

*A. Breach of Contract by the Seller*

The breach of contract by the seller refers to the seller's failure to deliver the goods or documents or delay delivery. If the delivery does not comply with the provisions of the contract, the third party has rights or a claim against the delivered goods.[1] According to the relevant evidence of delivery of goods provided by Dingfu, combined with the agreement between the two parties in the 'Sales Confirmation', the seller, Dingfu, had breached the contract due to delayed delivery, which violates art 33 of the CISG, and should bear the liabilities for breach of contract.

### *B. Fundamental Breach of Contract or Not?*

Fundamental breach is one of the most important terms in the CISG. Article 25 of the CISG stipulates that a breach of contract committed by one of the parties is fundamental 'if it results in such detriment to the other party as substantially to deprive him of what he is entitled to expect under the contract, unless the party in breach did not foresee and a reasonable person of the same kind in the same circumstances would not have foreseen such a result'. From this, the determination of fundamental breach of contract under the CISG should be judged by two criteria: one is objective criterion, which 'results in detriment to the other party as substantially to deprive him of what he is entitled to expect under the contract'. The second is the subjective criterion, that is, 'unless the party in breach did not foresee and a reasonable person of the same kind in the same circumstances would not have foreseen such a result'.

In the guiding case No.107: *Sinochem International (Overseas) Pte. Ltd. v. ThyssenKrupp*, the Supreme People's Court of the People's Republic of China held that, in an international sale of goods contract dispute, although the goods delivered by the seller may have defects, as long as the buyer can use the goods or resell the goods with reasonable efforts, it shall not be deemed to constitute a fundamental breach of contract under the CISG.[2] Similarly, in this case, although the seller, Dingfu, had breached the contract by delaying delivery, the email between Yuhai and Dingfu's employee, Gong Weiwan, indicated that it is not impossible that the buyer, Michyvic, could use the goods or resell the goods with reasonable efforts. Therefore, the delay in delivery by the seller did not constitute a fundamental breach of contract under the CISG.

### *C. Remedies for Breach of Contract by the Seller under the CISG*

When the seller breaches the contract, art 45 of the CISG provides the buyer with the following remedies: firstly, when the seller fails to perform its contractual obligations, the buyer may require the seller to actually perform its contractual obligations, including requiring the seller to submit goods that conform to the provisions of the contract or to repair, replace or submit substitutes for goods that do not conform to the provisions of the contract. Secondly, the seller may require a reduction in the price or, thirdly, claim damages for delay or non-performance of the contract. Lastly, the buyer may terminate the contract and claim damages. The buyer may also compel the seller to perform the above obligations through the court's coercive means. Thus, there are four main kinds of remedies: actual performance, price reduction, contract avoided, and damages claim.

---

[1] Wang [1], p. 66.

[2] See Guiding Case No. 107: Sinochem International (Overseas) Pte. Ltd. v. ThyssenKrupp.

The above remedies provided by the CISG are based on two principles of contract law. The first is of no-fault liability, the principle for contract law in the common law system. The CISG stipulates that, as long as the seller fails to perform any of his obligations under the contract and the Convention, his or her performance constitutes a breach of contract, and the buyer is entitled to the above remedies, regardless of whether the seller has subjective fault. Civil law countries generally hold that only when the breach of contract is due to the fault of the seller can they bear the liability for breach of contract. The second principle is that of combining avoiding contract with compensation for damages. The CISG stipulates that the buyer's right to claim damages may not be lost due to his or her exercise of other remedies. That is, when the seller breaches the contract, the buyer can enjoy several remedies at the same time.[3]

In this case, the seller, Dingfu, had violated the contract signed with the buyer, Michyvic, after which a new agreement about price reduction was reached. Thus, both parties agreed to remedy the seller's breach of contract through price reduction, and this new agreement should be performed as agreed.

### III. Buyer's Liability for Breach of Contract under the CISG

Pursuant to art 53 of the CISG, there are two obligations of the buyer, Michyvic, these being paying the price and taking delivery. In this case, although the seller's performance had constituted a breach of contract, according to the new agreement between the two parties, both parties had agreed to remedy the seller's delayed delivery by way of price reduction. Consequently, the buyer still has to bear the payment obligation after the price reduction.

The email correspondence between Michyvic and Dingfu and the statement issued by Jiangsu Zhonghai Container Transportation Co., Ltd., is sufficient evidence that Michyvic had taken possession of the goods, and therefore should undertake the corresponding obligations of payment.

However, Michyvic had not paid Dingfu for the goods, which violated the new agreement between the two parties on payment for goods. Therefore, it is reasonable to require Michyvic to pay for the goods. Given that both parties had agreed on the extent of price reduction, Michyvic should not have to pay the original contract price, but only the reduced price according to the new agreement.

## Issue 3 Whether the Defendant Yu Hai Should Bear Joint Liability

### I. Actual Purchaser of the Goods

Dingfu claims that Yu Hai was the co-purchaser of the goods involved in this case. However, Michyvic is the buyer's name stated in the contract, invoice and packing list involved. While Yu Hai is responsible for specific matters during negotiation, contacting and receiving emails, Dingfu has no evidence that Yu Hai is trading with it in his own name, so the actual buyer of the goods should be Michyvic rather than Yu Hai.

---

[3] See Guiding Case No. 107: Sinochem International (Overseas) Pte. Ltd. v. ThyssenKrupp.

### II. The Legal Status of Michyvic

The S.L. company in Spain, standing for Sociedad Limitada, is a private limited company. Therefore, the suffix 'S.L.' in the name 'Michyvic S.L.' means 'limited liability company', which can relieve the business owners of personal responsibility for their company's debts or liabilities and establishes the business as its own legal entity. Dingfu's claim that Yu Hai and Michyvic should jointly bear legal liability is lacking in factual and legal basis, and should not be supported.

### Closing Remark

The CISG is the most widely applicable international convention that applies to contracts for the international sale of goods and consequently has a far-reaching impact on the development of the international trade in goods. The CISG not only clearly stipulates its scope of application, but also has specific provisions for both buyers and sellers about their rights and obligations, any breach of contract and associated remedies and the risks involving the transfer of goods. This case involves the CISG remedy of price reduction following a breach of contract by the seller under the CISG, and which is related to reducing the price of the goods.

Article 50 of the CISG[4] stipulates the price reduction system, which the court can invoke in the judgement. Meanwhile, in addition to the calculation method prescribed by the CISG, the parties to the contract can negotiate with each other, based on their own demands, and agree on the price reduction. When the seller violates the contract, the regulations about price reduction stipulated by the CISG can be one of the relief measures for the buyer. However, the buyer still needs to perform its contractual obligations under the CISG after reaching a new agreement with the seller, otherwise it also needs to bear the corresponding liability for its breach of contract.

## Reference

1. Wang, C. (2015). *International Trade Law* (2nd ed.). China University of Political Science and Law Press

**Sarah Xiao Xun** is a post-doctoral fellow at Guanghua Law School, Zhejiang University. She specializes in company law, corporate governance, and interdisciplinary studies. She obtained her PhD from Erasmus University Rotterdam in the Netherlands and presented her works at academic conferences across Europe and the United States during that time. She received the degrees of LLM and LLB from China University of Political Science and Law. In addition to her academic

[4] Article 50 of the CISG: If the goods do not conform with the contract and whether or not the price has already been paid, the buyer may reduce the price in the same proportion as the value that the goods actually delivered had at the time of the delivery bears to the value that conforming goods would have had at that time. However, if the seller remedies any failure to perform his obligations in accordance with article 37 or article 48 or if the buyer refuses to accept performance by the seller in accordance with those articles, the buyer may not reduce the price.

experience, she has been practicing law at Beijing De Heng Law office in cross-border transactions, including takeovers and bank loans. She is also a visiting fellow at the University of New South Wales.

**Charles Caishun Guo** is a Judge Assistant at the High People's Court of Fujian Province (currently on a secondment to the Supreme People's Court of China). He is also a Ph.D. candidate at University of Cologne. He was a Visiting Scholar at Emory University School of Law in 2019 while he was pursuing his second LL.M. in Common Law at City University of Hong Kong (Chinese Judges Programme). Prior to that, he earned his first LL.M. in International Business Law from National University of Singapore in 2010. He obtained his LL.B. from Fujian Agriculture and Forestry University, China in 2008.

**Wenjing Lin** The Primary People's Court of Shishi City of Fujian Province

# XX Co., Ltd. (China) v. XX Company (Spain)

**Peng Wang and Yueshan Liu**

## Case Information

**Case Name:** *XX Co., Ltd. (China) v. XX Company (Spain)*

**Seller:** XX Co., Ltd. ('Company A')
**Place of Business:** China

**Buyer:** XX Company ('Company B')
**Place of Business:** Spain

**Details of First Instance:**
**Court:** Pudong New Area People's Court, Shanghai
**Date of Decision:** 20 June 2013
**Case No.:** (2012) Pu Min Er (Shang) Chu Zi No S749
**Judges:** Li Sun (Presiding Judge), Yi Xing (Judge), Wei Yang (Acting Judge)

**CISG Applied:** Yes
**Key CISG Provisions Interpreted and Applied:** Articles 1, 4, 53, 78

## Case Abstract

The seller, Company A, is a Chinese company, and the buyer, Company B, is a Spanish company. Company A had exported sofa components to Company B for a considerable period of time. From December 2009, Company B began to default on payments to Company A. On 28 November 2011, Company A entered into an

P. Wang · Y. Liu (✉)
Nankai University, Tianjin, China
e-mail: liuyueshan99@yeah.net



P. Guo et al. (eds.), *Selected Chinese Cases on the UN Sales Convention (CISG) Vol. 3*, Selected Chinese Cases on the CISG,
https://doi.org/10.1007/978-981-99-6851-0_30

Assignment of Claims Agreement with another company with its place of business in China, XX Limited ('Company C'), which assigned its claims against Company B, together with interest and penalty interest, to Company A. Without compensation, the amount totaled USD $40,563.56. According to the emails between the two parties, Company C had notified Company B of the assignment of claims, and Company B had confirmed the amount of the debt. Company A had instructed its lawyer to send a letter to Company B requesting payment, but Company B did not reply. Company A brought the defendant to court, requesting the Court to order Company B to pay the plaintiff the purchase price, the claim of the Assignment of Claims Agreement and the interest loss totaling USD $467,535.20.

The Court found that the invoices and related evidence issued by Company A showed that Company A had exported 17 batches of goods to Company B. The defendant paid part of the first batch of goods, totaling USD $11,750.31. For the second batch to the seventeenth batch of goods, the defendant owed the plaintiff for the cost of the goods. All invoices stated that payment would be made within 75 days after the invoice date, free on board (FOB) Shanghai. Seventeen invoices dated from December 26, 2009, to May 7, 2010.

The Court held that the case was a dispute over a foreign sales contract. Since the places of business of the plaintiff and the defendant are located in China and Spain respectively, and both China and Spain Contracting States to the United Nations Convention on Contracts for the International Sale of Goods ('CISG'), in this case the relevant provisions of the CISG are applicable to the issues of contract formation, contract performance and liability for breach of contract. As for the assignment of claims involved in the Assignment of Claims Agreement, since there is no relevant provision in the Convention, and both the assignor and the assignee of the claims are located in China, Chinese law is applicable according to the principle of closest connection.

The international contract for the sale of goods in this case is legal and valid, according to the provisions of art 53 of the Convention. After the supply of goods from Company A to Company B, Company B shall pay Company A for them. For the amount of supply claimed by the plaintiff, the invoice, bill of lading and export goods declaration (where the amount of the customs declaration and the amount of the invoice is different,) the Court declared the actual export amount recorded in the customs declaration shall prevail. The Court finally determined the amount of supply from the plaintiff to the defendant was USD $437,641.95.

For the Assignment of Claims Agreement signed between Company A and Company C, Company C sent a notice to Company B. The agreement became effective for Company B, and Company B should pay Company A. In the case that there was a slight difference between the agreement and the amount of the customs declaration, the Court determined the amount of USD $40,563 according to the Assignment of Claims Agreement. In summary, after deducting the amount of USD $11,750.31 already paid by Company B, the Court ruled that the defendant should pay Company A USD $466,454.64 for the goods and the loss of interest on late payment. The Spanish company was summoned by the Court and did not answer the lawsuit, so the Court, according to the law, conducted the trial in absentia.

## Commentary to the Key Issues Related to the CISG

### Issues

Issue 1 The Applicability of the CISG

Issue 2 The Determination of Interest Rate under the CISG

### Comments

### Issue 1 the Applicability of the CISG

This case involves the application of the governing law of two legal relationships. One is the application of the law of disputes involving foreign sales contracts and the other is the application of the law of disputes involving the assignment of foreign claims.

#### I. Legal application of the sales contract

For foreign sales contract disputes, the parties' places of business are located in China and Spain, both of which are Contracting States to the CISG. The parties have not excluded the application of CISG. According to the criteria listed in art 1(1)(a), if the parties' places of business are located in different Contracting States, the CISG should be 'directly' or 'automatically' applied, i.e., without recourse to private international law rules or a common agreement of the parties to the contract as to their application.[1]

Article 4 sets out the scope of application of the CISG. The Convention applies only to the formation of a contract of sale and to the rights and obligations of the buyer and the seller arising from such a contract. The validity of the contract or the effect which the contract may have on the property in the goods sold are not within the scope of application of CISG. While art 4 lists some matters in which the provisions of the CISG prevails over the application of domestic law, namely the formation of the contract and the rights and obligations of the parties, the matters mentioned arts 4(a) and 4(b) 4 are excluded from the scope of application of the Convention and need to be dealt with under the applicable domestic law as determined by the rules of private international law of the forum.[2] The contract of sale dispute in this relates to Company A requiring Company B to pay the price of goods and other corresponding interest. The request for payment of the goods is due to the rights and obligations of the buyer and seller after signing the contract, on the basis of the contract coming into force. Company A had already shipped goods to Company B, and Company B's failure to pay for the goods is a breach of contract. Therefore, matters relating to the conclusion and performance of the contract and liability for breach of contract between the parties should be directly applicable according to art 1(1)(a) of the CISG and need not be resolved according to domestic conflict of laws rules.

---

[1] UNCITRAL [1], p. 5.

[2] UNCITRAL [1], p. 24.

**II. Legal application of the Assignment of Claims Agreement**

As to the applicable law of the Assignment of Claims Agreement, the Court held that because there is no relevant provision in CISG, and the assignor and assignee of the claim are located in China, Chinese law should be applied according to the principle of closest connection. In the author's opinion, to solve the problem of legal application of foreign-related claims assignment, it is necessary to take two steps: firstly, to confirm whether the scope of application of CISG includes foreign-related claims assignment agreement; secondly, if not included in CISG, to confirm the application of the principle of party autonomy and the closest connection principle in order of priority according to the rules of private international law.

According to arts 1 and 4 of the CISG, the type of contract to which the CISG applies is 'a contract for the sale of goods concluded between parties whose places of business are in different countries', and 'only applies to the conclusion of a contract of sale and the rights and obligations of the buyer and seller arising from such a contract'. The subject matter of the contract of assignment of claims is money, which does not fall within the definition of the contract of sale of goods, and therefore the contract of assignment of claims is a matter not regulated by CISG.

For matters not provided for in the CISG, art 7(2) of the CISG provides that:

> Questions concerning matters governed by this Convention which are not expressly settled in it are to be settled in conformity with the general principles on which it is based or, in the absence of such principles, in conformity with the law applicable by virtue of the rules of private international law.

Through this provision, it can be seen that the application of law to matters not specified shall first be resolved according to the general principles of the Convention, and if it cannot be resolved through them, then it shall be resolved on the basis of the applicable law as determined by the rules of private international law.[3] The place of litigation in this case is China, according to art 41 of the Law of the People's Republic of China on Choice of Law for Foreign-related Civil Relationships ('Applicable Law'):

> The parties concerned may choose the laws applicable to contracts by agreement. If the parties do not choose the laws at the habitual residence of the party whose fulfillment of obligations can best reflect the characteristics of this contract or other laws which have the closest relation with this contract shall apply.

This article provides that the principle of party autonomy takes precedence over the principle of closest relation in foreign-related contract disputes.

The principle of party autonomy is that the parties to a contract are free to choose the law applicable to the contract by agreement, and the principle of party autonomy is an unanimously accepted principle in all countries in dealing with the governing law of international contracts.[4] Additionally, the law chosen by the parties by agreement usually refers to the substantive law norms of the country and region concerned,

[3] Fan and Chen [2], p. 46.

[4] Xiao [3], p. 189.

excluding conflict norms and procedural law norms. At the same time, the autonomy of the parties in choosing the applicable law should be subject to the necessary restrictions and should not be contrary to the international conventions to which China has acceded or ratified into force. The choice of applicable law should not violate the mandatory provisions of law and public order. If the parties do not choose the applicable law for the handling of the dispute in the contract, or if the chosen law is found to be invalid because it violates the public order or mandatory provisions of the forum, or if the chosen law cannot be applied because it cannot be identified, the law of the country with which the elements of the contract are most closely connected shall apply.

Before applying the principle of autonomy, it is necessary to clarify whether the parties to the Assignment of Claims Agreement in this case are Company A, Company B or Company C. In this case, Company A and Company C signed the Assignment of Claims Agreement, in which Company C assigned its claims on Company B to Company A. Company C notified Company B of the assignment in writing, and agreed that Company C's claims and rights of interest and penalty interest were assigned to Company A without compensation. The claim of Company A is to request Company B to settle the debt. Company C completes the notification obligation when the claim is transferred. It does not have any fault, so the parties in the dispute of claim transfer should be Company A and Company B. The Spanish company was summoned by the Court and did not answer the lawsuit, so there is no choice of law between the parties, and the principle of party autonomy cannot be applied. The next step is to apply the principle of closest connection.

Some scholars have pointed out that in recent years, Chinese courts have simply listed the number of points of connection in the selected jurisdictions without analyzing the distribution and quality of the points of connection in the unselected jurisdictions, i.e., there is no reason to explain why the unselected laws are not closely related to the case.[5] The case of *Shike Lin et al. v Yongquan Tan*[6] was a dispute over the contract of assignment of claims involving Hong Kong and Macao. The agreement stipulated that 'this agreement shall be governed by and interpreted in accordance with the laws of Hong Kong', but both the court of first and second instance held that 'both parties did not dispute the jurisdiction of this court and the application of the laws of the Mainland of the People's Republic of China as the law applicable to the substantive rights and interests of this case, and this court applied the laws of the Mainland of the People's Republic of China to the substantive handling of this dispute.' The judge disregarded the Hong Kong law agreed upon as the applicable law, and directly applied the Chinese law as the applicable law. 'No objection' indicates that the choice of the applicable law is not a law actively chosen by the parties by autonomy, but a 'passive' one after the judge determined it as the applicable law. Even if the judge determined Chinese law as the governing law of the Assignment of Claims Agreement based on the principle of closest connection, no relevant discussion of the connection point was seen in the decision. In *Societe*

[5] Xu and Zhang [4], p. 6.

[6] (2013) Zhu Zhong Fa Min Si Zhong Zi No. 18.

*Generale Asset Management SA v Fujian Chef Food Group Co., Ltd. and Tongjin Weng,* [7] the trial court found that the case was a dispute over a Hong Kong-related contract and applied the law of the Mainland as the applicable law based on the principle of closest connection, without analyzing and explaining factors such as the connection point. In the case of *Runfa Zhang v Junzhe Huang et al.*,[8] the parties were residents of Taiwan, so the case was a contract dispute involving Taiwan. The Court held that since the parties did not choose the applicable law to deal with the contract disputes, the law of the place where the contract is most closely connected should be applied. Since the place of performance of the contract in question was on the mainland, the law of the mainland should be used as the governing law.

These three cases only list the connecting points related to the case, but do not compare the various elements and select the best. Even in *Runfa Zhang v Junzhe Huang et al.*, the judges chose the law of the mainland as the applicable law only because the 'place of performance of the contract' was in the mainland. The legitimacy of such a choice of law process will be questioned, posing a threat to the legal value of conflict of laws justice. When applying the principle of the closest connection, attention should be paid to preventing the abuse of the judge's discretion and ensuring the fair and reasonable outcome of the case. Since the connection point of the closest connection principle is abstract and non-specific, and the certainty is insufficient, the court has great discretion in applying it, and cannot take the acquisition of jurisdiction as the factor of the closest connection. When applying the principle of closest connection, there are many connecting factors to be considered. These include factors connected with the subject of legal relationship such as domicile, residence, nationality, place of incorporation, and place of business of the company. Factors connected with the object of legal relationship are the location of the subject matter of the contract, the location of the property, and factors connected with the legal facts include the place of performance of the contract, and the place where the contract was signed.

For the issue of legal application of foreign-related claims transfer, Song pointed out that the transfer of claims simply cannot adopt a single and unified lineage but should apply different laws according to different issues. For example, when it comes to the attribution of the claim by the assignor and the assignee, the law applicable to the assignment contract is applicable. When it comes to the debtor's debt settlement, the law applicable to the assigned claim is applicable and when it comes to the question of which assignee gets the priority of the claim in repeated assignments, the law of the assignor's domicile is applicable. [9] The Court held that, as there was no relevant provision in CISG regarding the assignment of the claim involved in the case, and both the assignor and the assignee of the claim were located in China, Chinese law should be applied according to the principle of closest connection. From the Court's decision, it can be seen that the connection point considered by the Court was the assignor's and the assignee's place of business. As both connection points were in

[7] (2022) Zui Gao Fa Min Zhong No. 258.

[8] (2019) Yue 19 Min Zhong No. 4865.

[9] Song [5], p. 98.

China, Chinese law was applicable. The author agrees with the Court's thinking, but the judgment needs to add a complete argument and to be more rigorous and convincing.

The reason why the Court did not consider the relevant connection point of the debtor Company B in the Assignment of Claims Agreement may be because in the past, the assignment of claims often required the consent of the debtor. The debtor was the central party in the legal relationship of assignment of claims, and the debtor's property is usually located at the debtor's domicile. Under the combined effect of these factors, the assignment of claims should naturally apply the law of the debtor's domicile. However, in recent years, the laws of various countries have generally tended to facilitate the assignment of claims. The debtor is no longer the central figure in the assignment of claims relationship, and the legal importance of the debtor's consent and notification obligations is decreasing day by day. Art 546 of the Civil Code of the People's Republic of China ('Civil Code') provides that, '*Where a creditor assigns his claim but fails to notify the debtor thereof, the assignment is not effective against the debtor*'. This article clarifies that China adopts the principle of notice in the validity of the assignment of claims. The creditor's assignment of rights only needs to be notified to the debtor, at that time when it can be effective against the debtor.

Therefore, in disputes over assignment of claims agreements, according to the principle of closest connection, priority should be given to the place where the contract of assignment of claims was signed, the place where the contract was performed, and the place of business of the assignor and the assignee. In this case, the place of business of Company A and Company C are both in China, so it can be presumed that the place of signing of the contract is in China. Company B needs to pay the funds to Company A's account before the performance of the contract is completed. The place of performance of the contract can also be taken to be China. Therefore, according to the principle of closest connection and considering the above connection points, the Assignment of Claims Agreement involved in this case should be applied to Chinese law.

### Issue 2 the Determination of Interest Rate under the CISG

In its decision, the Court wrote that according to art 78 of the CISG, the plaintiff's claim for interest had a legal basis and the Court upheld it. Article 78 provides for the right of the parties to receive interest on the unpaid price. The specific stipulations are:

> If a party fails to pay the price or any other sum that is in arrears, the other party is entitled to interest on it, without prejudice to any claim for damages recoverable under Article 74.

Art 78 of the CISG provides for the parties' right to interest. However, this article only provides for the general right of the creditor to receive interest on late payment but does not elaborate on the specific time of interest, the specific method of determining the interest rate and other issues. This has led to disparity in the application of art 78 of the Convention in practice by different national adjudication bodies. Arts 4 and 5 of the CISG set out the matters excluded from the scope of adjustment under the

Convention. The standard determination of interest rate in the contract is a sub-issue of the interest issue. The Convention does not explicitly provide for, but still belongs to, the matters within the scope of adjustment of the Convention. Sun believes that the absence of the method of interest rate determination in the Convention is a kind of extra-statutory omission, which should first be resolved under the framework of the Convention by invoking its general principles. Where it is still impossible to determine the specific amount of interest rate, then the relevant provisions of private international law should apply. In general, the interest rate of commercial loans in the country where the debtor has its place of business should be used as the standard for deferred interest.[10]

In the judicial practice of various countries, most of the adjudicating bodies consider that the interest rate in art 78 of the Convention does not fall within the general scope of the CISG and courts directly invoke the provisions of private international law to determine the interest rate. Conversely, a small number of adjudicating bodies insist that the omission of art 78 of the Convention falls within the scope of the Convention and insist on invoking the general principles of the Convention to fill this omission, although there is no uniformity among the adjudicating bodies as to which general principles apply. When the general principles of the Convention are applied to determine interest rates, the issue is resolved by applying the general principle of full compensation, which leads to the application of the law of the creditor in favor of protecting the interests of the creditor. However, since the purpose of paying delayed interest is to deprive the debtor of unjust enrichment, generally speaking, if the interests of the debtor are to be protected, the country where the debtor has its place of business should be used as the connecting point for interest rate determination.

In this case, the Court did not state the legal basis for the application of the London Inter-bank Offered Rate (LIBOR), and whether the interest rate was determined in accordance with the general principles of the CISG or the rules of private international law. The Court did not apply either Chinese or Spanish law, rejecting the plaintiff's claim to convert the US dollars into RMB and to charge interest at the RMB loan rate, but rather charging interest at 3% above the one-year USD LIBOR base. The decision shows that the Court took a compromise approach by adjusting the interest rate issue as a matter within the scope of the Convention in accordance with art 9 or the general principles of the CISG. The specific stipulations of art 9 of the CISG are as follows:

> (1) The parties are bound by any usage to which they have agreed and by any practices which they have established between themselves.
>
> (2) The parties are considered, unless otherwise agreed, to have impliedly made applicable to their contract or its formation a usage of which the parties knew or ought to have known and which in international trade is widely known to, and regularly observed by, parties to contracts of the type involved in the particular trade concerned.

Opinions of Chinese court decisions differ on the issue of interest rate determination. In the case of *Huatai P&C Insurance Co., Ltd. Beijing Branch v. Zhejiang*

[10] Sun [6], p. 122.

*COSCO., International Freight Co., Ltd. Wenzhou Branch*[11], the Court found that the plaintiff's request for an order to pay interest on the compensation amount at the loan rate was reasonable. The Court determined that the interest rate in this case was calculated based on the closing price of the LIBOR at the date of the judgment, plus 3%, in accordance with the common practice of commercial banks. In the case of *Star Controls Engineering Co., Ltd. v. Guoping Tang*,[12] the contract did not agree on the standard for calculating the overdue interest rate. The Court held that since the settlement currency of both parties was the Euro, the court of first instance confirmed that the calculation was based on the five-year LIBOR of the Euro on the date of the court's judgment. However, in the case of *Shanghai An Pu Information Technology Co., Ltd. v. Unity Technologies Finland Oy Advertising*,[13] the Court held that since the parties had not agreed on the standard of interest for late payment, the interest rate of LIBOR chosen by the Finnish company was not based on law and should be determined in accordance with the Bank of China's deposit rate for the same period. In *Shanghai Yiman Knitting Co., Ltd. v. Jade Marketing Group, LLC*,[14] Jade owed Yiman USD $207,767.16 for goods under the sales contract. The plaintiff requested that Jade be ordered to pay interest at the loan rate, and the Court supported the plaintiff's request. The Court held that because since September 21, 2000, the People's Bank of China no longer announced a unified foreign currency loan interest rate, the current Chinese commercial banks used LIBOR as the basic rate of foreign currency loans, plus a certain percentage of the formation of foreign currency loan interest rate. Accordingly, the Court determined that the interest rate in this case was calculated on the basis of the closing price of LIBOR on October 13, 2005, and then increased this amount by 3%. In the case where the principal amount is in U.S. dollars, this line of thinking also treats the adoption of LIBOR as a commercial practice to determine the interest rate standard.

Peng has pointed out that in recent years, the world's major international commercial banks have gradually unified the terms and standards of international loan agreements and formed a secondary market for the transfer of international loans in the location of international financial centers. Commercial banks generally decide on floating loan rates based on LIBOR; thus, all types of international loan agreements have a common scale of value.[15] It is more appropriate to use commercial interest rates compared to statutory interest rates because statutory interest rates are relatively stable compared to commercial interest rates, while commercial interest rates change frequently according to market conditions and more accurately reflect the returns of the parties. As for the question of whether the commercial interest rate should be applied to the deposit rate or the loan rate, the loan rate should normally be applied. Essentially, in the field of international trade, a rational businessperson would not have idle funds, and a late payment by a debtor would mean an additional loan on the

[11] (2010) Hu Hai Fa Shang Chu Zi No. 349.

[12] (2020) Hu 01 Min Zhong No. 8077.

[13] (2020) Hu Min Zhong No. 37.

[14] (2006) Hu Er Zhong Min Wu (Shang) Chu Zi No. 28.

[15] Peng [7], p. 142.

balance sheet. However, based on the principle of the CISG, the deposit rate is more appropriate if the debtor can prove that it did not need to borrow, or that the delay in payment was caused by an exculpatory circumstance (e.g., *force majeure*).[16]

In addition, if the parties have agreed on an interest rate, the agreed rate will apply. If the trade usage under art 9 of the CISG allows a party to fix the interest rate, that rate applies instead of the rate determined on the basis of the law applicable under the rules of private international law.

## References

1. UNCITRAL. (2016). *Digest of Case Law on the United Nations Convention on Contracts for the International Sale of Goods* (Chinese version). Publications and Libraries Section, United Nations Office at Vienna
2. Fan, J. H., & Chen, K. R., et al. (2017). *Contract Law for the International Sale of Goods*. Law Press China
3. Xiao, Y. (2002). *On Conflict of Law*. Wuhan University Press
4. Xu, W. & Zhang, Y. (2022). The Predicament and Relief of Unagreed Governing Law in Cross-border Contract Disputes under the Belt and Road Initiative. *Journal of Gansu University of Political Science and Law*, 5, 1–15
5. Song, X. (2011). The Path of Interpretation of the Law Applicable to the Assignment of Foreign Claims. *Law Review*, 29(04), 93–99
6. Sun, H. (2012). A Study of the Calculation of Interest Rate under Article 78 of The United Nations Convention on Contracts of International Sales of Goods. *Journal of Jiangxi University of Finance and Economics*, 80(02), 122–128
7. Peng, Y. (2016). Foresight on the Legal Application of the Asian Infrastructure Investment Bank Loan Agreement. *Studies in Law and Business*, 33(01), 139–147
8. Koneru, P. (1997). The International Interpretation of the UN Convention on Contracts for the International Sale of Goods: An Approach Based on General Principles. *Minnesota Journal of International Law*, (6), 105–152

**Peng Wang** the associate professor of Nankai University Law School. He graduated from Peking University with a doctor of Law degree in 2003. His main areas of research include Public International Law, International Economic Law and Legal Professional Ethics. Professor Wang has published one monograph On the Nature of International Mixed Arbitration in 2007. He participated in the National Social Science Foundation's project, Research on the Development of Human Rights with Chinese Characteristics in 2012. He is a director of Tianjin Sports Law Society and a director of Tianjin International Economic Law Society.

**Yueshan Liu** graduated from Nankai University with a master of International Law degree in 2023. Prior to that, she graduated from Nankai University with a bachelor of Law degree in 2021, double-majoring in Business Management in Tianjin University. Her research interests lie in Public International Law and International Economic Law.

[16] Koneru [8], p. 125.

# Shanghai Yuqing Clothing Company v. Corporate Funding Partners

**Mengsha Yang**

**Case Information**

**Case Name:** Shanghai Yuqing Clothing Company v Corporate Funding Partners

**Seller:** Shanghai Yuqing Clothing Company
**Place of Business:** China

**Buyer:** Corporate Funding Partners
**Place of Business:** United States

**Details of First Instance:**
**Court**: Shanghai Pudong New Area People's Court
**Date of Decision:** 18 November 2013
**Case No:** (2012) Pu Min Er (Shang) Chu Zi No. S2384
**Judges:** Li Sun, Hongyi Zhang, Wei Yang

**Details of Second Instance:**
**Court**: Shanghai First Intermediate People's Court
**Date of Decision**: 3 July 2014
**Case No:** (2014) Hu Yi Zhong Min Si (Shang) Zhong Zi No. S786
**Judges:** Ying Huang, Mingyan Ren, Su Yang

**CISG Applied**: Yes
**Key CISG Provisions Interpreted and Applied**: Articles 1, 53, 78

M. Yang (✉)
Tianjin University, Tianjin, China
e-mail: mengsha.yang@tju.edu.cn



P. Guo et al. (eds.), *Selected Chinese Cases on the UN Sales Convention (CISG) Vol. 3*, Selected Chinese Cases on the CISG,
https://doi.org/10.1007/978-981-99-6851-0_31

## Case Abstract

The seller, a garment company operating in China, had entrusted a Chinese shipping company to export a batch of women's trousers as an agent. On May 8, 2011, the shipping company signed a sales contract for women's trousers with the buyer based in the United States. The contract stipulated that the total value of the goods was USD $621,000, the mode of transportation and expenses was FOB, and the settlement method was L/C at sight. If the buyer breached the payment obligation, it would pay the seller interest of 2 ‰ per day as overdue payment.

The seller informed the buyer that its L/C limit was insufficient. It could only issue the L/C for half of the contract value. The seller also required the plaintiff to ship half of the goods. On July 30, 2011, the plaintiff loaded 50,000 pieces of the goods, contained in 1,043 boxes, to the value of USD $310,500 at the port of Shanghai. However, due to the expiry of the L/C issued by the seller at this time, the buyer required the seller to transfer the goods to another company Leefungg Trading Ltd. The buyer promised the plaintiff and the shipping company in written form, twice, that the seller, Leefungg Trading Ltd., Leefungg Trading Ltd.'s agent Jetnet Company, and Leefungg Trading Ltd.'s director Liuqiang would be jointly liable for the payment obligation. In case the payment was not made, a late performance penalty, as much as 1% of the outstanding payment daily, should be paid to the shipping company. In September 2011, the seller transferred the goods to Leefungg Trading Ltd. as requested by the buyer, and provided Jetnet Company with the bill of lading for the goods. However, after receiving the goods, the buyer only paid USD $30,000 to the seller through Jetnet Company. The remaining payment was delayed. The buyer filed a lawsuit requiring the seller to pay USD $280,500 in arrears, overdue fees, and legal costs.

The court of first instance held that the case was a contract dispute over the international sale of goods. Both parties agreed that the CISG should be applied, while the Contract Law of the People's Republic of China and other domestic laws should be applied if they were out of scope of the CISG. According to art 41 of the Law of the People's Republic of China on Choice of Law for Foreign-related Civil Relationships, 'The parties concerned may choose the laws applicable to contracts by agreement', and the Court confirmed it.

As for the payment of goods and interest losses claimed by the plaintiff, the Court supported this according to arts 53 and 78 of the CISG. As for the calculation of interest, the Court opposed the plaintiff's argument that the calculation standard should be the standard for overdue fees stipulated by the People's Bank of China. The Court determined that as the People's Bank of China did not specify the US dollar's standard for overdue fees, the interest rate based on the one-year dollar London Interbank Offered Rate ('LIBOR') on the effective date of the ruling was to be applied.

In the second instance case, the Court held that the judgement of the court of first instance on the payment of goods and interest calculation of the sale contract dispute was correct.

## Commentary on the Key Issues Related to CISG

### Issues

Issue 1 The Applicability of the CISG
Issue 2 Determination of Interests Rate under the CISG.

### Comments

#### Issue 1 the Applicability of the CISG

According to the semantic and systematic interpretations of Ch. 1 of the CISG, the application paths of the CISG has an order of priority. Firstly, the CISG will automatically and directly apply according to art 1(1)(a); Secondly, according to art 1(1)(b), the CISG can be applied indirectly in countries where no reservation has been made, provided that the conditions for indirect application are met. Finally, under art 6 of the CISG, the parties may agree to exclude the application of the CISG in whole or in part.

Under the paradigm of private international law, the determination of the agreement of the parties is often the first element of legal choice that judges or arbitrators need to examine. Because 'the autonomy of the parties principle' itself is one kind of conflict rule, especially in the legal relations of international commercial contracts. However, under the international uniform law paradigm, judges from Contracting States to the CISG should give priority to the application of international commercial treaties. Examination of the agreement of the parties' legal choice should be made after establishing the preliminary applicability of international commercial treaties. This is because 'the autonomy of the parties principle' will, as in the paradigm of conflict laws, have been excluded from the application of international commercial treaties. In the legal system of international commercial treaties, the parties' legal choice of agreement only plays a role in changing the initial applicability of international commercial treaties. Therefore, it should be emphasized again that the examination of the parties' choice of law is the second step of the application method of international commercial treaties.[1]

In this case, since the business places of the buyer and seller are located in China and the United States respectively, it meets the conditions of direct application of the CISG. The CISG should be automatically applied without considering the application of private international law. However, it can be seen from the reasoning on the applicable law of the court of first instance in this case that, although the CISG was correctly applied as the applicable law, it was based on art 41 of the Law of the People's Republic of China on the Application of Law on Foreign-related Civil Relations: 'the parties may choose the applicable law of the contract by agreement'. Therefore, the judges' choice of the applicable law as the CISG was a confirmation of the parties' choice of law by agreement under the paradigm of private international

[1] Yang [1], p. 43.

law, rather than out of respect for the priority and direct application of the CISG as a Uniform Substantive Law. Therefore, the decision has defects is defective in reasoning concerning the applicable law.

**Issue 2 Determination of Interest Rate Under CISG**

## I. Whether the Determination of Interest Rate can be Governed by the CISG

Article 78 of the CISG provides for the recovery of interest on the unpaid price (if overdue) and 'any other sum that is in arrears.' However, this provision does not specify the calculation method of the interest rate.[2] To determine the interest rate, one prerequisite issue should be paid attention to in advance, i.e., whether the determination of the interest rate falls within the scope of the CISG. To be specific, whether the determination of the interest rate is a *lacuna praeter legem* that is governed by the CISG but without explicit provision, or a *lacuna intra legem* outside the scope of the CISG. There are two mutually conflicting views on this issue. Some tribunals have held that, even though art 78 does not provide a specific formula for interest rate calculation, it is still governed by the CISG. However, other tribunals have held that domestic law, instead of the CISG should be applied to solve this issue.[3]

## II. The Development of Case Law on Determination of Interest Rate under the CISG

The issue of whether the determination of interest rate falls within the scope of the CISG has led to different approaches to the calculation of the interest rate. On the one hand, if the determination of interest rate falls within the application scope of the CISG but is not expressly provided, art 7 of the CISG should be applied to fill the gap of the CISG, i.e. this issue should be solved firstly on the basis of general principles, and only in the absence of such general principles then the domestic law chosen by the rules of private international law should be applied. On the other hand, if the CISG does not govern the determination of the interest rate, then the appropriate domestic law should be applied. Thus, even though there are many different specific methods used in the case law of the CISG, they can all be generally divided into two categories: uniform law approaches and domestic law approaches.

### A. *Uniform Law Approaches*

**a**. General Principles of the CISG

The purpose for using general principles to interpret art 78 is to promote a uniform interpretation and application of the CISG. Its underlying logic is to regard the determination of the interest rate as a treaty loophole which falls within the application scope of the CISG but is not expressly provided. Some cases have followed the general principles of the CISG to find a solution to the interest rate calculation issue. One

[2] Eiselen [2], para b.

[3] Greece 2008 Decision 43,945/2007 of the Single-Member Court of First Instance of Thessalonika, http://cisgw3.law.pace.edu/cases/080002gr.html.

view is that interest on arrears under art 78 is a full compensation for damages under art 74.[4] Hence, under art 7(2), some tribunals have relied on the general principles of full compensation for damages to fill the gap in art 78.

For example, in one arbitral case in Austria, the tribunal held that the determination of the interest rate was a matter governed by the CISG but not yet expressly provided for, and that the rate should be determined in accordance with the general principles on which the CISG is based. Additionally, the tribunal also held that in commerce, the seller may obtain a loan from a bank due to delayed payment, and the interest rate shall be calculated according to the interest rate prevailing in the country for the currency used in payment. This currency can be either the currency of the seller's country or any other foreign currency agreed upon by the parties.[5]

**b.** UNIDROIT Principles of International Commercial Contracts

While art 78 of the CISG sets out the basic principle for the granting of interest, it does not give sufficient guidance on how to determine the interest rate to be granted. In contrast, the UNIDROIT Principles of International Commercial Contracts ('UNIDROIT PICC') also a uniform law, provides a more specific and clearer method for determining the interest rate in its art 7.4.9, which is particularly beneficial in filling the gap in the CISG. For example, in a case before the Supreme Economic Court of the Republic of Belarus, the tribunal held that the seller was entitled to claim the interest for delayed payment of the price of the goods.

The rate of interest should be determined according to art 7.4.9 of the 1994 UNIDROIT PICC.[6]

**c.** Trade Usages

A number of courts and arbitral tribunals have invoked art 9 of the CISG to determine the interest rate. For example, Argentina's 10th National Commercial Court of First Instance has repeatedly invoked art 9(2) of the CISG to fill the gap in determining the interest rate. In one decision, the tribunal held that it is a widely recognized trade usage in international trade to pay interest at the rate that is generally known and internationally used (such as the bank's minimum interest rate), even if the parties have not reached a clear agreement on this.[7] In another decision, the court held the same view, and commented that the CISG gives international trade usages a higher position than its provisions.[8]

If the trade usages allow one party to set the interest rate, then that rate can be applied. In the Italian Plant Case, the tribunal pointed out that the CISG only provided for interest claims according to the actual situation but did not mention the

---

[4] Corterier [3], p. 35.

[5] CLOUT case No. 93 [International Tribunal of the Federal Chamber of Commerce and Industry of Vienna, Austria, 15 June 1994] (For the purpose of solving the matters not covered in Article 78 in accordance with Article 7(2), the general principles are deduced from Article 74).

[6] CLOUT case No. 499 [Supreme Economic Court of the Republic of Belarus, 20 May 2003].

[7] Argentina 10th National Commercial Court of First Instance, 23 October 1991, Unilex.

[8] Argentina 10th National Commercial Court of First Instance, 6 October 1994, Unilex.

specific interest rate. If both parties fail to agree on the specific interest rate in a sales contract governed by the CISG, it is not until art 9 cannot be applied that the interest rate should be decided according to the domestic law.[9] This reasoning indicates that trade usages related to the determination of the interest rate in art 9 of the CISG takes precedence over domestic law. When there is a trade usage in determining the interest rate, art 9 of the CISG should be applied to confirm it.

**d.** Reasonable Commercial Interest Rate

In *Zapata Hermanos, S.A. v Hearthside Banking Co., Inc., d/b/a Maurice Lenell Cooky Company*, the tribunal held that there was no universally applicable rate for delayed payment. The interest rate to be applied should be determined based on the 'reasonableness' principle of the CISG.[10] This method of applying general principles indirectly suggests that the reasonable commercial rate is deemed as an issue that falls within the scope of the CISG. What is a 'reasonable' commercial rate is often decided ex officio by the court or arbitration tribunal directly on its own. Some judges and arbitrators believe that since the commercial interest rate changes frequently in response to market conditions, it can more accurately reflect the returns of parties.[11] The LIBOR and Euro Interbank Offered Rate (EURIBOR) are usually chosen by judges or arbitrators as the reasonable commercial rate in practice.

*B. Domestic Law Approaches*

When the interest rate is deemed as a *lacuna intra legem* outside the scope of the CISG, judges and arbitrators will choose the appropriate domestic law as the applicable law for the interest rate standard. For example, a German court held that the issue of interest should resort to the applicable domestic law, since it is beyond the scope of the Convention.[12]

**a**. Conflicts of Law Rules Approach

Most courts use domestic law guided by the place of the forum's private international law rules as the applicable law in determining the interest rate. A court in New Jersey held that the CISG did not provide a 'uniform rule' that could be used to determine the interest rate, so the legislative purpose of the CISG was to refuse to choose a specific interest rate. The issue should be resolved through the rules of private international law.[13]

[9] District Court, Bamberg, Germany,23 October 2006, English translation available at www.cisg.law.pace.edu.

[10] Li [4], p. 81.

[11] Gotanda [5], p. 59.

[12] CLOUT case No. 1399 [Oberlandesgericht Hamburg, Germany, 25 January 2008], English translation available on the Internet at www.cisg.law.pace.edu.

[13] District Court, New Jersey, United States, 15 April 2009, available at www.cisg.law.pace.edu.

**b.** Other Domestic Law Approaches

It should be noted that the following approaches for determining the interest rate are also determined according to domestic law, but they are different from the conflicts of law rules approach. Courts or arbitral tribunals no longer determine the interest rate through the guidance of private international law rules, but directly determine the interest rate through domestic law. However, their commonality is that the determination of interest rate is outside the scope of adjustment of CISG Convention.

*(1) Interest Rate in the Venue of the Court*

Several courts directly apply the interest rate in the venue of the court for calculation of interest. A New York court held that as art 78 of the CISG did not provide a specific interest rate to be applied, the determination of the interest rate was an issue under the discretion of the Court. The Court ultimately applied the United States Treasury Bill rate, for calculation of the interest.[14]

*(2) Interest Rate Provided by Creditor's Domestic Law*

There are also some courts directly apply the creditor's domestic law as the basis for determining interest rates. A Belgian commercial tribunal held that art 78 of the CISG did not provide for a specific rate of interest, and since interest was a compensation to creditors, so it was more appropriate to set the rate according to the domestic law of creditors.[15] Some scholars also believe that the creditor's place is where the seller (creditor) often invests, so the creditor's domestic law should be applied to determine the interest rate.[16]

*(3) Interest Rate Provided by Debtor's Domestic Law*

There are also courts that directly specify the interest rate based on the debtor's domestic law. A German court pointed out that the application of the creditor's domestic law will result in the creditor receiving greater benefit than it should have from contract performance. This is not consistent with the principle of full compensation of damages, so it is more appropriate to apply the debtor's domestic law.[17] Some scholars also believe that the purpose of paying deferred interest is to deprive the debtor of unjust enrichment, so generally speaking, the debtor's domestic law should be taken as the connection point for determining the interest rate. Of course, if the debtor's financial activity is in another country, the connection point should be that country.[18]

---

[14] Delchi Carrier, SpA v. Rotorex Corp., 71 F 3d 1024 (2nd Cir, 1995).

[15] Rechtbank van Koophandel Hasselt, Belgium, 20 September 2005, English translation available on the Internet at www.cisg.law.pace.edu

[16] Ana [6].

[17] Landgericht Kiel, Germany, 27 July 2004, English translation available on the Internet at www.cisg.law.pace.edu

[18] Sun [7], p. 126.

*(4) Interest Rate Provided by Domestic Law of Legal Currency*

The International Court of Commercial Arbitration has pointed out in a decision that, although there are many ways to determine interest rates in international commercial cases, the it believes that the application of the domestic law of the legal currency is the most appropriate and reasonable way at present.[19] In China International Economic and Trade Arbitration Commission ('CIETAC') practice, if the currency used by both parties in the case is RMB, the CIETAC arbitrators will tend to apply the interest rate issued by the People's Bank of China.[20]

**II. Comments on the Determination of Interest Rate**

In this case, the court of first instance denied the method of interest rate calculation advocated by the plaintiff in the trail proceedings, which was to use the standard set by the People's Bank of China for calculating late payment fees. The Court held that since the People's Bank of China had not set a standard for late payment of US dollars, the interest rate should be set at 3% above the one-year US dollar LIBOR on the effective date of the judgement.

In this case, there was neither a trade usage of interest rate calculation nor an agreement on the applicable interest rate between the parties. There was only a claim made by the seller in the proceedings. The judges did not rely on domestic law to determine the interest rate but chose to directly apply LIBOR as the standard for interest rate calculation. Since LIBOR is commonly applied in international commerce, the judges' determination of interest rate in this case is to a large extent, a uniform law approach, which exhibits respect for international usages.

## References

1. Yang, M. (2020). *A Study on the Priority Application of the United Nations Convention on Contracts for the International Sale of Goods*. Law Press
2. Eiselen, S. (2002). Remarks on the Manner in which the UNIDROIT Principles of International Commercial Contracts May Be Used to Interpret or Supplement Article 78 of the CISG. *Pace International Law Review*, 14, 379–384 Retrieved from http://www.cisg.law.pace.edu/cisg/principles/uni78.html
3. Corterier, A. (2000). A New Approach to Solving the Interest Rate Problem of Art 78 CISG. *International Trade and Business Law Annual*, 5, 33–42
4. Li, B. (2011). On the determination of interest rate in Article 78 of the CISG - Reflection on the determination of interest rate by domestic law. *Heihe Journal*, 164(04), 80–81
5. Gotanda, J. (1996). Awarding Interest in International Arbitration. *American Journal of International Law*, 90(40), 40–63
6. Ana, M. (2005). The Duty to Pay Interest on Advance Payment under Art. *Nordic Journal of Commercial Law*, 2, 1–9

[19] Court of Arbitration of the International Chamber of Commerce, France, December 1998 (Arbitral award No. 8908), available on the Internet at www.unilex.info.

[20] Lu [8], p. 719.

7. Sun, H. (2012). A Study of the Calculation of Interest Rate under Article 78 of The United Nations Convention on Contracts of International Sales of Goods. *Journal of Jiangxi University of Finance and Economics*, 2, 122–128
8. Lu, S. (2007). Award of Interest in Arbitration under Article 78 CISG. *Uniform Law Review*, 12(4), 719–731

**Mengsha Yang** is a lecturer and master supervisor in Law School at Tianjin University, China. Prior to that she got her graduated degree and doctoral degree in Nankai University. Her research area is international trade law and international commercial law.

# Jiaxing Haoneng Packaging Co., Ltd. v. Print-Service Ltd.

**Hongzhi Hu**

## Case Information

**Case Name:** *Jiaxing Haoneng Packaging Co., Ltd. v Print-Service Ltd.*

**Seller:** Jiaxing Haoneng Packaging Co., Ltd.
**Place of Business:** China

**Buyer:** Print-Service Ltd.
**Place of Business:** Ukraine

**Details of First Instance:**
**Court:** Shanghai Pudong New Area People's Court
**Date of Decision:** 5 May 2014
**Case No:** (2012) Pu Min Er (Shang) Chu Zi No S2851 Civil Judgment
**Judges:** Zhang Haijuan (Presiding Judge), Yang Wei (Acting Judge), Zhang Xiaoxian (People's juror)

**CISG Applied:** Yes
**Key the CISG Provisions Interpreted and Applied:** Arts 1(1)(a), 6, 53, 61, 62

## Case Abstract

The seller, Jiaxing Haoneng Packaging Co., Ltd. ('Jiaxing'), with its place of business in Zhejiang, China, agreed to sell aluminized paper products to the buyer, Print-Service Ltd., with its place of business in Ukraine. According to the contract, Jiaxing

H. Hu (✉)
Nankai University, Tianjin, China
e-mail: hongzhihu@126.com

 
P. Guo et al. (eds.), *Selected Chinese Cases on the UN Sales Convention (CISG) Vol. 3*, Selected Chinese Cases on the CISG,
https://doi.org/10.1007/978-981-99-6851-0_32

would provide 395,304 tons of aluminized paper products. The total amount was USD $1,221,489.36, the payment period was 25 days from the date of the bill of lading, and the payment method was wiring transfer. From June to July 2010, Jiaxing sold five batches of goods to the defendant Print-Service Ltd. Between January and November 2011, Jiaxing received six payments totalling USD $647,000. The defendants, Print-Service Ltd. still owed USD $574,489.36. Jiaxing repeatedly demanded payment, but the defendant refused to pay the remaining amount. A dispute arose when the seller stated the buyer did not pay the price as required by the contract and the CISG.

In determining the governing law, Shanghai Pudong New Area People's Court held that this case should apply the CISG. This case is a dispute over an international sale of goods contract. The business places of the buyer and the seller are located in the Ukraine and the People's Republic of China. Both countries are Contracting Parties to the CISG.

With respect to the buyer's contractual obligations, the Court stated that the contract was legal and valid. The contract was legally binding on the parties. Thus, the parties should perform their obligations in accordance with the agreement. The seller delivered the goods and handed over documents within the time limit agreed in the contract and performed its contractual obligations. After the buyer had taken delivery of all the goods, they should pay the price according to the agreed amount. Their failure to pay constituted a breach of contract, and the buyer should bear breach of contract liability. The buyer must continue with performance.

## Commentary to the Key Issues Related to the CISG

### Issues

Issue 1 Direct Application of the Convention.
Issue 2 Determination of the Buyer's Breach of Contract.

### Comments

### Issue 1 Direct Application of the Convention

According to arts 1(1)(a), 2, 3, 4 and 5, when parties whose places of business are in different Contracting States, and all the CISG's requirements of applicability are met, the CISG does not necessarily apply. This is because freedom of contract, as a basic principle in the context of international trade, has been recognized by the drafters of the CISG. According to art 6 of CISG, the parties may exclude the application of the Convention. Thus, subject to the conditions of application of the Convention, the court must determine whether the CISG has been excluded by the parties[1]. If the parties have not designated a given law with the intention to exclude the Convention, it is 'directly' or 'autonomously' applicable. If the Convention has been excluded, the agreement shall be governed by the laws chosen by the parties.

[1] Ferrari, F. (2005). Remarks on the UNCITRAL digest's comments on Article 6 CISG. Journal of Law and Commerce, 6, p.15.

In this case, Print-Service Ltd. is a corporate entity organized and existing under the laws of the Ukraine with its regular and principal place of business located at 92 Aplekhanovskaya Str. UA-61001, Kharkov. Jiaxing is a corporate entity organized and existing under the laws of the People's Republic of China. Thus, the dispute is a foreign-related commercial case. Shanghai Pudong New Area People's Court ruled that the CISG only governs the formation of contracts and the rights and obligations of the parties. Within its scope, the parties' contract was governed by the Convention, because the parties had their places of business in two different Contracting States (Ukraine and China) pursuant to art 1(1)(a) of the CISG.

However, there are certain flaws in the analysis of the application of the Convention in this case. This is because when all the CISG's requirements of applicability are met, the court must look into whether the parties have or have not designated a given law with the intention to exclude the Convention.

In China's judicial practice, most courts will be concerned with whether the Convention is excluded. For instance, in *Nanjing Dingfu Toys & Gifts Co., Ltd. v Michyvics Ltd.*,[2] Nanjing Intermediate People's Court of Jiangsu Province concluded that in this case, one party to the contract had its place of business in China and the other party had its place of business in Spain. The parties had their places of business in two different Contracting States. Moreover, the parties did not unanimously exclude the application of the CISG. According to arts 1(1)(a) and 6 of the CISG, the contract is silent as to the applicable law; the Convention is 'directly' or autonomously applicable.

In *ЗАО «БЭЛСИГрупп» v Tianjin Zhonglian Weitian Trading Co.*,[3] *ЗАО «БЭЛСИГрупп»* is a corporate entity organized and existing under the laws of Russia. Tianjin Zhonglian Weitian Trading Co., Ltd. is a corporate entity organized and existing under the laws of the People's Republic of China. Thus, the dispute is a foreign-related commercial case. The parties had their places of business in two different Contracting States. Both Russia and China are parties to the Convention. The parties had not agreed to exclude the application of the Convention in the contract. Thus, Tianjin High People's Court concluded that the parties' contract was governed by the Convention.

In *Yangzhou Ruitian Pipe Fittings Manufacturing Co., Ltd. v UGRINEKSD.O.O.*,[4] Yangzhou Ruitian Pipe Fittings Manufacturing Co., Ltd. is a corporate entity organized and existing under the laws of the People's Republic of China. UGRINEKSD.O.O. is a corporate entity organized and existing under the laws of the Republic of Croatia. Thus, the dispute is a foreign-related commercial case. Both parties expressly did not exclude the application of the CISG. Therefore, in addition to the provisions that China has declared reservations, the relevant provisions of the CISG should pre-empt in this case. In this case, both parties expressly invoked the law of the People's Republic of China during the court hearing, which should be regarded as an express choice of the law by both parties. According to art 3 of the Law of

[2] (2012) Ning Shang Wai Chu Zi No. 46 Civil Judgment.

[3] (2011) Jin Gao Min Si Zhong Zi No. 181 Civil Judgment.

[4] (2015) Jin Gao Min Si Zhong Zi No. 2 Civil Judgment.

the People's Republic of China on the Application of Law to Foreign-related Civil Relations, 'the parties may expressly choose the law applicable to foreign-related civil relations in accordance with the provisions of the law; if there is no provision in the CISG, the laws of the People's Republic of China shall apply'.

In *Mohamed El Sayed Helmelmenawey v Xu Jianhui,*[5] Guangzhou Intermediate People's Court concluded that Mohamed El Sayed Helmelmenawey is a citizen of Egypt and Xu Jianhui is a citizen of the People's Republic of China. Both the People's Republic of China and Egypt are Contracting States to the CISG. In addition, the parties did not exclude the application of the Convention or make another choice of law in the sales contract, so the relevant provisions of the Convention should be automatically applied to the sales contract.

**Issue 2 Determination of the Buyer's Breach of Contract**

The core issue in this case is whether the buyer breached the contract during performance, in particular, whether the buyer should pay the remaining price.

Compared to the great variety of obligations of the seller and the different kinds of breach of contract by the seller, the obligations of the buyer are relatively simple.[6] Pursuant to art 53 of the CISG, the buyer must pay the price for the goods and take delivery of them as required by the contract and the Convention. Paying the price for the goods is an important obligation of the buyer. Article 53 describes the general responsibilities of the buyer in an international sales transaction. This provision recognizes the primacy of the contract in defining the parties' obligations, and applies absent a contractual agreement between the parties to the contrary.[7] The buyer must also, pursuant to art 59, 'pay the price on the date fixed by or determinable from the contract and this Convention without the need for any request or compliance with any formality on the part of the seller'.

In this case, the Court concluded that the contract was legal and valid. Jiaxing had delivered the goods to Print-Service Ltd. Print-Service Ltd. received and accepted the goods delivered by Jiaxing and did not give notice to Jiaxing of any lack of conformity of the goods it had ordered or described in the invoices and shipping documents. However, Print-Service Ltd. failed to pay the price for the goods as agreed in the contract.

From the facts and evidence outlined by the Court in its judgment, which included six copies of invoices, seven copies of 'Export Goods Declaration', four copies of certificates and Jiaxing's statement, the Court concluded that the total amount of the goods was USD $1,221,489.36. The plaintiff received six payments totalling USD $647,000 from January to November 2011. The defendants, Print-Service Ltd. still owed USD $574,489.36. Therefore, Print-Service Ltd. is in breach of this important obligation.

Pursuant to art 61(1)(a) of the CISG, 'if the buyer fails to perform any of his obligations under the contract or this Convention, the seller may exercise the rights

[5] (2014) Sui Zhong Fa Min Si Zhong Zi No. 64 Civil Judgment.

[6] Sevón [1], p. 203.

[7] Gabriel [2], p. 273.

provided in articles 62 to 65.' According to art 62 of the CISG, 'the seller may require the buyer to pay the price, take delivery or perform his other obligations, unless the seller has resorted to a remedy which is inconsistent with this requirement.' In accordance with arts 61 and 62 of the CISG, where the buyer fails to fulfil any of its obligation under a contract, the seller shall be entitled to demand the payment of the price from the buyer. Moreover, failure on the part of the buyer to perform any one of its obligations is the only prerequisite for the seller's recourse to the remedies referred to in art 61(1). As one decision stated, an aggrieved seller's recourse to such remedies is not subject to the requirement that the seller prove that the buyer was at fault.[8]

As a result of Print-Service Ltd.'s material breaches of its contractual obligations, Jiaxing is entitled to demand payment of the remaining price from the buyer. Accordingly, the Court ruled in favour of Jiaxing Co's claim on the grounds that Print-Service Ltd. was in breach of paying the price obligation. The Court ruled that the seller was entitled to the remaining USD $574,489.36 of the purchase price.

Moreover, pursuant to art 78 of the CISG, 'if a party fails to pay the price or any other sum that is in arrears, the other party is entitled to interest on it.' Entitlement to interest requires only that the sum for which interest is sought is due, and that the debtor has failed to comply with its obligation to pay the sum by the time specified either in the contract or, absent such specification, by the Convention.[9] However, the plaintiff did not claim interest for late payment.

## References


1. Sevón, L. (1986). Obligations of the Buyer under the UN Convention on Contracts for the International Sale of Goods, in Sarcevic, P. & Voken, P. (Eds.), *International Sale of Goods: Dubrovnik Lectures* (pp. 203–238). Oceana Publications United
2. Gabriel, H. D. (2005). The Buyer's Performance Under the CISG: Articles 53-60 Trends in the Decisions. *Journal of Law and Commerce*, 6, 273–283
3. Nations Commission on International Trade Law (UNCITRAL). (2016). *UNCITRAL Digest of Case Law on the United Nations Convention on Contracts for the International Sale of Goods.* https://uncitral.un.org/en/case_law/digests


**Hongzhi Hu** holds a LL.B. (U. Nankai), LL.M (U. Nankai), and Dr. iur. (U. Nankai). His research focuses on the CISG, International Financial Law. He has published "China-EU Monetary Cooperation in the process of RMB Internationalization: Motivations and Prospects" 7 Intertrade (2020); "International Legal Basis and Obligations of RMB Internationalization: From the Perspective of the International Monetary Fund Legal System" 5 Legal Forum (2020); and "On the Developments and Influence of the Currency Provisions of the United States-Mexico-Canada Agreement (USMCA)" 4 Social Sciences in Chinese Higher Education Institutions (2020).

[8] UNCITRAL [3], p. 284.

[9] UNCITRAL [3], p. 364.

# Guangzhou Fanyunanxing Limited v. J & H International Inc. & Merion Kitchenware (Suzhou Industrial Park) Co., Ltd.

**Kaiwei Cui and Peng Guo**

## Case Information

**Case Name:** *Guangzhou Fanyunanxing Co., Ltd. v. J&H International, Inc. & Merion Kitchenware (Suzhou Industrial Park) Co., Ltd.*

**Seller:** Guangzhou Fanyunanxing Co., Ltd. ('Fanyunanxing Company')
**Place of Business:** China

**Buyer:** J&H International, Inc. ('J&H Company') & Merion Kitchenware (Suzhou Industrial Park) Co., Ltd. ('Merion Company')
**Place of Business:** USA

**Details of First Instance:**
**Court:** People's Court of Yantian District, Shenzhen City, Guangdong Province
**Date of Decision:** 31 October 2013
**Case No.:** (2012) Shenzhen Fa Min Chu Zi No.310
**Judges:** Guo Ninghua (Presiding Judge), Sun Yan (Acting Judge), Li Mingming (People's Juror)

**CISG Applied:** Yes
**Key the CISG Provisions Interpreted and Applied:** Arts 25, 35(2)(c), 42(1), 74

K. Cui (✉)
University of International Business and Economics, Beijing, China
e-mail: 13663719268@163.com

P. Guo
Swinburne University of Technology, Melbourne, VIC 3000, Australia
e-mail: pguo@swin.edu.au



P. Guo et al. (eds.), *Selected Chinese Cases on the UN Sales Convention (CISG) Vol. 3*, Selected Chinese Cases on the CISG,
https://doi.org/10.1007/978-981-99-6851-0_33

## Case Abstract

In 2010, Fanyunanxing Company (plaintiff) signed a 'Purchase Order' with Merion Company (agent of J & H Company & defendant 2) and J & H Company (buyer & defendant 1) in China, and agreed that the plaintiff, as the seller, would sell goods to the defendant J & H Company. The parties agreed that the seller would sell 36,330 flasks to the buyer for the total amount of USD $119,162.40. The delivery date was August to September 2010, with the goods to be shipped in two batches and delivered to China. The defendant, J & H Company, was to be responsible for international transportation. The plaintiff delivered the goods in batches between the end of August 2010 and mid-September 2010, J & H Company delivered the flasks to the US retail department store Macy's (the customer of J & H Company), which sold them online. In early October 2010, Macy's found that the flasks had a weak handle which could easily fall off the bottle. In late October and November 2010, the U.S. Consumer Product Safety Commission recalled the flasks and then destroyed the goods in batches. J & H Company refused to pay Fanyunanxing Company after the destruction of the goods. In view of this fact, the plaintiff requested: 1. The two defendants pay the price of USD $71,575.84 and overdue interest; 2. The two defendants jointly bear liability for the first claim; 3. The two defendants bear all litigation costs. The defendant believed that the safety and quality problems of the flasks were the primary cause of the dispute, the related products had to be destroyed according to United States law (19 of the *Consumer Product Safety Act 1972* and § 2068 of Code 15), and that J & H Company suffered losses due to the product's defects. As for the application of the law, the defendant further stated that according to arts 25, 35(2)(c), 42(1) and 74 of the CISG, and the fact that the place of sale of the thermos bottles is in the United States, it was apparent that the hidden danger of the safety defect threatened United States consumers. Therefore, sales and dispute settlements are bound by United States law.

After cross-examination and the trial, the Court found that the main dispute in the case involved two issues. One concerned the application of the law, the other relates to liability for breach of contract. As for the application of law, the Court held that since the parties did not agree in the contract on which country's law is the applicable law, according to the relevant provisions of Chinese judicial interpretation, the law of the country or region most closely related to the contract should be applied. The sales contract in this case was concluded in China by fax, the seller was the plaintiff, and the delivery method was FOB Shenzhen. Therefore, the seller's domicile law, Chinese law, should be applied. As for the liability for breach of contract, the Court held that both the defendant and plaintiff had breach of contract in the performance of the sales contract, so each should bear corresponding responsibilities. The Court judged the plaintiff and the defendants responsible for 50% of the losses according to the evidence from both parties. According to Chinese law, if the defendant in this case believes that the quality of the seller's products is defective, he may choose to continue to perform the contract by means of repair, rework, replacement, etc. Even if the purpose of the contract cannot be realized due to serious quality problems, he may also choose to terminate the contract, return goods for refund, or restore the other party to their original state. The plaintiff's act of destroying the goods without technical identification is improper performance, so the plaintiff should bear the corresponding liability. The plaintiff failed to provide a qualification certificate or product materials, and there was a delay in delivery, so it shall also bear the corresponding liability for the breach of contract. In the plaintiff's claim that the defendants J & H Company and Merion Company assume joint liability, the Court did not support a view of principal-agent relationship between them.

## Commentary on the Key Issues Related to the CISG

### Issues

Issue 1 The Applicability of the CISG.
Issue 2 Differentiation between Fundamental Breach of the Contract and Product Flaw Guarantee.
Issue 3 Allocation of Liability for Breach of Contract by Parties.

### Comments

#### Issue 1 the Applicability of the CISG

The parties involved in this case are Fanyunanxing Company, located in Guangzhou, China, J & H International Inc., and Merion Company, where J & H Company and Merion Company were in a principal-agent relationship as defendants. In the case of the principal-agent relationship between the two defendants, the ultimate parties to the rights and obligations of the sale of goods involved in the contract was Fanyunanxing Company (plaintiff) and J & H Company (defendant). From the content of the judgment, the defendant claimed that the CISG should be the applicable law in the case, however the judge was clear that the contract did not explicitly chose the applicable law to the dispute. He then chose, art 5 of the *Supreme People's Court on Foreign Civil or Commercial Contract Dispute Cases Legal Provisions,*[1] the most closely related to the country or regional law. The judge further held that the sales contract was subject to the seller's domicile law at the time the contract was concluded. In this case, the sales contract was concluded in China by fax, and the delivery method was FOB Shenzhen, so the seller's domicile law, namely Chinese law, should be applied. In the judgment, the judge in this case did not directly respond to the defendant J & H Company's request to directly apply the CISG to resolve the relevant disputes, but identified Chinese Law as the applicable law in accordance with the relevant judicial interpretation of the Supreme People's Court of China.

In a contract for the international sale of goods, if the parties fail to agree on the applicable law to apply in the contract, the court will preferentially determine the

[1] Provisions of the Supreme People's Court on Several Issues Concerning the Application of Law in the Trial of Civil or Commercial Contract Disputes Involving Foreign Affairs (promulgated by The Supreme People's Court of the People's Republic of China, Jun.11, 2007, Effective Aug 8, 2007).

law to be applied according to national procedural law. There is a large number of relevant cases heard by Chinese courts in which the CISG is applied. For example, among the 22 cases with final citations for the CISG included in China Judgements Online, 13 judgements are those cases where the parties did not select the proper law (at least not as indicated by the judgements, and not selected at trial), but the court still applied the law according to international private procedure law. This accounted for 59% of cases to 1 January 2023 (due to differences in search conditions, the cases were not completely counted).[2] In this case, the defendant had clearly stated in the claim:

> Articles 25, 35(2)(c), 42(1), 74 of the CISG and the fact that the sales place of the thermos flasks in this case are in the United States, it can be seen that the safety hazards threaten consumers in the United States, regardless of their sales, the handling of disputes, etc., and must be subject to the laws of the United States.

J & H Company hoped to invoke the above provisions to address the security risks of the products and argued that they should be subject to U.S. law. Although this claim did not directly assert that the CISG should be applied to the case, and the correlation between the proof and the above content was not high, it also implicitly expressed the intention to apply the CISG. From the judgment, the Court did not respond positively to the application of the CISG. If the parties to the contract for the sale of goods do not specify in the contract which law shall be the applicable law in case of disputes, if the countries of the parties to the contract are States Parties to the CISG and the parties have not excluded the application, the CISG shall be given priority application.

[2] Haier International Business Co., Ltd. v. EUROBUSINESS-CARGO Co., Ltd. (2018) Lu 02 Min Chu No.821 (Qingdao Intermediate People's Court, Shandong Province, March 10, 2020); Danson Décor Inc. v Linhai Xinhui Handicrafts Co., Ltd. (2021) Zhejiang 10 Minchu No.75 (Taizhou Intermediate People's Court, Zhejiang Province, November 12, 2021); Ningbo Fengya Import and Export Co., Ltd. v STARPRINT S.R.L. (2020) Zhejiang 02 Minchu No.872 (Ningbo Intermediate People's Court, Zhejiang Province, August 12, 2022); Zhejiang China-Africa International Economic and Trade Port Service Co., Ltd. v CER-MEC SRL, (2020) Zhe 10 Min Chu No.603 (Taizhou Intermediate People's Court, Zhejiang Province, March 15, 2022); Dongguan Tecway Technology Co., Ltd. ××, LLC, (2020) Yue 19 Min Zhong No.9930 (Dongguan Intermediate People's Court, Guangdong Province, November 10, 2021); Ningbo Zhenyu Technology Co., Ltd. v DA Technology Co., Ltd., (2019) Zhejiang 02 Minchu No.587 (Ningbo Intermediate People's Court, Zhejiang Province, October 22, 2021); Jiangyin Longguang Aluminum Co., Ltd. v Triton mental supplies Pte Ltd. (2020) Su 02 Minchu No.125 (Wuxi Intermediate People's Court, Jiangsu Province, June 15, 2021); Haier International Business Co., Ltd. v EURO BUSINESS-CARGO, (2018) Lu 02 Min Chu No.821 (Qingdao Intermediate People's Court, Shandong Province, March 10, 2020); Shanghai Junyao Glasses Co., Ltd. v FLAMINGOVENTURESSL, (2021) Hu 0115 Minchu 38,888 (Shanghai Pudong New Area People's Court, May 16, 2022); Dashun Food (Shanghai) Co., Ltd. v IDEALLEADER INTERNATIONAL SRL, (2020) Hu 0115 Minchu No.42206 (Shanghai Pudong New Area People's Court, May 31, 2021); Motion Tech Automation, LLC v Guangzhou Kesheng Measurement and Control Equipment Co., Ltd. (2020) Yue 0191 Minchu No.2906 (People's Court of Nansha District, Guangdong Free Trade Zone, July 30, 2020); Shanghai Jialing Wind Instrument Co., Ltd. v ERANOMUSICALINSTRUEMENTS, INC, (2014) Pumin Er (Shang) Chu Zi No.S2228 (Shanghai Pudong New Area People's Court, June 5, 2015); Shanghai Xufu Industrial Co., Ltd. v MindsInSync Inc. (2013) Pumin Er (Shang) Chu Zi No.S1846 (Shanghai Pudong New Area People's Court, July 18, 2014).

From the practice of applying the CISG in China in recent years, with *ThyssenKrupp Mentallurgical Products Gmbh v Sinochem International (Overseas) Pte Ltd.* as an important precedent,[3] Chinese courts have made advancements in the number of cases 'directly applying or self-applying' the CISG. Chinese judges generally apply the CISG through 'comparison'. It is clear that when the provisions of the CISG are inconsistent with the provisions of domestic law, the CISG has the legal status of priority application. From the perspective of the CISG objective requirements, the court should directly apply it when meeting the applicable conditions of the Convention. The *UNCITRAL Summary on the Case Law of the United Nations Convention on the International Sale of Goods* also states that the application of the CISG takes precedence over the use of private international law rules.[4] Some scholars believe that, in terms of the direct application of the CISG, the court should first determine whether the contract involved falls within the jurisdiction of the CISG, then the international nature of the contract involved, and finally whether the parties effectively exclude the CISG.[5]

In the case of Fanyunanxing Co., v J & H International, Inc., despite the defendant's request for the application of the CISG and the absence of exclusion, the Court chose to rely on private international law rules of *lex fori* to hear the facts in dispute. This frustrated the defendant's expectation of the CISG as the applicable law. The method of law application in the case is quite different from the claim of the direct application of the CISG in China. What needs to be further considered is that even under the application mode of private international law, the CISG should still have the possibility of 'transformation' to application, but at the same time, due to the requirement of the treaty law, if it has transformed into domestic law, it should obtain special legal status over the general law. The judicial interpretation and guidance cases of Chinese courts play an important role in the applicable practice of the CISG. *The Minutes of the National Symposium on Foreign Commercial and Maritime Trials of Courts* issued in January 2022 clarified the mode of automatic application of the CISG, and required the People's Courts to ask the parties for specific opinions on the application of the Convention before the end of the court debate.[6] In fact, Chinese judicial institutions are promoting the application of the CISG consciously. During the trial, when the parties put forward the application of the CISG, the judge should give them a positive response.

This case was concluded in 2012. Considering the judge's grasp of the application of law to this case, he did not choose 'automatic application', but chose to use private international law rules to apply Chinese law. Today this method of law application seems deviant in understanding. If the parties do not explicitly exclude the CISG adaptation, the court should respond to the reasons for not applying the CISG. When

[3] ThyssenKrupp Mentallurgical Products Gmbh v. Sinochem International (Overseas) Pte Ltd. Min Four Zhong No.35 (The Four Civil Trial Chamber of the Supreme People's Court, June 30, 2014).

[4] UNCITRAL [1].

[5] Zhang [2], p. 104.

[6] Minutes of the National Symposium on Foreign-related Commercial and Maritime Trials of Courts (promulgated by The Supreme People's Court of the People's Republic of China, June 10, 2021).

China joined the CISG, China retained the application of art 1(2), excluding the application of the CISG according to the rules of private international law. This may be one of the reasons for the deviation of application of this case. Presently many scholars in China believe that China should withdraw its reservation to subparagraph (1)(b) of art 1 of the Convention.[7]

## Issue 2 Differentiation Between Fundamental Breach of the Contract and Product Flaw Guarantee

### I. Fundamental Breach of the Contract

From the cross-examination of the plaintiff and the defendant on the evidence, the buyer and seller of the goods recognized the quality problems of the product. Where a plaintiff demands payment from a defendant and the defendant refuses the demand, the performance of the seller's obligation to deliver the goods and the quality guarantee obligation will determine whether the plaintiff can fully obtain the consideration agreed to in the contract. The defendant claimed to apply arts 25, 35(2)(c), 42(1) and 74 of the CISG, but did not present further arguments as to whether this constituted a fundamental breach. The corresponding judgment did not provide a direct response, but on the basis that the plaintiff sold goods with a large defect risk, according to Chinese law, the existing quality defaults, can be remedied through repair, rework, replacement and other remedies and performance of the contract can continue. The defendant claimed that the defendant J&H Company lost USD $242,987.89 due to product quality problems, and argued that the amount of USD $79,620.88 already paid to the plaintiff should be returned.

Whether there is a fundamental breach depends on whether the breach caused the buyer to suffer a loss that '*deprives him of what he is entitled to expect under the contract*' and the breaching party subjectively foresaw that it would lead to damages. The Court held that the product was in breach of contract due to quality problems, and remedy was available to continue to perform the contract. Even the breach of a collateral duty can give rise to a fundamental breach.[8] The seller is responsible for the guarantee of the quality of the product, and when there is a problem with product quality which makes it impossible to continue performance of the contract, there is the possibility of fundamental breach of contract. According to the CISG, where the goods have already been delivered, the breach must reach the point where '*the delivered goods irrevocably need to be replaced*' to constitute a fundamental breach, and the seller may still take remedial action at its own expense if it does not cause the buyer unreasonable inconvenience or delay. Based on the principle of good faith, the spirit of encouraging transactions and contract maintenance, the CISG gives the seller the right to remedy its failure in performance.[9] As to whether the seller subjectively predicted the occurrence of the damage caused by the product quality problems, the plaintiff in the case had explained that the product will be sold

---

[7] Han [3], p. 218.

[8] UNCITRAL [1].

[9] Wang [4], p. 55.

to the United States. Thus, the quality of the product is bound by US law. Even if the quality of the goods sold by the seller were to be adjusted by US legal norms, it does not prove that the product is so defective that it constitutes a fundamental breach under art 25 of the CISG.

## II. Product Flaw Guarantee

Even if it does not constitute a fundamental default, the plaintiff is still liable for the defective product. Article 46 (3) of the CISG stipulates that:

> If the goods do not conform with the contract, the buyer may require the seller to remedy the lack of conformity by repair, unless this is unreasonable having regard to all the circumstances. A request for repair must be made either in conjunction with notice given under article 39 or within a reasonable time thereafter.

The flasks delivered by the seller could meet the market quality requirements of relevant products through repair. Even if the product had been destroyed by the U.S. Consumer Product Safety Commission, the relative contract relationship still does not exempt the seller from the post-contractual obligations or ancillary obligations caused by the product quality problems. When ancillary obligations are not performed, there is still the possibility of constituting a fundamental default.[10] In view of the fact that the product delivered by the seller had been destroyed and the actual repairs could not be undertaken, the judge clarified the responsibilities of both parties based on the discretion and the proof of both parties. The CISG provides the actual source of law, displacing the territorial contract laws of different countries, in order to create a unique and uniform body of CISG law.[11] The CISG's distinction between liability for breach of contract and liability for quality defects has been supported by the broadest range of countries, and the most critical factor in distinguishing between the two is whether the breach of contract has caused a significant risk that the purpose of the contract will not be achieved. In this case, the quality defects of the product did not reach the point where the contractual and post-contractual obligations agreed to by both parties could not be performed due to product defects, both parties should bear the corresponding responsibility for their respective breaches of contract. Article 107 of the *Contract Law of the People's Republic of China* stipulates the liability of the parties if they fail to perform the contract or fail to perform the contract in accordance with the regulations. This provision states that:

> If a party fails to perform its contractual obligations or fails to perform its contractual obligations in accordance with the agreement, it shall be liable for breach of contract, such as continuing to perform, taking remedial measures or compensating for losses.

According to the facts verified by the Court, the department store Macy's, the defendant's client, found that the flasks had a weak handle prone to easily fall off

[10] CLOUT case No.2 [Oberlandesgericht Frankfurt a.M., Germany, 17 September 1991]; See also CLOUT case No.217 [Handelsgericht des Kantons Aargau, Switzerland, 26 September 1997]; CLOUT case No.154 [Courd'appel Grenoble, France, 22 February 1995]; CLOUT case No.282 [Oberlandesgericht Koblenz, Germany, 31 January 1997].

[11] Lee [5], p. 8.

the bottle, reflecting defective product quality, in early October 2010. Therefore, the seller was obliged to maintain the contract. The CISG stipulates that if the seller defaults, the buyer can require the delivery of alternative goods (fundamental default), repair, at his own remedy, declare the contract invalid, reduce the price, reject early delivery, reject more than the agreed amount of goods, and demand damages, such as contract remedy method. In the Fanyunanxing case, the defendant was faced with various measures such as repair, remedy and price reduction of the defective products. Before the case was prosecuted, the defendant refused to make the remaining payment, which is the result of the defendant's self-help remedy contract. Another important factual situation is that the buyer had unilaterally destroyed the goods involved in the case under United States law. The problem is whether the seller has an obligation to provide goods consistent with the buyer's national law or art 35 of the CISG to solve this problem. The product purpose way as to the final law which should apply, and which national standard evaluation is used is not unified. Examples such as the 'New Zealand mussel case'[12] and the 'Belgium pork case'[13] respectively adopted the 'seller country standard' and the 'buyer's country' standard.

**Issue 3 Allocation of Liability for Breach of Contract by Parties**

On the basis of affirming the breach of both the buyer and the seller in the performance of the contract, the determination of the share of the buyer and the seller for breach of contract is another important issue in regard to settlement of the case. In this case, the Court clarified the responsibilities of both parties, that is, J & H Company believed that the plaintiff sold quality products, neither required the other party to continue to perform the contract nor conducted the necessary technical appraisal of the defective products; the plaintiff failed to provide the product quality qualification certificate or product quality test report on the product, and delayed the delivery of the contract. Finally, the Court ordered the plaintiff and the defendant to bear 50% of the loss. In determining the liability of the parties, the Court exercised discretion based on the fault of the buyer and seller.

The amount of assuming half of the value of the object of the contract separately seems to take into account the actual performance of the contract by both parties. However, if the CISG is taken as the applicable law, and the defendant clearly states that the seller should bear the liability for damages with the help of the counterclaim system, the resulting judgment may be differentiated. Article 74 of the CISG stipulates that:

> Damages for breach of contract by one party consist of a sum equal to the loss, including loss of profit, suffered by the other party as a consequence of the breach.

The judgment indicated that J & H Company lost USD $242,987.89 due to the quality problems of the goods sold by the seller, resulting in the recall and removal of

[12] Germany 8 March 1995 Supreme Court (New Zealand mussels case), available at: http://cisgw3.law.pace.edu/cases/950308g3.html.

[13] Germany 2 March 2005 Federal Supreme Court (Frozen pork case), available at: http://cisgw3.law.pace.edu/cases/050302g1.html.

the products and related expenses. Although the judgment disclosed limited information, it at least shows that the default of the seller caused the buyer to suffer calculated losses, including profits. Given the need to promote the Convention's international character and the need to promote uniformity in the Convention's application, and in light of the purposes and policies of art 74, the aggrieved party bears the burden of proving with reasonable certainty it has suffered a loss as a result of the breach.[14] If the buyer can clearly prove that it suffered a reasonable loss of profit due to the quality problems of the seller's products, the court at least should take into account the expected loss of profit when distributing the liabilities of both parties as appropriate.

In addition, the division of primary and secondary obligations in a contract is also of positive significance to the allocation of liability for breach of contract. The primary and secondary obligations of the contract are not unchanged. It is generally believed that the delivery of quality test data of the products sold is a secondary obligation relative to the delivery of the goods itself. Article 30 of the CISG stipulates the relevant obligations of the seller in relation to the *Delivery of the goods and handing over of documents*, but it does not specify the main obligation of said goods and documents. Some scholars actively advocate the trend to consider the application of domestic law as *ultima ratio* is necessary,[15] but for judges, it should be a general choice to complete the 'Gap-Filling' with the assistance of the UNIDROIT Principles, unless the provisions of domestic law have more obvious advantages of filling in. However, this is not always the case. In disputes over the international sale of goods contract involving trade terms, the applicable order of international commercial practice, international commercial treaties and domestic law is international commercial practice gives priority, followed by the CISG, and then domestic law again.[16]

Because the judgment does not reflect whether the two parties' special quality inspection obligations are the main contractual obligations, therefore without the CISH being specified, the relevant provisions of art 598 of *Chinese Civil Code* can apply.[17] The seller has completed the main obligations, even if the product had quality defects, and should also maximise the contract consideration. Although it is too concise to equally assign the liabilities of both parties within the limit of the contract subject amount, the above deduction is based on the parties having clear propositions and sufficient evidence. Even if the court does not directly apply the relevant provisions of the CISG for judgment, the final judgment also clarifies the fault of both parties for breach of contract.

[14] CISG Advisory Council. (2013). CISG-AC Opinion No.6: Calculation of Damages under CISG Article 74. http://www.cisgac.com/cisgac-opinion-no6/.

[15] Viscasillas [6], p. 16.

[16] Zuo [7], p. 58.

[17] Civil Code of the People's Republic of China (promulgated by The Third Session of the 13th National People's Congress of the People's Republic of China, May 28,2020, Effective Jun.1, 2021).

## References


1. United Nations Commission on International Trade Law (2016). *UNCITRAL Digest of Case Law on the United Nations Convention on Contracts for the International Sale of Goods*. https://uncitral.un.org/en/case_law/digests
2. Zhang, P. (2022). The Application of the CISG in Chinese Courts: Also on the Application of Treaties after Implementation of Civil Code. *Journal of Northeastern University (Social Science)*, 24(4), 100–108
3. Han, S. (2016). Application of the CISG in China's International Commercial Arbitration. *China Legal Science*, 2016(05), 28–238
4. Wang, J. (2017). On the Seller's Right to Cure under CISG Article 48. *International Business Research*, 2017(02), 55–65
5. Lee, E. (2005). The new canon: using or misusing foreign law to decide domestic intellectual property claims. *Harvard International Law Journal*, 46(1), 1–66
6. Viscasillas, P. (2017). Interpretation and Gap-Filling under the CISG: Contrast and Convergence with the Unidroit Principles. *Uniform Law Review*, 22(1), 4–28
7. Zuo, H. (2021). The Application of the CISG and Incoterms in risk Transfer from Neuromed Case. *Journal of Henan University of Economics and Law*, 36(01), 54–59


**Kaiwei Cui** Ph.D. candidate in International Law at the University of International Business and Economics, majoring in International Business Law and International Trade Law. Prior to that, he got his LL.M. from Zhengzhou University. He participated in projects of the National Social Science Fund, and projects of the Department of Commerce of Henan Province, among others.

**Peng Guo** is Lecturer in Law at the Swinburne University of Technology. He has worked across several Australian universities and has held visiting positions at different European universities. He has received scholarships awarded by renowned research institutions and international organisations, including the Max Planck Institute for Comparative and International Private Law, the International Institute for the Unification of Private Law (UNIDROIT), the Swiss Institute of Comparative Law, and the European Union. He specialises in the international sale of goods, international commercial arbitration, comparative contract law, and law and technology.

# Taiwan Semiconductor Co., Ltd. v. Shenzhen SANG DA Bai LI Electric Co., Ltd.

**Shaotang Wang**

## Case Information

**Case Name:** *Taiwan Semiconductor Co., Ltd. v Shenzhen SANG DA Bai LI Electric Appliance Co., Ltd.*

**Seller**: Taiwan Semiconductor Co., Ltd.
**Place of Business**: Taiwan, China

**Buyer**: Shenzhen SANG DA Bai LI Electric Appliance Co., Ltd.
**Place of Business**: Shenzhen, China

**Details of First Instance:**
**Court:** Nanshan District People's Court, Shenzhen
**Case No.:** (2012) Shen Nan Fa Min Er Chu Zi No. 134

**Details of Second Instance**:
**Court**: Shenzhen Intermediate People's Court
**Date of Decision**: Nov.13, 2012
**Case No.**: (2012) Shen Zhong Fa She Wai Zhong Zi No.186
**Judges**: Mingyan Qiu (Presiding Judge), Ping Zhu (Acting Judge), Lele Liang (Acting Judge)

**CISG Applied:** No
**Key CISG Provisions Interpreted and Applied:** None

S. Wang (✉)
Nankai University, Tianjin, China
e-mail: wstwell@163.com



P. Guo et al. (eds.), *Selected Chinese Cases on the UN Sales Convention (CISG) Vol. 3*, Selected Chinese Cases on the CISG,
https://doi.org/10.1007/978-981-99-6851-0_34

**Case Abstract**

The appellant, Taiwan Semiconductor Co., Ltd. ('Semiconductor Company') and the appellee, Shenzhen SANG DA Bai LI Electric Co., Ltd. ('SANG DA Bai LI Company') were in dispute over a sales contract between them. Semiconductor Company did not accept the civil judgment of the first instance made by Nanshan District People's Court, Shenzhen and appealed to the Shenzhen Intermediate People's Court.

The Semiconductor Company claimed that SANG DA Bai LI Company issued a purchase order to it on November 6, 2007, in order to purchase electronic components worth USD $19,800. The Semiconductor Company delivered the goods to the consignee designated by SANG DA Bai LI Company on November 8, 2007. SANG DA Bai LI Company did not make payment for the goods. The court of first instance held that, according to the facts claimed by the Semiconductor Company, the limitation of action period for the dispute in this case had expired on January 9, 2010, and there was no evidence to show that the limitation of action period had been suspended or interrupted. The Semiconductor Company failed to exercise the right of claim within the statutory limitation period of action and could not request the Court to protect its corresponding civil rights.

The Semiconductor Company appealed to the Nanshan District People's Court of Shenzhen against the first-instance judgment, believing that according to the provisions and spirit of the Minutes of the Second National Conference on Foreign-related Commercial Maritime Justice (Fa Fa (2005) No. 26), the Supreme People's Court's Provisions on Several Issues Concerning the Application of Law in the Trial of Foreign-related Civil or Commercial Contract Disputes (Fa Shi (2007) No. 14) and other relevant laws and regulations, sales contracts involving Hong Kong, Macao and Taiwan should refer to relevant provisions applicable to contracts for international sales of goods, that is, the dispute in this case should be subject to a four-year limitation of action.

The court of second Instance held that the case was a dispute over a Taiwan-related sales contract, and the focus of the dispute was whether the case had exceeded the legal limitation period of two years. The Semiconductor Company filed a lawsuit on January 9, 2012, which already exceeded the statutory limitation of action, without providing evidence to support the suspension or interruption of the limitation of action in this case. The first-instance judgment rejected its claim, which was not improper, and the court of second instance supported the first-instance judgment according to law.

The court of second Instance held that according to art 1 of the United Nations Convention on Contracts for the International Sale of Goods ('CISG'), the CISG applies to contracts for the sale of goods concluded between parties having their places of business in different countries. The contract involved is not an international contract for the sale of goods. Secondly, there are no laws, administrative regulations and relevant provisions that stipulate that the limitation of action for bringing a lawsuit in respect of a dispute over a sales contract involving Hong Kong, Macao and Taiwan should refer to the four-year limitation of action period applicable to contracts for the international sale of goods. Therefore, the court of first instance applied the limitation of action for two years, and there was no error in applying the law.

## Commentary on the Key Issues Related to the CISG

### Issue

Issue 1 Whether the CISG is Applicable to Parties whose Places of Business are in Mainland, China and Taiwan.

### Comments

### Issue 1 Whether the CISG is Applicable to Parties Whose Places of Business Are in Mainland, China and Taiwan

As of October 2022, the CISG had 95 contracting countries worldwide and has entered into force in 93 contracting countries. Therefore, the CISG is an international convention widely accepted by most trading countries. On January 1, 1988, the CISG came into force in China (excluding Hong Kong, Macao Special Administrative Region, and Taiwan). On May 5, 2022, China deposited a statement with the Secretary-General of the United Nations to expand the territorial application of CISG to the Hong Kong Special Administrative Region. The territorial application took effect in Hong Kong on December 1, 2022. However, China has not made a statement on whether Taiwan applies the CISG.

Article 1(1) of the CISG stipulates its basic rules of application:

> This Convention applies to contracts of sale of goods between parties whose places of business are in different States:
>
> (a) when the States are Contracting States; or
>
> (b) when the rules of private international law lead to the application of the law of a Contracting State.

Taiwan belongs to the territory of China, and its dispute over the international sale of goods with mainland of China is a domestic dispute in nature, which does not meet the definition of 'international dispute' in the CISG, and certainly does not meet the concept of 'contracting state' in the CISG. Therefore, in principle, art 1(1) of the Convention does not apply to disputes between parties whose places of business are in Taiwan, China and mainland China. The court of second instance made an accurate judgment on this case. However, if the CISG cannot be applied directly, the parties can jointly choose to apply the CISG according to their autonomy of will. Although the parties in mainland China and the parties in Taiwan are both parties with their places of business in China, as long as the parties have the intention to apply CISG, the People's Court will generally follow the principle of party autonomy, respects the wishes of the parties, and apply the CISG to resolve disputes.

**Shaotang Wang** is a Lecturer in Law from Law School of Nankai University. He holds a Master in Law and a Ph.D. from Peking University. He specialises in international investment law and international trade law. He has published related articles in some core journals in China.

# Cai Puzhong v. Huang Xiaobin, Liu Liya

**Shao Long and Suqing Shi**

## Case Information

**Case Name:** *Cai Puzhong v Huang Xiaobin, Liu Liya*

**Seller:** Cai Puzhong
**Place of Business:** China

**Buyer:** Huang Xiaobin
**Place of Business:** Romania

**Buyer:** Liu Liya (also named Liu Liduo)
**Place of Business:** Romania

**Details of First Instance:**
**Court:** Ruian People's Court, Zhejiang Province
**Date of Decision:** 10/05/2013
**Case No.:** (2012) Wen Rui Shang Wai Chu Zi No.18
**Judges:** Huang Pingping (Presiding Judge), Cai Yonglin (People's Juror), Zhang Weiping (People's Juror)

**CISG Applied:** Yes.
**Key the CISG Provisions Interpreted and Applied:** Articles 53, 54, 74

S. Long (✉) · S. Shi
Hunan University, Changsha, Hunan, China
e-mail: longshao@hnu.edu.cn

S. Shi
e-mail: ssq2002@hnu.edu.cn



P. Guo et al. (eds.), *Selected Chinese Cases on the UN Sales Convention (CISG) Vol. 3*, Selected Chinese Cases on the CISG,
https://doi.org/10.1007/978-981-99-6851-0_35

### Case Abstract

Cai Puzhong ('Cai'), the plaintiff, filed a lawsuit to Ruian People's Court, Zhejiang Province on 16 April 2012 for an international sales dispute with Huang Xiaobin and Liu Liya ('Huang' and 'Liu').

Huang and Liu were a couple residing in Romania who divorced in 2012. In 2010, they successively purchased various specifications of socks from Cai. On 29 May 2011, the parties settled the account as Huang and Liu owed Cai €25,300. Huang wrote an IOU to Cai, agreeing on a monthly payment of €1,000 on the 15th of each month plus overdue interest in case of delay. It was ascertained by the Court that the central parity of the RMB exchange rate of €100 was 918.24 yuan on 30 May 2011 (the following working day) according to the State Administration of Foreign Exchange. The two defendants thus owed the plaintiff a converted sum of 232,314.72 yuan. Yet the arrears were not paid, in spite of several demands by the plaintiff.

The Court confirmed the existence of a valid sales contract between the parties governed by the CISG. The sales contract reflected the parties' true intention and involved no null and void circumstances. The two defendants were obliged to pay the price pursuant to arts 53 and 54 of the CISG. The defendants' nonfulfillment of this obligation incurred a liability for breach including payment of damages and loss of interest according to art 74 of the CISG. Concerning the loss of interest, since the parties did not agree on a specific interest rate in the IOU, the Court adopted a monthly rate of 0.4875% calculated on the benchmark one-year lending rate. The plaintiff's claim for the application of a monthly rate of 1% was not supported due to lack of legal basis.

### Commentary to the Key Issues Related to the CISG

#### Issues

Issue 1 The Applicability of the CISG
Issue 2 The Seller's Right to Remedies Including Claim for Incurred Loss of Interest
Issue 3 The Determination of Interest Rate.

#### Comments

#### Issue 1 the Applicability of the CISG

The Court did not expound the applicability of the CISG to the current case. Its judgment pursuant to the CISG reflects its opinion that both the sales contract and the disputed issues fall under the applicable scope of the CISG.

The Convention applies only to contracts for the international sale of goods. When determining what an 'international sale' is, the parties' nationalities are disregarded according to art 1(3) of the CISG. The Convention conversely requires that the parties' places of business are in different States in art 1(1). This is the sole criterion adopted by the CISG, so as to avoid complexity in determining internationality, thus reducing controversy on the applicability of the CISG in this regard.[1] The civil or commercial character of the parties is irrelevant in applying the CISG and natural persons can also be eligible subjects of a CISG contract.[2] The CISG does not limit contract parties to commercial subjects since there is no uniform definition of 'merchants' worldwide and the distinction between commercial and civil contracts is unclear in many jurisdictions.[3] Since natural persons do not have places of business, their habitual residences substitute in determining foreign connection pursuant to art 10(b) of the CISG. In this case, the seller, Cai, and the buyers, Huang and Liu, are all natural persons. The disclosed habitual residences of the parties are in different Contracting States of the CISG, China and Romania respectively. This suffices discerning of the contract as an international sales contract in the sense of the CISG and entitles the autonomous application of the Convention based on an objective test.

For sales contracts concluded between natural persons, it should be made clear that the goods concerned are not purchased for personal, family or household use since these sales are otherwise excluded from the applicable scope of the CISG. Though the CISG does not positively define 'goods', it excludes certain types of sale in art 2 based on the aim of the sale, the method of the sale, and the specific goods concerned. Sales for personal, family or household use are excluded since these consumer sales are subject to special consumer-protection laws and the CISG governs only commercial sales.[4] Consumer sales are to be excluded unless the seller neither knew, nor ought to have known, that the goods were bought for such use before or at the conclusion of the contract. In this case, though the buyers are natural persons, the socks to the value of €25,300 they purchased were obviously not for personal, family or household use. The sale qualifies as a sale governed by the CISG.

In addition, the Convention limits its governing issues in art 4 only to the formation of a qualified contract and the rights and obligations of the seller and the buyer arising therefrom. It does not regulate all contractual matters, expressly excluding in particular the validity of the contract and the effect the contract may have on the property in the goods being sold. In this case, the validity of the contract was not challenged. The plaintiff, the seller, contended the buyers' nonperformance of their contractual obligation to pay the price, and claimed for damages resulting from this nonperformance. The plaintiff proved the claimed breach by submitting the original handwritten IOU as evidence, without the submission of a copy of the contract. The Chinese Civil Procedural Law was applied in determining procedural matters, including verifying evidence, yet the substantive issues of the case, the buys' obligation and the seller's remedy, were considered to be governed by the CISG and were determined relying solely on provisions of the Convention.

In conclusion, though the Chinese Court did not expound its deliberation of the applicability of the CISG to this case, it in practice inclined to directly applying

[1] Schwenzer [1], p. 250.
[2] Schwenzer [1], p. 250.
[3] Schwenzer [1], p. 250.
[4] Schwenzer [1], p. 262.

the Convention rather than Chinese domestic law. The obligation to implement the CISG, an international treaty, has been generally observed.

**Issue 2 the Seller's Right to Remedies Including Claim for Incurred Loss of Interest**

The CISG leaves the validity issue to domestic laws, but it specifies, directly and clearly, the rights and obligations of the seller and the buyer arising from a valid sales contract under its applicable scope. Chapter III, Part III (arts 53–65) of the Convention specifically addresses obligations of the buyer and remedies for breach of contract by the buyer. Article 53 sets the buyer's obligation of paying the price and taking delivery. In practice, the obligation of paying the price matters most, which is further elaborated in arts 54–59, specifying clearly the determination of the time and place of the payment and other requirements on the buyer's performance of this obligation.[5] In this case, the fact of the buyers' complete non-payment of the price was confirmed by the Court relying on the evidence, namely the original IOU submitted by the plaintiff. The defendants neither defended nor attended the trial. Their breach of the obligation in arts 53 and 54 CISG was decided in absentia.

Breach of contract by the buyer entitles the seller's right to remedies provided generally in art 61 of the CISG. In the case of nonpayment, the seller may require the buyer to pay the price and claim for damages. Damages are a universally applied monetary remedy compatible with other remedies. An aggrieved party can resort to damages as long as his loss has not been fully compensated. Article 74 of the CISG adopts a general principle of 'full compensation', which establishes damages as 'a sum equal to the loss, including loss of profit, suffered by the other party as a consequence of the breach'. The loss should actually be incurred by the aggrieved party but predictable to the party in breach at the time of conclusion. The full compensation principle provides for the recovery of interest.[6] Moreover, art 78 of the CISG further explicitly stipulates the obligation to pay interest if a party fails to pay the price or defaults on any other payment.[7]

In this case, the plaintiff, the aggrieved seller, claimed for the defendants' paying of the arrears and compensation for his loss of interest. His right to remedies was confirmed by the Court after its establishment of the buyers' nonperformance of the obligation of paying the price. The claim for the arrears and interest loss was also generally upheld. The claimed amount, however, was not supported by the Court since both the exchange rate and the interest rate were corrected by it. For the exchange rate, the Court verified that the central parity of RMB exchange rate of €100 was 918.24 yuan, rather than 926.79 yuan claimed by the plaintiff on 29 May 2011. It thus awarded the defendants' payment of 232,314.72 yuan in arrears, instead of the claimed 234,477.80 yuan. Concerning the calculation of loss of interest, the Court diverged from the plaintiff on the interest rate to be applied. The complexity of this matter suffices specific elaboration below.

---

[5] Lookofsky [2], p. 102.

[6] Schwenzer [1], p. 366.

[7] Schwenzer [1], p. 1628.

## Issue 3 the Determination of Interest Rate

The CISG provides in art 78 the general right of creditors to interest on delayed payment, but does not specify the rate of interest to be applied. The rule is considered to act as a compromise, bridging irreconcilable differences of opinion to prevent the failure of the conclusion of the Convention.[8] The determination of the amount of interest loss is characterized as a *gap praeter legem*, i.e. the Convention applies to the issue but does not expressly resolve it, which is to be settled in conformity with the general principles on which the Convention is based.[9] Some scholars instead argue for applying domestic law to fill the gap.[10] There are even courts which regard the issue as not governed by the Convention.[11]

Often-cited awards of interest loss exist where the tribunal held that the interest rate is a matter governed but not expressly settled by the CISG.[12] For example, in an Austrian arbitral award, No. SCH-4318 in 1994,[13] the following opinion was conveyed:

> As far as interest is concerned, the sole arbitrator held that the interest rate is a matter governed but not expressly settled by CISG. Therefore, it must be determined according to the general principles on which CISG is based (Art. 7(2) CISG). Referring to Arts.78 and 74 CISG, the arbitrator found *that full compensation* is one of the general principles underlying CISG.

However, the various opinions on interest loss calculation make it a most complex issue in applying the CISG. Some argue that the principle of full compensation should be used[14]; others prefer using the usual rate at the debtor's place of business or the places of performance[15]; while yet others suggest distinguishing between cases where the creditor had to use credit or not.

Among all these divergent views, the CISG-AC prefers the interest rate relevant at the creditor's place of business, suggesting applying the national rate of that State.[16] The national rate, however, may be influenced by public policy and preconditions of the claim itself, and it thus seems more appropriate to apply an interest rate determined by the market.[17] Yet according to Schwenzer, 'the market price criteria'

---

[8] Schwenzer [1], p.1628.

[9] Schlechtreim [3], p. 279.

[10] Kröll et al. [4], p. 1118.

[11] UNCITRAL [5], p. 365.

[12] UNCITRAL [5], p. 365.

[13] Internationales Schiedsgericht der Bundeskammer der gewerblichen Wirtschaft—Wien, Arbitral awards No.SCH-4318,15 June 1994.UNILEX.

[14] CISG-AC Opinion No.14, Interest Under Article 78 CISG, Comments 3.35 et seq.

[15] LG Berlin, 21 March 2003, CISG-online 785; Regional Court Bratislava, 1 February 2007, CISG-online 1758; see also Wuhan Intermediate People's Court of Hubei Province, 11 May 2004, CISG-online 1499; Regional Court Bratislava, 15 December 2005, CISG-online 1754; Yugoslav Chamber of Commerce, 28 January 2009, CISG-online 1856.

[16] CISG-AC Opinion No.14, Interest Under Article 78 CISG, Comments 3.36.

[17] Schwenzer [1], p. 1636.

is more difficult to use because it varies in borrowing and saving, short-term or long-term investments, etc.[18] She suggests that when the sum is paid in Euros, the court or arbitral tribunal may apply the minimum bid rate for main refinancing operations fixed by the European Central Bank.[19]

In this case, the Court decided that the interest accrual period began on 16 June 2011, the day after the first repayment date, conforming to the plaintiff's request. For the interest rate, it denied the plaintiff's request for 1% per month, but held, in the absence of an agreement on this rate in the IOU, it was appropriate to calculate the loss of interest based on the current benchmark one-year lending rate in China, the creditor's place of business. A converted monthly rate of 0.4875% per month was applied. Though the Court did not explain the underlying rationale, its decision is general justified.

## References

1. Schwenzer, I. (2016). *Schlechtriem & Schwenzer: Commentary on the UN Convention on the International Sale of Goods* (4th ed.). Oxford University Press
2. Lookofsky, J. M. (2017). *Understanding the CISG: A Compact Guide to the 1980 United Nations Convention on Contracts for the International Sale of Goods* (5th ed.). Kluwer Law International
3. Schlechtreim, P. (2004). Interpretation, Gap-Filling and Further Development of the UN Sales Convention. *Pace International Law Review*, 16(2), 279–306
4. Kröll, S., Mistelis L. & Viscasillas, P. (2018). *UN Convention on Contracts for the International Sale of Goods (CISG): A Commentary* (2nd ed.). Hart Publishing
5. United Nations Commission on International Trade Law (UNCITRAL). (2016). *UNCITRAL Digest of Case Law on the United Nations Convention on Contracts for the International Sale of Goods*. Retrieved June 20, 2023, from https://uncitral.un.org/en/case_law/digests

**Shao Long** is an Assistant Professor in Law at Hunan University. She holds a doctoral degree in law, specialising in the field of international law, from Vienna University. Dr. Long's research interests lie in international trade law, WTO law, and international commercial arbitration. She teaches International Economic Law to LLB students and acts as the coach of HNU CIETAC Cup (pre-vis) moot team.

**Suqing Shi** LL.B. (Hunan University). The author majors in international economic law and competition law; participated in the 19th annual CIETAC Cup International Commercial Arbitration Moot and helped the team to win the Best Memo Award.

[18] Schwenzer [1], p. 1636.

[19] Schwenzer [1], p. 1636.

# A/S Harald Nyborg Co., Ltd. v. Wuxi Anjiu Automatic Vehicle Co., Ltd.

**Kaiwei Cui and Peng Guo**

**Case Information**

**Case Name:** *A/S Harald Nyborg Co., Ltd. v Wuxi Anjiu Automatic Vehicle Co., Ltd.*
**CISG Applied:** No
**Key the CISG Provisions Interpreted:** Arts 1(1)(a), 2, 3, 6

**Seller:** Wuxi Anjiu Automatic Vehicle Co., Ltd. ('Anjiu Company')
**Place of Business:** China

**Buyer:** A/S Harald Nyborg Co., Ltd. (Harald Company')
**Place of Business:** Denmark

**Details of First Instance:**
**Court:** Wuxi Intermediate People's Court of Jiangsu Province
**Date of Decision:** 17 January 2013
**Case No.:** (2012) Xi Shang Wai Chu Zi No. 0037
**Judges:** Lu Chao (Presiding Judge), Li Jun (Acting Judge), Su Qiang (Acting Judge)

K. Cui (✉)
University of International Business and Economics, Beijing, China
e-mail: 13663719268@163.com

P. Guo
Swinburne University of Technology, Melbourne, VIC 3000, Australia
e-mail: pguo@swin.edu.au



P. Guo et al. (eds.), *Selected Chinese Cases on the UN Sales Convention (CISG) Vol. 3*, Selected Chinese Cases on the CISG,
https://doi.org/10.1007/978-981-99-6851-0_36

**Case Abstract**

In April 2010, the plaintiff, Harald Company, and the defendant, Anjiu Company, entered into an international contract for the sale of goods which agreed that Anjiu Company would provide electric motorcycles, batteries and chargers to Harald Company, and Anjiu Company would promise in a Proforma Invoice that all electric motorcycles should have an EU compliance certificate. In June 2010, Anjiu Company delivered the goods to the carrier designated by Harald Company at Shanghai Port, and issued the commitment of a commercial invoice, a packing list and a European Union compliance certificate. In the same month, Harald Company issued a letter of credit and made the payment in accordance with the contract. After the agreed goods in the contract arrived at the receiving port, Harald Company found that the electric scooter of the agreed model delivered by Anjiu Company was not accompanied by the EU compliance certificate, and there were quality problems with the goods. On June 15, 2011, Harald Company claimed that Anjiu Company had violated its quality assurance commitments, and that the goods delivered by Anjiu Company had serious quality problems. Harald Company requested the contract be cancelled and the goods be returned for a refund, however Anjiu Company refused.

During the trial, both parties unanimously requested to exclude the application of the CISG, and chose Chinese law as the applicable law. According to the Court, the focus of the dispute centered around two issues. The first is whether Anjiu Company has breached the contract, and the second is whether Harald Company has the right to terminate the contract. The plaintiff believed that, in accordance with art 94(2), 94(3) and 94(4) of the Chinese Contract Law,[1] the defendant failed to provide the EU conformity certificate, refused to perform after-sales maintenance obligations, pay maintenance fees, and provided unqualified products. These and other behaviors constituted a fundamental breach of contract. The Court did not recognize the above claim. It reasoned that the product had a normal sale at the location of the buyer, Harald Company did not raise any objection after receiving the goods, the two parties did not expressly agree on the warranty period or the assumption of after-sales maintenance services, and the relevant inspection reports were not valid. Invalid inspection reports could not indicate that there were quality problems in the products that prevented the normal use of the goods, and the purpose of the contract involved could not be achieved. The Court finally made a judgment in accordance with Chinese law, holding that the evidence submitted by Harald Company was insufficient to prove that the goods provided by Anjiu Company did not constitute a fundamental breach of contract The Court finally rejected Harald Company's claim for termination of the contract and degradation of the payment for goods.

---

[1] Contract Law of the People's Republic of China (promulgated by NPC Standing Committee, December 28, 2013, Effective July 1, 2013, repealed on January 1, 2021, and replaced by the Civil Code of China).

## Commentary to the Key Issues Related to the CISG

### Issues

Issue 1 Exclusive Application of the CISG
Issue 2 Fundamental Breach and Post-contractual Obligations
Issue 3 Termination of Rights and Obligations after Completion of Contract Performance.

### Comments

### Issue 1 Exclusive Application of the CISG

The plaintiff, Harald Company, and the defendant, Anjiu Company, are legal persons located in Denmark and China respectively. Since Denmark and China are both Contracting Parties to the CISG, art 1(1)(a) of the CISG certainly applies to adjust the sales contract relationship between the buyer and the seller in this case. Article 6 of the CISG allows the contract to exclude the CISG on the basis of autonomy, but it is still worth discussing through what form of exclusion this can occur, and whether the application of the CISG has further requirements in terms of form and time. In this case, the buyer and seller of the goods unanimously requested the exclusion of the application of the CISG and chose Chinese law. In the case that the buyer and the seller do not specify what law is the applicable law in the sales contract, the choice to exclude the CISG during the trial constitutes express exclusion. The exclusion effect of the trial practice of Chinese courts has been recognized in the case *of Jingjin Electric Technology Co., Ltd. v Semikron Automotive Systems GmbH &Co., KG* where the parties applied for confirmation of the validity of the arbitration judged in China.[2] The decision stated:

> With regard to the application of law, the terms and conditions stipulated in this package order and the relevant procurement issuance and this package order are only governed by the substantive laws of England and Wales, and "the United Nations Convention on Contracts for the International Sale of Goods (CISG)" is expressly excluded.

Article 6 of the CISG allows the parties to exclude the relevant provisions of the CISG in the corresponding rules system. The court of the contracting party is obliged to apply the CISG according to arts 1–3 which stipulates whether the contract involved is within the scope of the CISG adjustment. Only after determining the validity of the application of the CISG to the case can, it be determined whether the parties may effectively exclude the application of the CISG. In the case o9f express exclusion, the parties may either choose to directly agree in the contract, or unanimously claim exclusion to the judge under the conditions of the litigation procedure, such as the conclusion of the court debate required in China's trial practice.

[2] Jingjin Electric Technology Co., Ltd. and Semikron Automotive Systems GmbH & CoKG applied for confirmation of the validity of the arbitration. (2018) Jing 04 Min Te No.145 (Beijing Fourth Intermediate People's Court, March 25, 2020).

For example, the *Minutes of the National Court Symposium on Foreign-Related Commerci8al and Maritime Trials* issued by the Supreme People's Court in January 2022, stipulates that[3]:

> The provisions of the United Nations Convention on Contracts for the International Sale of Goods shall automatically apply to contracts for the international sale of goods concluded by parties whose places of business are located in different Contracting States, unless the parties expressly agree to exclude the application of the Convention. The people's court shall, before the end of the court debate, ask the parties for specific opinions on the application of the Convention.

Neither the provisions nor the legislative history of the CISG require that exclusion must be expressed. As the chairman of the First Committee of the Diplomatic Conference in Vienna establishing the CISG said to the delegates present, exclusion can be expressed or implied.[4] In the case of implied exclusion, the parties may choose the laws of non-CISG parties as the final application of the contract. Of course, the legal effects of the two parties in choosing the laws of Contracting Parties, non-contracting parties or specific departmental laws of Contracting Parties are different. According to the interpretation rule of Article 8 of the CISG, if there is sufficient evidence indicating that the party wants to exclude the application of CISG, for example, the party chooses the specific legal department of the State party and specifies the full name, the CISG convention has the possibility of being excluded then.[5] Article 6 of the CISG does not specify the specific way to apply the exclusion, and there are considerations to avoid abuse of the exclusion clause.

In the case of Harald Company v. Anjiu Company, although the parties unanimously requested the exclusion of the CISG in the trial, and the Court also chose to apply Chinese law, due to the particularity of the CISG exclusion clause, this explicit exclusion method did not actually affect the exclusion effect of arts 1–3 of the CISG in the logical judgment level. In China, the effect of the CISG with priority or automatic application has been generally recognized.[6] In the situation of the parties excluding the CISG based on the unanimous choice of intention, the Court actually expanded the exclusion stipulated in art 6 in practice. As a unified law on international commerce, the CISG has formed a special paradigm for the treaty's application. The automatism and autonomy of the CISG application has the effect of hard law application and the flexibility of soft law. If the parties do not agree to exclude the CISG, and do not fall within the scope of prohibited application, the

---

[3] Minutes of the National Symposium on Foreign-related Commercial and Maritime Trials of Courts] (promulgated by The Supreme People's Court of the People's Republic of China, June 10, 2021).

[4] Liu [1], p. 73.

[5] Zuo [2], p. 191.

[6] Qingdao Huijintong Power Equipment Co., Ltd. v HJTSTEELTOWER(NORTHAMERICA) CO., Ltd. (2020) L02 Minchu No.872(Qingdao Intermediate People's Court of Shandong Province, October 19, 2021).

court should apply the CISG to resolve the disputes involved in the case. In *Danson Decor Inc. v. Xinhui Company*,[7] the relevant judgment documents stated that:

The plaintiff Danson Décor Inc. is a Canadian registered enterprise, so this case is a foreign-related commercial dispute. The business places of the plaintiff Danson Décor Inc. and the defendant Xinhui Company are respectively in Canada and the People's Republic of China, both of which are contracting countries of the CISG. However, the plaintiff Danson Décor Inc. and the defendant Xinhui Company have not agreed to exclude the application of the CISG, and the goods bought and sold by both parties are not within the scope of the CISG prohibition. Therefore, the disputes arising from the sales contract of the original defendant in this case should be handled by CISG.

Similar accounts have repeatedly appeared in the narratives of Chinese judgment documents, such as *Ningbo Zhenyu Technology Co., Ltd. v. DA Technology Co., Ltd.*,[8] *Steeltrade S.R.L. v. Xi'an Litonglian Steel Pipe Co., Ltd.* amongst others.[9] As far as the exclusion and application of the CISG is concerned, if the contract agreement or the trial expression of meaning is true and effective, the court will generally choose to respect the autonomy of its meaning at the time and apply the legal norms it chooses.

## Issue 2 Fundamental Breach and Post Contractual Obligations

In the case of Harald Company v Anjiu Company, the confirmation of the fundamental breach and post-contractual obligations is the key to resolution of the dispute. Although the case excluded the application of the CISG as the standard law, it does not prevent application of the fundamental default clause of the CISG and the seller's obligations in Chapter II. Article 25 of the CISG defines a fundamental default as '*A breach of contract committed by one of the parties is fundamental if it results in such detriment to the other party as substantially to deprive him of what he is entitled to expect under the contract*'. It does not only require damage to the buyer (or seller), but also requires the actual deprivation of the goods expected as agreed upon in the contract. Generally, in an international sale of goods contract, if the seller has delivered the goods in accordance with the agreement, and the buyer has completed the inspection of the goods within the agreed, reasonable or a negotiated period, the probability of fundamental breach will be greatly reduced.

In this case, the Court summarized the disputed focus of the case as whether defendant had a breach of contract and whether plaintiff had exercised the statutory discharge right. From the available evidence, both plaintiff and defendant recognized the fact that the goods had been delivered as required by the contract. According to the provisions of Chinese Contract Law (art 91),[10] the Court held that the debt has been

[7] Danson Decor Inc. v. Linhai Xinhui Crafts Co., Ltd. (2021) Zhe 10 Min Chu No.75 (Taizhou Intermediate People's Court of Zhejiang Province, November 12, 2021).

[8] Ningbo Zhenyu Technology Co., Ltd. v. DA Technology Co., Ltd., (2019) Zhe 02 Min Chu No.587 (Ningbo Intermediate People's Court of Zhejiang Province, October 22, 2021).

[9] Steeltrade S.R.L. v. Xian Litonglian Steel Pipe Co., Ltd., (2020) Shan 01 Min Chu No.662 (Xi'an Intermediate People's Court of Shaanxi Province, September 14, 2021).

[10] Contract Law of the People's Republic of China (promulgated by NPC Standing Committee, December 28, 2013, Effective July 1, 2013).

performed as agreed, and the rights and obligations of the contract are terminated. According to the situation reflected in the existing text, neither the plaintiff nor the defendant clearly agreed on the commitment of the warranty period or after-sales maintenance service in the contract text. From the general theory of contract law, the obligation of quality assurance is similar to the obligation of assistance and confidentiality, and belongs to post-contractual obligation. Some scholars regard this obligation as an attached obligation, but no matter what it is qualitatively, without special agreement it is generally difficult to achieve the '*actual deprivation of the goods*' for the main obligation of the contract. In the Austrian Supreme Court of case 1517,[11] the Court held that the seller violated the exclusive sales contract, the seller signed the exclusive sales contract with the buyer, and signed with another store in buyer's city shortly after in order to sell the goods. The buyer did not lose all opportunities to sell the goods in the original store, therefore, the relevant behavior does not constitute a fundamental breach of contract.

According to the UNCITRAL Secretariat's *Commentary on the Draft Convention on Contracts for the International Sale of Goods*, the seriousness standard of default is the '*basic standard*' for fundamental breach.[12] Although the statistics are incomplete, UNCITRAL's CLOUT case law database, the CISG database and the UNILEX database have included more than 100 cases involving fundamental breach of contract, with most cases involving defective performance. Cases involving the seller accounted for about 30%, where it was generally believed that the goods were defective but could still be resold, even at a low price, which generally does not constitute a fundamental default. A summary of case 171 from the German Federal Supreme Court included in the CLOUT database shows that[13]:

> The delivery of goods which do not conform with the contract either because they are of lesser quality or of different origin does not constitute non-delivery.

There are legal loopholes in the provisions of contractual obligations, resulting in violations of the system, and the connotation and extension of the theory are highly uncertain.[14] Regardless of the legal legitimacy of the post-contractual obligation itself, even if the post-contractual obligation has the nature of an obligation derived after the termination of the contractual right and obligation, it cannot be excluded from giving such an obligation an important contractual status in a specific contract for the sale of goods. It should at least be preceded by a clear contractual agreement or stable commercial customs. In this case, the buyer and seller of the goods neither agreed on the content of the after-sales maintenance service, nor did the contract specify whether the service had a special nature. Therefore, after the buyer received the goods and delivered the goods on FOB basis as agreed in the contract, it may be preliminarily considered that the seller has fulfilled the obligation of quality assurance

---

[11] UNCITRAL [3].

[12] UNCITRAL Secretariat [4], p. 14.

[13] UNCITRAL [3].

[14] Li [5], p. 1295.

of the goods implied in the underlying contract, provided that there are no other special requirements.

Even if the contract does not expressly stipulate the post-contractual obligation or ancillary obligation of the product quality guarantee, the implied obligations in the contract and the mandatory obligations stipulated by law cannot be excluded. The CISG is not stipulated by national law in respect of art 7(1)'s 'uniformity' interpretation and the convention of international principle on the basis of the legal rules of the 'fill'. Article 39(2) of the CISG stipulates that *'the buyer to notify the goods inconsistent during the longest two years'*, which aims to encourage the buyer to actively fulfill the obligation of inspection of the goods, but it does not (and is unlikely to) stipulate the seller's warranty obligations if the agreed quality guarantee period is too short (the agreed period is shorter than the period stipulated by the national compulsory law) or the parties have not agreed to a quality guarantee period.

The UNCITRAL Secretariat notes that it is important to protect the buyer's right to claim a remedy, but that protecting the seller prevents the buyer from making a claim long after the delivery.[15] For products without a set expiration date, in the absence of the mandatory provisions of the national regulations of the CISG and the case, the setting of the warranty period of the goods sold by the seller shall conform to the habit of international commercial trading or the purpose of the contract. Article 622 of the Civil Code of China stipulates that[16]:

> Where a period of inspection agreed by the parties is excessively short, and it is difficult for the buyer to complete a comprehensive inspection within such a period by virtue of the nature of the subject matter and in accordance with the course of dealing such period shall be deemed only as a period for the buyer to raise objections on the patent defects of the subject matter.

In this case, the plaintiff claimed the product quality problems, but from the international commercial trading norms, it cannot be denied that it still belongs to the contract obligations or attached obligations. If there is a problem with the quality of the goods between the delivery of the goods by the seller and the buyer's claim, it may be clear that the seller is liable for repairs if this is in accordance with international commercial customs, and if it can be proved that the product itself is defective. In addition, in the absence of an agreement between both parties on the after-sales maintenance, Harald Company required that Anjiu Company should conduct after-sales maintenance in Denmark, the place of sale, which would greatly increase the cost of the realization of the contract, making subsequent contractual obligations not incidental. This is contrary to the purpose of the contract.

---

[15] UNCITRAL Secretariat [4], p. 15.

[16] Civil Code of the People's Republic of China (promulgated by The Third Session of the 13th National People's Congress of the People's Republic of China, May 28, 2020, Effective Jun. 1, 2021).

**Issue 3 Termination of Rights and Obligations After Completion of Contract Performance**

Although the parties in Harald Company v. Anjiu Company clearly excluded the application of the CISG, it is not denied that the CISG's provisions on the declaration of the invalidation system are more targeted for international contracts for the sale of goods. The most serious cases concerning the Convention are usually strict on essential breach, and these cases usually plead the remedy of avoidance since it is the only defence available.[17] The Court's adjudication method was to prove that Harald Company did not have the right to rescind the contract by relying on the provisions of art 91 of the Chinese Contract Law on the termination of contractual rights and obligations, and the provisions on contractual obligations after termination of art 92 of the Contract Law. (These provisions have lapsed and are otherwise stipulated by the Civil Code of the People's Republic of China).[18] Article 49(2) of the CISG provides that *'in cases where the seller has delivered the goods, the buyer loses the right to declare the contract avoided'*, and is logically consistent with the provisions of Chinese law. According to the provisions of arts 49 and 64 of the CISG, *'Declare the contract avoided'* is limited to two types of situations in which the contracting party fundamentally breaches the contract, or the defaulting party still fails to perform or declares it will not perform its contractual obligations within the grace period. Article 64(1)(a) of the CISG equals *'perform any of his obligations'* to 'fundamental breach', and it can be understood that the delivery of the goods will not constitute a fundamental breach.

Based on the stability of the performance, the CISG sets several restrictive provisions on the invalidation of the contract, such as arts 39, 43 and 49. If the fundamental breach is established, it can avoid the occurrence of the termination of the contract as long as the seller provides sufficient and effective remedy. Even if the products delivered by the seller have serious defects, the benefits available to the buyer can be repair or replacement.[19] If a cure has not yet been effect but is a possibility, what might otherwise be a fundamental breach is not so until that possibility has been tried and has failed.[20] In addition, in order to avoid fundamental default, the right of cure should also be restricted; the CISG bars any purported exercise to cure which is not authorized by the buyer.

In a specific civil contract, even if the delivery of goods is not agreed upon, case 992 of the Copenhagen District Court on the fundamental breach of contract caused by pony soft tissue damage is a typical case.[21] Article 91(1)(1) of the Chinese Contract Law adjusts the debt relationship, which can include both the delivery of goods covered by the sales contract and the provision of services required by the service contract. Article 3(2) of the CISG explicitly excludes situations applicable to 'the

---

[17] Malkawi [6], p. 36.

[18] Contract Law of the People's Republic of China (promulgated by NPC Standing Committee, December 28, 2013, Effective July 1, 2013).

[19] Ferrari [7], p. 389.

[20] Bridge [8], p. 928.

[21] UNCITRAL [3].

preponderant part of the obligations of the party who furnishes the goods consists in the supply of labour or other services'. Therefore, when both the buyer and seller of the goods have agreed on after-sales maintenance services as their main obligation, the provisions of art 49(2) of the CISG will lose their adjustment effect. In addition, the buyer shall return the goods after declaring the contract invalid and claim the necessary damages as the non-breaching party. Articles 75 and 76 of the CISG stipulate the calculation method of damages, and specify the compensation liability of the breaching party based on the actual losses and the expected market losses. Harald Company's request to refund the payment for goods, and the seller bearing the inspection, repair and transportation costs, generally falls under the 'breach of contract by one party consist of a sum equal to the loss' stipulated in art 74 of the CISG.

## References

1. Liu, Y. (2019). Exclusion Clause and Application of the CISG. *Journal of Political Science and Law*, 2019(4), 68–84
2. Zu, H.C. & Lin, S. S. (2017). On the implied exclusion of the United Nations Convention on Contracts for the International Sale of Goods: from the perspective of the choice of law clause. *Jiangxi Social sciences*, 10, 191–199
3. United Nations Commission on International Trade Law (UNCITRAL). (2016). *UNCITRAL Digest of Case Law on the United Nations Convention on Contracts for the International Sale of Goods*. Retrieved June 20, 2023, from https://uncitral.un.org/en/case_law/digests
4. UNCITRAL Secretariat. (March 1979). *Commentary on the Draft convention on Contracts for the International Sale of Goods*. Retrieved June 20, 2023, from https://uncitral.un.org/sites/uncitral.un.org/files/media-documents/uncitral/en/a-conf-97-19-ocred-eng.pdf
5. Liu, Y. (2019). Review of post-contract obligations. *Peking University Law Review Journal*, 31(5), 1270–1298
6. Malkawi, B. H. (2020). CISG: The Relation among Cure, Fundamental Breach, and Avoidance. *Journal of Law, Policy and Globalization*, 93, 24–44
7. Ferrari, F. (2005). Fundamental Breach of Contract under the UN Sales Convention 25 Years Article 25 CISG. *International Business Law Journal*, 3, 389–400
8. Bridge, M. (2010). Avoidance for Fundamental Breach of Contract under the UN Convention on the International Sale of Goods. *International and Comparative Law Quarterly*, 59(4), 911–940

**Kaiwei Cui** Ph.D. candidate in International Law at the University of International Business and Economics, majoring in International Business Law and International Trade Law. Prior to that, he got his LL.M. from Zhengzhou University. He participated in projects of the National Social Science Fund, and projects of the Department of Commerce of Henan Province, among others.

**Peng Guo** is Lecturer in Law at the Swinburne University of Technology. He has worked across several Australian universities and has held visiting positions at different European universities. He has received scholarships awarded by renowned research institutions and international organisations, including the Max Planck Institute for Comparative and International Private Law, the International Institute for the Unification of Private Law (UNIDROIT), the Swiss Institute of Comparative Law, and the European Union. He specialises in the international sale of goods, international commercial arbitration, comparative contract law, and law and technology.

# Wooree ETI Co., Ltd. v. Beijing Shiyuanda Electronic Technology Co., Ltd.

**Long Shao and Sichen Lu**

## Case Information

**Case Name**: Wooree ETI Co., Ltd. v. Beijing Shiyuanda Electronic Technology Co., Ltd.

**Seller**: Wooree ETI Co., Ltd.
**Place of Business**: Korea

**Buyer**: Beijing Shiyuanda Electronic Technology Co., Ltd.
**Place of Business**: China

**Details of First Instance**:
**Court**: Beijing No.1 Intermediate People's Court
**Date of Decision**: 5 November 2012
**Case No.**: (2012) Yi Zhong Min Chu Zi No 5062
**Judges**: Chang Jie (Presiding Judge), Liang Rui (Assistant Judge), Wu Yangxin (Assistant Judge)

## Case Abstract

Wooree ETI Co., Ltd. ('Wooree ETI') is a company incorporated in Korea, and Beijing Shiyuanda Electronic Technology Co., Ltd. ('Shiyuanda') is a Chinese company. Between January 2010 and August 2011, the parties entered into 13 contracts with a total amount of USD $712,848.70. In all contracts, Shiyuanda was obliged to make corresponding payments in 90 days upon receiving the invoice. However, Shiyuanda began to fall behind on payments from December 2010, and

L. Shao (✉) · S. Lu
Hunan University, Changsha, Hunan, China
e-mail: longshao@hnu.edu.cn



P. Guo et al. (eds.), *Selected Chinese Cases on the UN Sales Convention (CISG) Vol. 3*, Selected Chinese Cases on the CISG,
https://doi.org/10.1007/978-981-99-6851-0_37

the arrears had reached USD $712,848.70 by December 2011. Park Chung Seok, Shiyuanda's investor and director, signed a confirmation statement of accounts receivable. Wooree ETI informed Shiyuanda of the outstanding payments by phone calls and lawyer's letters, but to no avail. As a result, Wooree ETI sued Shiyuanda, in the hope that the Court would order Shiyuanda to pay the balance of USD $712,848.70, as well as overdue interest and litigation costs.

To prove delivery of the goods, Wooree ETI presented 13 sets of receipts, packing lists, waybills, and contracts. It also provided the signed statement and relevant business registration files to prove that Shiyuanda had confirmed the arrears with the authentic signature of Park Chung Seok. It also presented pages 290–315 of the No. 8, 1990 State Council of the People's Republic of China Gazette and notarization from Shanghai Oriental Notary Public Office to prove that both China and Korea had ratified the CISG. Shiyuanda neither defended itself nor appeared in court.

The Court confirmed the authenticity, legality, and relevance of Wooree ETI's evidence and the company's interest calculation. The Gazette presented was a record of the full article of the CISG and the Chinese government's instrument of approval. The Court stated that relevant articles of the CISG were arts 1, 2, 7, 11, 14, 15, 30, 33, 38, 39, 53, 54, 62, 78, and 95. Wu Xueqian, former Minister of Foreign Affairs, forwarded the instrument of approval to the United Nations Secretary-General on November 26, 1986, marking China as a Contracting State to the CISG. The notarization showed that Korea was recorded as having approved the CISG with no restriction on the UNCITRAL official website.

According to Article 142 of the General Principles of Civil Law of the People's Republic of China, if any international treaty concluded or acceded to by the People's Republic of China contains provisions differing from those in the civil laws of the People's Republic of China, the provisions of the international treaty shall apply unless the provisions are ones on which the People's Republic of China has announced reservations. The Court stated that the applicable law in this case was the CISG since Shiyuanda and Wooree ETI's places of business were China and Korea respectively, and both countries are Contracting States to the CISG. The Court confirmed the exact content of the CISG by referring to the Gazette, and therefore the Convention could directly be the legal basis of the case.

The Court considered the contracts between the parties valid since their conclusion conformed to arts 14(1) and 15(1) of the CISG, and their content did not violate relevant rules of the Convention. Because Wooree ETI delivered the goods in batches as agreed, and Shiyuanda was required to pay the balance in 90 days after receiving the invoice, Shiyuanda's delay of payments constituted a breach of the contracts. Wooree ETI's request for arrears and interest was justified by arts 53 and 78 of the CISG. Since the Convention makes no reference to interest rates, the Court applied Chinese law to weigh the issue and supported Wooree ETI's claim to calculate the interest on the arrears of the loan at the lending rate of the People's Bank of China for the same period. Following the reasoning above, the Court fully upheld Wooree ETI's claims.

## Commentary on the Key Issues Related to the CISG

### Issues

Issue 1 The Parties of the Disputed Contracts and the Applicability of the CISG
Issue 2 The Defendant's Fulfillment of its Obligations under the Contracts
Issue 3 The Plaintiff's Claim for the Price and the Calculation of Interest

### Comments

#### Issue 1 The Parties of the Disputed Contracts and the Applicability of the CISG

This case concerns a contractual dispute, therefore firstly the disputed contractual relationship should be identified. Based on all submitted relevant evidence, it was confirmed that the Korean Plaintiff Wooree ETI concluded 13 international sales contracts with the Chinese defendant Shiyuanda.

The sphere of application of the CISG, that means its applicability to certain contracts and specific contractual issues is to be determined according to its own rules of application set out in arts 1 to 6 of the CISG. To determine its applicability, the CISG relies on the following five aspects: (a) the internationality of the contract concerned (art 1); (b) the connection of the contract to Contracting States to the CISG (art 1); (c) the subject goods of the contracts (arts 2 and 3); (d) the issues governed by the CISG (arts 4 and 5) and (e) the parties' autonomy to exclude or vary the application of the CISG (art 6). In this case, the applicability determination was made principally on the deliberation of the three factors below.

#### I. Place of Business

The CISG is applicable to international sales contracts. Regarding internationality, the CISG adopts a sole criterion, i.e., the parties have their respective places of business in different states [art 1(1)]. This broad rule is, however, restricted by art 1(2) according to which the internationality of the contract is to be disregarded where it was not apparent to both parties from the contract or surrounding circumstances when concluding the contract.[1] In this case as previously analyzed, the disputed contracts are the 13 contracts concluded between Wooree ETI and Shiyuanda. The two parties' places of business are China and Korea respectively. This fact undisputedly satisfies the internationality requirement of the CISG.

Moreover, China and Korea are both are Contracting States to the CISG, as correctly presented by the plaintiff during the hearing. According to art 1(1)(a), this fact establishes the connection of the contracts with the CISG and leads to the autonomous application of the Convention.[2] If this requirement is not met, the court would then need to resort to its private international law to determine the applicable law. Once the law of a Contracting State is directed, the CISG should again be applied

---

[1] Schwenzer and Hachem [1], p. 28.

[2] UNCITRAL [2], p. 5.

according to art 1(1)(b), which is called the indirect application.[3] The indirect application based on art 1(1)(b), however, is reserved by many Contracting States to the CISG including China.[4]

### II. Sale of Goods

The CISG does not define 'goods', but excludes certain types of sales from its sphere of application in art 2.[5] The exceptions enumerated in art 2 are exhaustive and may not be applied by way of analogy to other cases.[6] For instance, art 2(a) excludes almost all 'consumer sales' from the Convention's ambit. Other transactions specifically excluded by art 2 include sales by auction, forced sales, sales of negotiable instruments, ships and vessels, aircraft, and electricity. Moreover, art 3 specifies mixed contracts which involve the buyer's obligation to supply materials for the production or manufacture of the goods concerned. The nature of mixed contracts, i.e., being sales contracts or service contracts, depends on whether the preponderant obligation of the party who furnishes the goods consists in the supply of goods or the supply of labor or other services. In case law, the two most frequently used benchmarks are economic value of different obligations and the principal purpose of the contract.[7] The items concerned in this case are LED assembly, which is tangible, falling under the ordinary meaning of 'goods' The transaction involves neither the buyer's supply of materials nor the sales explicitly excluded by art 2. The sale constitutes an applicable 'sale of goods' under the CISG.

### III. Parties' Autonomy

The CISG, throughout its text, 'affirms and preserves the absolute autonomy of the parties to determine the content of their contract'.[8] Article 6 explicitly specifies the parties' autonomy in respect of the applicability of the CISG. It confirms that the parties may, expressly or impliedly, choose to derogate from some or all of the provisions.[9] It is undisputed that provisions of the CISG can be excluded by explicit or implicit agreement.[10] CISG formation provisions incontrovertibly apply to both *ex ante* and *ex post* exclusions, while the latter also constitutes a modification of the original contract and thus art 29of the CISG must also be satisfied before the CISG's application is excluded at the stages of contractual performance or legal proceedings alike.[11] In this case, the CISG is applicable based on an objective test evaluating the places of business and the goods concerned. The parties did not choose the governing

---

[3] Ibid.

[4] CISG Advisory Council [3].

[5] Schlechtriem and Butler [4], p. 3.

[6] Schwenzer and Hachem [1], p. 47.

[7] CISG Advisory Council [5].

[8] Schlechtriem and Butler [4], p. 3.

[9] CISG Advisory Council [6].

[10] Hachem [7], p. 36.

[11] CISG Advisory Council [6].

law of the disputed contracts, nor did they exclude the application of the CISG. The CISG should therefore be applied.

Further, the CISG clarifies that it governs only the formation of the contract, i.e., the 'objective agreement', and the rights and obligations of the parties established under the sales contract (art 4). This case concerns disputes arising from the seller's performance of its obligations and the buyer's remedies for breach of contract by the seller. Rules on these issues are specifically set out in Chapter II, Part III of the CISG.

**Issue 2 The Defendant's Fulfillment of Its Obligations Under the Contracts**

With regard to the formation of sales contracts, the correct and often repeated standard phrasing is 'mutual consent'.[12] The CISG generally uses the traditional mechanism of offer and acceptance in arts 14–24 to form contracts. The CISG is generally 'not concerned' with validity (art 4). Most problems under the validity heading—such as duress, mistake or the unreasonableness of contract terms—must be resolved in accordance with domestic (non-CISG) rules of law.[13] In this case, the Court confirmed the formation and validity of the contracts according to the evidence presented by the plaintiff. Disputes arose from the implementation of the two validly concluded contracts, where the defendant's performance of its general obligations under art 59 to make payments on time as required by the contracts and the Convention. The disputed performance is the defendant's delayed payments.

Article 53 affirms the duty to pay the purchase price, generally stipulated in the sale of goods contract. Article 59 clearly sets out the rule whereby the buyer must pay the price as soon as it becomes due, without the need for any request or compliance with any other formality by the seller.[14] In this sense, late payment is a breach of contract, which triggers the legal consequences set out in arts 61 *et seq*. In this case, the parties agreed that the price shall be paid in 90 days after receiving the invoice. The first unpaid contracts were concluded on 11 August 2010, and the last were concluded on 26 January 2011. All payments agreed upon in the contracts were due when the plaintiff filed this lawsuit, as the 90-day period had already passed. While party agreement or trade usages and practices often determine that the payment is only due after the seller sent the invoice, the plaintiff had sent the invoices of all the contracts on time.[15] The time that payment is due can be extended on some occasions, such as when the buyer takes advantage of his right to examine the goods under art 58(3), when the buyer did not know or was under no obligation to know when the goods or documents would be available to the buyer during a step-by-step performance, or when the buyer does not know the exact amount of the purchase at the time the purchase price is due.[16] This case contains no such exceptional circumstances.

---

[12] Case No. 4 R 224/98p, Oberlandesgericht, Austria, 24/02/1999.

[13] Lookofsky [8], p. 22.

[14] UNCITRAL [2], p. 276.

[15] CISG-online 1218, Oberlandesgericht Köln, Germany, 03 April 2006.

[16] Kröll et al. [9], p. 860.

Therefore, the defendant was obligated to make payments with interest according to arts 62 and 78, and such obligation cannot be waived.

**Issue 3 The Plaintiff's Claim for the Price and the Calculation of Interest**

### I. Plaintiff's Claim for the Price

According to art 62, the seller may require the buyer to pay the purchase price, take delivery or perform his other obligations. Of primary practical importance is the seller's action for the price. However, art 62 also stipulates that the seller loses his right to require performance of the contract if he resorts to a remedy inconsistent with this requirement. Remedy includes the declaration of avoidance of contract and damages claim for the performance interest.[17] In this case, the plaintiff repeatedly demanded the defendant to pay the arrears plus interest, instead of declaring avoidance of the contracts or claiming any performance interest. Therefore, Wooree ETI's requests before the Court were justified, and Shiyuanda should at least pay for the price of the goods.

Article 28 applies to the seller's action for the price. According to art 28, a court is not obliged to grant specific performance under the Convention if it would not do so for similar sales contracts under its domestic law.[18] One US court mentioned art 28 of the CISG in its ruling, finding that the complaint stated sufficient facts to justify an order of specific performance under art 46(1) of the CISG and domestic law.[19] There was little controversy over this provision in practice, and all the speculation that art 28 would lead to forum shopping, and hence undermine the uniform sales law. has not proven to be correct. As a mere option, art 28 was designed specifically for common law courts, and it has never been mentioned in cases dealing with the seller's right to demand the price.[20] In this case, a claim for specific performance can be upheld under both the CISG and domestic Chinses law.

### II. The Determination of Interest Rate

The right to claim interest on amounts due and not paid by a contractual party under the CISG is governed by arts 78 and 84(1). There was so little consensus on the issue of interest rate in the CISG that one commentator in 1981 remarked that it was 'more conspicuous for the questions it fails to answer than the questions it answers'.[21] Interest rate is considered as a 'gap' intentionally left open by the drafters of the CISG. Some courts and scholars, including the CISG Advisory Council, hold the opinion that the rate should be based on the loss suffered by the non-defaulting party and that the place of business of the *creditor* should therefore be decisive.[22]

[17] Mohs [10], p. 909.

[18] UNCITRAL [2], p. 122.

[19] CLOUT case No. 417, U.S. District Court, Northern District of Illinois, United States, 7 December 1999.

[20] Zeller [11], pp. 60–61.

[21] Ziegel and Samson [12].

[22] CLOUT case no. 911, Cour De Justice, Switzerland, 12 May 2006; CISG Advisory Council [13].

Other courts hold that since the provision is aimed at providing compensation for benefits unjustifiably received, they therefore argue that the rate of interest should be based on the *debtor*'s place of business.[23] There are also some courts that link the rate of interest to the *currency* in which the debt is to be paid, because the usual rate of interest is normally related to a particular currency, in particular the relevant inflation rate for that currency.[24] Many courts and tribunals choose their domestic law to govern the issue of interest, in consideration of art 7(2) of the CISG and relevant private international law rules.[25] Despite precedents for each of these approaches, it would seem that the general tendency in the decided cases is to regard the issue as one not regulated by the CISG, and therefore that it consists of a gap that should be fulfilled by local law.[26]

In this case, the Court resorted to relevant Chinese law to determine the interest rate, which is in accordance with art 7(2) of the CISG. By choosing Chinese law, the Court was choosing the law of debtor's place of business, which does not conform to CISG-AC Opinion No. 14. As discussed above, this is an approach supported by many courts and tribunals over the world. However, as courts have broad discretion to set a rate of pre-judgment interest sufficient to compensate the plaintiff for the true costs of the money damages incurred, the decision made in this case is appropriate. Such calculation was brought forward by the debtor (plaintiff), which means that Wooree ETI tacitly agreed with this calculation. In conclusion, the Court was justified to use the lending rate of the People's Bank of China for the same period as the interest rate for the arrears.

### III. The Time when Interest Accrues

The CISG is also silent on the period during which interest accrues.[27] Interest begins to accrue as soon as the payment is in arrears, such as when the payment of the purchase price ought to have been made.[28] This position is derived from art 74's principle of full compensation and from the text of art 59, which states that the buyer has an obligation to make payment without the seller having to make a formal demand.[29] In this case, the Court calculated the interest in the aforementioned way,

---

[23] CLOUT case no. 215, Bezirksgericht, Switzerland, 3 July 1997, in which the court mentioned the possibility of determining the rate of interest in application of the law at the debtor's place of business; CISG-online 659, Amtsgericht Duisburg, Germany, 13 April 2000.

[24] CISG-online 164, Arbitration Court attached to the Hungarian Chamber of Commerce and Industry, Hungary, 05 December 1995; CISG-online 765, Rechtbank van Koophandel Veurne, Belgium, 25 April 2001; CISG-online 671, Oberlandesgericht Rostock, Germany, 10 October 2001; CISG-online 2918, High Court of Uganda, Uganda, 03 October 2017.

[25] CLOUT case no. 1881, Nejvyšší soud České republiky, Czechia, 29 January 2019; CISG-online 2269, Foreign Trade Court of Arbitration attached to the Serbian Chamber of Commerce, Serbia, 15 September 2008; CISG-online 5503, Rechtbank, Amsterdam, Netherlands, 20 November 2020; CISG-online 6111, District Court, New York, United States, 1 November 2022.

[26] Eiselen [14], p. 233.

[27] Gotanda [15], p. 40.

[28] CISG Advisory Council [13].

[29] Kröll et al. [9], p. 1032.

where the period extended from 90 days upon receiving the invoice to the actual date of payment.

## References


1. Schwenzer, I. & Hachem, P. (2016). Ch.I Sphere of Application, Article 1, in Schwenzer, I. (Ed.), *Schlechtriem & Schwenzer: Commentary on the UN Convention on the International Sale of Goods* (4th edition, p.28). Oxford University Press
2. United Nations Commission on International Trade Law (UNCITRAL). (2016). *UNCITRAL Digest of Case Law on the United Nations Convention on Contracts for the International Sale of Goods*. Retrieved June 20, 2023, from https://uncitral.un.org/en/case_law/digests
3. CISG Advisory Council. (21 and 22 October 2013). *Opinion No. 15, Reservations under Articles 95 and 96 CISG*. CISGAC. Retrieved June 20, 2023, from https://cisgac.com/opinions/cisgac-opinion-no1-copy-copy-4-copy-copy-copy-6/
4. Schlechtriem, P. & Butler, P. (2009). U*N Law on International Sales: The UN Convention on the International Sale of Goods* (1st ed.). Springer-Verlag Berlin Heidelberg
5. CISG Advisory Council. (24 October 2004). *Opinion No. 4, Contracts for the Sale of Goods to Be Manufactured or Produced and Mixed Contracts (Article 3 CISG)*. CISGAC. Retrieved June 20, 2023, from https://cisgac.com/opinions/cisgac-opinion-no1-copy-copy/
6. CISG Advisory Council. (30 May 2014). *Opinion No. 16, Exclusion of the CISG under Article 6*. CISGAC. Retrieved June 20, 2023, from https://cisgac.com/opinions/cisgac-opinion-no1-copy-copy-4-copy-copy-copy-7/
7. Hachem, P. (2014). Applicability of the CISG – Articles 1 and 6, in Schwenzer, I., Atamer, Y. M. & Butler P. (Eds.), *Current Issues in the CISG and Arbitration* (1st ed.). Eleven International Publishing
8. Lookofsky, J. (2017). *Understanding the CISG: A Compact Guide to the 1980 United Nations Convention on Contracts for the International Sale of Goods* (5th ed.). Kluwer Law International
9. Kröll, S., Mistelis L. & Viscasillas, P. (2018). *UN Convention on Contracts for the International Sale of Goods (CISG): A Commentary* (2nd ed.). Hart Publishing
10. Mohs, F. (2016). Ch.III Obligations of the Buyer, S.III Remedies for Breach of Contract by the Buyer, Article 62, in Schwenzer, I. (Ed.), *Schlechtriem & Schwenzer: Commentary on the UN Convention on the International Sale of Goods* (4th ed.). Oxford University Press
11. Zeller, B. (2007). *CISG and the Unification of International Trade Law* (1st ed.). Routledge-Cavendish
12. Ziegel, J. S. & Samson, C. (1981, July). *Report to The Uniform Law Conference of Canada on the Convention on Contracts for the International Sale of Goods*. Pace Edu. Retrieved June 20, 2023, from https://iicl.law.pace.edu/sites/default/files/bibliography/english2_0.pdf
13. CISG Advisory Council. (21 and 22 October 2013). *Opinion No. 14, Interest under Article78 CISG*. CISGAC. Retrieved June 20, 2023, from https://cisgac.com/opinions/cisgac-opinion-no1-copy-copy-4-copy-copy-copy-5/
14. Eiselen, S. (2007). Interest on sums in arrears: Remarks on the manner in which the UNIDROIT Principles of International Commercial Contracts may be used to interpret or supplement Article 78 of the CISG, inFelemegas, J. (Ed.), *An International Approach to the Interpretation of the United Nations Convention on Contracts for the International Sale of Goods (1980) as Uniform Sales Law* (1st ed.). Cambridge University Press
15. Gotanda, J. Y. (1996). Awarding Interest in International Arbitration. *The American Journal of International Law*, 90(1), 40–63

**Long Shao** is an Assistant Professor in Law at Hunan University. She holds a doctoral degree in law, specialising in the field of international law, from Vienna University. Dr. Long's research interests lie in international trade law, WTO law, and international commercial arbitration. She teaches International Economic Law to LLB students and acts as the coach of HNU CIETAC Cup (pre-vis) moot team.

**Sichen Lu** LL.B. (Hunan University). The author majors in private international law; participated in the 19th annual CIETAC Cup International Commercial Arbitration Moot and helped the team to win the Best Memo Award.

# Wooree LED CO., Ltd. v. Beijing Shiyuanda Electronic Technology Co., Ltd.

**Junkai Fan, Chaolin Zhang, and Shu Zhang**

**Case Information**

**Case name**: Wooree LED Co., LTD v Beijing Shiyuanda Electronic Technology Co. LTD.

**Seller**: Wooree LED Co., LTD.
**Place of business**: Korea
**Buyer**: Beijing Shiyuanda Electronic Technology Co., LTD.
**Place of Business**: China

**Details of First Instance**:
**Court**: The First Intermediate People's Court of Beijing Municipality
**Date of Decision**: November 2012
**Case No**: (2012) Yi Zhong Min Chu Zi No. 5063
**Judges**: Jie Chang (Presiding Judge), Rui Liang (Acting Judge), Yangxin Wu (Acting Judge)

**CISG Applied**: Yesn
**Key CISG Provisions Interpreted and Applied**: Article 14(1), 15(1), 53, 78.

J. Fan (✉)
Qingdao Maritime Court, Qingdao, Shandong, China
e-mail: fan_junkai@163.com

C. Zhang
Qufu Normal University, Rizhao, Shandong, China

S. Zhang
Deakin University, Geelong, VIC 3220, Australia
e-mail: shu.zhang@deakin.edu.au



P. Guo et al. (eds.), *Selected Chinese Cases on the UN Sales Convention (CISG) Vol. 3*, Selected Chinese Cases on the CISG,
https://doi.org/10.1007/978-981-99-6851-0_38

## Case Abstract

Wooree LED Co., LTD. (hereinafter referred to as Wooree LED) is a company incorporated in South Korea, while Beijing Shiyuanda Electronic Technology Co., LTD. (hereinafter referred to as Shiyuanda) is domiciled in China. The two companies have been trading together for several years as Wooree LED has long supplied Shiyuanda with goods.

From February 22, 2011 to August 12, 2011, the two companies have signed 14 contracts, agreeing that Wooree LED will supply the specified type of goods to Shiyuanda, and have made specific agreements in terms of the quantity of goods, unit price, total price, shipment date, export port, destination, payment method, etc.

After the signing of each contract, Wooree LED will ship the agreed goods from the export port of Incheon, Korea to the destination of Tianjin, China by shipping according to the contract.

The terms of payment stipulated in the contract are monthly payment by t/t after 90 days. However, at the end of May 2011, Shiyuanda began to default on Wooree LED payments, and a total of USD 203,174.14 was owed by December 2011. Park Jung-seok, an investor and director of Shiyuanda, signed the account receivable statement to confirm this. In addition, Wooree LED has been asking for payment through phone calls and lawyer letters, but Shiyuanda Company has not returned the arrears.

Therefore, Wooree LED filed a lawsuit with the First Intermediate People's Court of Beijing Municipality. The plaintiff has three claims: First, order Shiyuanta Company to pay Wooree LED arrears, a total of USD 203,174.14; Second, order Shiyuanda Company to pay arrears interest; Third, the litigation costs shall be borne by Shiyuanda Company.

Among them, Wooree LED provides a specific plan for the calculation of interest, including four parts: the first part, starting from May 29, 2011, based on USD 96,122.14; The second part, starting from 29 June 2011, is based on USD 745,23.6; The third part is based on USD 27,728.4 as of July 29, 2011; The fourth part starts on November 29, 2011 and is based on USD 4,800. The four parts are calculated according to the benchmark interest rate of one-year loans of the People's Bank of China for the same period until the date of actual payment.

The court held that the plaintiff's three claims had factual and legal basis, and therefore supported all of them. The law on which the court made its decision includes the *United Nations Convention on Contracts for the International Sale of Goods*, Articles 14(1), 15(1), 53 and 78, the *General Principles of the Civil Law of the People's Republic of China*, Article 142 (2), the *Law of the People's Republic of China on the Application of Law to Foreign-related Civil Relations*, Articles 8 and 14, the *Civil Procedure Law of the People's Republic of China*, Article 22(2), 130 and 235.

## Commentary to the Key Issues Related to the CISG

### Issues

Issue 1: Identification of the CISG as the applicable law.
Issue 2: Interest on outstanding amounts.

## Comments

### Issue 1: Identification of the CISG as the Applicable Law

According to the provisions of Chap. 9 of the *Contract Law of the People's Republic of China* on the contract of sale and purchase and the relevant provisions of the *Decision of the Supreme People's Court of the People's Republic of China on Amending the Provisions of Civil Cases*, this case belongs to the dispute of international contract of sale and purchase of goods. On the issue of ascertaining the contents of the CISG, the Court held that Wooree LED submitted to the Court its copy of the *Gazette of the State Council of the People's Republic of China* [No. 8 of 1990, (General No. 617)], which was reproduced at the Shanghai Institute of Science and Technology Information of the Shanghai Library. The aforementioned Gazette contains on pages 290–315 the entire text of the CISG and the instrument of ratification of the aforementioned Convention by the Government of the People's Republic of China. After examination, the Court held that the *State Council Gazette of the People's Republic of China* is a publication of the Central People's Government of the People's Republic of China edited and published by the General Office of the State Council of the People's Republic of China for public distribution at home and abroad (domestic uniform publication number cn11-1611, domestic code 2–2, foreign code n311), and the contents of the CISG and the *Approval Letter* published in it is a standard text and is authoritative. Therefore, the Court considers that the contents of the CISG have been ascertained and can be directly used as the legal basis of this case.

This case is a typical dispute of international contract of sale of goods, China and Korea are both contracting parties to the CISG, and the CISG should be taken as the applicable law to resolve the dispute in the absence of express exclusion of application to CISG by the parties. The court's application of the applicable law turned out to be correct, but there may be flaws in the application procedure.

Firstly, China's constitutional laws do not provide for the relationship between international treaties ratified by China and domestic laws. As a special law regulating foreign-related civil legal relations, the *Law on the Legal Application of Foreign-Related Civil Relations* also does not directly regulate the application of international treaties.[1] Article 4 of the Interpretation of the Supreme People's Court on *Several Issues Concerning the Application of the Law of the People's Republic of China on Foreign-related Civil Relations (I)* states that where the application of the law on foreign-related civil relations involves the application of international treaties, the court shall apply the provisions of Article 142(2) of the *General Principles of the Civil Law* and other legal provisions. Paragraph 2 of Article 142 of the *General Principles of the Civil Law* provides: "Where an international treaty concluded or entered into by China has different provisions from Chinese civil law, the provisions of the international treaty shall apply, except for those provisions which the People's Republic of China has declared to be reserved".With regard to the application of

[1] Liu [1], p. 193.

CISG, the Supreme People's Court has adopted relevant documents to clarify the direct applicability of CISG in China's justice.[2]

A general point that emerges from the above is that international treaties concluded or acceded to by China are directly applicable in the trial activities of Chinese courts. Specifically in the practice of applying the CISG justice, when determining the CISG as the applicable law for hearing cases, the correct order should be to first determine whether CISG is applicable, that is, it is necessary to find out whether the location of both parties is a CISG member state, whether it is agreed in the contract to exclude the application and other factors, and on the basis of determining the application, the court should take the initiative to find out the content of the relevant law *ex officio*, instead of applying it as the applicable law only after it is provided by the parties and identified by the court according to Article 10 of the *Law on the Application of Law to Foreign-related Civil Relations*. Usually, the application of foreign law in a narrow sense in our courts requires two conditions to be met: 1. the parties agree to apply it; 2. the parties provide the text. In contrast, the application of international treaties concluded or participated by China, especially in the absence of reservations, in our courts does not require the parties to provide the text.

According to the standard understanding of private international law, the object of "identification" of the above-mentioned clause is the foreign law that the parties have agreed to apply, which is essentially the autonomy of the parties in terms of the standards and criteria to be applied in dealing with their disputes, and has nothing to do with the authority of the court. In the case that the parties provide foreign law and does not conflict with China's compulsory law, our court will take its agreed foreign law as the governing law is to respect the autonomy of the parties, and the parties are certainly obliged to provide foreign law. However, the CISG as an international convention to which China has acceded, is a part of our legal sources and has direct applicability. In addition, given the worldwide influence of the CISG and the need for active compliance in China, it would be contrary to this trend if the courts were to avoid using it because "the parties are unable to provide it". In this case, according to the court's understanding, it is obviously inaccurate to equate the CISG or even international conventions to which China is a party with "foreign law", which needs to be provided by the parties and identified by the court before it can be used as the applicable law.

The trial of this case took place in 2012, when China's foreign law identification mechanism was not perfect, and the degree of specialization of the foreign-related trial team was generally low, which led some judges to rely highly on the parties to provide foreign law identification, and seldom took the initiative to identify ex officio, and a certain habit was formed over time, and it is because of this habit that some judges lacked research and judgment on the definition of foreign law. Moreover, the judge's application of the law and the judgment based on it often have to be combined with the context, legislative background, legislative purpose and other factors, and the parties will of course provide the legal provisions in favor of their own side, and to a certain extent this does not guarantee the fairness of the trial. In recent years, with

[2] Wang and Shen [2], p. 138.

the continuous improvement of China's foreign law identification mechanism and the increasing specialization of judges, Chinese courts are bound to play a greater function of authority in the identification of foreign law.

**Issue 2: Interest on Outstanding Amounts**

Article 53 of the CISG provides that the buyer must pay the price and take delivery of the goods in accordance with the contract and the provisions of this Convention, and Article 78 provides that if a party fails to pay the price or any other sum in arrears, the other party shall be entitled to interest on those sums, without prejudice to any claim for damages that may be obtained in accordance with Article 74.

Article 53 of the CISG regarding the buyer's obligation to pay the price of the goods in accordance with the contract and Article 78 regarding the right of the other party to charge interest on the price or any other sums in arrears if one party fails to pay them. As for the interest rate, since the CISG did not provide for the interest rate, the court held that the interest rate in this case should be determined in accordance with the relevant laws and regulations of the People's Republic of China. Wooree LED claimed that the interest rate on the arrears was calculated at the benchmark one-year loan rate of the People's Bank of China for the same period, and the court held that the claim was in accordance with the relevant laws and regulations of the People's Republic of China.

Article 53 of the CISG sets forth in general terms the buyer's obligations in the contract of international sale of goods, namely: payment for the goods and acceptance of the goods. The buyer's obligations are based on the proper performance of the seller, e.g. when the seller fails to properly perform its delivery obligations,[3] or delivers the goods in advance or in excess,[4] the buyer has the right to refuse to accept the goods, and there is no obligation to accept the goods. However, Article 53 of the Convention requires the buyer to take over the goods in accordance with the contract and the provisions of the Convention. This obligation is closely related to the issue of ownership of the goods, and the Convention deliberately avoids the relationship between taking over the goods and accepting the goods, in order to be consistent with the provisions of Article 4, which does not involve the issue of ownership, but the distinction between the two has important practical significance.[5] Obviously, Article 53 clearly stipulates that merely receiving the goods cannot be regarded as accepting the goods. The above two concepts of behavior also have obvious differences in legal effects. In international trade, receiving the goods is the act of receiving the goods made by the buyer in accordance with the contract or convention, and its purpose is to ensure the performance of the contract, while accepting the goods is the act of the buyer acknowledging the transfer of ownership of the goods, and the contract has been performed in the case of payment of the goods. Similarly, the buyer's obligation to pay for the goods as stipulated in Article 53 is also an act requiring the buyer to guarantee the performance of the contract, which does not mean that the

[3] The CISG, Article 31, 32.

[4] The CISG, Article 52.

[5] Li [3], p. 260.

buyer has recognized the goods, accordingly, Article 36 of the Convention stipulates the seller's responsibility for the existence of hidden defects in the delivered goods, and the buyer has the right to exercise the right to remedy, including the return of the goods, while Articles 49 and 82 further make arrangements for the buyer to exercise the right of return. However, this does not mean that the Convention gives discretion to the buyer to accept the goods or pay for the goods, other articles of the Convention make restrictions accordingly, for example, Article 38 requires the buyer to examine the goods in time, and Article 39 requires the buyer to notify the seller in time after discovering the non-conformity of the goods, otherwise the buyer loses the right to claim the non-conformity of the goods, which is equivalent to the buyer's acceptance of the goods.

The essence of interest under Article 78 is the cost of capital occupation. In international trade, the buyer's default in payment of goods will inevitably cause the seller to suffer interest losses caused by the default of payment, and the buyer shall pay interest. Similarly, Article 84 provides that the buyer is entitled to claim interest from the seller if the seller is required to return the price to the buyer in the transaction and fails to do so. However, the issue of interest was disputed by the framers of the Convention at the Vienna Conference,[6] and in the context of this case, two issues need to be determined: 1. the time of accrual of interest; 2. the criteria for calculating the interest rate. With respect to the first issue, Article 78 grants the right to receive interest without depending on the creditor giving notice of payment to the debtor, and interest begins to accrue as soon as the debt becomes due and payable.[7] This provision is not difficult to understand, usually, the performance of the contract, that is, the delivery of the other party to pay the price, after the seller in accordance with the provisions of the contract and the Convention delivery, it is reasonable for the buyer to pay the full amount of the goods on time and expected to dominate, at this time, if the buyer does not pay the full amount or delayed payment of the goods, from the moment it should be paid but not paid, the buyer is actually the seller's funds occupied, should pay the corresponding funds occupancy charges, that is, interest, the interest does not depend on the time of the seller to the buyer to send a notice of reimbursement, which is also in line with the buyer's obligation to pay as stipulated in Article 53.

With regard to the criteria for calculating the interest rate, due to the disagreement during the Vienna Diplomatic Conference, article 78 of the Convention does not provide for a fixed interest rate, which is quite different from the provision in the *Hague Convention on the Uniform Law of International Sale of Goods.*[8] In this regard, most countries apply the domestic law of a particular country according to the private international law rules of the forum, and a small number of countries apply

[6] The differences between the parties at the Vienna Conference, see Li [4], pp. 333–334.

[7] Li [3], p. 377.

[8] *1964 Hague Convention on the Uniform Law of International Sale of Goods*, Article 83: Where the breach of contract consists of delay in the payment of the price, the seller shall in any event be entitled to interest on such sum as is in arrear at a rate equal to the official discount rate in the country where he has his place of business or, if he has no place of business, his habitual residence, plus 1%.

the domestic law of the creditor's country, not necessarily the law chosen according to the private international law rules.[9] The law chosen based on the rules of private international law is usually also the law of the country where the seller has its place of business, i.e. the law with which the contract is most closely connected, and the "most closely connected" law is the law of the country where the party performing the characteristic performance has its place of business, i.e. the law of the country where the seller has its place of business. Similarly, it has been argued that since the price owed should have been transferred to the seller in a timely manner but was not, the interest rate in the country where the seller has its place of business should be used to calculate the amount of interest that the seller can earn in the abstract, and this should be used to calculate the amount of interest that the buyer should return.[10]

This case is a typical dispute over an international contract for the sale of goods. In the absence of agreement and exclusion by the parties on the governing law for resolving the contract dispute, the court did not err in applying the CISG as the governing law for this case, but there were certain flaws in the allocation of the obligation to ascertain. The court ordered the buyer to pay the interest on the arrears according to Article 78, and the application of the law was accurate, but for the part of interest calculation which was not stipulated by the CISG, the calculation was made by applying the law of the forum/the law of the buyer's location, which deviated from the current mainstream theoretical view and international judicial practice.

## References


1. Liu, Y. (2019). Application of CISG by Domestic Courts of Contracting States. *Science of Law (Journal of Northwest University of Political Science and Law*, 03, 191–201.
2. Wang, H. & Shen, W. (2016). Fixing the Failure of Ascertainment of Foreign Law——An Empirical and Economics Study. *International Business*, 05, 135-149.
3. Li, W. (2009). *A Commentary on CISG*, 2nd edition. Law Press.
4. Li, W. (2002). *A Commentary on CISG*, 1st edition. Law Press.
5. United Nations Commission on International Trade Law (UNCITRAL). (2016). *UNCITRAL Digest of Case Law on the United Nations Convention on Contracts for the International Sale of Goods*. https://uncitral.un.org/sites/uncitral.un.org/files/media-documents/uncitral/en/cisg_digest_2016.pdf.
6. Bianca, C. M. & Bonell, M. J. (1987). *Commentary on the international sales law: the 1980 Vienna sales convention*. Giuffrè Milan.


**Junkai Fan** is a judge assistant at Qingdao Maritime Court. He hears cases on admiralty law, maritime law and international trade law. He also served as an executive officer and is familiar with the mechanism of the enforcement of ship arrest and auction as well as the protection of international seafarers' rights and interests. His cases were selected as The Top Ten Typical Cases of National Admiralty and Maritime in 2020. He holds an LLM by research from Tongji University.

---

[9] UNCITRAL [5], Article 78, para. 10.

[10] Bianca and Bonell [6], p. 611.

**Chaolin Zhang** is a lecturer in Law at the Qufu Normal University. She obtained a Ph.D. in International Law from Nankai University, China. Prior to that, she obtained an LLM in International Economic Law from the School of Law at the City University of Hong Kong, China. Her research interests lie in international trade law, data law, and law and technology.

**Shu Zhang** is a lecturer in commercial law at Deakin Law School, Deakin University (Australia) and coached Deakin Law School's Vis Moot team. Prior to joining Deakin Law School, Dr. Zhang was a post-doctoral fellow in the Chinese International Business and Economic Law Initiative, Law School, University of New South Wales (Australia). Her research interests include international commercial law, dispute resolution and international arbitration, as well as comparative contract law. She also completed internships at both the Australian Centre for International Commercial Arbitration (ACICA) and the Chinese International Economic and Trade Arbitration Commission (CIETAC). She is also admitted to practice in New South Wales, Australia. Dr. Zhang obtained her PhD in Law from University of New South Wales (Australia), and her LLM, LLB and BA in Economics (Double Degree) from Peking University (China). She has published various manuscripts with leading journals in this area, such as the Journal of Contract Law, Vindobona Journal of International Commercial Law and Arbitration, China Quarterly.

# KOYJ Co., Ltd. v. Beijing Shiyuanda Electronic Technology Co., Ltd.

Geng Wang and Shu Zhang

**Case Information**

**Case Name**: KOYJ Co., Ltd. v. Beijing Shiyuanda Electronic Technology Co., Ltd.

**Seller**: KOYJ Co., Ltd.
**Place of Business**: Republic of Korea.

**Buyer**: Beijing Shiyuanda Electronic Technology Co., Ltd.
**Place of Business**: China.

**Details of First Instance**:
**Court**: The First Intermediate People's Court of Beijing Municipality.
**Date of Decision**: 5 November 2012.
**Case No**: (2012) Yi Zhong Min Chu Zi No. 5442.
**Judges**: Chang Jie (Presiding Judge), Liang Rui (Acting Judge), Wu Yangxin (Acting Judge).

**CISG Applied**: Yes.
**Key CISG Provisions Interpreted and Applied**: Articles 14, 15, 53.

G. Wang (✉)
University of International Business and Economics, Beijing, China
e-mail: wanggeng_aoi@163.com

S. Zhang
Deakin University, Geelong, VIC 3220, Australia
e-mail: shu.zhang@deakin.edu.au



P. Guo et al. (eds.), *Selected Chinese Cases on the UN Sales Convention (CISG) Vol. 3*, Selected Chinese Cases on the CISG,
https://doi.org/10.1007/978-981-99-6851-0_39

## Case Abstract

From April to July 2011, Shiyuanda Company purchased 16 batches of prism sheets from KOYJ Company, with payment due via wire transfer 60 days after the delivery of the goods. KOYJ Company performed its duty to deliver the goods as required, but Shiyuanda failed to pay for them. After deducting reimbursement for defective products, Shiyuanda Company still owed KOYJ Company USD$ 233,967.61. Consequently, KOYJ Company filed a lawsuit.

The Court first determined that pt 4 of the Civil Procedure Law of the People's Republic of China, as well as other relevant provisions of the law, should be applicable to procedural aspects. The Court then held that both companies have capacity for civil rights and capacity for civil conduct under art 14 of the Law of the People's Republic of China on Choice of Law for Foreign-related Civil Relationships and the Company Law of the People's Republic of China. Concerning the applicable law, the Court found that the CISG is the applicable law for resolving the dispute in this case. Further, the Court stated that the law of the forum, namely Chinese law, should apply to determining the nature of the legal relationship between Shiyuanda Company and KOYJ Company. According to Chinese law, the legal relationship between the two parties is a contract relationship for the international sale of goods. In terms of ascertaining the contents of the CISG, the Court noted that KOYJ Company had submitted to the Court all of the content of the CISG, which was copied from the Science and Technology Novelty Retrieval Center of the National Library of the People's Republic of China, and published in the Gazette of the State Council of the People's Republic of China. Therefore, the contents of the CISG had been ascertained and could be used directly as the legal basis of this case.

Later, the Court discussed the substantive issues of the case. The Court stated that the legal relationship between Shiyuanda Company and KOYJ Company was a contract relationship, and that the contract was valid because the contract was concluded in accordance with the contract formation procedures stipulated in arts 14(1) and 15(1) of the CISG, and its terms did not conflict with the provisions of the CISG. The failure of Shiyuanda Company to make the required payments for the goods constituted a breach of contract, and KOYJ Company had the right to demand the arrears under art 53 of the CISG. Consequently, Shiyuanda Company was sentenced to pay KOYJ Company US $233,967.61 within seven days from the date on which the judgment was effective.

## Commentary to the Key Issues Related to the CISG

### Issues

Issue 1 The Applicability of the CISG
Issue 2 Determination of the Nature of the Legal Relationship
Issue 3 Determination of the Breach of Contract and its Consequences.

## Comments

In this case, Shiyuanda Company, the defendant, neither made any reply nor attended the trial. According to art 147 of the Civil Procedure Law of the People's Republic of China, if the defendant refuses to appear in court without justifiable reason after being summoned, or leaves the courtroom during a court session without the permission of the court, the court may make a judgment by default.[1] Therefore, the case was decided in absentia. Nowadays, the litigant's litigation behaviour has emerged as the primary driving force behind the lawsuit process. The litigant usually participates in the litigation in order to obtain a favourable judgment outcome, but sometimes the litigant can be voluntarily absent from trial for the sake of his own interests.[2]

### Issue 1 The Applicability of the CISG

The Court correctly determined that the CISG was the applicable law in this case, but its reasoning process for determining the applicable law was flawed. Before invoking art 1(1)(a) of the CISG, the Court applied art 142(2) of the General Principles of the Civil Law of the People's Republic of China.[3] Article 142(2) is a special provision in Chinese law governing the application of international treaties in China. It stipulates that: "If any international treaty concluded or acceded to by the People's Republic of China contains provisions differing from those in the civil Laws of the People's Republic of China, the provisions of the international treaty shall apply, unless the provisions are ones on which the People's Republic of China has announced reservations." As noted in the case of China Yituo Group Co., v. Germany Gerhard Freyso LTD. GmbH & Co., KG,[4] this line of reasoning is not only unnecessary, but could also result in misinterpretation.

Firstly, the CISG, as a substantive uniform law, should be directly applied without resorting to private international law rules.[5] However, the nature of art 142(2) of the General Principles of the Civil Law of the People's Republic of China is ambiguous. Some scholars believe that this is not a rule of private international law, but rather a principle of the provisions made by China's highest legislative body on the domestic implementation of treaties,[6] whereas others believe that this provision cannot be called a principle of treaty application in China,[7] but still falls under the purview of China's private international law rules. The practice of invoking art 142(2) of the General Principles of the Civil Law of the People's Republic of China before

[1] Civil Procedure Law of the People's Republic of China (2021 Amendment) (promulgated by the Standing Comm. Nat'l People's Cong., Apr. 9, 1991, effective Apr. 9, 1991, rev'd by the Standing Comm. Nat'l People's Cong., Dec. 24, 2021).

[2] Qu and Suo [1], p. 26.

[3] General Principles of the Civil Law of the People's Republic of China (2009 Amendment) (promulgated by the Nat'l People's Cong., Apr. 12, 1986, effective Jan. 1, 1987, amended Aug. 27, invalid Jan. 1, 2021).

[4] Wang et al. [2], pp. 49–57.

[5] UNCITRAL [3], p. 4.

[6] Li [4], pp. 316–317.

[7] Han [5], p. 226; Shi [6], p. 84.

implementing the CISG may be contrary to the spirit of art 1(1)(a) of the CISG's autonomous applicability.

Secondly, the wording of art 142(2) of the General Principles of the Civil Law of the People's Republic of China is prone to ambiguity, leading to the conclusion that international treaties only apply when they conflict with domestic legislation. In this case, the Court made such an error. The Court held that, except for the provisions to which China declared reservations, all international treaties concluded or acceded to by China, and which have entered into force for China, have different provisions on the same matter than Chinese laws, and the provisions of international treaties shall prevail. In fact, this notion runs counter to the basic legal principle of "*pacta sunt servanda*", as it is a conditional application of treaty terms, which is incompatible with the original intent of the States parties to establish international treaties.[8] Furthermore, most foreign parties only know that China has signed the CISG, but it is difficult to determine whether the specific provisions of Chinese domestic law are consistent with the terms of the CISG.[9] Foreign parties must use more effort to ascertain the law, which is unjust to them. In addition, determining whether international treaties are consistent with Chinese law is subjective, and who will assess this is contentious.[10] A regional court in China may not be an appropriate judge. In this case, the Court did not demonstrate its method of determining how provisions of international treaties and those of Chinese law differ from one another, instead ruling in general terms that international treaties should apply.

Thus, the correct reasoning path should be to assess whether the CISG is directly applicable in this circumstance under art 1(1)(a) of the CISG. Since Shiyuanda Company has its place of business in China and KOJY Company has its place of business in Korea, both of which are Contracting States to the CISG, the CISG is the applicable law for settling the issue in this matter.

### Issue 2 Determination of the Nature of the Legal Relationship

The applicable law to determine the nature of the parties' legal relationship is another intriguing topic that the case poses. The answer to this question will also affect the application of the CISG, as one of the premises of CISG application is that the parties have a legal relationship of contracts for the international sale of goods. If the court concludes that the legal relationship in question is not a contract relationship for the international sale of goods, the CISG cannot be applied.

In this case, the Court chose to apply Chinese private international law rules. According to art 8 of the Law of the People's Republic of China on Choice of Law for Foreign-related Civil Relationships, *lex fori* shall apply to the determination of the nature of foreign-related civil relationships.[11] *Lex fori* is Chinese law in this

---

[8] Song and Zhang [7], p. 107.

[9] Xuan and Wang [8], p. 129.

[10] Xuan and Wang [8], p. 12; Liu [9], p. 194.

[11] Law of the People's Republic of China on Choice of Law for Foreign-related Civil Relationships (promulgated by the Standing Comm. Nat'l People's Cong., Oct. 28, 2010, effective Apr. 1, 2011).

instance. Subsequently, the Court stated that this case involves a dispute over contracts for international sales of goods pursuant to ch 9 of the Contract Law of the People's Republic of China[12] and the relevant provisions of the Notice by the Supreme People's Court of Issuing the Decision to Amend the Provisions on the Causes of Action of Civil Cases.[13] In other cases, Chinese courts have also tended to use Chinese law to determine the nature of the legal relationship between the parties, such as the appeal case of the contract dispute between Shanghai Jiamupu Industrial Co., Ltd. and Moraglis S.A.[14] However, there are some differences between the definition of contract for the international sale of goods in Chinese law and in the CISG, particularly some contracts that are considered contracts for work in Chinese law but are sales contracts according to art 3(1) of the CISG, which leads to some Chinese courts that judge the nature of the legal relationship in this way failing to apply the CISG correctly.[15] Fortunately, in this case, notwithstanding the Court's imperfect reasoning, the legal relationship between the parties is reasonably straightforward and unambiguous, and it falls inside the contract relationship of the international sale of goods under the CISG. Yet the Court's line of reasoning is not one that should be supported. The CISG has priority over all domestic civil laws in China, and this priority extends not only to the provisions of the CISG but also to interpretations of such provisions and general principles.[16] When determining the applicability of the CISG, the factors mentioned in the CISG must first be examined in characterising the contract. As stressed in art 7 of the CISG, when it comes to concerns relating to contract characterisation that are not expressly addressed by the CISG, the general principles of the CISG should be considered before resorting to private international law rules.

**Issue 3 Determination of the Breach of Contract and Its Consequences**

According to the evidence presented by KOJY Company, Shiyuanda Company failed to pay for the goods as contracted, clearly violating art 53 of the CISG. Article 53 of the CISG provides that the buyer must pay the price and take delivery of the goods as required by the contract and the CISG. The Court correctly applied art 53 of the CISG and determined that Shiyuanda Company did not fulfill its contractual payment obligations and constituted a breach of contract. However, the Court did not cite art 61 or art 62 of the CISG to explain the consequences of the Shiyuanda Company's breach of contract, but instead directly supported KOJY Company's claim. In this

[12] Contract Law of the People's Republic of China (promulgated by the Nat'l People's Cong., Mar. 15, 1999, effective Oct. 1, 1999).

[13] Notice by the Supreme People's Court of Issuing the Decision to Amend the Provisions on the Causes of Action of Civil Cases (promulgated by the Sup. People's Ct., Feb. 18, 2011, effective Apr. 1, 2011), Fa [2011] No. 41.

[14] Shanghai Jiamupu Shiye Youxian Gongsi Su Moraglis S.A. Chenglan Hetong Jiufen Shangsu An—Dispute Concerning Contracts for Work, (2012) Hu Gao Min Er (Shang) Zhong Zi No. 4 Civil Judgment, CLI.C.853584 (Chinalawinfo) (Shanghai High People's Ct. May 28, 2012).

[15] He [10], p. 23.

[16] Liu and Ren [11], p. 893.

regard, the Court's reasoning is not perfect. Furthermore, if one party fails to pay the price, the other party is entitled to interest on those amounts under art 78 of the CISG. The interest, nevertheless, can be waived. In this case, KOJY Company only requested that Shiyuanda Company reimburse the purchase price, which was considered as relinquishing the interest. As a result, the Court ultimately ruled that Shiyuanda Company must repay the purchase price, which came to USD $233,967.61 according to KOJY Company's claim.

## References


1. Qu, W. & Suo, Z. (2015). A Comparative Analysis of Default Judgment: In the Perspective of Protecting the Interests of the Parties. *Tianjin Legal Science,* 31(03), 26-31
2. Wang, G., Guo, P. & Zhang, S. (2022). Chapter 6: China Yituo Group Company v Germany Gerhard Freyso Ltd GmbH & Co. KG, in Guo, P., Zuo, H. C., & Zhang, S. (Eds.), *Selected Chinese Cases on the UN Sales Convention (CISG) Vol. 1* (pp.49–57). Springer
3. United Nations Commission on International Trade Law (UNCITRAL) (2016). *UNCITRAL Digest of Case Law on the United Nations Convention on Contracts for the International Sale of Goods*. Retrieved June 20, 2023, from https://uncitral.un.org/en/case_law/digests
4. Li, H. (2003). *Introduction to Treaty Law* (2nd Ed.). Law Press
5. Han, S. (2016). Application of the CISG in Chinese International Commercial Arbitration. *China Legal Science*, 5, 218-238
6. Shi, H. (2015). On the path of the court's application of the United Nations Convention on Contracts for the international sale of goods: the relationship with the rules of conflict law. *Law Science Magazine*, 36(12), 81-88
7. Song, X. & Zhang, Q. (2008). Problems in the Application of United Nations Convention on Contracts for the International Sale of Goods and its practice in China. *Law Science*, 1, 103-110
8. Xuan, Z. & Wang, Y. (2013). Application of UN Convention of International Sale of Goods (CISG) in China Courts. *Law Science Magazine*, 33(05), 125-131
9. Liu, Y. (2019). On the Application of the United Nations Convention on Contracts for the International Sale of Goods in Chinese Courts. *Science of Law*, 37(03), 191-201
10. He, X. (2017). An Analysis on Divergences in the Application of CISG in Courts of PFTZs. *International Business Research*, 38(01), 19-29
11. Liu, Q. & Ren, X. (2017). CISG in Chinese courts: The issue of Applicability. *American Journal of Comparative Law*, 65(04), 873-918



**Geng Wang** is a Ph.D. candidate in law at University of International Business and Economics. Prior to that, she earned her LL.M. in International Law from Nankai University and LL.B. from Shandong University, respectively. Her areas of research are international trade law and international treaty law.

**Shu Zhang** is a lecturer in commercial law at Deakin Law School, Deakin University (Australia) and coached Deakin Law School's Vis Moot team. Prior to joining Deakin Law School, Dr. Zhang was a post-doctoral fellow in the Chinese International Business and Economic Law Initiative, Law School, University of New South Wales (Australia). Her research interests include international commercial law, dispute resolution and international arbitration, as well as comparative contract law. She also completed internships at both the Australian Centre for International

Commercial Arbitration (ACICA) and the Chinese International Economic and Trade Arbitration Commission (CIETAC). She is also admitted to practice in New South Wales, Australia. Dr. Zhang obtained her Ph.D. in Law from University of New South Wales (Australia), and her LLM, LLB and BA in Economics (Double Degree) from Peking University (China). She has published various manuscripts with leading journals in this area, such as the Journal of Contract Law, Vindobona Journal of International Commercial Law and Arbitration, China Quarterly.

# m.c.or-shy Ltd. Company v. Hangzhou Fuming Refrigeration Technology Co., Ltd. and Hangzhou Silk Garment Import and Export Co., Ltd.

**Kaiwei Cui and Peng Guo**

**Case Information**

**Case Name**: m.c.or-shy Ltd. v. Hangzhou Fuming Refrigeration Technology Co., Ltd. and Hangzhou Silk Garment Import and Export Co., Ltd.

**Seller**: Hangzhou Fuming Refrigeration Technology Co., ('Fuming Company').
**Place of Business:** China.

**Buyer**: m.c.or-shy Ltd. ('m Company').
**Place of Business**: Israel.

**Details of First Instance**:
**Court**: Hangzhou Intermediate People's Court of Zhejiang Province.
**Date of Decision**: 22 December 2014.
**Case No.**: (2012) Zhe Hang Shang Wai Chu Zi No. 281.
**Judges**: Yu Sheng (Presiding Judge), Miao Lei (Acting Judge), Wang Jianying (People's Jurors).

**CISG Applied**: Yes.
**Key the CISG Provisions Interpreted and Applied**: Articles 23, 30, 35.

---

K. Cui (✉)
University of International Business and Economics, Beijing, China
e-mail: 13663719268@163.com

P. Guo
Swinburne University of Technology, Melbourne, VIC 3000, Australia
e-mail: pguo@swin.edu.au



P. Guo et al. (eds.), *Selected Chinese Cases on the UN Sales Convention (CISG) Vol. 3*, Selected Chinese Cases on the CISG,
https://doi.org/10.1007/978-981-99-6851-0_40

## Case Abstract

From April to October 2010, the employees of the defendant, Fuming Company, negotiated refrigerant transactions with the plaintiff m Company by email. The parties determined that the seller of the goods would provide the buyer with multiple specifications of refrigerant, and agreed on the price, packaging and transportation responsibilities of the goods. Subsequently, the buyer sought the services of Hangzhou Silk Garment Import and Export Co., ('Silk Company') a goods export agency. After m Company paid for the goods, the seller provided the goods and quality inspection report to the buyer in accordance with the agreement, and issued the corresponding invoice for each specification of the goods sold. From October 2011 to March 2012, the plaintiff claimed to the defendant through a lawyer's letter that the product quality was problematic, but Fuming Company did not make a positive response.

After the dispute in this case was litigated, m Company appealed to the Court to order the plaintiff to return the price it paid for the purchase of the defective products, to reimburse the bank interest charged, to pay related expenses caused by the direct loss and requiring Fuming Company and Silk Company to assume joint and several liability in the trial. The Court held that since the parties agreed on the application of Chinese law in the trial, both the plaintiff and the defendant were States Parties to the CISG. It was decided to give priority to the application of the CISG for judgment. If the CISG was not applicable, Chinese law would be applied.

After cross-examination between the plaintiff and the defendant, the Court found that Fuming Company and Silk Company had an entrusted relationship, and that the evidence provided by the plaintiff could not prove that the goods it commissioned for inspection had quality defects. Similarly, it could not be completely proved that the tested gas and the refrigerant supplied by the plaintiff to the customer were produced and sold by Fuming Company. Therefore, the Court dismissed the claims of the plaintiff m Company under arts 23, 30 and 35 of the CISG.

## Commentary on the Key Issues Related to the CISG

### Issues

Issue 1 Conclusion and Effectiveness of Sales Contract
Issue 2 The Seller's Obligation to Guarantee the Conformity of the Goods
Issue 3 Limitation on Avoidance of the Contract.

### Comments

### Issue 1 Conclusion and Effectiveness of Sales Contract

In the case of m Company v. Fuming Company and Silk Company, to determine whether there is an effective contractual relationship between the buyer and the seller of international goods, it should be judged by the objective offer and acceptance behavior of both parties. Only an offer containing all of the requisite terms, thus making it suitable for acceptance, can lead to the successful formation of a contract.[1] Part II of the CISG systematically specifies the related issues of contract conclusion. Article 14 (1) of the CISG provides that:

> A proposal for concluding a contract addressed to one or more specific persons constitutes an offer if it is sufficiently definite and indicates the intention of the offeror to be bound in case of acceptance.

As the primary issue that the parties to the case should resolve, determining the existence of a genuine and effective contractual relationship between the parties to the case will help clarify the basic rights and obligations. In view of defendant Fuming Company's opinion that there was no sales contract between it and m Company, defendant Silk Company believed that the goods were involved and sold them to m Company. Therefore, the determination of the true entity responsible as the seller of the goods should be based on the judgment of the identity of the payer.

During the contract conclusion phase, the employees of m Company and Fuming Company determined the specifications, prices and quantities of the goods to be traded by email, making Fuming Company the real counter party to the contract. Evidence showed that although Silk Company issued the bill of lading, packing list and commercial invoice, it was Silk Company which was involved in the sales of the goods and the corresponding goods agent service object is Fuming Company. Based on the relativity of the contract, the agency relationship between Silk Company and Fuming Company does not affect the fact that m Company entered into a valid contract with Fuming Company for the sale of the goods.

In an international contract for the sale of goods, one of the steps to determine the validity of the contract is to clarify the subject suitability of the parties to sign the contract. The CISG adjusts the sales contract relationship concluded between contemporaries in different countries, and with regard to the handling of the principal-agent relationship between the two defendants. In this case, the judge, in the absence of relevant CISG provisions, found that the legal consequences arising from Silk Company's export agency activities were borne by Fuming Company pursuant to art 402 of the Chinese Contract Law (lapsed and replaced by art 925 of the Chinese Civil Code).[2] The CISG allows both general principles and rules of private international law to fill the loopholes in the Convention.[3] Article 7(2) of the CISG provides the method by which non-statutory legal issues are filled in accordance with the general principles on which the Convention is based, but it is clear that the general principles are less effective in filling gaps in specific issues than existing domestic law provisions.

Article 23 of the CISG states that '*A contract is concluded at the moment when an acceptance of an offer becomes effective*'. It is therefore essential to confirm that the parties to the contract accept the offer. Although the commercial invoices and

---

[1] Cvetkovic [1], p. 122.

[2] Contract Law of the People's Republic of China (promulgated by NPC Standing Committee, December 28,2013, Effective July 1, 2013).

[3] Luo [2], p. 137.

money orders provided by the plaintiff listed Silk Company, due to the principal-agent relationship of the goods between Fuming Company and Silk Company, the existing evidence can confirm that the offer had been accepted and the contract is true and valid. The identification of the truth and validity of the evidence by the Court in this case is based on the Court's judgment. Article 23 of the CISG makes the confirmation of the offer a requirement for the contract to be valid, but the acceptance of an offer can be accompanied by more or less obvious additional terms.[4] It can be seen from the situation reflected in the corresponding judgment documents that the buyer and seller of goods did not set any other obvious additional conditions for the validity of the contract in addition to the provision of test reports. Therefore, the setting of additional conditions in this case did not actually affect the validity of the contract.

Article 24 of the CISG stipulates the meaning of 'delivery' to the other party, but does not explain the relationship between the acceptance of the delivery price and 'delivery'. According to the Chinese Civil Code,[5] a contract becomes effective when the acceptance becomes effective, and the acceptance becomes effective when the notice of acceptance reaches the offeror. The acceptance becomes effective when it is made in accordance with the customs of the transaction or the requirements of the offer without notice. If acceptance and acceptance at the offered price are understood as the same thing, both acceptance and acceptance at the offered price will lead to the validity of the contract.

While art 18(2) of the CISG provides that '*acceptance of the notice upon the issuer*', art 18(3) makes exceptions to the same issue. If acceptance is expressed by a particular act of the offeree on the basis of the offer or in accordance with the customs and usages established between the parties, the acceptance takes effect at the time, without notice to the offeror. It can be considered that the above practice of confirming the effective time of the receiving price according to customary practices and practices is actually a typical practice to respect the autonomy of the parties. This kind of custom and practice directed by autonomy of will only constrain the parties to the contract of sale of goods, and generally needs to be supported by previous business conduct. Article 18(3) of the CISG has been invoked in several decisions with regard to the suggestion that a contract may be concluded by a particular act of the offeree, for example CLOUT cases No. 416 [Federal District Court of Minnesota, March 9,1999], No. 193 [Commercial Court of Zurich, Switzerland, July 10,1996] and No. 1452 [High Court of the Czech Republic, March 29,2006].[6] In the m Company case, although the parties agreed to trade multiple types of products, the relevant acts were not sufficient to establish customary practices and usages, and the parties did not object to the timing of accepting the offer.

[4] Hahnkamper [3], p. 149.

[5] Civil Code of the People's Republic of China (promulgated by The Third Session of the 13th National People's Congress of the People's Republic of China, May 28,2020, Effective Jun.1, 2021).

[6] UNCITRAL [4], p. 94.

### Issue 2 The Seller's Obligation to Guarantee the Conformity of the Goods

After the parties have established a valid international contract for the sale of goods, the seller has the obligation to ensure that the goods it delivers are consistent with the provisions of the contract. Article 30 of the CISG sets out the seller's obligations to deliver the goods, hand over the relevant documents and transfer ownership of the goods. Article 35 specifies that the quantity, quality and specifications of the goods delivered by the seller are in conformity with the requirements of the package contract, and the typical circumstances of the goods being in conformity agreed upon by the parties. ULIS and CISG have significantly different provisions on goods conformity. ULIS stipulates that if the quality of delivery by the seller is not in conformity with the contract, the seller shall be deemed to have failed to fulfill the delivery obligation.[7] In the m Company case, the parties did not dispute the quantity and packaging of the traded goods sold, but the buyer claimed that the quality problem of the refrigerant gas produced by the plaintiff required him to bear the liability for breach of contract and compensate for losses. The settlement of the dispute in this case requires determination of whether the products provided by Fuming Company met the quality requirements of the contract, so that the seller shall be liable. In order to prove this problem, it is necessary to guarantee: first, the goods that m Company claims have quality problems are the goods agreed in the contract; second, that there is sufficient evidence to prove that the goods agreed upon in the contract do not meet the agreed standards; third, the damage caused by the use of the goods is not caused by any non-goods quality problems.

Judging from the evidence provided by both parties, the buyer cannot obtain a positive result, for the reason that the standards for inspecting the goods and corresponding supporting materials are not applicable to the goods actually traded between the parties, and it cannot be proved that the goods actually agreed to be traded did not meet national or industrial standards. During the same period, m Company also purchased refrigerant gas from other manufacturers apart from Fuming Company. Therefore, even if the tested goods did have quality problems, it cannot be explained that the corresponding products were provided by the defendant. In addition, m Company employees stated that the customer's reaction cooling effect when using specific refrigerant did not match the gas pressure with the original safety valve and catheter, which cannot rule out that the damage caused by the goods is caused by non-cargo quality problems.

The buyer has the right to fully demand what the seller has agreed to do, and the buyer's knowledge of the actual state of the goods cannot change the content of the seller's obligation.[8] Article 35(2)(a) of the CISG indicates that the contract complies with the goods requiring '*are fit for the purposes for which goods of the same description would ordinarily be used*'. Article 35(2)(c) requires the goods to '*possess the qualities of goods which the seller has held out to the buyer as a sample or model*'. In the m Company case, a Fuming Company employee indicated that 'a

[7] Convention relating to a Uniform Law on the International Sale of Goods, (The Hague, 1 July 1964).

[8] Saidov [5], p. 532.

quality inspection report is attached to the sample of each gas', but the sample here is not a sample of the actual goods agreed to in the contract. This can be verified in the email between the two parties. The product characteristics of the replacement gas actually traded by the parties was different from those of the refrigeration pure gas, but the plaintiff m Company did not prove that the replacement gas actually traded could not meet the purpose of the contract. Article 35(2) of the CISG, which stipulates that goods must meet the criteria for commercial sale, has seen different approaches in practice as to assessing which criteria should be applied to criterion (a). CLOUT Case No. 123 of the Federal Supreme Court of Germany and CLOUT case 426 of the Austrian Supreme Court held that the assessment should generally be based on the criteria of the seller's country, while CLOUT case No. 774 of the German Federal High Court and CLOUT case 1097 of China's CIETAC opted for the resaleability criterion.[9] Article 35 of the CISG as the core clause has accumulated a large number of cases in the practice of international goods sales. Delivery by the seller shall be judged through this article, and the parties in this case have clearly agreed in accordance with art 35(1), otherwise the '*Commercial Sales Standard*' of art 35(2) shall apply. CIETAC tribunals in different cases have found various situations in which the goods delivered did not conform with the contract, the quality of the goods not conforming to the contractual requirements being an oft-found example. If there has no sample had been considered by the parties, the tribunal would be inclined to employ other criteria, such as those set out in art 35(2)(a) of the CISG.[10]

In this case, the burden of proof is the key factor affecting its final direction. The Court chose to assign the burden of proof to the plaintiff when determining whether the relevant evidence could prove that Fuming Company knew of the product quality problem, and whether the quality of the product involved conformed to the contract. The CISG contains a general principle that the party who is asserting or affirming a fact bears the burden of proving it, resulting in an allocation of the burden of proof to a buyer who asserts that goods did not conform to the contract.[11] If the plaintiff cannot prove that the goods delivered by the seller are not consistent with the contract, the seller shall suffer from unclear burden of proof. The conformity of goods is determined not only by their quantity, quality, description, or packaging, but also by compliance with standards affecting the use of the goods, such as public law regulations and industry codes.[12] The plaintiff claimed that the goods delivered by the defendant violated the national standards of China as well as international standards, but it did not provide evidence on the matters claimed.

[9] CLOUT case No.123 [Bundesgerichtshof, Germany, 8 March 1995]; CLOUT case No.426 [Oberster Gerichtshof, Austria, 13 April 2000]; CLOUT case No.774 [Bundesgerichtshof, Germany, 2 March 2005]; CLOUT case No.1097 [China International Economic and Trade Arbitration Commission, China, 6 March 2003]. Available at: https://www.uncitral.org/clout/search.jspx.

[10] Wu [6], p. 16.

[11] Linne [7], p. 34.

[12] Michael [8], p. 39.

### Issue 3 Limitation on Avoidance of the Contract

The CISG gives parties the right to 'declare the contract avoided' for a material breach of contract by the other party in the course of performance.[13] In this case, the plaintiff m Company's claim includes not only asking the defendant to return the price paid and the bank interest for the period, but also requesting the payment of direct losses and the recovery of defective products, which achieves an effect similar to termination of the contract. Although the full text of the judgment does not reflect the plaintiff's claim, the result of the seller's obligation to refund the price is the content of CISG section 5 *"Effects of avoidance"*. Article 49(1) of the CISG provides for a fundamental breach by the seller and the buyer's avoidance in the event of a fundamental breach of the contract. Article 46(2) provides for the seller's right to demand delivery of substitute goods in the event of a fundamental breach of the contract, which is the legal consequences of the seller's fundamental breach under the CISG. Article 49(2) of the CISG provides for *'in cases where the seller has delivered the goods, the buyer loses the right to declare the contract avoided'*. This means that the invalidation of the contract is limited to the seller's failure to deliver the goods. After the seller delivers the goods, and except for late delivery in Article 49(2)(a) and specifications in Article 49(2)(b), the buyer has no right to terminate the contract even if the product has serious quality problems.

From the perspective of the above provisions, the fundamental breach 'gives' the buyer the right to declare the contract invalid and then to claim return of the price paid. In the case that the seller has completed the delivery, the possibility of requiring the seller to return payment has lost the legal level. The problem is that even if it does not choose to declare invalidity or fundamental default, can the buyer demand that the seller return payment with interest for other reasons?

Some courts have held that the invalidation of a contract should serve as a 'final' remedy.[14] Article 45 of the CISG sets out the rights of the buyer in the event of non-performance by the seller. It further requires the seller to perform its obligations, deliver substitute goods (in the event of a fundamental breach), repair the contract, remedy at its own expense, declare the contract avoided, reduce the price, refuse in the case of early delivery, reject goods exceeding the agreed quantity under arts 46–52, and damages under arts 74–77. Although art 45 stipulates the rights of the buyer where the seller is in breach, it does not specify whether the buyer has the right to demand the return of the full price. In the case of m Company v. Fuming Company, although the plaintiff did not directly express the direct rescission of the contract, or assert that the seller had committed a fundamental breach of contract, it could not be ruled out that the plaintiff had a right of action to claim the exclusion of the full price.

Whether under the CISG or the relevant provisions of domestic law, judges are generally very cautious in upholding requests for the return of all prices paid in cases

[13] Li [9], p. 91.

[14] CLOUT case No.747 [Oberster Gerichtshof, Austria, 23 May 2005] (see full text of the decision); CLOUT case No.428 [Oberster Gerichtshof, Austria, 7 September 2000].

of non-fundamental breach of contract or avoidance of contract, such as Germany's 'grace period' mechanism designed to severely limit contract rescission.[15] This is similar to the application of limiting fundamental breaches and avoidance contracts, both in the pursuit of effective international contracts for the sale of goods, but also because these requests are the most severe remedy for breach of contract and the last resort of 'remedies' They also set a number of conditions limiting their application, and relate to arts 25, 45, 49, 51, 61 and 64 of the CISG. In the m Company case, since the seller delivered the goods, unless it has in effect deprived the buyer of what it was entitled to expect under the contract, it is difficult to ask the court to uphold a claim for non-conforming quality. Where there are many limitations to asserting avoidance, it may be easier for the buyer of the goods to opt for a more realistic contractual remedy.

## References

1. Cvetkovic, P. (2002). The Characteristics of an Offer in CISG and PECL. *Pace International Law Review*, 14(1), 121-132.
2. Luo, J. (2008). General principles of international trade and the filling of gaps in CISG. *Theory Monthly*, 2008(11), 134-138.
3. Hahnkamper, W. (2005). Acceptance of an offer in light of electronic communications. *Journal of Law and Commerce*, 25(1), 147-152.
4. United Nations Commission on International Trade Law (UNCITRAL) (2016). *UNCITRAL digest of case law on the United Nations convention on contracts for the international sale of goods*. Retrieved from https://uncitral.un.org/en/case_law/digests.
5. Saidov, D. (2013). Article 35 of the CISG: reflecting on the present and thinking about the future. *Villanova Law Review*, 58(4), 529-552.
6. Wu, D. (2005). CIETAC's Practice on the CISG. *Nordic Journal of Commercial Law*, 2005(2), 1-46.
7. Linne, A. L. (2008). Burden of proof under article 35 of the CISG. *Pace International Law Review*, 20(1), 31-44.
8. Michael, B., Yesim, A., Eric, B., et al. (2019). CISG advisory council opinion no.19 standards and conformity of the goods under article 35 CISG. *Nordic Journal of Commercial Law*, 2019(2), 34–63.
9. Li, J. & Liu, N. (1999). On the System of "Invalidation of Contract" in the United Nations Convention on Contracts for the International Sale of Goods: Also comment on the relevant provisions of China's contract legislation. *Studies in Law and Business*, 1999(3), 90-96.
10. Chen, S. (2011), A Comparative Study of the System of Rescission of the United Nations Convention on the International Sale of Goods. *Tsinghua Law Journal*, 5(5), 115-135.

**Kaiwei Cui** Ph.D. candidate in International Law at the University of International Business and Economics, majoring in International Business Law and International Trade Law. Prior to that, he got his LL.M. from Zhengzhou University. He participated in projects of the National Social Science Fund, and projects of the Department of Commerce of Henan Province, among others.

[15] Chen [10], p. 116.

**Peng Guo** is Lecturer in Law at the Swinburne University of Technology. He has worked across several Australian universities and has held visiting positions at different European universities. He has received scholarships awarded by renowned research institutions and international organisations, including the Max Planck Institute for Comparative and International Private Law, the International Institute for the Unification of Private Law (UNIDROIT), the Swiss Institute of Comparative Law, and the European Union. He specialises in the international sale of goods, international commercial arbitration, comparative contract law, and law and technology.

# Grand Resources Group Co., Ltd. v. STX Corporation

**Peng Wang and Yueshan Liu**

**Case Information**

**Case Name**: Grand Resources Group Co., Ltd. v STX Corporation – Dispute Arising from a Sale of Goods Contract

**Seller**: Grand Resources Group Co., Ltd.
**Place of Business**: China

**Buyer**: STX Corporation
**Place of Business**: Korea

**Details of First Instance**:
**Court**: Ningbo Intermediate People's Court, Zhejiang
**Date of Decision**: 28 January
**Case No.**: (2012) Zhe Yong Min Yi Chu Zi No.1
**Judges**: Weidong Lv (Presiding Judge), Zhenyu Liu (Judge), Xindi Hu (People's Assessor)

**Details of Second Instance**:
**Court**: Zhejiang High People's Court
**Date of Decision**: 20 August 2014
**Case No.**: (2014) Zhe Shang Wai Zhong Zi No 48

P. Wang (✉) · Y. Liu
Nankai University, Tianjin, China
e-mail: wppku@163.com

Y. Liu
e-mail: liuyueshan99@yeah.net



P. Guo et al. (eds.), *Selected Chinese Cases on the UN Sales Convention (CISG) Vol. 3*, Selected Chinese Cases on the CISG,
https://doi.org/10.1007/978-981-99-6851-0_41

**Judges**: Fanhong Kong (Presiding Judge), Wei Chen (Acting Judge), Tong Huo (Acting Judge)

**CISG Applied**: Yes
**Key CISG Provisions Interpreted and Applied**: Articles 1, 6, 81, 86, 87

### Case Abstract

Grand Company, a Chinese company is the seller, and STX Company, a Korean company, is the buyer. On April 29, 2008, the two companies signed a sales contract under which STX Company would purchase from Grand Company special steel plates for shipbuilding that were to be certified by an independent company, DNV, with the port of discharge in India. The parties agreed that the handling of any contract disputes should be submitted to the Hong Kong International Arbitration Centre ('HKIAC') for settlement. On May 2, 2008, STX Company also entered into a steel plate sales contract with Pipavav Shipyard Limited ('PSL') in India, under which STX Company resold the steel plates it had purchased from Grand Company to PSL. The sales price agreed in the two sales contracts was respectively paid to the seller on September 18, 2008. The steel plates arrived at the Indian discharge port on October 18, 2008. After receiving the goods, PSL had doubts relating to the documents and quality of the goods, and the parties commenced a dispute. According to the test report issued by DNV India, 783 pieces of the steel plates in the batch were found to be non-conforming.

On May 18, 2009, STX Company refused to accept the goods delivered by Grand Company on the grounds that they did not meet the contractual requirements, and initiated arbitration with the HKIAC. During the Hong Kong arbitration, STX Company and PSL conducted arbitration in Singapore regarding the contract dispute between them. The Singapore Arbitration Tribunal ruled that STX Company should pay PSL a total of USD $2883,174 in damages and interest. PSL was to hand over the steel plates to STX Company after settling the dispute between STX Company and Grand Company, and PSL would keep the steel plates properly until that time.

The HKIAC ruled that the letter sent by STX Company to Grand Company on 30 December 2008 showed that Grand Company's bad faith breach of contract was justified and that there was no obligation for STX Company to take any action to mitigate damages before finding Grand Company's breach of contract. The arbitration award entitled STX Company to damages of USD $292,486, KRW 4,457,613,35, S $21,355.25, and interest thereon. Grand Company applied to the HKIAC for return of the steel plates in question, and the HKIAC held that it had no jurisdiction over the request. From September to October 2011, the court of first instance enforced the compensation amount determined by the HKIAC award based on the application of STX Company. Grand Company applied for non-enforcement of the arbitration award, which was later rejected by the Court. Subsequently, because of the dispute in this case, the execution amount was applied for preservation by Grand Company.

**First Instance:**

In order to solve the problem of returning the steel plates involved in the case, Grand Company appealed to the court of first instance on February 17, 2012, requesting that STX Company be ordered to return 783 pieces of steel plates (worth USD $2,437,877, equivalent to RMB16,663,621, calculated according to the exchange rate base price of USD $1 = RMB6.8353 on December 30, 2008) and compensate Grand Company for the corresponding interest loss. If STX Company was unable to return the steel plates, it should compensate Grand Company for the loss of USD $2,437,877. If there was any shortage of the steel plates returned to Grand Company by STX Company, there would be compensation for the price as agreed in the contract.

STX Company argued that it, as a no-fault party to the contract, had received the storage fee bill sent by PSL and had communicated with Grand Company several times about the storage fee. Grand Company had refused to retrieve the steel plates and pay the storage fee, resulting in increased storage fees and overdue interest.

As to the application of the law, the parties had their places of business in the People's Republic of China and the Republic of Korea respectively, both of which are Contracting States of the United Nations Convention on Contracts for the International Sale of Goods ('CISG'). The parties did not agree to exclude the application of the CISG, and the goods bought and sold by the parties did not fall within the scope of the CISG's prohibited application. The parties also applied or invoked the Convention in the HKIAC and in the court, so the dispute in this case should be handled by the CISG.

The Court held that as to whether the steel plates in question should be returned and the compensation in case of failure to return them, the subject matter of the case was a special steel plate subject to certification by DNV: not a simple kind of object, but a specific object with certain properties. The responsibility for the fundamental breach of contract in this case lay entirely with Grand Company. The ruling of the HKIAC can be interpreted as a partial exercise of the right to rescind the contract by STX Company. The corresponding compensation, and the 783 pieces of non-conforming steel plates should be returned to Grand Company. If any of the steel plates were lost due to poor storage by PSL, STX Company should settle the matter with PSL on its own. Any issues relating to lost steel plates would not affect the transfer of the steel plates to Grand Company on the date set by the judgment, and Grand Company should not refuse to accept the steel plates due to the loss.

With regard to the subject of retrieving the goods from PSL and the calculation of the storage fee when the goods were returned, the Court held that according to the principle of relativity of contract, STX Company, as an intermediary, had a contractual relationship with PSL. STX Company should settle the storage fee first, so that Grand Company could recover the 783 steel plates from PSL's warehouse in the Indian port without any obstacles.

The Court ruled that STX Company should return 783 pieces of steel plates to Grand Company, and that this should be fulfilled within three months from the effective date of the judgment. If the steel plates could not be returned as scheduled, or if STX Company could not return the steel plates due to failure to fulfill the necessary assistance obligations, STX Company should be compensated for the steel plates that could not be returned at the rate of USD $1312/ton, which was calculated at the exchange rate on the last day of the performance period determined by the judgment.

**Second Instance:**

Both Grand Company and STX Company appealed to the court of second instance against the original judgment. The controversial points of the second trial were: firstly, whether there were defects in the procedure and application of the law by the court of first instance; secondly, the return of the non-conforming steel plates and the calculation of storage fees; and thirdly, whether the base price for the calculation of the exchange rate should be based on that of December 30, 2008.

I. Problems with procedure and application of law in the court of first instance

The Court held that Grand Company had expressly agreed to the application of the law of the People's Republic of China in the reply to the jurisdictional objection submitted by it and twice in the trial court hearing, so its claim that the laws of the Hong Kong Special Administrative Region should be applied was not accepted. Since the two countries where the parties are domiciled are both Contracting States to the CISG, and the goods in question did not fall within the scope excluded by arts 2 and 3 of the Convention. As Grand Company and STX Company did not explicitly agree in the contract to exclude the application of the Convention, the original judgment automatically and preferentially applied the CISG according to the provisions of art 1, which was confirmed. As to how to calculate the actual value of the steel plates to be returned is a substantive issue, the Court was not defective in the procedural dealing of this issue.

II. The return of the non-conforming steel plate and the calculation of storage fee

As to whether STX Company had the obligation to return the steel plates in question, the Court held that the contract should be terminated because the contract purpose could not be realized due to Grand Company's malicious breach of contract. According to art 81 of the CISG, Grand Company had the right to request STX Company to return the unacceptable steel plates it had received after paying full compensation for STX Company's losses. STX Company's obligation to return is limited to handing over the non-conforming steel plates to Grand Company at the Indian port. STX Company only need to perform the necessary incidental obligations such as assisting in customs clearance. The relevant costs should be borne by Grand Company itself.

According to art 86(1) of CISG, in the case of bad faith breach of contract by Grand Company, STX Company, as the buyer of the goods, was obliged to take reasonable measures to preserve the non-conforming steel plates in order to avoid the expansion of losses. At the same time, it had the right to keep the steel plates until Grand Company reimbursed the reasonable costs paid by it in full. However, since the non-conforming steel plates in question were stored in PSL's warehouse and therefore involved the payment of storage fees to a third party, PSL handed over the steel plates to STX Company rather than Grand Company. STX Company should first settle the storage and custody fees with PSL according to the principle of contractual relativity before charging Grand Company for a reasonable portion. However, STX Company should still fulfill the obligation of returning the non-conforming steel plates to Grand Company.

Regarding compensation in the case of failure to return, the non-conforming steel plates in question belonged to specific objects in nature, and if STX Company failed to return them in full, it should compensate Grand Company for the corresponding loss. The Court held that since STX Company could not prove the difference in price between the non-conforming steel plates and the steel plates with complete certificates as agreed in the contract, the court of first instance was not wrong to calculate the compensation based on the contract price of USD $1,312/ton from the perspective of no obvious quality problems of the steel plates and prompting STX Company to actively return them.

III. Criteria for calculating the exchange rate

Grand Company claimed that December 30, 2008 (the date when STX Company refused to accept the goods) was the date when STX Company should return the steel plates and calculated the exchange rate based on this date. The Court held that although the HKIAC had determined that date as the date from which interest in damages could be recovered, the determination was only for the breach of contract claims of the parties involved. For the issue of damages in the event of failure to return the original property, the calculation should still be based on the exchange rate on the last day of the return period as determined by the Court.

In conclusion, after paying the compensation and the corresponding interest to STX Company, Grand Company had the right to request STX Company to return the non-conforming steel plates it had obtained and stored in PSL's warehouse, but Grand Company should first pay to STX Company the storage and custody fees and the corresponding interest loss and other costs incurred by the steel plates in India. STX Company failed to prove the reasonable standard of the above costs and the fact that they had been actually incurred, so it should bear the adverse consequences of not being able to prove this. Therefore, in the case that Grand Company did not pay the above expenses, STX Company should still fulfill the obligation to return the non-conforming steel plates involved. The court of second instance upheld the original judgment.

## Commentary to the Key Issues Related to the CISG

### Issues

Issue 1 The Applicability of the CISG
Issue 2 Preservation of the Goods under the CISG.

## Comments

### Issue 1 The Applicability of the CISG

Regarding the jurisdiction of this case, STX Company argued during the appeal that the trial court lacked legal basis for jurisdiction when the parties explicitly agreed to submit disputes related to the performance of the contract to the arbitral tribunal for settlement. After the Court filed the case, during the defense period, STX Company raised jurisdictional objection, and the Court finally ruled that STX Company's jurisdictional objection was not established. After the parties re-determined the defense period, STX Company filed a counterclaim, and both parties appeared in court to participate in the proceedings, indicating that STX Company agreed to the jurisdiction of the trial court over its case, so the jurisdiction of this case was correctly applied.

As for the application of law in this case, there are two controversial points at issue: firstly, whether Chinese substantive or Hong Kong substantive law should be applied in this case, and secondly, when the parties choose to apply the domestic law of a certain country, if the CISG is not explicitly excluded, whether the CISG can be applied at the same time, and how to determine the sequence of application of the CISG and domestic law.

Regarding the first point of dispute, Grand Company and STX Company agreed in the contract that 'all disputes relating to this contract shall be settled amicably, and if they cannot be settled, they shall be submitted to the HKIAC, and the HKIAC award made under the Arbitration Act shall be final and binding on both parties.' This clause should not be interpreted as a choice of law clause, but only a choice of dispute resolution. The parties agreed to submit the dispute to the HKIAC, and the 'Arbitration Act' agreed in the clause is also the procedural law, i.e., when the HKIAC deals with the dispute, the procedure applies to the Arbitration Act, not on the application of Hong Kong substantive law. The Arbitration Act is the procedural law, not the substantive law of Hong Kong. Under the correct application of jurisdiction in this case, the choice of the applicable law should be made in accordance with art 41 of the Law of the People's Republic of China on the Application of Law to Foreign-related Civil Relations ('Applicable Law'), and the parties should choose the applicable law by agreement in accordance with the principle of autonomy.

Grand Company claimed that on the issue of application of law, the HKIAC award confirmed that the sales contract in question was governed by Hong Kong law and that Hong Kong substantive law would apply to the dispute between the parties in this case, except for the choice of law rule. The choice of the applicable law between the HKIAC and the Chinese court is independent of each other, and the applicable law should be based on the choice of the parties. Grand Company had twice explicitly agreed that the law of the People's Republic of China applied in this case, both in its jurisdictional objection brief and in the original trial. Therefore, the court of second instance was correct and did not support Grand Company's claim that the laws of the Hong Kong Special Administrative Region were applicable according to the agreement of the arbitration clause.

As to the second point of contention, during the first instance defense, STX Company cited the relevant provisions of arts 86 and 87 of the CISG as the legal basis, thus showing that STX Company expressly agreed to the application of the CISG. The court of first instance also took the CISG as the legal basis for the case. The Court held that the parties in this case had their places of business in China and Korea respectively, both of which are Contracting States to the CISG, that the parties had not agreed to exclude the application of the CISG, that the goods bought and sold by the parties did not fall within the scope of the CISG's prohibition of application, and that the parties had applied or invoked the Convention in the arbitration and the litigation in the court, so the CISG should be applied to this dispute.

In the original trial, Grand Company agreed to apply the laws of the People's Republic of China but argued that since it had not reached agreement with STX Company on the application of the CISG, the Convention should be excluded from application. The court of second instance held that both countries where the parties were domiciled were CISG Contracting States, and the goods in question did not fall within the scope of the exclusion of arts 2 and 3 of the CISG. Under the circumstance that Grand Company and STX Company had not explicitly agreed in the contract to exclude the application of the Convention, the original judgment automatically applied the CISG in accordance with the provisions of art 1 of the CISG and was not improper.

It can be seen that both the court of first and second instance preferentially applied the CISG according to art 1, making it clear that the CISG is not applicable only when the parties expressly exclude its application, and that if it is not expressly excluded, the CISG shall be applied automatically and in preference to domestic law even if the parties have not expressly chosen to apply the CISG at the same time. The question of whether the parties' agreement to choose Chinese law constitutes a valid exclusion of the CISG or only applies to matters in dispute not provided for in the CISG has become one of the most important issues to be resolved by the courts in the process of applying the CISG. The resolution of this issue involves the interpretation and application of the CISG exclusion clause (art 6).[1] There is a clear order of precedence in the system of rules in the applicable part of the CISG. The court of the Contracting State first needs to examine the provisions of art 1 of the CISG to determine whether the contract dispute in question should apply the CISG from the perspective of the contracting party, and then rely on arts 2 and 3 of the CISG to determine whether the goods and the manner of sale and purchase in the contract in question are within the scope of adjustment of the CISG. Only after concluding that the CISG should apply to the contract in question, the last step is to determine whether the parties have effectively excluded the CISG under art 6.[2] The process of examining art 6 of the CISG includes determining whether the choice of law clause in the contract meets the art 6 requirements to exclude the application of the CISG, and in particular, when the contract does not contain an express exclusion

[1] Lian [1], p. 136.

[2] Liu [2], p. 69.

clause, examining whether the implied intent to exclude can exclude the application of the CISG.

In this case, STX Company took the initiative to invoke the CISG as the legal basis for its claim, and Grand Company did not agree to the application of the CISG. However Grand Company did not expressly exclude the application of the CISG in the contract. It is a question worth exploring whether the situation that Grand Company did not agree to apply the CISG in the litigation can also be regarded as the party's explicit exclusion of the CISG. Most judicial cases and papers now focus on the situation where the parties do not expressly exclude the application of the CISG, but the court does not give priority to the application of the CISG. Few cases are similar to this case, i.e., where one party agrees to apply the CISG and the other party does not agree to apply it, the court still automatically gives priority to the application of the CISG according to art 1.

In the author's view, Grand Company's consent to the application of the CISG can already be found as it did not explicitly exclude the application of the CISG in the contract and in the first trial. Its reasons for not agreeing to the application mentioned in the appeal process are also not valid, because for the same contractual relationship two laws can be applied at the same time, but there is an order of application of these two laws, i.e., the CISG is automatically and preferentially applied, and the domestic law is applied after the CISG to resolve the matters not covered by the CISG. In the case of *Shenzhen Wellfaith Electronic Technology Co., Ltd. v. Shenzhen Sheng Hui Huang Electronics Co., Ltd.*,[3] the Court's thinking was similar to this case. The defendant argued that the parties did not choose to apply the CISG in the purchase order and that the Chinese Contract Law should be applied. The Court held that the parties in this case had their places of business in Hungary and the People's Republic of China, both of which are CISG Contracting States, and that the parties had not agreed to exclude the application of the CISG, nor did the goods bought and sold by the parties fall within the scope of CISG's prohibited application. It can be seen through the judgment that the Court did not adopt the defendant's claim, considering it unreasonable. The Court held that the parties not expressly agreeing in the contract to apply the CISG did not mean that the application of the CISG was excluded, that the CISG could be applied at the same time as Chinese law was applied in this case, and that the CISG was applied in priority. The defendant's claim violates the principle of the application of law that international treaties take precedence.

In addition, it should be noted that Grand Company and STX Company agreed in the contract that the contract dispute would be submitted to the HKIAC for settlement, the HKIAC award confirmed that the sales contract in question was governed by Hong Kong law, and that Hong Kong substantive law would be applicable to the dispute between the parties. Can the CISG then be directly applicable in the Hong Kong arbitration where the parties have not expressly excluded the application of CISG? This should be done in two steps: firstly, to clarify whether the CISG can be applied in Hong Kong, and secondly, if the CISG can be applied in Hong Kong arbitration, will it be applied in a direct or indirect manner? In the case of *Yinshon Development*

[3] (2019) Yue 03 Min Zhong No.3155.

*Hong Kong Limited v. Zhejiang Zhongda Technical Export Co., Ltd.*,[4] the parties' places of business were located in Hong Kong and Zhejiang Province respectively. Before the handover of Hong Kong, the UK was not a party to the CISG, and after the handover of Hong Kong, the Central Government did not declare that the CISG was applicable to the Hong Kong SAR. Therefore, before the CISG came into force in the Hong Kong SAR,[5] the parties agreed to choose Hong Kong law, which would have the legal effect of excluding the application of the CISG. As this case occurred before 2022, the HKIAC should not apply the CISG after using Hong Kong substantive law as the governing law. For cases after 1 December 2022, it is also necessary to consider whether the HKIAC's application of the CISG, if applicable, is direct or indirect.

In response to that question, should art 1(1)(a) of the CISG be invoked as a direct application of the Convention in the case of arbitral institutions as in the case of courts of contracting states? Most western scholars believe that the CISG cannot be applied directly, and that the status of an arbitral tribunal in such cases is similar to that of a court in a non-contracting state, even if both parties to a contract have their places of business in the Contracting State. The arbitral tribunal cannot directly apply the convention by invoking art 1(1)(a), as it should first apply the rules of private international law. The CISG applies only if the rules of private international law led to the application of the law of the contracting state. On the contrary, the CISG does not apply if the rules of private international law lead to the application of the law of a non-contracting state.[6] According to art 1(1)(b) 'Indirect application' of the CISG, a contract concluded between parties whose places of business are in different states, provided that the parties to the contract have chosen the law of a contracting state as the law applicable to the contract, the CISG should apply. Therefore, most foreign arbitral awards tend to apply the CISG indirectly through art 1(1)(b). In this case, under the rules of private international law, the HKIAC held that Hong Kong substantive law would apply to contractual disputes between the parties and that Hong Kong, as part of the territory of China, could also be regarded as a Contracting 'State' of the CISG. Therefore, according to the rules of private international law, the CISG can be applied indirectly at this time.

### Issue 2 Preservation of the Goods Under the CISG

In this case, in accordance with arts 86 and 87 of the CISG, STX Company held that Grand Company should first compensate it for its losses and pay the corresponding storage costs before returning the steel plates. Otherwise, STX Company had the right to retain or even dispose of the goods. The specific stipulations of arts 86(1) and 87 of the CISG are as follows:

> Article 86(1) If the buyer has received the goods and intends to exercise any right under the contract or this Convention to reject them, he must take such steps to preserve them as are

---

[4] (2010) Zhe Shang Wai Zhong No.99.

[5] On 5 May 2022, China deposited with the secretary-general of the United Nations a declaration extending the territorial application of CISG to the Hong Kong Special Administrative Region of China. Under Sect. 97(3) of CISG, the declaration came into effect on 1 December 2022.

[6] Du [3], p. 90.

reasonable in the circumstances. He is entitled to retain them until he has been reimbursed his reasonable expenses by the seller.

Article 87 A party who is bound to take steps to preserve the goods may deposit them in a warehouse of a third person at the expense of the other party provided that the expense incurred is not unreasonable.

Chapter 5, Section 6 of the CISG deals with the preservation of goods. Arts 85 – 88 describes the obligation of parties to preserve the goods in several situations and the manner of their restitution. Art 86(1) sets out the buyer's obligation to take reasonable steps to preserve the goods when it has received them but intends to return them, and the party obliged to preserve the goods is entitled to recover from the other party the various costs incurred in preserving the goods. Art 87 provides a means by which a party may satisfy its obligation to preserve the goods by placing them in the warehouse of a third party 'at the expense of the other party, provided that the expense is reasonable. Article 87 is also used as a partial basis for the buyer to recover the costs of holding the goods in its warehouse when the buyer declares the contract void. The word 'reasonable' appears in both articles, and the reasonableness of the cost may depend on the nature of the goods (perishable, preservable, odoriferous, fragile, etc.), the likelihood of damage and its magnitude, and other circumstances 'unreasonable' mainly refers to the cost of preservation rather than the value of the goods themselves. How to grasp this scale, the preservation costs to reach the value of the goods under the circumstances of how much can be a self-help sale and other circumstances need more judicial guidance to improve interpretation of these CISG provisions.[7]

Citing this case in the UNCITRAL Digest of Case Law on the CISG, UNCITRAL notes that few decisions have invoked or addressed the provisions of art 86, with most cases focusing on the buyer's claim to recover the costs of preserving the goods it refused to accept. The Court therefore invoked art 86 as a legal basis for the buyer's claim to recover the costs of preservation of the goods after he had declared the contract void. The defective steel plates rejected by STX Company were stored in the warehouse of the second buyer, PSL, and STX Company was required to settle and pay the preservation costs to PSL before it was entitled to recover the preservation costs from the seller, Grand Company.[8] In analyzing art 87, UNCITRAL also agreed with the Court's line of reasoning in this case, commenting that the buyer who resold and delivered the defective steel plates at the time the contract was declared void had a duty to take reasonable steps to preserve the goods because they were safely kept in the second buyer's warehouse.[9]

In Chinese judicial practice, if the buyer, after receiving the goods, believes that the goods are defective, he is also required to assume the obligation to preserve the goods before returning them in order to prevent further expansion of damages. In the case of *Shenzhen Wellfaith Electronic Technology Co., Ltd. v. Shenzhen Sheng Hui*

---

[7] Lv and Huang [4], p. 58.

[8] UNCITRAL [5], p. 406.

[9] UNCITRAL [5], p. 408.

*Huang Electronics Co., Ltd.*,[10] the Court held that the buyer had the right to keep the Christmas lights until the seller paid the relevant fees, according to art 86(1) of the CISG. After the seller paid the relevant fees, the plaintiff buyer should return the Christmas lights to the defendant seller.

In *Hang Tat Foods USA Inc. v. Rizhao Aquatic Products Group Corporation, Rizhao Rirong Aquatic Products Co., Ltd.*,[11] the Court held that the plaintiff, as the buyer, was entitled to return the frozen shrimp and claim the purchase price and related expenses, as well as damages, including profits and interest, as agreed upon by the defendant. However, according to the CISG, while the plaintiff was entitled to retain the goods, it also had a duty to preserve them. The plaintiff was primarily responsible for the failure to take reasonable measures in a timely manner and allowed the loss to expand until the value of the frozen shrimp was eventually lost. The Court held the plaintiff liable for 70% of the loss of the value of the frozen shrimp under arts 86(1) and 88 of the CISG. In this case, the court distinguished the meaning of the words 'retain' and 'preservation', and Du has pointed out that the purpose of preserving the goods is to protect their safety and integrity in order to mitigate the possible loss suffered, while the purpose of retaining the goods is to ensure the possession of the goods and to take further action after ensuring possession.[12] It can be seen that retaining the goods is similar to taking possession of the goods, which is an exercise of a right to minimize one's loss, while preserving the goods is an obligation that reflects the principle of harm mitigation. When a party defaults, the non-defaulting party is obligated to preserve the goods until the other party has been reimbursed for the reasonable costs paid.

In this case, STX Company argued that arts 86 and 87 of the CISG follow the principle of 'compensation before taking the goods'. The buyer has the right to keep the goods until the seller has paid the costs of preserving the goods, including but not limited to storage fees, custody fees and interest costs. Therefore, Grand Company should fulfill its obligations since the contract was cancelled, i.e., it should recover the subject goods and compensate the storage fee punctually. Secondly, in spite of repeated reminders from STX Company, Grand Company did not communicate or negotiate with STX Company regarding retrieval of the goods, which allowed the expansion of the loss. Considering that its own losses would be extended if left unattended for a long period of time, STX Company had to hand over the goods to a third party, PSL India. Therefore, without receiving the relevant storage and custody fees from Grand Company, STX Company should not return the steel plates to Grand Company.

The Court held that Grand Company had broken the contract in bad faith and the purpose of the contract could not be realized and should be cancelled. After Grand Company had paid full damages to STX Company in accordance with the Hong Kong arbitration, it was entitled to request the buyer of the contract to return the non-conforming steel plates it had received. This request is a return of the buyer's

[10] (2019) Yue 03 Min Zhong No.3155.

[11] (1997) Ri Jing Chu Zi No.29.

[12] Du [6], p. 203.

property acquired by the contract after it had been cancelled. Its purpose is to restore the parties to the legal state before the contract was signed, and its nature should be a right of the obligatory claim. Therefore, STX Company's defense that Grand Company should claim the return from PSL, the custodian of the steel plates in question, based on the ownership of the goods cannot be established. STX Company had stored the non-conforming steel plates in PSL's warehouse in accordance with the ruling of the Singapore Arbitration Tribunal, which fulfilled the condition of 'reasonable measures' as stated above. STX Company has the right to request Grand Company to pay the reasonable costs incurred for the preservation of the goods before returning the non-conforming steel plates in accordance with arts 86 and 87 of the CISG.

However, according to the principle of contract relativity, the steel plates involved in the case had been resold by STX Company to, and kept at, PSL. Only STX Company, as an intermediary, had a contractual relationship with PSL. Since there is no clear and reasonable basis for calculating the storage fee and its interest, it is obviously unreasonable for Grand Company to pay a determined amount of storage fees to STX Company first. Additionally, the storage fee was not actually incurred by STX Company, but needed to be settled separately with PSL, the other party to the contract, in order for the goods to be cleared. Therefore, the storage fee should be handled by STX Company and PSL first, so that Grand Company can retrieve the 783 steel plates from PSL's warehouse in India without any obstacles, and then claim the reasonable part of the fee from GRAND Company in separate negotiations. If the steel plates need to be shipped back to China, Grand Company should resolve the problem by itself and bear the related costs, however STX Company is obliged to assist. Grand Company has the obligation to retrieve the unqualified steel plates from PSL's warehouse in India, and its delay in doing so was the main reason for the large amount of storage and storage fees incurred for the steel plates. Grand Company should not refuse to accept the steel plates due to wear and tear in favor of reducing the continued expansion of losses.

## References

1. Lian, J. Y. (2023). A Study on the Problems in the Application of CISG in China's Judicial Practice and Suggested Solutions: From the Perspective of Parties' Choice of Chinese Law. *Chinese Review of International Law*, 1, 129-144
2. Liu, Y. (2019). Exclusion Clause and Application of CISG. *Journal of Political Science and Law*, 4, 68-84
3. Du, T. (2009). Application of CISG in the Arbitration. *Oriental Law*, 3, 88-101
4. Lv, G. M. & Huang, L. X. (2013). Commentary on Article 86, paragraph 2, of the United Nations Convention on Contracts for the International Sale of Goods. *Forward Position*, 22, 57-88
5. United Nations Commission on International Trade Law (UNCITRAL) (2016). *UNCITRAL digest of case law on the United Nations convention on contracts for the international sale of goods*. Retrieved from https://uncitral.un.org/en/case_law/digests
6. Du, Z. J. (2007). A legal Analysis of the Legislative Purpose of Preservation of the goods Clause in CISG. *Legal System and Society*, 7, 203-204

**Peng Wang** the associate professor of Nankai University Law School. He graduated from Peking University with a doctor of Law degree in 2003. His main areas of research include Public International Law, International Economic Law and Legal Professional Ethics. Professor Wang has published one monograph On the Nature of International Mixed Arbitration in 2007. He participated in the National Social Science Foundation's project, Research on the Development of Human Rights with Chinese Characteristics in 2012. He is a director of Tianjin Sports Law Society and a director of Tianjin International Economic Law Society.

**Yueshan Liu** graduated from Nankai University with a master of International Law degree in 2023. Prior to that, she graduated from Nankai University with a bachelor of Law degree in 2021, double-majoring in Business Management in Tianjin University. Her research interests lie in Public International Law and International Economic Law.

# Guangzhou Gulangma Co., Ltd. v. WS Invention Trade Gmbh

**Shao Long and Siyuan Yu**

**Case Information**

**Case Name**: Guangzhou Gulangma Co., Ltd. v. WS Invention Trade Gmbh

**Seller**: Guangzhou Gulangma Trade Co., Ltd.
**Place of Business**: China

**Buyer**: WS Invention Trade Gmbh
**Place of Business**: Austria

**Details of First Instance**:
**Court**: Primary People's Court of Yuexiu District of Guangzhou City, Guangdong Province
**Date of Decision**:
**Case Number**: (2011) Sui Yue Fa Min Si Chu Zi No. 141
**Judges**:

**Details of Second Instance**:
**Court**: Intermediate People's Court Guangzhou, Guangdong Province
**Date of decision**: 20 October 2014
**Case Number**: (2013) Sui Zhong Fa Min Si Zhong Zi No. 91
**Judges**: Xiaokai Zhang (Presiding Judge), Runzhi Guan (Judge), Yu He (Assistant Judge)

**CISG Applied**: No
**Key CISG Provisions Interpreted and Applied**: Article 6

S. Long (✉) · S. Yu
Hunan University, Changsha, Hunan, China
e-mail: longshao@hnu.edu.cn



P. Guo et al. (eds.), *Selected Chinese Cases on the UN Sales Convention (CISG) Vol. 3*, Selected Chinese Cases on the CISG,
https://doi.org/10.1007/978-981-99-6851-0_42

**Case Abstract**

On 19 May 2010, WS Invention Trade Gmbh ('WSI') ordered a batch of cell phones, model PROVXXXL, from Guangzhou Gulangma Trade Co., Ltd. ('Gulangma') through two purchase orders, No. 10002118 and No. 10002119. WSI also informed Gulangma that the goods would be later resold to DS Produkte Co., in Germany.

With regard to the increasing quantity of goods, WSI received an email from skye-Glomarket, requesting the modified orders. On the same day, there were two purchase orders attached to the reply sent by WSI, which respectively required Gulangma to provide 20,106 and 7,232 cell phones. Both orders stipulated that the goods were expected to be shipped by FF HONOUR LANE and FF Nisko respectively no later than 2 and 5 July. The content of invoices issued by Gulangma on 12 July 2010 consisted of the details of the goods listed in the orders, and stated that the goods were to be delivered to Hongkong, referring to the INCOTERM EX Works (EXW). The price terms stipulated that WSI was obliged to pay a 30% deposit in advance through wire transfer, and then pay 70% before shipment. The warranty period for the goods was one year and the failure rate ought to be 0.5%.

WSI claimed that it had paid the full price for the goods in accordance with the contract through three wire transfers, which amounted to USD $486,421, of which only USD $304,038.73 US had been proved through evidence. Nevertheless, after receiving the payment, Gulangma sent only 6240 overdue products for order No. 10002118 with no goods sent for order No. 1002119 until 13 January 2011.

On September 28, 2010, Gulangma sent a 'Notice of Urgent Disposal of Goods' to WSI, which stated that there were disagreements between WSI and Gulangma due to WSI's delay in payment, leaking of trade secrets, and repeated requests for changes in goods. As WSI did not determine whether to accept refund or continuous delivery, Gulangma decided to take urgent measures to deal with the remaining goods to avoid expanding losses.

The Court of First Instance confirmed that WSI is a legal entity founded in Austria and the Plaintiff and the Defendant did not explicitly choose the governing law of the dispute in the contracts. Under this circumstance, the 'Doctrine of the Most Significant Relationship' should be applied in accordance with art 126 of the Contract Law of the People's Republic of China. In view of the fact that Gulangma is domiciled in China, therefore the law of China shall govern this case.

The Court of First Instance confirmed that the Plaintiff and the Defendant had entered into two sales contracts by means of sending emails with orders and invoices attached. The sales contracts reflect both parties' true intention and are valid. Gulangma was to pay USD $187,002.13 for the undelivered goods. Due to a lack of factual and legal grounds, the Court did not support the Plaintiff's claim for damages caused by extra transportation costs.

Gulangma appealed against the decision, claiming that there was no contractual relationship between WSI and itself. The facts found by the Court of First Instance were confirmed by the Intermediate Court. The Intermediate Court reasoned that Austria and China are both Contracting States to the CISG and its application should be given priority. However, the appealer and the appellee both objected to applying the CISG, and since art 6 of the CISG allows for parties' exclusion of the Convention, it is correct to apply Chinese law as the First Instance Court decided. The Intermediate Court confirmed that it was the appealer who used email to make the acceptance, and for lack of a factual basis did not support the claim that a third party, GLM Ltd., was the actual counterparty of the disputed contract.

## Commentary to the Key Issues Related to the CISG

### Issues

Issue 1 The Parties to the Disputed Contracts
Issue 2 The Autonomous Applicability of the CISG
Issue 3 The Exclusion of the CISG.

### Comments

#### Issue 1 The Parties to the Disputed Contracts

This case deals with disputes arising from two sale of goods contracts. Among the conflicts WSI and Gulangma have debated, the parties actually involved in the contractual relationship should be given priority in accordance with the principle of privity of contract. In this case, it was ascertained by the Court of First Instance that the contracts, order No. 10002118 and order No. 10002119, were concluded through emails between WSI and another party, whose email address suffix was @glomarket.com. Given that the suffix is consistent with the name of Gulangma's website, and the address listed on the invoices issued also conformed to the registered business address of Gulangma, the Court of First Instance and the Intermediate Court correctly identified Gulangma as the counter party of the contracts.

Furthermore, Gulangma would not be relieved of the contractual duties that the third party, GLM Ltd., received payments from WSI and provided the goods. The performance of the contracts could be carried out in a suitable and punctual manner by the parties. Based on the evidence submitted by WSI, Gulangma designated the specific account for payment and ought to bear the corresponding legal consequences. It was Gulangma which entrusted the third party to deliver the goods, and the contractual relationship only existed between Gulangma and the third party, which has no connection with this case. Due to insufficient evidence, GLM Ltd. did not express its intent to enter into a contract with WSI and thus was not bound by the disputed contracts.

#### Issue 2 The Autonomous Applicability of the CISG

As for the applicable law, there was inconsistency between the Court of First Instance and the Intermediate Court. The applicable law was not challenged in the first instance and Chinese law was invoked under the Doctrine of the Most Significant Relationship pursuant to art 126 of the Contract Law of the People's Republic of China, while the Intermediate Court firstly reasoned the applicability of the CISG. The essence of the conflict on the applicable law ought to fall on the prevailing application of recourse to the CISG once it has been determined that the application of the CISG is possible.

### I. The Applicability of the CISG

Given the fact that the CISG is a self-executing treaty, the CISG itself governs its sphere of application and automatically applies once the objective requirements for its application are met.[1] Therefore, to determine whether the CISG could apply to certain contracts, the articles of Chapter I of the CISG should be referred to, amongst which art 1 of the CISG defines the sphere of application in terms of persons involved and territory, the substantive coverage of the CISG.[2] In the current case, there were two factors essential for the applicability determination pursuant to art 1 of the CISG.

#### *A. Internationality and Place of Business*

The CISG's basic requirement that a contract to which it applies must be an international one is manifested in the fact that the parties' place of business ought to be situated in different States. It would not meet the requirement if the places of business are located in the territory of the same State, or the contract was concluded in one State by parties located in the State even if the contract is performed in another State. The time point of the criteria ought to be limited to the time of the conclusion of the contract.[3]

Regarding the place of business, it is acknowledged that a place of business exists if a party uses it openly to participate in trade and if it displays a certain degree of duration, stability and independence.[4] There is no need for a place of business to represent the center of a party's business activities.[5] Nevertheless, a particular place where a party merely intends to conclude some sales contracts could not be regarded as a place of business. The aforementioned requirements hold true for the location of the server used if the contract is concluded via the Internet.[6]

Given the evidence and the analysis above, it is clear that the disputed contracts were concluded through emails between WSI and Gulangma, whose places of business are Austria and China respectively, satisfying the 'internationality' requirement regulated by the CISG.

#### *B. Goods*

The CISG does not define 'goods' but some of the exclusions specified in art 2 and other provisions of the Convention provide guidance for construing this basic concept. In line with art 7(1), the concept should be interpreted autonomously. According to the case law, 'goods' are moveable and tangible objects at the time of delivery, irrespective of whether they are solid, used or new. At some time, it is sufficient for them to become moveable as a result of the sale even though they

---

[1] Schwenzer et al. [1].

[2] Enderlein and Maskow [2].

[3] Kröll et al. [3], Art 1, para 42.

[4] Honnold [4], p. 43.

[5] Schwenzer [5], p.36.

[6] Schwenzer [5] Art 1, para 23.

are not corporeal.[7] The CISG is applicable to contracts for the delivery of goods by installments, as can be derived from art 73 of the CISG and contracts providing for the delivery of the goods sold directly from the supplier to the customer of the seller.[8]

From the contents of the disputed contracts, the subject matter is cell phones, which meet the 'tangible and moveable' criteria and constitute goods in the sense of the CISG. Furthermore, even though there is potential for GLM Ltd. to act as the final supplier and provide the delivery of the goods in the name of Gulangma, the CISG still covers the disputed contracts as analyzed above.

### II. The Prevailing Application of the CISG

As long as a contract for the sale of goods is international, the court shall not settle a dispute arising out of the contract simply by resorting to domestic law. Instead, the court must determine which substantive rules are adopted to resolve these disputes. In case law, when faced with a situation international in nature, the court adopts the rules of private international law to determine which substantive rules apply. However, for Contracting States to the CISG, the judge must examine whether the CISG is applicable to any given issue before resorting to the rules of private international law. According to art 1(1)(a) of the CISG, the CISG automatically applies to contracts of sale of goods between parties whose place of business are in different CISG Contracting States. This means that the CISG prevails over recourse to private international law unless excluded by the parties.

As already mentioned, the parties in this case both met the requirement of 'place of business' pursuant to art 1(1)(a), as China and Austria are Contracting States to the CISG. Therefore, the CISG was autonomously applicable. The Court of First Instance wrongly resorted to private international law without considering the applicability of the CISG. The Intermediate Court corrected this error of the first-instance judgment.

### Issue 3 The Exclusion of the CISG

If the requirements for its application are met, the CISG applies. The only remaining question is whether the Convention has been excluded from application by a prior agreement between the parties in accordance with art 6 of the CISG.[9] In the current case, the differentiation between the first instance and the second instance judgments concentrated on the agreement made by the parties regarding the exclusion during the proceedings, which needs further analysis to ascertain whether the agreement meets the exclusion criteria set in the CISG.

### I. No Exclusion of the CISG in First Instance

Within its scope of application, the CISG supersedes national law, and art 6 of the CISG deals with the exclusion.[10] Nevertheless, art 6 of the CISG does not explicitly stipulate the manner in which the contracting parties may define the law applicable to

[7] Schwenzer [5], Art 1, para 23.

[8] UNCITRAL [6], Art.1, para 22.

[9] Schwenzer et al. [1].

[10] CLOUT case No.2845 Italian knitwear case III [Oberster Gerichtshof, Austrian, 29 June 2017].

their contractual relationships and exclude the CISG. Due to the ambiguous wording of the article, there are two sorts of exclusion in the case law and scholarly commentary: express exclusion and implied exclusion. In general, two contrary opinions exist. According to one school of thought, the CISG as a uniform set of rules allows only express exclusion.[11] Nevertheless, many a tribunal expressly admits the possibility of implicit exclusion.[12] Regardless of express or implicit exclusion, it is acknowledged that a clear and real intent to exclude is required according to CISG Advisory No. 16.

Apart from express exclusion of the CISG, it is unanimously accepted that the choice of law of a non-contracting State constitutes an implied exclusion.[13] A clear intent to exclude could be also manifested in the choice of an express specific domestic statue or code which would be contentious to the CISG's application. Nevertheless, whether such a choice-of-law is sufficiently clear depends on the scope of the rules of law validly chosen, for some domestic statutes may indeed have the CISG enacted into law in that Contracting State, where the choice-of-law could not be regarded as the clear intent to exclude and other more specific expressions should be necessary.[14] Likewise, under art 6, a choice-of-law clause designating the law of a CISG Contracting State without further specifications is not an exclusion of the CISG but indeed leads to the application of the Convention.

Regarding the evidence, the parties had not incorporated the choice-of-law term into the underlying contracts or expressly excluded the CISG. Consequently, there were two aspects remaining to be determined: whether the parties have implicitly excluded the CISG through other conduct and whether the Court of First Instance was obliged to autonomously invoke the CISG.

In the invoices, the parties referred to INCOTERM Ex Works (EXW), standardized international trade terms published by the International Chamber of Commerce. However, according to some courts, the fact that the parties incorporated INCOTERMS Ex Works (EXW) into their agreement does not sufficiently constitute an implicit exclusion of the Convention. The selection of an INCOTERM only represents mere derogation from some provisions at some time rather than the exclusion of the entire CISG, such as risk, documentation, and payment terms.[15] Therefore, there was no clear intent to exclude expressed by the parties' conduct.

However, neither of the parties plead or present arguments based on the CISG during the litigation, which leaves suspended whether this can be seen as an implied exclusion. In line with the view of the CISG Advisory No. 16, failure to invoke the CISG in proceedings can only constitute an implied agreement, which does not sufficiently amount to clear intent to exclude the CISG.

---

[11] Felemegas [7].

[12] CLOUT case No. 904 [Tribunal Cantonal du Jura, Switzerland, 3 November 2004]. Oberlandesgericht Linz, Austria, 23 January 2006; CLOUT case No. 575 [U.S. Court of Appeals (5th Circuit), United States, 11 June 2003, corrected on 7 July 2003].

[13] Bonell and Liguori [8], p. 360.

[14] CISG Advisory Council [9].

[15] CISG Advisory Council [9].

Furthermore, a court is obliged to resort to the applicable law irrespective of whether parties have invoked it, according to the principle *iura novit curia* ('the court knows the law'.[16] In Contracting States, courts must apply the CISG to an existing contract once it falls in the sphere of the application of the CISG.[17]

Thus, under the circumstance where the contracting parties did not exclude the CISG expressly or implicitly, the applicability of the CISG was overlooked in the first instance, leading to decisions based on domestic law.

## II. The Clear Intent to Exclude the CISG

The exclusion of the CISG can be made at the time of concluding a contract or at the post-contractual stage. While the parties can agree on the exclusion during litigation, only if the conduct of legal proceedings amounts to the agreement to modify the choice of law of the underlying contract can the prior applicability of the CISG be potentially altered. This means the CISG is only excluded if such conduct results in an agreement that modifies the original contract in accordance with arts 6, 8, 11, 14 to 24 and 29 of the CISG.[18]

In accordance with art 14 of the CISG, *ex post* offers to exclude should manifest an 'intent to be bound'. It could not be seen as intent to be bound concerning absence of argument on applicable law in litigation or failure to mention the substantive rules that should be excluded in anticipation. Likewise, the intent to exclude ought to be tested objectively under art 8 of the CISG, as understood by a reasonable person. In line with art 29 of the CISG, silence or inaction rarely constitutes assent to the modification. The same is true for failure to object to the purported modifying offers.[19]

Although *ex ante* and *ex post* both request clear and real intent,[20] it is realistic that the evidentiary record is not static during the legal proceedings. The court judge could continuously enquire about the parties or their counsels to produce more specific proof. If the parties both present an express agreement to exclude upon being informed by the court, this will meet the requirement of clear intent to modify by agreement.[21]

In the case at hand, the parties presented an express agreement of excluding the CISG through enquiry by the Intermediate Court during litigation. On such a basis, the Intermediate Court held that the agreement between both parties shall be deemed as a valid exclusion of CISG application. In cases of total exclusion without indication of the applicable law, both legal scholars and international case practice unanimously state that the rules of private international law should determine the applicable law.[22] Hence, although the prior application of the 'Doctrine of the Most

[16] Sass [10], pp.334–5.

[17] Schwenzer and Hachem [11], pp. 104–5.

[18] Schlechtriem and Butler [12]; Viscasillas [13], p.171; Gabriel [14].

[19] Magnus [15], p. 324.

[20] CLOUT case No. 904 [Tribunal Cantonal du Jura, Switzerland, 3 November 2004].

[21] CISG Advisory Council [9].

[22] Ferrari [16].

Significant Relationship' by the Court of First Instance was incorrect, the application of Chinese Law on the merit of this case was correct regarding the express exclusion and the choice-of-law made by the parties. Above all, the Intermediate Court ruled that since the facts were clearly ascertained and the decision of the First Instance was correct, the appeal of the appealer must be rejected, and the original judgment sustained.

## References

1. Schwenzer, I., Atamer, Y. M., & Butler, P. (2014). *Current issues in the CISG and arbitration*. Eleven International Publishing
2. Enderlein, F., & Maskow, D. (1992). *International sales law: United Nations Convention on Contracts for the International Sale of Goods: Convention on the Limitation Period in the International Sale of Goods: commentary*. Oceana
3. Kröll, S., Mistelis, L., & Viscasillas, P. (2011). *UN Convention on Contracts for the International Sale of Goods (CISG)*. München: CH Beck
4. Honnold, J. O. (2009). *Uniform Law for International Sales under the 1980 United Nations Convention* (4th Ed.). Kluwer Law International
5. Schwenzer, I. (2016). *Schlechtriem & Schwenzer: Commentary on the UN Convention on the International Sale of Goods* (4th Ed.). Oxford University Press
6. United Nations Commission on International Trade Law (UNCITRAL). (2016). *UNCITRAL Digest of Case Law on the United Nations Convention on Contracts for the International Sale of Goods*. Retrieved from https://uncitral.un.org/en/case_law/digests
7. Felemegas, J. (2013). *An International Approach to the Interpretation of the United Nations Convention on Contracts for the International Sale of Goods (1980) as Uniform Sales Law*. Cambridge University Press
8. Bonell, M. J., & Liguori, F. (1996). The U.N. Convention on the International Sale of Goods: A Critical Analysis of Current International Case Law - 1997 (Part 1). *Uniform Law Review*, 1, 359-376
9. CISG Advisory Council. (2014). *Opinion No. 16: Exclusion of the CISG under Article 6*. Retrieved from https://cisgac.com/opinions/cisgac-opinion-no1-copy-copy-4-copy-copy-copy-7/
10. Sass, S. L. (1968). Foreign law in civil litigation: a comparative survey. *American Journal of Comparative Law*, 16, 332-371
11. Schwenzer, I. & Hachem, P. (2010). Art. 6, in Schwenzer, I. (Eds.), *Schlechtriem & Schwenzer: Commentary on the UN Convention on the International Sale of Goods (CISG)* (3rd Edition, pp.104–105). Oxford University Press
12. Schlechtriem, P. & Butler, P. (2008). *UN Law on International Sales: The UN Convention on the International Sale of Goods*. Springer
13. Viscasillas, P. (2005–2006). Modification and Termination of the Contract. *Journal of Law and Commerce*, 25, 167–179
14. Gabriel, H. D. (2008). *Contracts for the Sale of Goods: A Comparison of U.S. and International Law* (2nd Ed.). Oxford University Press
15. Magnus, U. (2008). Incorporation of Standard Contract Terms under the CISG, in Andersen, C. B. & Schroeter U. G. (Eds), *Sharing International Commercial law across National Boundaries: Festschrift for Albert H. Kritzer on the Occasion of his Eightieth Birthday*. Wildy, Simmonds & Hill Pub
16. Ferrari, F. J. (1995). Specific Topics of the CISG in the Light of Judicial Application and Scholarly Writing. *Journal of Law and Commerce*, 15, 1–126

**Shao Long** is an Assistant Professor in Law at Hunan University. She holds a doctoral degree in law, specialising in the field of international law, from Vienna University. Dr. Long's research interests lie in international trade law, WTO law, and international commercial arbitration. She teaches International Economic Law to LLB students and acts as the coach of HNU CIETAC Cup (pre-vis) moot team.

**Siyuan Yu** LL.B. (Hunan University) and LLM (Xiamen University). The author majors in international tax law and participated in the 19th annual CIETAC Cup International Commercial Arbitration Moot to win the Best Memo Award.

# Allied Pacific Motor (Malaysia) Sdn. Bhd v. Chongqing Jieyadi Technology Development Co., Ltd.

**Alex Wan**

## Case Information

**Case Name**: *Allied Pacific Motor (Malaysia) Sdn. Bhd v. Chongqing Jieyadi Technology Development Co., Ltd.*

**Seller**: Chongqing Jieyadi Technology Development Co., Ltd. ('Jieyadi Company')
**Place of Business**: China

**Buyer**: Allied Pacific Motor (Malaysia) Sdn. Bhd ('APM Company')
**Place of Business**: Malaysia

**Details of First Instance**:
**Court**: The First Intermediate People's Court of Chongqing Municipality
**Date of Decision**: 1 January 2004
**Case No.**: (2004) Yu Yi Zhong Min Chu Zi No. 395
**Judges**: N/A

**CISG Applied**: No
**Key CISG Provisions Interpreted and Applied**: N/A

## Case Abstract

On July 16, 2003, the buyer, APM Company, and the seller, Jieyadi Company, concluded a contract for the purchase of 7000 sets of motorcycle frames and fuel

A. Wan (✉)
Swinburne University of Technology, Melbourne, VIC 3000, Australia
e-mail: awan@swin.edu.au



P. Guo et al. (eds.), *Selected Chinese Cases on the UN Sales Convention (CISG) Vol. 3*, Selected Chinese Cases on the CISG,
https://doi.org/10.1007/978-981-99-6851-0_43

tanks, stipulating that the goods were to be transported by Jieyadi Company and the quality of the goods had to comply with Chinese industry standards. After signing the contract, Jieyadi Company shipped all the goods under the contract to APM Company in July and August 2003, respectively. APM Company paid RMB1.32 million for the goods but still owed RMB150,000. After receipt of the goods, APM Company found that the goods had serious quality problems and then negotiated with Jieyadi Company. Jieyadi Company subsequently contacted the manufacturer of the goods, Jiujiu Company, and they signed a document on August 14, 2003, which mentioned that Jiujiu Company provided the goods to Jieyadi Company, and dents and deformities were found in these motorcycle frames upon the goods' arrival in Malaysia. On October 10, 2003, the representatives of Jieyadi Company and Jiujiu Company went to Malaysia where APM Company was located to have consultations with APM Company for a settlement of this matter, and the three parties signed an inspection report, which confirmed that the goods were of poor quality. However, Jiujiu Company stated that its representative Zhou Guangji's passport was confiscated after arriving in Malaysia which was proved by newspaper reports at the time, so Zhou Guangji signed that inspection report under duress and the signature did not have legal effect. In 2004, in accordance with the contractual provisions and the provisions of the CISG, the Contract Law of the People's Republic of China, and the Product Quality Law of the People's Republic of China, APM Company filed a lawsuit against Jieyadi Company with the Court, requesting that the contract between the two parties be terminated and that Jieyadi Company ship the goods back to China and pay compensation for losses, including direct losses of RMB1.32 million, loss of available profits of RMB9,939,636.40, and inventory losses. The Court stated that it had jurisdiction over this case because the buyer and seller agreed in the contract that if a dispute arises, it shall be under the jurisdiction of the court where the defendant is located. As to the applicable law, the Court noticed that the two parties specified the applicable laws in the contract, including Chinese laws, so the Court would apply Chinese laws. The Court claimed that according to the litigation request of the plaintiff APM Company, the main issues of this case were the effectiveness and performance of the contract between APM Company and Jieyadi Company, not the contract between Jieyadi Company and Jiujiu Company, and the dispute between Jieyadi Company and Jiujiu Company was being arbitrated by the CIETAC. The contract between APM Company and Jieyadi Company was valid because the two parties had no objection to the validity and the contract did not violate the prohibitive provisions of Chinese laws, so both parties should fulfill their respective obligations in line with the contract. APM Company discovered quality problems with the goods after receiving them and asked an appraisal agency to issue a report. The representative of Jieyadi Company also went to APM Company and confirmed that the goods had quality problems, and during the trial, Jieyadi Company did not take opposing claims about the goods' quality. Thus, the Court held that Jieyadi Company was responsible for the quality problems of the goods. The court also emphasized that Jieyadi Company's self-admission of responsibility to APM Company does not extend to the third-party Jiujiu Company. According to the relevant provisions of the Contract Law of the People's Republic of China, the Court stated that Jieyadi

Company is liable for breach of contract because it causes APM Company's failure to realize the purpose of the contract, so APM Company's claim to terminate the contract is legitimate, and that Jieyadi Company should bear the cost of transporting the goods back. With regard to the issue of losses, the Court held that only APM Company's payment of RMB1.32 million was its loss. The claims of asking for the loss of available profits of RMB9,939,636.40 and inventory losses was dismissed pursuant to the Contract Law of the People's Republic of China, because the court believed that APM Company did not provide evidence to prove that the loss of available profits was foreseeable or should have been foreseen by Jieyadi Company and it also could not prove that there is inventory loss.

**Commentary to the Key Issues Related to the CISG**

**Issues**:

Issue 1 Application of the CISG to the contract

Issue 2 Did the court have the discretion to apply domestic law when one of the contracting parties is from a non CISG country?

**Comments**:

This contract dispute involves one party from a CISG contracting state (China—Jieyadi Company) and another from a non CISG contracting state (Malaysia—APM Company). Since one of the contracting parties is from a non-contracting state, is there still an obligation for the CISG to be applicable to the contract or is the choice determine by the contract clause itself? What is the appropriate approach?

**Issue 1 Application of the CISG to the Contract**

In any international sales of goods contract, the aims of the United Nation Convention on Contracts for the International Sale of Goods ('the Convention' or 'CISG') is to provide "a neutral, uniform, harmonized sales law around the world"[1] which promotes the removal of legal barriers in international commercial sales contracts between international contracting parties.[2] In the event of a contractual dispute, the courts in a contracting state and, arguably, in non-contracting states[3] are expected to determine whether the conditions in Article 1 of the CISG are met or not, independent of the conflict of laws rules of the forum.[4] And where the CISG is applicable, national law would be superseded.[5] In this respect, the CISG is positioned as a *lex specialis* involving contracts for the international sale of goods and accords with the CISG's objective of unifying international sale of goods law. Unless, of course, the conditions

[1] Spagnolo [11, p. 145].

[2] One of the preambles to the CISG for contracting member States hold that "the adoptions of uniform rules which govern contracts for the international sale of goods and take into account, the different, social, economic and legal systems would contribute to the removal of legal barriers in international trade and promote the development of international trade".

[3] Bell [1, p. 247], UNCITRAL [12, p .6].

[4] Ferrari [3, p. 34].

[5] Rosett [7, p. 273].

for the CISG's application are not met, then there is no other choice but to refer to the conflict of laws rules.[6] Similarly, this scenario would also materialised where the contracting parties have chosen to opt out of the CISG's application.[7]

There are 2 ways to satisfy the conditions for the application of the CISG: (a) autonomous application (direct) using Article 1(1)(a) CISG, or (b) indirect application under Article 1(1)(b) CISG which accords with the conflict of laws rules of the forum. The prerequisite criteria for the application of the CISG is that the contract for the sale of goods must be international in the sense that the places of business of the contracting parties must be located in different states.[8] Autonomous application is only possible where the contracting parties are from the contracting states of the CISG.[9]

In this contractual dispute, the application of the CISG may be possible through an indirect application under Article 1(1)(b) when the conflict of laws rules of the forum refers to the law of a contracting state. As part of the ratification by the contracting state, the provision of the CISG is implemented as part of applicable domestic law affecting international sale of goods contract, the appropriate *lex specialis*.[10] It, therefore, follows that the court should identify and apply the CISG provisions to the contract dispute regardless of the commercial parties' 'status'.[11] China, however, have made a reservation to Article 95 of the CISG that allows a contracting state to declare that it will not be bound by matters relating to formation of contracts and the rights and obligations of the buyer and seller. The Article 95 reservation meant that Article 1(1)(b) is not applicable to contracts made between Chinese parties and parties in non-contracting states.[12]

**Issue 2 Did the Court Have the Discretion to Apply Domestic Law When One of the Contracting Parties is from a Non CISG Contracting State?**

In the light of China's Article 95 reservation, the only way the CISG would apply is if the contracting parties have chosen to opt in to the CISG in their contract. The court in this instance have applied Chinese law to the contract dispute by referring only to the contract's clause stipulating the applicable law to be domestic Chinese law. As there was no acknowledgement of the CISG by the court, this may be suggestive of the court not taking cognizance of its effect on the contract and have simply followed private international law, through the choice of law clause, when applying Chinese law here.

In this respect, despite the seemingly correct outcome of applying Chinese law in this contract dispute involving a contracting party from a non CISG contracting state, the appropriate approach by the court should have been to acknowledge and apply

[6] Ferrari [3, p. 34].

[7] Article 6 of the CISG.

[8] Article 10 of the CISG.

[9] This must be in accordance with the meaning stipulated in Article 99 and 100 of the CISG.

[10] Spagnolo [11, p. 143].

[11] Schwenzer [10, p. 20].

[12] Xiao and Long [13, p. 81].

the CISG instead of Chinese law. This is particularly relevant in this dispute when Jieyadi Company accepted liability for the breach of contract when they sent the defective goods to APM Company in Malaysia. As the breach of contract occurred in Malaysia, a non CISG contracting state, and under the conflict of laws rules and by virtual of the choice of law clause in the contract stipulating Chinese law, the court in this instance should have referred to the CISG since the reserving state should not be seen as a non-contracting state, despite the Article 95 reservation.[13] This is not due to any obligation under Article 1(1)(b) CISG but the result of complying with China's private international law.[14] The court, therefore, should have applied the CISG as long as there was no express exclusion of the CISG in the contract and that domestic law does not prevent them from doing so. The CISG as a *lex specialis* is also clearly better suited to govern this contract dispute than domestic Chinese contract law since it is an international sale of goods contract.

It should be noted that having a choice of law clause in a contract is not an implicit exclusion of the CISG.[15] A case example from the United States that has clearly articulated the intention of the Convention is *Easom Automation Systems Inc v Thyssenkrupp Fabco Corp.* The US District Court in Michigan have held that it is insufficient to exclude the application of the CISG to an agreement on the basis of a choice of law clause which provided for the law of one of the contracting parties' jurisdictions to prevail over the contract.[16]

Further, the CISG has *lex mercatoria* as it "finds its subjective sphere of application in the field of contracts, and particularly in… international sale of goods."[17] As a *lex mercatoria*, the CISG conveys a more appropriate approach than any predisposition made toward domestic law.[18] This is not to imply that the outcome of this contractual dispute would necessarily yield a different or more favourable outcome under the CISG than under domestic Chinese law, but rather the application of the CISG would be allowed to fulfill its purpose as a uniform law for the international sale of goods.[19]

**Issue 3 Should Malaysia Ratify the CISG?**

Lastly, I like to make a quick comment about the benefit of Malaysia ratifying the CISG. The CISG is a substantiative international law treaty that has been adopted by 95 countries to date.[20] In Malaysia's context, its main import and export partners

---

[13] Ferrari [3, p. 46], Schlechtriem [8, p. 783].

[14] Li [5, p. 305].

[15] Article 6 of the CISG.

[16] United States District Court, Eastern District Michigan. (2007, September 28). *Easom Automation Systems, Inc. v. Thyssenkrupp Fabco, Corp. No. 06–14,553.* UNILEX. Retrieved June 23, 2023, from https://www.unilex.info/cisg/case/1224.

[17] Dawwas and Shandi [2, p. 832].

[18] Mustill [6, p. 108].

[19] Article 7 of the CISG.

[20] There have been 95 ratification, accession, approval, acceptance of succession, with only Ghana and Venezuela not having brought the CISG into force yet. See *Status: United Nations Convention on Contracts for the International Sale of Goods (Vienna, 1980) (CISG),* https://uncitral.un.org/en/texts/salegoods/conventions/sale_of_goods/cisg/status. Accessed 23 June 2023.

are China, Singapore, the United States and Japan[21] which are all CISG contracting states. The aim of the CISG is to be the legal regime for transnational sale contracts that eliminate transnational legal barriers. Malaysia's domestic laws dealing with the sales of goods are governed by its own *Sales of Goods Act 1957* and the *Consumer Protection Act 1999.* These legislations are limited to the protection of domestic consumer rights in Malaysia and were never designed to deal with the issues affecting contracting parties in an international sale of goods setting.

As mentioned above, for contracting states, the CISG legal regime applies automatically when the conditions stipulated in Article 1(1)(a) are met without the parties having to opt-in to it, thereby making private international law rules redundant. This is a desirable legal framework that is binding and predictable for commercial parties to adjudicate obligations and contractual disputes.

Even when dealing with a non-contracting state, Malaysian commercial parties could still ensure that the CISG applies by using private international law in this situation, and then applying a subjective connecting factor in Article 3 and 4 CISG. This occurs when the contracting parties use the choice of law clause in their contract to select the law of the CISG contracting state under Article 1(1)(b). This adds to the consistency in legal approach for international sale contracts and allows domestic sale of goods contracts to be dealt with separately under domestic legislations.

Although contracting states implements the Convention as part of their national law, the contracting parties' autonomy are still protected under Article 6 CISG which allow the parties to opt-out of its application or derogate from or even vary the effect of any of its provisions in their contract, if they wish. This is an express recognition of the basic principle of freedom of contracting in the international sale of goods space. It is achieved through an explicit provision in the contract stipulating a different applicable regulatory framework or by an implicit exclusion of the CISG utilising a choice of law clause which has chosen the law of a non-contracting state or by a choice of forum selection located in a non-contracting state and the contracting parties' intention is to have the law of the state where the forum is located apply to the contract.[22]

To ensure consistency of the CISG's application across jurisdiction, Article 7(1) CISG sets the interpretive framework by encouraging courts and tribunals to look beyond their national legal concepts and domestic interpretations by taking into account the international nature of commercial transactions which are governed by the CISG. Furthermore, Article 7(2) CISG provides a non-exhaustive list of interpretive aids covering the Convention's international character, the need to promote good faith contracting and the relevant international trade usages. These inclusions empower commercial parties, in cross-border transactions, with the ability to rely on a common set of rules, and the further reliance on general legal principles such as good faith and party autonomy which ensures that the Convention continues to evolve with the needs of international business.

[21] Information available from https://wits.worldbank.org/CountrySnapshot/en/MYS. Accessed 23 June 2023.

[22] Johnson [4, p. 220].

In conclusion, the CISG functions as the *lex mercatoria* and it is designed to move away from the restrictions of national law and to facilitate the creation of a unification of the law governing the international sale of goods between international commercial parties regardless of their jurisdictional background.[23] And in this sense, the CISG becomes the *lex specialis* for the international sale of goods contract. As cross-border transactions have increased tremendously since the start of the twenty-first century and international transactional formalities are now no longer restricted to the domain of multi-national enterprises but also increasingly frequented by small and medium enterprises, these characteristics in the CISG should be tremendously beneficial for commercial parties in having a settled and predictable legal regime involving international sale of goods contracts. This should be sufficient incentive for Malaysia to take the step to ratify the CISG.

## References

1. Bell, K. (1996). The Sphere of Application of the Vienna Convention on Contracts for the International Sale of Goods. *Pace International Law Review*, 8(1), 237–258.
2. Dawwas, A. & Shandi, Y. (2011). The Applicability of the CISG to the Arab World. *Uniform Law Review*, 16(4), 813–842.
3. Ferrari, F. (1995). Specific Topics of the CISG in the Light of Judicial Application and Scholarly Writing. *Journal of Law and Commerce*, 15(1), 1–126.
4. Johnson, W. (2011). Understanding the Exclusion of the CISG: A New Paradigm of Determining Party Intent. *Buffalo Law Review*, 59(1), 213–292.
5. Li, W. (2014). On China's Withdrawal of its Reservation to CISG Article 1(b). *Renmin Chinese Law Review: Selected Papers of the Jurist*, 2, 300–318.
6. Mustill, M. (1988). The new Lex Mercatoria: The First 25 Years. *Arbitration International*, 4(3), 86–119.
7. Rosett, A. (1984). Critical Reflections on the United Nations Convention on Contracts for the International Sale of Goods. *Ohio State Law Journal*, 45(2), 265–306.
8. Schlechtriem, P. (2005). Requirements of Application and Sphere of Applicability of the CISG. *Victoria University of Wellington Law Review*, 36(4), 781–794.
9. Schmitthoff, C. (1988). International Business Law: A New Law Merchant, in Cheng, C. J. (Eds), *Clive M Schmitthoff's Select Essays on International Trade Law*. Martinus Nijhoff Publishers.
10. Schwenzer, I. (2010). Introduction to Articles 1–6, in Schwenzer, I. (Eds), *Schlechtriem & Schwenzer: Commentary on the UN Convention on the International Sale of Goods* (3rd editions). Oxford University Press.
11. Spagnolo, L. (2009). The Last Outpost: Automatic CISG Opt Outs, Misapplications, and the Costs of Ignoring the Vienna Sales Convention for Australian Lawyers. *Melbourne Journal of International Law*, 10(1), 141–216.
12. United Nations Commission on International Trade Law (UNCITRAL) (2016). *UNCITRAL Digest of Case Law on the United Nations Convention on Contracts for the International Sale of Goods*. Retrieved June 20, 2023 from https://uncitral.un.org/sites/uncitral.un.org/files/media-documents/uncitral/en/cisg_digest_2016.pdf.
13. Xiao, Y. & Long W. (2008). Selected Topics on the Application of the CISG in China. *Pace International Law Review*, 20(1), 61–104.

[23] Schmitthoff [9, p. 28].

**Dr. Alex Wan** is Lecturer in Law at the Swinburne University of Technology. He received his degrees in law from universities in the UK, New Zealand and Australia. He has taught law for about twenty years at Swinburne, including two and half years at the Swinburne's Sarawak campus in Malaysia. Dr Wan's industry experience, which spanned nearly a decade, saw him work for both private and public-listed companies in Malaysia where his area of practice was primarily centred on corporate and construction legal work. He was also actively involved in the corporate listing and restructuring of two companies during this time. His current research interests are in the areas of commercial law, corporate law and Public Private Partnerships (PPPS) contracts. He has taught a wide range of law units in both undergraduate and postgraduate programs in the business degrees and in the Bachelor of Laws degree. The law units that he has taught have included Law in Global Business, Law of Commerce, Marketing Law, Contract Law, Torts 2, Company Law and Corporations and Contract Law.

# P.H. "PODLASIAK" Andrzej Cylwik v. Yiwu Entuo Import and Export Firm

**Alex Wan and Peng Guo**

## Case Information

**Case Name**: *P.H. "Podlasiak" Andrzej Cylwik v. Yiwu Entuo Import and Export Firm.*

**Seller**: Yiwu Entuo Import and Export Firm
**Place of Business**: China

**Buyer**: P.H. "Podlasiak" Andrzej Cylwik
**Place of Business**: Poland

**Details of First Instance**:
**Court**: Yiwu Primary People's Court, Zhejiang
**Date of Decision**: 31 August 2018
**Case No.**: Zhe 0782 Min Chu No. 2064
**Judges**: Chenbo Wu (Presiding Judge), Qindi Ye (Juror), Jiannian Wang (Juror)

**Details of Second Instance**:
**Court**: Jinhua Intermediate People's Court, Zhejiang
**Date of Decision**: 9 November 2018
**Case No.**: Zhe 07 Min Zhong No. 5356

A. Wan (✉)
Swinburne University of Technology, Melbourne, VIC 3000, Australia
e-mail: awan@swin.edu.au

P. Guo
Swinburne University of Technology, Melbourne, VIC 3000, Australia
e-mail: pguo@swin.edu.au



P. Guo et al. (eds.), *Selected Chinese Cases on the UN Sales Convention (CISG) Vol. 3*, Selected Chinese Cases on the CISG,
https://doi.org/10.1007/978-981-99-6851-0_44

**Judges**: Naiping Dong (Presiding Judge), Huizhen Yu (Judge), Linjun Zheng (Judge)

**CISG Applied**: No
**Key CISG Provisions Interpreted and Applied**: N/A

### Case Abstract

In January 2016, the plaintiff, a Polish company P.H. "Podlasiak" (Podlasiak) signed a contract on the import of tents, sleeping bags, picnic mats and other outdoor products with the defendant, a Chinese company 'Pinfirst Import & Export Co Ltd' (Pinfirst Company), totalling USD$48,355. On 23 February 2016, Podlasiak paid USD$15,477. On 7 March 2016, the plaintiff purchased another batch of mattresses for USD$1,164, and the plaintiff paid the full price for the mattresses. On 25 April 2016, the plaintiff paid another USD$32,908 making a total payment of USD$49,519 to the defendant. The two parties agreed to deliver the goods within 30 days after ordering, however shipment only commenced on 21 May 2016. This was due to the defendant's failure to ship the goods on time. In order to compensate the plaintiff for the loss caused by the delayed delivery, the defendant agreed to compensate the plaintiff 5% of the total order price of the first batch of goods amounting to USD$2,417.75. After receiving the goods on 28 June 2016, the plaintiff found that the goods received were actually less than half of the ordered goods. The plaintiff negotiated with the defendant several times, requesting the defendant to either deliver the goods or refund the money, but the defendant did nothing. The plaintiff then filed a lawsuit in court against the defendant claiming an overpayment of USD$25,734.36. The plaintiff, Podlasiak's legal claims include: (1) The defendant shall refund the excess payment of USD$25,734.36 to the plaintiff; (2) The defendant shall pay interest to the plaintiff on the excess payment; (3) The defendant shall pay the plaintiff the sum of RMB¥ 20,000, being expenses incurred which includes attorney fees, notary fees and translation fees.Regarding the applicable law, the court of first instance held that Chinese law should apply. According to Article 41 of the Law of the People's Republic of China on Choice of Law for Foreign-related Civil Relationships, where the plaintiff and the defendant did not specify the applicable law for the contract, the mode of delivery of the goods can represent the characteristics of the contract and as it occurred in the territory of China, Chinese law should be applied in this case.The other key issue in this case was whether the defendant, Pinfirst Import & Export Firm (Pinfirst Firm) was the counterparty in the contract and the correct defendant in the contractual dispute. The plaintiff claimed that Pinfirst Company was the English name of Yiwu Entuo Import and Export Firm (Entuo), and there was evidence proving the connection between the Pinfirst Company and the Entuo Firm. However, the court of first instance held that the plaintiff did not provide sufficient evidence to prove that Entuo was a party to the contract and the appropriate defendant in this case. Therefore, the plaintiff's claim was dismissed. The buyer, Podlasiak, appealed to the Jinhua Intermediate People's Court, Zhejiang. The court of second instance corrected the relevant applicable law and held that this case was a dispute over a contract for the international sale of goods. Since the parties did not agree on the applicable law (and both China and Poland are members of the CISG), the CISG should be applied first. However, in the court of the first instance, both parties cited the laws of the People's Republic of China and have not objected to its application. Therefore, it may be concluded that the parties have made a specific choice of the applicable law on the contract dispute. The court of first instance may, under the circumstance, apply the laws of the People's Republic of China in its ruling although the reasoning given for choosing the applicable domestic law was inappropriate.The court of appeal further made a distinction between "firm" and "company" and upheld the decision of the court of first instance regarding the appropriate identity of the defendant/respondent and rejected the plaintiff/appellant's claims on the same basis.

**Commentary on the Key Issues Related to the CISG**

**Issues**:

Issue 1 Application of the CISG to the contract.
Issue 2 Whether the failure of the contracting parties' legal representatives to plea their arguments on the CISG is sufficient to indicate their intention to exclude the CISG?
Issue 3 Is the CISG an integral part of the Chinese law?

**Comments**:

**Issue 1 Application of the CISG to the Contract**.

In order to determine if the contract dispute is governed by the United Nations Convention on Contracts for the International Sale of Goods ('the Convention' or 'CISG'), it is important to establish that the contract arose under an international contract for the sale of goods. Both the plaintiff, Podlasiak, and the defendant, Entuo, have their respective places of business in two different contracting states of the CISG, namely Poland and China[1] and the agreement possessed the characteristic of an international sale of goods contract. Article 1(1)(a) of the CISG was, therefore, fulfilled and the Convention's prerequisites of direct or autonomous application were satisfied.[2]

When this case was brought before the court of first instance, the Yiwu Primary People's Court's presiding Judge never considered the application of the CISG. Instead, the court applied Article 41 of the Law of the People's Republic of China on the Choice of Law for Foreign-related Civil Relationships. The reason for this was apparently due to the contracting parties not having a choice of law clause in their contract and the fact that the characteristic connection of the contract is within China's territory. This has caused the court to conclude that Chinese law was applicable to this contract.

[1] Both China and Poland have ratified the CISG in 1986 and 1995 respectively.

[2] UNCITRAL [9, p. 5].

It is an established convention for ratifying states of the CISG to implement and integrate the Convention's provisions into their respective national legal system.[3] As such, when the prerequisites for the CISG' application are met, its provisions should have priority over any non-unified domestic laws of the state. In this sense, the presiding Judge should have applied the CISG *ex officio* regardless of the contracting parties' contract position.[4]

In this respect, the Jinhua Intermediate People's Court, on appeal, have indeed held that the court of first instance should have considered applying the CISG first rather than proceeding with the application of Chinese law from the outset, as the prerequisites of Article 1(1)(a) of the CISG were met. This is the correct interpretation and application of the CISG. As a court in a CISG contracting state, the judge is required to apply the CISG as the applicable governing law when the prerequisites are fulfilled and a failure to do so is tantamount to a breach of international obligations.[5] It is also the court's implicit duty as prescribed by public international law.

**Issue 2: Whether the Failure of the Contracting Parties' Legal Representatives to Plea their Arguments on the CISG is Sufficient to Indicate their Intention to Exclude the Convention?**

The Yiwu Primary People's Court have pointed out that both the contracting parties at the first instance hearing have not only referred to Chinese non-uniform domestic law but have also not objected to its application on the contractual dispute. Since there was no clause indicating the choice of law in the contract, does this mean that the parties have implicitly made the decision to choose Chinese law and have thus implicitly excluded the application of the CISG – presumably by virtual of Article 6 CISG? The appellate Jinhua Intermediate People's Court has concluded that the failure of the contracting parties' legal representatives to object to the exclusive use of Chinese law could be seen as an implicit exclusion of the CISG and upheld the application of Chinese law on the dispute. The author believes that when Article 1(1)(a) is satisfied, its initial application is not diminished by the contracting parties' intent; only its subsequent application may be excluded by the parties in their contract. The presiding Judge should have assessed the contract under the CISG first and then look for evidence of the contracting parties' use of their Article 6's autonomy to exclude the application of the CISG.

The exclusion of the CISG is governed by Article 6 which requires the contracting parties to have (1) intended it, and (2) reached a mutual agreement for it. This agreement to exclude the CISG must conform with the requirements of Articles 6, 11, 14 to 24, and 29 of the CISG.[6] The exclusion of the CISG under Article 6 can

---

[3] Schlechtriem [4, p. 5].

[4] Schwenzer [5, p. 20].

[5] Spagnolo [8, p. 286]; Article 26 Vienna Convention on the Law of Treaties: '[e]very treaty in force is binding upon the parties to it and must be performed by them in good faith'; Article 27 Vienna Convention on the Law of Treaties: 'A party may not invoke the provisions of its internal law as justification for its failure to perform a treaty'.

[6] Schlechtriem [4, p. 91], CISG Advisory Council [1], para, 2.

only be achieved through an explicit agreement declaring the parties' intention to use a different applicable regulatory framework or by an implicit exclusion of the CISG involving a choice of law clause that has chosen the law of a non-contracting state or by a choice of forum selection located in a non-contracting state in which the contracting parties have decided that the law of the state where the forum is located applies to the contract.[7] In order to exclude the CISG during legal proceedings when the Convention applies, the contracting parties must, in addition to having mutually agreed to its exclusion, also ensure that the particular procedural law of the *lex fori* allowed it.[8]

In this contractual dispute, since there was no choice of law clause found in the contract, there must be evidence of an actual agreement to exclude the CISG in order to comply with the requirements of Articles 14 to 24 CISG. In Article 18 CISG, a statement made by or other conduct of the offeree indicating assent to an offer would be sufficient for an acceptance.[9] Other conduct may suggests that an implicit agreement could be made out, however, silence or mere inactivity would not have amounted to acceptance.[10] It, therefore, follows that where the CISG applies by operation of law, the contracting parties cannot exclude it without evidence of actual agreement.[11] As such, a failure to object to the use of non-uniform domestic law during legal proceedings is not sufficient for an implied exclusion of the CISG as it may be based on mere ignorance – it requires a much stronger evidence of the parties' actual intent to exclude the application of the CISG.[12] The appropriate approach for the court (as long as procedural law allows it) is to draw the disputing parties' attention that the CISG applies before ruling on the applicability of domestic law.[13] This would allow the parties to decide on whether to change their legal submission or if they need to reach a separate agreement to exclude the CISG.

With respect, both the court of the first instance and the appellate court have made an incorrect decision to exclude the CISG on the ground that their legal representatives have not plea or base their arguments on the applicable CISG provisions nor on the lack of objection to the application of Chinese law. The success of the CISG is very much dependent on national courts or tribunals applying and interpreting the provisions correctly. If domestic laws are allowed to invade the domain of the CISG repeatedly, whether in interpretation or gap-filling, the integrity and structure of the CISG will eventually breakdown. The CISG rules should always be interpreted and applied uniformly in line with the principles of Article 7(1).

In conclusion, the author believes that at a practical level, when contracting parties made legal submissions on the basis of non-unified domestic law in which the CISG

---

[7] Johnson [3, p. 220].

[8] Fawcett et al. [2, p. 917. p. 922].

[9] Article 18(1) CISG—first sentence of the provision.

[10] Article 18(1) CISG—second sentence of the provision.

[11] CISG Advisory Council [1], para 3.5, 5.11, 5.12, 6.3.

[12] CISG Advisory Council [1], para 5, Schwenzer and Hachem [6, p. 113], para 21; Spagnolo [8, p. 305].

[13] Spagnolo [8], p. 308, Schwenzer and Hachem [6, pp. 113–114].

clearly applies to their contract dispute, the court should be able to, first of all, draw the parties' attention to the Convention's application and then ask the contracting parties whether they have agreed to exclude its application. If they have not excluded the CISG's application and continue to ignore the application of the CISG, the court should decide the case based on the CISG or to request the legal representatives of the parties to re-lodge their legal submissions.[14] This ensures a consistent outcome with the application of the CISG's provisions and in line with the uniformity prescribed in Article 7 CISG.

**Issue 3: Is the CISG an Integral Part of Chinese Law?**[15]

The application of Chinese law in this case should address the relationship between international treaties and the domestic legal system. In other words, should the CISG be considered a part of Chinese law? This part focuses on judicial practice in China. China is a party to the CISG, so when the parties to the contract choose Chinese law as the governing law, should this choice automatically exclude the CISG? There is no positive response to this issue as Chinese law does not clarify where the CISG is positioned in the Chinese legal system, but the former Ministry of Foreign Economic Relations and Trade (MOFTEC) responded to this issue in an official document,

> (A)ccording to the provision of Article 1 of the Convention, from 1 January 1988, the contracts for the sale of goods reached between the Chinese companies and the companies in the aforementioned countries ... will be automatically governed by the provisions of the Convention, and the disputes or litigations should be also settled under the Convention, unless otherwise agreed.[16]

It can be specifically interpreted that, in the settlement of a China-related CISG dispute, even if the parties do not make a choice, if there is no clear agreement on the exclusion, the CISG should be automatically applied between the contracting parties. That is to say, if the parties do not explicitly exclude the CISG, but believe that only Chinese law is chosen, this cannot be regarded as an exclusion of the CISG.[17]

This MOFTEC document was notified and forwarded by the Supreme People's Court, requiring courts to correctly implement the CISG in foreign-related economic trials,[18] and this method has indeed been repeatedly followed in judicial practice.[19] According to Chinese trial experience, when both parties have their place of business in the contracting states, the CISG have been actively invoked by the court, and there was no need to examine whether the parties have chosen to apply Chinese law. On

---

[14] Spagnolo [7, p. 221].

[15] Zhang et al. [11, pp. 70–73].

[16] Certain Issues in Connection with the Implementation of the United Nations Convention on Contracts for the International Sale of Goods. (4 December, 1987). (87) Wai Jing Mao Fa Zi No. 22.

[17] Yang [10, p. 99].

[18] Circular of the Supreme People's Court on Transmitting Certain Issues of the MOFTEC in Connection with the Implementation of United Nations Convention on Contracts for the International Sale of Goods. (10 December, 1987). Fa (Jing) Fa < 1987 > No. 34.

[19] Zheng [12, p. 80].

the premise of meeting the applicable conditions in Article 1, judges not only "can" but also "should" invoke CISG to resolve disputes.

In addition, it should be noted that, if the parties expressly agree to apply certain specific domestic laws, such as the Chinese Civil Law Code, whether it should be considered that the parties exclude the application of the CISG is still unclear. Further clarification from the Supreme People's Court is needed.

## References

1. CISG Advisory Council. (2014, May 30). *Opinion No 16 Exclusion of the CISG under Article 6*. CISGAC. Retrieved June 20, 2023, from www.cisgac.com/wp-content/uploads/2023/02/CISG_AC_Opinion_no_16.pdf.
2. Fawcett, J., Harris J. & Bridge, M. (2005). *International Sale of Goods in the Conflict of Laws*. Oxford University Press.
3. Johnson, W. (2011). Understanding the Exclusion of the CISG: A New Paradigm of Determining Party Intent. *Buffalo Law Review*, 59(1), 213–292.
4. Schlechtriem, P. (2005). Introduction, in Schlechtriem, P & Schwenzer, I. (Eds), *Commentary on the UN Convention on the International Sale of Goods* (2nd ed.). Oxford University Press.
5. Schwenzer, I. (2010). Introduction to Articles 1–6, in Schwenzer, I. (Eds), *Schlechtriem & Schwenzer: Commentary on the UN Convention on the International Sale of Goods (CISG)* (3rd ed.). Oxford University Press.
6. Schwenzer, I. & Hachem, P. (2010). Article 6, in Schwenzer, I. (Eds), *Schlechtriem & Schwenzer: Commentary on the UN Convention on the International Sale of Goods (CISG)* (3rd ed.). Oxford University Press.
7. Spagnolo, L. (2011). Iura Novit Curia and the CISG: Resolution of the Faux Procedural Black Hole, in Schwenzer, I. & Spagnolo L. (Eds.), *Towards Uniformity: The 2nd Annual MAA Schlechtriem CISG Conference* (1st ed., pp.181–221). Eleven International Publishing.
8. Spagnolo, L. (2014). *CISG Exclusion and Legal Efficiency*. Kluwer Law International.
9. United Nations Commission on International Trade Law (UNCITRAL) (2016). *UNCITRAL Digest of Case Law on the United Nations Convention on Contracts for the International Sale of Goods*. Retrieved June 20, 2023 from https://uncitral.un.org/sites/uncitral.un.org/files/media-documents/uncitral/en/cisg_digest_2016.pdf.
10. Yang, M. S. (2020). *Study on the priority application of the United Nations Convention on contracts for the international sale of goods*. Law Press China.
11. Zhang, C., Guo, P. & Zhang, S. (2022). Chapter 8: Tunghang (Asia) Co., Ltd v Shenzhen Haizhongbao Aquatic Products Trading Co., Ltd, in Guo, P., Zuo, H. & Zhang, S. (Eds.), *Selected Chinese Cases on the UN Sales Convention (CISG) Vol. 1* (pp. 67–77). Springer.
12. Zheng, X. Y. (2018) A study on the application of the CISG in Chinese courts based on 108 judgments of Chinese courts. *Journal of Weinan Normal University*, 33(2), 79–84.

**Dr. Alex Wan** is Lecturer in Law at the Swinburne University of Technology. He received his degrees in law from universities in the UK, New Zealand and Australia. He has taught law for about twenty years at Swinburne, including two and half years at the Swinburne's Sarawak campus in Malaysia. Dr. Wan's industry experience, which spanned nearly a decade, saw him work for both private and public-listed companies in Malaysia where his area of practice was primarily centred on corporate and construction legal work. He was also actively involved in the corporate listing and restructuring of two companies during this time. His current research interests are in the areas of commercial law, corporate law and Public Private Partnerships (PPPS) contracts. He has taught a wide range of law units in both undergraduate and postgraduate programs in the business degrees and in the Bachelor of Laws degree. The law units that he has taught have included Law in Global Business, Law of Commerce, Marketing Law, Contract Law, Torts 2, Company Law and Corporations and Contract Law.

**Dr. Peng Guo** is Lecturer in Law at the Swinburne University of Technology. He has worked across several Australian universities and has held visiting positions at different European universities. He has received scholarships awarded by renowned research institutions and international organisations, including the Max Planck Institute for Comparative and International Private Law, the International Institute for the Unification of Private Law (UNIDROIT), the Swiss Institute of Comparative Law, and the European Union. He specialises in the international sale of goods, international commercial arbitration, comparative contract law, and law and technology.

# Index

**A**
Acceptance, 33, 283, 306
Additional period of time fixed, *see* Nachfrist
Agency, 2, 306
Amendment, *see* Modification of contract
Arbitration agreement, 271, 316
Auction sales, 282
Autonomy of will, *see* Party autonomy
Avoidance of contract, 284, 312

**B**
Bill of lading, 38, 110, 117
Breach, 21, 38
- anticipatory, 148, 150
- fundamental [Art. 25], 97, 255, 273, 312

Burden of proof, 310
Buyer's obligations, 293

**C**
Cancellation, *see* Avoidance of contract
Carriage, *see* Delivery, of goods
Case law under the Sales Convention, 332
Choice of law, 185, 226, 320, 334
Circular of the Supreme People's Court on Transmitting Certain Issues of the MOFTEC in Connection with the Implementation of United Nations Convention on Contracts for the International Sale of Goods, 11
Civil Code of the People's Republic of China, 39, 62, 276, 308
Civil Procedure Law of the People's Republic of China, 298
Commercial invoice, 270
Company Law of the People's Republic of China, 206
Compensation, full, 91, 119, 134, 168, 224, 237, 267, 285
Conclusion of contract, 332
Conflict of laws, 5, 61, 133, 193, 202, 212, 225, 228
Conformity
- [Art. 35], 149, 255, 308
- [Art. 36], 294
- Notice period [Art. 39], 165, 270, 294

Contract
- formation, 34, 265, 282, 307
- mixed, 194, 282

Contracting States, 70, 330, 333
Contract Law of the People's Republic of China, 11, 47, 48, 168, 270, 330

**D**
Damages
- calculation of, 168, 193
- punitive, 169

Declarations
- Buyer [Art. 49], 48, 270, 311
- Seller [Art. 64], 132, 273, 307

Defective goods, 166, 250, 274, 311, 318
Delivery
- of goods, 109
- of goods by instalments, 333
- time of, 164

Direct loss, 306


P. Guo et al. (eds.), *Selected Chinese Cases on the UN Sales Convention (CISG) Vol. 3*, Selected Chinese Cases on the CISG,
https://doi.org/10.1007/978-981-99-6851-0

Domestic law, 3, 58, 294, 307, 320
Duty to preserve goods, 324, 325

E
Examination of goods, 283, 294
Exclusions from the CISG, 282, 332
Ex officio, 89, 162, 292
Exemption (*force majeure*), 232

F
Full compensation, *see* Compensation, full
Fundamental breach, *see* Breach, fundamental

G
General Principles of Sales Convention [Art 7(2)], 267, 307
General Principles of the Civil Law of the People's Republic of China, 38, 48, 49
Grace period for performance, *see* Reasonable period

H
Hong Kong, 24, 46, 180, 316

I
INCOTERMS, 40, 334
Inspection, *see* Examination of goods
Intention to be bound, 34, 307
Interest
  calculation of, 193, 266, 290
  rate, 38, 41, 42, 264, 266–268, 280, 284, 285, 290, 293–295
Interpretation of the CISG
  [Art. 7(1)], 275, 330
  [Art. 8], 331
Interpretation of the Supreme People's Court on Issues Concerning the Application of Law for the Trial of Cases of Disputes over Sales Contracts, 41
Interpretations of the Supreme People's Court on Several Issues Concerning Application of the Law of the People's Republic of China on Choice of Law for Foreign-Related Civil Relationships (I), 100, 163

J
Joint liability, 217

L
Law of the People's Republic of China on Choice of Law for Foreign-related Civil Relationships, 298
Lex causae, 4, 12, 41, 116
Lex fori, 4, 253, 300

M
Mandatory rules, *see* Validity
Maritime Law of the People's Republic of China, 89
Market price, 267
Minutes of the National Symposium on the Foreign-related Commercial and Maritime Trial Work of Courts, 67
Mitigation of damages, 180, 182, 325
Modification of contract, 164, 282

N
Natural person, 265
Non-conformity, *see* Conformity
Notice of
  non-conformity, 165
  suspending performance, 141

O
Offer, 11, 15, 33, 34, 306
Opting-out of the CISG, 14
Overdue payment, *see* Payment, overdue
Ownership, 66, 293, 309

P
Pacta Sunt Servanda, 300
Party autonomy, 61, 109, 150, 162, 261
Payment
  obligation, 54, 210, 218, 301
  overdue, 38, 41, 169
PIL, *see* Conflict of law
Place of business, 25, 260
Preservation of the goods, 319
Principle of the closest connection, 228
Principles of International Commercial Contracts, 92, 187, 237
Private international law, *see* Conflict of law

**R**
Reasonable period, 51, 103
Remedy, 91, 134, 157, 165, 208, 220, 247, 254, 266, 276, 284, 311
Repair, 165, 219, 250, 277
Reservation, 20, 34, 39, 89, 133, 185
Revocation of acceptance of goods, *see* Avoidance of contract
Risk transfer, *see* Passing of risk

**S**
Sample or model of goods, 309
Scope of application of Sales Convention, 26, 71
Seller's obligation, 164, 254
Services, *see* Contract, mixed
Specific performance, *see* Compelling performance
Statute of limitations, 75
Storage costs, 128

**T**
Take delivery, buyer's obligation to, 55, 134, 198, 207, 208, 218, 246, 284, 293, 301
Termination of contract, 48
Trade usage, *see* usage
Trial in absentia, 266

**U**
UNCITRAL Digest, 48, 51, 324
UNIDROIT Principles of International Commercial Contracts, *see* IPCC
Uniform Law for the International Sale of Goods (ULIS), 309

**V**
Validity, 206, 211, 265, 283, 307